Complete Xhosa

CW01647580

Beverley Kirsch
and Silvia Skorge

in consultation with
Sindiwe Magona and Theresa Soci

PRODUCTION DEPARTMENT
FILE COPY
DO NOT REMOVE

For UK order enquiries: please contact Bookpoint Ltd, 130 Milton Park, Abingdon, Oxon OX14 4SB. *Telephone:* +44 (0) 1235 827720. *Fax:* +44 (0) 1235 400454. Lines are open 09.00–18.00, Monday to Saturday, with a 24-hour message answering service. Details about our titles and how to order are available at www.teachyourself.co.uk

For USA order enquiries: please contact McGraw-Hill Customer Services, PO Box 545, Blacklick, OH 43004-0545, USA. *Telephone:* 1-800-722-4726. *Fax:* 1-614-755-5645.

For Canada order enquiries: please contact McGraw-Hill Ryerson Ltd, 300 Water St, Whitby, Ontario L1N 9B6, Canada. *Telephone:* 905 430 5000. *Fax:* 905 430 5020.

Long renowned as the authoritative source for self-guided learning – with more than 50 million copies sold worldwide – the *Teach Yourself* series includes over 500 titles in the fields of languages, crafts, hobbies, business, computing and education.

British Library Cataloguing in Publication Data: a catalogue record for this title is available from the British Library.

Library of Congress Catalog Card Number: on file.

First published in UK 1999 as Teach Yourself Xhosa by Hodder Education, part of Hachette UK, 338 Euston Road, London, NW1 3BH.

First published in US 1999 as Teach Yourself Xhosa by The McGraw-Hill Companies, Inc.

This edition published 2010.

The *Teach Yourself* name is a registered trade mark of Hodder Headline.

Copyright © 1999, 2003, 2004, 2010 Beverley Kirsch and Silvia Skorge.

In UK: All rights reserved. Apart from any permitted use under UK copyright law, no part of this publication may be reproduced or transmitted in any form or by any means, electronic or mechanical, including photocopy, recording, or any information, storage and retrieval system, without permission in writing from the publisher or under licence from the Copyright Licensing Agency Limited. Further details of such licences (for reprographic reproduction) may be obtained from the Copyright Licensing Agency Limited, of Saffron House, 6–10 Kirby Street, London EC1N 8TS.

In US: All rights reserved. Except as permitted under the United States Copyright Act of 1976, no part of this publication may be reproduced or distributed in any form or by any means, or stored in a database or retrieval system, without the prior written permission of the publisher.

Typeset by Transet Limited, Coventry, England.
Printed in Great Britain for Hodder Education, an Hachette UK Company, 338 Euston Road, London, NW1 3BH, by CPI Group (UK) Ltd, Croydon, CR0 4YY.

The publisher has used its best endeavours to ensure that the URLs for external websites referred to in this book are correct and active at the time of going to press. However, the publisher and the author have no responsibility for the websites and can make no guarantee that a site will remain live or that the content will remain relevant, decent or appropriate.

Hachette's policy is to use papers that are natural, renewable and recyclable products and made from wood grown in sustainable forests. The logging and manufacturing processes are expected to conform to the environmental regulations of the country of origin.

Impression number 10 9 8 7 6 5 4 3
Year 2014 2013 2012

Contents

Credits

Front cover: © EggImages/Alamy

Back cover and pack: © Jakub Semeniuk/iStockphoto.com, © Royalty-Free/Corbis, © agencyby/iStockphoto.com, © Andy Cook/iStockphoto.com, © Christopher Ewing/iStockphoto.com, © zebicho – Fotolia.com, © Geoffrey Holman/iStockphoto.com, © Photodisc/Getty Images, © James C. Pruitt/iStockphoto.com, © Mohamed Saber – Fotolia.com

Pack: © Stockbyte/Getty Images

Acknowledgements

It is impossible to quantify the late Ralph Kirsch's part in helping us to bring the original *Teach Yourself Xhosa* to fruition. His interest, support, technical advice and especially his generosity of spirit over the years, were unfailing. We would also like to thank Ms Theresa Soci for her help with proof reading and for the many useful suggestions she made and for acting as consultant for this new edition.

We are grateful to the following copyright owners for permission to reproduce texts and/or photographs:

Amathole Museum, Kingwilliam's Town
David Philip Publishers (Pty) Ltd, Cape Town
Fort Hare University, Alice, Eastern Cape
John Murray, London
Witwatersrand University Press, Johannesburg
Heinemann Publishers (Pty) Ltd, Johannesburg
Struik Publishers, Cape Town
Sunday Independent, Johannesburg
Maskew Miller Longman, Cape Town
Little, Brown, UK
Educum Publishers, Halfway House
Bona Magazine, Durban
TV Bulpin, Muizenberg, Cape Town
Cape Argus, Cape Town
Cape Times, Cape Town
Sunday Times, Johannesburg
National Botanical Institute, Kirstenbosch, Cape Town
Department of Water Affairs, Pretoria
United Cricket Board of South Africa, Northlands, Johannesburg
National Gallery, Cape Town
Mayibuye Centre, University of the Western Cape
Touchline Photo
Fair Lady, Cape Town
Imvo
Ian Lusted

Meet the authors

South African-born Beverley Kirsch and German-born Silvia Skorge who has a doctorate in linguistics from the Freie Universität, Berlin, first met, as mature students, in 1974 while studying Xhosa at the University of Cape Town. Beverley was completing a Bachelor's degree and Silvia was keen to add an African language to her collection of some four Romance and three Scandanavian languages. In 1976, their final year, feeling the need for some extra coaching, they had the singular good fortune of being referred to a dynamic teacher at the South African College for Higher Education, Sindiwe Magona (now a celebrated author and much in demand as a motivational speaker).

Realizing that a more communicative approach to learning Xhosa was needed, Beverley and Silvia drew on their knowledge of the challenges facing non-mother-tongue speakers learning a new language and wrote their first book, ***Masithethe isiXhosa*** *Let's Speak Xhosa* in 1979 which they initially published themselves.

Silvia has written several text books and grammars in German and was an associate professor in the Department of German at the University of the Western Cape, specializing in the methodology of foreign language teaching. Beverley has taught Xhosa at the medical schools of the Universities of Cape Town and Stellenbosch (as well as extra-murally) which resulted in the publication of ***An English-Xhosa Companion for Health Care Professionals*** with Dr Nosisa Matsiliza acting as both language and medical consultant.

This was followed by ***Teach Yourself Xhosa*** and then a phrase book entitled ***Clicking with Xhosa,*** again with Sindiwe Magona acting as language consultant. The Zulu version of this phrase book, entitled ***Zooming in on Zulu*** with Dr Nonhlanhla Khumalo acting as language consultant, was published a year later.

In 2007 Silvia, Beverley and Sindiwe were jointly awarded the Molteno Medal [Gold] for their 'lifetime achievement in literature by the promotion of the Xhosa language […] that has made the learning of the Xhosa language, together with an understanding of Xhosa traditions and culture, a wonderful and pleasurable experience.'

The language consultant for **Complete Xhosa** is Theresa Soci, who taught Xhosa at the National Language Project and at various schools in Cape Town. She has also taught Xhosa to the staff at a number of companies as well as to several private groups.

Only got a minute?

The **Xhosa** language, former President Mandela's mother tongue, is spoken by about eight million people mainly in the Eastern and Western Cape of South Africa and it is one of the 11 official languages of South Africa. It uses the Latin alphabet and its writing and literature go back to the beginning of the 19th century.

Xhosa is a *tone* language with high, low and high falling tones which mark a difference in meaning of words with the same spelling:

> **Úthetha isiXhosa kakuhle**. =
> *He / she speaks Xhosa well.*
> **Ùthetha isiXhosa kakuhle.** =
> *You speak Xhosa well.*

The influence of the Khoi and San languages spoken by the indigenous herders and hunters of Southern Africa, with whom the various **Xhosa** groups had early and intimate contact, explains the incorporation of **click** sounds. The name **Xhosa** itself and many other words in the lexicon, for example names of Xhosa chiefs and geographical names, bear testimony to this contact.

There are also quite a number of words borrowed from English and Afrikaans which facilitate the learning of vocabulary, e.g. *i***kofu** < *coffee*, *i***venkile** < Afrikaans winkel = *shop*.

Another characteristic is that **Xhosa**, as an *agglutinative* language, *laces words together*:

NdinguJohn	one word
I am John	three words.

However, the most striking feature of the **Xhosa** language is **the grouping of nouns into classes** (instead of gender) according to their **prefix** from which other elements in the sentence are derived, e.g. subject and object concords which, unlike English pronouns, never stand alone but are attached to the predicate. The **stem** carries the meaning and does not change. Different prefixes usually alter the meaning of a stem:

*um***ntu**	*a person**
*aba***ntu**	*people*
*ulu***ntu**	*community*

It is important to be able to identify this division between prefix and stem as nouns are listed in dictionaries according to their stem.

*Context indicates whether the meaning of, for example, '*um***ntu**' is ***the*** *person* or ***a*** *person*.

10 Only got ten minutes?

In addition to English and Afrikaans, there are nine official languages in South Africa. These nine, like several hundred other Sub-Saharan languages, belong to the family of **Bantu languages** of which Swahili (East Africa) has the most speakers. *Aba***ntu,** meaning *people*, is a common word in many of these languages (which also have similar grammatical structures, i.e. nouns which dominate the sentence and which are grouped into classes according to prefixes). They have hence been internationally classified as the Bantu family of languages.

Of the nine African languages spoken in South Africa, Xhosa, Zulu, Ndebele and Swati constitute the Nguni group; Southern Sotho, Pedi (Northern Sotho) and Tswana constitute the Sotho group. Venda and Tsonga (Shangaan) do not belong to either the Nguni or the Sotho group.

After Zulu, Xhosa is the most widely spoken language in South Africa. It is spoken by approximately 18 per cent of South Africans as their first language. The vast majority of Xhosa speakers live in the Eastern and Western Cape.

Xhosa, the mother tongue of former President Mandela, is the southernmost of the nine African languages and has been enriched in sounds and vocabulary by the San and Khoi languages spoken by the indigenous hunters and herders of Southern Africa with whom the various Xhosa groups had early and intimate contact over several centuries. Wives of the 18th-century Xhosa chiefs were often Khoikhoi.

This influence is reflected in the incorporation of **click** sounds and the sound 'rh' – pronounced like the Afrikaans 'g' in 'goed' or the German 'ch' in 'nach', cf. *i***Rhini** (Grahamstown). There are about

2,400 click words in Xhosa compared with fewer than 400 in Zulu. They are found in basic vocabulary, e.g. **-cela** = *ask*, **-nceda** = *help* as well as in names of chiefs, such as **Ngqika**, and also in geographical names like *i***Qonce** (King William's Town).

Sometimes Xhosa words and those taken from the Khoi language coexist:

*in***gca**/*u***tyani**	=	*grass*
*im***vu**/*i***gusha**	=	*the fat-tailed African sheep*
*i***gqirha**/*um***thakati**	=	*sorcerer*

In more recent years, many English and Afrikaans words have been 'Xhosalized':

*isi***kolo**	=	*school*
*ii***bhokisi**	=	*box*
*u***matshini**	=	*machine*

In some instances '*i-*' is simply prefixed to an English word:

*i***Red Cross**
*i***personnel manager**

Xhosa is a heterogeneous and complex language originating from a large and diversified group with many chiefs and clans. Until the mid-1950s the Xhosa spoken by *ama***Gcaleka** and *ama***Rharhabe**** (also known as '*ama***Ngqika**' or **'Tshiwo' Xhosa**) was regarded as standard literary Xhosa – '*isi***Xhosa** esithethwa ngama**Ngqika** omgquba' (lit. Xhosa spoken by *ama***Ngqika** of old manure [of the kraal]), i.e. pure **Xhosa** also termed as *isi***Xhosa** somthonyana (*of very, very old manure*).

Nowadays the variations of the dialects of the other groups further north, namely *aba***Thembu**, *ama***Bomvana**, *ama***Mpondo** and *ama***Mpondomise**, as well as *aba***Mbo** or *ama***Mfengu (Fingoes)**, are also accepted in the written language.

Ama*Gcaleka** and *ama***Rharhabe** were named after the two brothers, chiefs **Gcaleka** and **Rharhabe**. **Ngqika** was **Rharhabe**'s grandson.

It was the Scottish missionary, the Reverend Dr John Bennie of Lovedale, who first recorded the Xhosa language and produced the first written texts using the Latin alphabet with the letters **c**, **q**, **x** representing the three clicks. Since then many literary texts have been published and much of the rich oral literature of former times has been preserved.

Like all languages, everyday colloquial Xhosa differs from that found in literature and grammars. Similarly, language use often differs not only from region to region, but also from generation to generation.

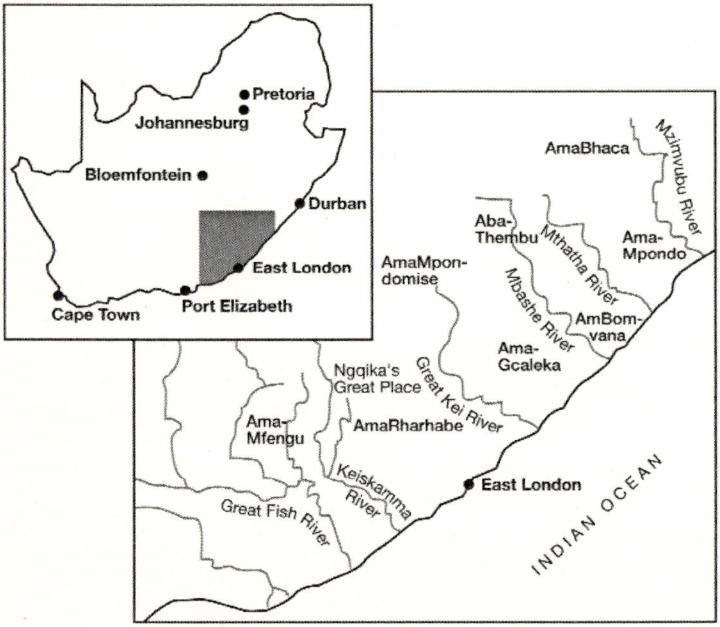

Striking characteristics of the Xhosa language

Most of these characteristics are in common with other Bantu languages. They include the following:

The *lacing together of words* where English has separate words, often resulting in lengthy word formations:

Ndiya**vuya** uku*kw***azi**	two words
I **am glad** to **know** *you*	six words

All nouns consist of two parts, namely a **prefix** and a **stem**, and are *grouped into noun classes according to their prefix* (unlike most Indo-European languages which have grammatical gender, i.e. masculine, feminine and neuter). The **prefix** generally indicates whether a noun is singular or plural unlike in English where, in most cases, the addition of 's' makes a noun plural. The **stem** carries the **meaning**:

*um***ntu**	*a / the person**
*aba***ntu**	*people*

(*Context indicates whether the meaning of, for example, '*um***ntu**' is ***the** person* or ***a** person.*)

Different prefixes usually alter the meaning of the stem:

*isi***ntu**	dress, language, custom of *aba***Ntu**	*isi***Xhosa**	Xhosa **language**
*ulu***ntu**	community		
*ubu***ntu**	common **human** decency	*ubu***Xhosa**	'Xhosa**ness**'

It is important to be able to identify this division between prefix and stem as nouns are listed in dictionaries according to their stem.

The **prefix** of a noun determines not only the class or group to which a noun belongs, but also the **formation of concords**, i.e. **subject concords** which are the equivalent of English pronouns '*he, she, it, they*'. Unlike English pronouns, subject concords cannot stand on their own but are always attached to the verb even if it is preceded by a noun.

A noun with the **prefix** '*um-*' has the **subject concord** '*u-*' = '*he, she, it*':

*Um***ntwana** *u***thetha** *isi***Xhosa**.	The **child** (*he / she*) **speaks Xhosa**.

*Um***thi** *u***khula** kakuhle. The **tree** (*it*) is **growing** well.

A noun with the **prefix** '*aba-*' has the **subject concord** '*ba-*' = '*they*':

*Aba***ntwana** *ba***thetha** *isi***Xhosa**. The **children** (*they*) **speak Xhosa**.

In the same way, **adjectives** and **relative clauses** must agree with the noun they refer to by prefixing **adjectival** and **relative concords**:

*Aba***ntwana** *ba***m**	*My children* (lit. ***children** of **my***)
*Aba***ntwana** *aba***hle**	*Beautiful children* (lit. ***children** who [are] **beautiful***)
*Aba***ntwana** *aba***thetha** *isi***Xhosa** *ba***ninzi**.	*The **children** who **speak Xhosa** (they) are **many**.*

The equivalent of the English pronouns *him*, *her*, *them* are known as **object concords** and precede the verb:

Ndiya*ba***thanda** (*aba***ntwana** *ba***m**) *I **love** them* (*my* **children**).

Verbs in Xhosa have many tenses and moods. Verb endings are the same for all persons, singular and plural, and all tenses:

*Ndi*ya**thetha**	*I am **speaking***	*Ndi***thethile**	***I spoke***
*Si*ya**thetha**	*We are **speaking***	*Si***thethile**	*We **spoke***
*Ù*ya**thetha**	*You (s.) are **speaking***	*Ù***thethile**	*You (s.) **spoke***
*Ni*ya**thetha**	*You (pl.) are **speaking***	*Ni***thethile**	*You (pl.) **spoke***
*Ú*ya**thetha**	*He / she is **speaking***	*Ú***thethile**	*He / she **spoke***
*Ba*ya**thetha**	*They are **speaking***	*Ba***thethile**	*They **spoke***

Many verbs can be extended in a number of different ways thereby altering their meaning or translating the equivalent of an English preposition or forming the passive voice:

Ndiya**funda**	*I am **learning***
Ndiya**fundisa**	*I am **teaching*** (lit. *I **cause to** learn*)

Ù**fundela** ntoni?	*What are you* ***studying for****?*
Ndiya**fundiswa**	*I am* ***taught*** (passive voice)

As you can see from the above examples, the *word order* can differ from that of English:

Question words (interrogatives) usually *follow the verb* (or predicate):

Ùphila **njani**?	***How*** *are you?* (lit. *You live* ***how****?*)
Ùhlala **phi**?	***Where*** *do you live?* (lit. *You live* ***where****?*)

Similarly, *qualificatives* such as adjectives, numerals and possessives are usually placed after the word they describe:

*um***ntu** *om***tsha**	*a young* ***person*** (lit. *a* ***person*** *who* is *young*)
*um***ntu** *om***nye**	*one* ***person*** (lit. *a* ***person*** *who* is *one*)
*um***ntwana** *wa***m**	*my* ***child*** (lit. ***child*** *of* ***my***)

Like all the Southern Bantu languages, **Xhosa** is a *tonal language* with *high, low* and *high falling tones* which mark a difference in the meaning of words with the same spelling:

Ùya**vuya**:	ù with a *low tone* means *You (s.)* ***are glad***
Úyavuy**a**:	ú with a *high tone* means *He/she* ***is glad***

Tone is not usually marked in dictionaries. When listening to or speaking Xhosa, context will help to impart the intended meaning.

Introduction

About this book

Complete Xhosa is intended for all who are interested in learning one of the most widely spoken African languages in South Africa.

It is aimed at both South Africans and visitors to South Africa, and at those who are learning Xhosa from scratch as well as those who would like to brush up their existing skills. As such, it should benefit students at high school and university level, as well as those involved in adult education.

Wherever possible, the communicative aspect of the language has been emphasized which has hopefully resulted in a course which is useful and practical. Cultural background and information forms an integral part of the course.

The book is divided into 16 units which range from basic functions and language usage in the initial units to more varied and complex usage in the later units. The inclusion of material from Xhosa literature and magazines is aimed at encouraging further reading.

Each unit consists of a:

- list of functions
- dialogue (*in*coko) setting out the situation and functions
- vocabulary (*isi*gama) box with all new words and expressions
- 'How to …' section which summarizes and expands upon the functions dealt with in the conversation
- 'How it works' section which explains the grammatical structures as they occur in the conversations and exercises
- 'How to apply it' section comprising a number of exercises to help you to evaluate your progress and your ability to apply the new vocabulary and structures you have learned
- Test yourself questions.

In the initial units, useful idiomatic expressions and phrases which crop up in the conversations are highlighted in a 'Try to memorize' box. You will understand their grammatical structure as you progress through the course.

Insight boxes, cultural information and songs are included throughout the course. Translations of the dialogues of each unit and the key to exercises and Test yourself questions are found after the last unit followed by a Xhosa–English vocabulary, an English–Xhosa vocabulary, a bibliography and an index.

The use of contrasting typefaces

One of the most striking features of **Xhosa** is the combination of different parts of speech into a 'single' word. Thus the equivalent of 'I ***am*** **Jenny**' is 'Ndi***ngu*****Jenny**'. We have used contrasting typefaces to identify the components of **Xhosa** words and sentences as illustrated here. In order to establish this usage, these are used in all components of Units 1–3. In Units 4–16 contrasting typefaces only appear in certain sections where they are useful in explaining grammar. English translations are in the same typefaces as the corresponding **Xhosa**, and therefore almost always self-explanatory.

Key to the use of typefaces

To find examples, consult the index.

Italics:

- *noun prefixes*
- *object concords*, *subject concords* of vowel verbs
- *negative subject concords* and final *-i*
- *adjectival, relative, possessive concords* and *suffix* '*-yo*'
- *recent past tense suffixes* '*-ile*' and '*-e*'
- *-ni in instructions*
- *emphatic pronouns* preceded by **na**-, **ku**-, **nga**- and followed by -**na**
- *locative prefixes* and *suffixes*
- *palatalised forms* of the *passive, locative* and *diminutive*
- *ideophones* and *idioms*.

continued …

Bold:

- **stems** of **nouns, verbs, adjectives, relatives**
- **interrogatives**
- **possessive adjectives**
- final -**e** of **subjunctive**
- **negative -nga-; -nge-**
- elements with shortened emphatic pronoun **na**-, **ku**-, etc.

Italicised bold:

- ***copulatives***
- ***two juxtaposed components***.

Underlining:

- added emphasis.

Symbols and abbreviations

🔊 recorded material

→ cf. / see **Unit** ...

SC	subject concord
OC	object concord
AC	adjectival concord
RC	relative concord
s.	singular
pl.	plural
adj.	adjective
lit.	literally

A hyphen preceding an element, e.g. '-na', means something must be attached before. Following an element, e.g. 'na-', means something must follow. On either side of an element, e.g. '-ng-', means something must precede and follow.

Pronunciation guide

It goes without saying that a written guide to pronunciation can at best only give an approximation of sounds. Therefore, to 'tune in' to the language try, as much as possible, to listen to mother-tongue speakers (radio and television are excellent resources) and to the CD that accompanies this book.

Tone

CD 1, tr 1, 01:06

Xhosa is a **tone language**. Its range of **tones** makes Xhosa the beautiful, musical language that it is. The **three** tonal distinctions are:

high ´ tone	falling ^ tone	low ` tone

Examples of some tonal patterns are:

high / falling / low	**ékhâyà**	at home
high / high / low	**ábántù**	people
high / low / low	**ízòlò**	yesterday
high / low	**mólò**	hello
low / high	**èwé**	yes

This difference in tone can change the meaning of two words or elements that are written identically, e.g.:

ùnjani?	How are **you**? (s.)	úl**ù**s**ú**	*skin*	íthàng**á**	thigh
únjani?	How is **he/she**?	úl**ú**s**ù**	*intestine*	íthàng**à**	pumpkin

Notwithstanding these differences in tone, learners should not allow concern regarding the use of 'the correct tone' to inhibit their efforts to speak, especially as a word may have different tone patterns in different dialects of Xhosa. As is the case with all languages, the context will, in most cases, help the listener to understand the intended meaning.

Stress

CD 1, tr 1, 03:00

The penultimate syllable of most Xhosa words is **lengthened** (stressed):

nam**hla**nje	today	ibho**to**lo	butter
um**hlo**bo	friend	kulun**gi**le	all right

The penultimate syllable in a sentence structure is often lengthened beyond the single word limit:

Ùve<u>**la**</u> phi?	Where do you come from?
Hayi, akukh**o n**to.	No, there is nothing bad. (i.e. I'm fine.)

A working guide to Xhosa pronunciation

CD 1, tr 1, 03:50

Vowels

Letter	***Approximate sound***		***Example***	
a	English	f**a**st	l**a**la	(sleep)
e (open)	English	**e**gg	**e**we	(yes)
e (closed)	English	**e**(i)ght	iv**e**ki	(week)
i	English	b**e**	n**i**n**i**	(when?)
o (open)	English	l**a**w	iz**o**lo	(yesterday)
o (closed)	English	**o**wn	ng**o**ku	(now)
u	English	r**u**le	**u**mntu	(person)

In Xhosa, two vowels never follow one another within a word. Double vowels only occur in the **plural prefixes**, *oo-* and *ii-*:

*oo***mama** (mothers) *ii***veki** (weeks)

Double vowels also occur in some **demonstratives**:

l**oo** nto (**that** thing) ab**aa** *ba***ntu** (**those** people over there)

In words adopted from English and Afrikaans, vowels are often separated by a hyphen:

<u>*i-*</u><u>**e**</u>ropleni (aeroplane) <u>*i-*</u><u>**o**</u>fisi (office)

Xhosa speakers tend not to pronounce the final vowel of a word, especially when the following word starts with a vowel:

Yiz' apha	instead of	Yiz<u>a</u> apha (Come here)
Nceda ùlind' ithuba		Nceda ùlind<u>e</u> ithuba! (Wait your chance!)
Enkos' kakhulu		Enkos<u>i</u> kakhulu (Many thanks)

Consonants

CD 1, tr 1, 06:18

Single consonants similar to English in pronunciation are:

d	f	g
h	j	l
n	s	v
w	y	z

The Xhosa consonants **b**, **k**, **p**, **t** are very interesting. Followed by '*h*' (aspirated) they are pronounced as they are in English, i.e. accompanied by a puff of air:

B*h*ala! (Write!)
K*h*a**p***h*a! (Go with!)
P*h*a**p***h*a! (Be alert!)
T*h*a**t***h*a! (Take!)

However, when they are not followed by '*h*', air is drawn into the mouth. Compare the following:

B*h*ala! (Write!)	**B**ala (Count!)
K*h*a**p***h*a! (Go with!)	i**K**a**p**a (Cape Town)
P*h*a**p***h*a! (Be alert!)	i**p**a**p**a (porridge)
T*h*a**t***h*a! (Take!)	u**t**a**t**a (father)

In order to ascertain whether you are pronouncing:

b or **b***h*   **k** or **k***h*   **p** or **p***h*   **t** or **t***h*

you might find it helpful, in the beginning, to hold your hand in front of your mouth when pronouncing these consonants. If you feel a puff of air, you will be pronouncing an aspirated consonant and vice versa.

m, when not followed by a vowel or the consonants b / p / v, is pronounced as a syllable:

ú / **m** /ntù (person)	3 syllables
ú / **m** / fu / ndi (student, pupil)	4 syllables

As **p***h* represents an aspirated 'p' it and is **not** pronounced like the English '**f**'; similarly, **t***h* represents an aspirated **'t' not English** 'th' as in 'thing'.

n is never followed by an aspirated consonant, cf. *in***kwenkwe** (boy) BUT *ama***khwenkwe** (boys)

Some consonant combinations similar to English

ng	i**ng**oma (song) pronounced like English	‘**ng**’in si**ng**
sh	i**sh**i**sh**ini (factory)	‘**sh**’ in **sh**ine
tsh	ikhi**tsh**i (kitchen)	‘**tch**’ in ki**tch**en
ntsh	i**ntsh**onalanga (west)	‘**nch**’ in i**nch**
ny	u**ny**ana (son)	‘**ny**’ in ca**ny**on
ths	**ths**u (pitch-black)	‘**ts**’ in i**ts**

Consonant combinations with no English equivalents

CD 1, tr 1, 08:30

Because there are no English equivalents of the following consonant combinations it might take you a little longer to master them:

dl	um**dl**alo (game, play)	
hl	**hl**ala (sit, stay [as in reside])	(cf. Zulu ‘**Hl**uh**l**uwe’ or Welsh **Ll**andudno. Don’t insert an ‘s’ making it sound like ‘shl’)
ntl	i**ntl**anzi (fish)	
dy	-**dy**u**dy**uza (pour with rain)	
ty	uku**ty**a (to eat)	(cf. ‘Cape’ Afrikaans ‘**tjie**’)
ts	iin**ts**apho (families)	(‘t’ is not aspirated)
rh	i**Rh**awuti (Johannesburg)	(< Afrikaans ‘goud’ = gold; cf. Gauteng [Sotho]; Scottish ‘loch’)
kr	-**kr**ele**kr**ele (sharp < i**kr**ele = sword)	

kr as well as **rh** and the **clicks** are sounds taken over from the Khoi and San languages.

The clicks

CD 1, tr 1, 09:36

The **three clicks** are represented by the letters:

c **q** **x**

When Xhosa became a written language in the 1800s, these three letters were chosen to represent the three click sounds because the letter **k** could replace each one:

cat	could be written **k**at
queen	could be written **k**ween
a**x**e	could be written a**k**s

C – the '*what a pity*' click

This is a **dental click** produced by pressing the **tip** of the **tongue** against the **upper front teeth** where these meet the gum and rapidly pulling it away with a '*tut-tutting*' sound.

Q – the '*champagne cork popping*' click

This is a **palatal click** produced by pressing the **front part of the tongue** against the **hard palate behind the front teeth** and rapidly pulling it away with a '*popping*' sound.

X – the '*cantering horse*' click

This is a **lateral click** produced by placing the **side of the tongue** against the **upper side teeth** and rapidly pulling it away with a '*clucking*' sound.

Clicks may also be aspirated, i.e. followed by '*h*':

c*h* -**c***h*a**c***h*a (recuperate)	**c** -**c**a**c**a (be clear)
q*h* -**q***h*uba (drive)	**q** -**q**ubha (swim)
x*h* -**x***h*o**x***h*a (mash)	**x** -**x**o**x**a (discuss)

Remember that '**c***h*' is not pronounced like the English 'ch' therefore '**c***h*a**c***h*a' = 'recuperate' is not pronounced like the Latin American dance!

Non-aspirated clicks can be preceded by the following consonants and consonant combinations:

	*g***c** (voiced)	*n***c** (nasalised)	*ng***c** (nasalised voiced)	*nk***c***
c	um*g***c**a (row)	u*n***c**edo (help)	ii*ng***c**ango (doors)	i*nk***c**itho (expenditure)
	*g***q**	*n***q**	*ng***q**	*nk***q**
q	u*g***q**irha (doctor)	i*n***q**welo-moya (aeroplane)	i*ng***q**ondo (intelligence)	*nk***q**o*nk***q**oza (knock)
	*g***x**	*n***x**	*ng***x**	*nk***x**
x	i*g***x**alaba (shoulder)	u*n***x**ano (thirst)	i*ng***x**oxo (discussion)	i*nk***x**aso (support)

*In these nasalized voiceless sounds 'k' is not pronounced.

🔊 **CD 1, tr 1, 12:10**

Practise the **q** clicks by listening to the first few lines of the '*Click Song*' made famous by the late **Miriam Makeba**. Try singing along:

'I*g***q**irha lendlela ngu**q**o*ng***q**othwane,	*The witchdoctor of the road is a black beetle.*
Ebe**q**abel' e*g***q**ith' apha u**q**o*ng***q**othwane!'	*It has gone past here, the black beetle.*

Here are some phrases or words you'll come across in this course. Take special note of the implosives **b**, **t**, **k**, the **consonant combinations** with no English equivalents and the **clicks**:

So**b**onana!	*We'll see each other!*
Bekumnandi ukudi**b**ana nawe	*It was nice to meet you*
Ham**ba** kakuhle!	*Go well!*
Nam**k**ele**k**ile e**K**apa	*Welcome to Cape Town* (lit. *You are welcome in Cape Town*)
Siza kufi**ka** e**K**apa **k**amsinyane	*We'll arrive in Cape Town shortly*
Kulungile	*All right*
Molo **t**a**t**a!	*Hello, father!*
Ndisa**t**o**t**oba	*I'm still tottering along, i.e. I'm well*
Siphi isibhe**dl**ele?	*Where's the hospital?*
Aba**dl**ali ba**dl**ala um**dl**alo	*The players are playing a game*
Masi**hl**ale ngaphandle nam**hl**anje	*Let's sit outside today*
Mhlawumbi, yonke imi**hl**a	*Perhaps, every day*
Intle le **ntl**anzi	*It's beautiful, this fish*
Intle **intl**akohlaza	*It's beautiful, spring*
Tyala ezi zi**ty**alo ehlo**ty**eni	*Plant these plants in summer*
Ikomi**ty**i enye kuphela	*One cup only*
Na**nts**i ikofu!	*Here's the coffee!*
U**kr**ele**kr**ele gqitha	*He's very sharp*
Uhlala e**Rh**awutini	*He lives in Johannesburg*
Ndingaku**nc**eda?	*Can I help you?*
Zi**nc**ede!	*Help yourself!*
U**c**han' u**c**wethe!	*You're spot on!* (lit. *You've taken aim and hit the shrew!*)
Cheba i**ngc**a!	*Cut the grass!*

Ndi**gq**ibile!	*I've finished!*
Eku**gq**ibeleni!	*At last!*
Qhuba uye ku**Q**obo**q**obo!	*Drive and go to Keiskammahoek!*
Masi**q**abule u**nx**ano!	*Let's quench the thirst!*
Ndi**nx**aniwe	*I'm thirsty*
U**x**olo!	*Sorry!* (lit. *peace)*

1 Ukwazana *kwi*-eropleni*
Getting acquainted on an aeroplane

In this unit you will learn how to:

- exchange greetings
- welcome a group
- ask how someone is and respond to being asked how you are
- introduce yourself and respond to an introduction
- ask where someone lives and respond to being asked where you live
- say goodbye to a group and individuals

Incoko (*Dialogue*)

CD 1, tr 2

Thandi Thamsanqa and Jenny Murray are seated next to each other on a flight from Port Elizabeth. The stewardess greets the passengers.

Umququzelelikazi	Molweni *ma***nene** n*ama***nenekazi**! **Namkelek***ile ku*flight 301 *o***ya** *e***Kapa**!
UThandi	Molo **sisi**, **ùnjani** namhlanje?
UJenny	Ewe **sisi**, si**khona**!
UThandi	Oo! Ù*si***thetha** kakuhle *isi***Xhosa**, sisi! Ndi*ngu***Thandi** Thamsanqa.
UJenny	Ndi*ngu***Jenny** Murray. Ndiya**vuya** uku*kw***azi**, Thandi. Wena, **uphila njani**?
UThandi	Hayi, si**phil***ile* enkosi. Nam, ndiya**vuya** uku*kw***azi**, **Jenny**.
UJenny	**Ùhlala** *e***Kapa**, **Thandi**?
UThandi	Ewe, si**hlala** *e***Pinelands**.

*Anglicised version of the much more picturesque '*in***qwelo-moya**' (lit. wagon [of the] air).

UJenny	Oo! Nam ndi**hlala** *e***Pinelands**!
UThandi	Ndawoni kanye?
UJenny	Ngase*e***Forest Drive**. Wena u**hlala** **ndawo***ni*?
UThandi	Ngase*e***Pinelands** High School.

For the duration of the flight Thandi and Jenny get to know each other and agree to make contact again soon.

Umququzelelikazi	*U***xolo**, *ma***nene** n*ama***nenekazi**. **Qhobosha***ni* *ama***bhanti**. Siza ku**fika** *e***Kapa** kamsinya. Enkosi kakhulu ngoku**khetha** i-*Rainbow Airlines*. Ndiya**themba** so**bonana** kwakhona kamsinyane! **Namkelek***ile* *e***Kapa**! **Hamba***ni* kakuhle!
UJenny	**Hamba** kakuhle Thandi. Beku**mnandi** kakhulu uku**thetha** nawe.
UThandi	So**bonana** sisi, beku**mnandi** uku**dibana** nawe!

Isigama (*Vocabulary*)

*um***ququzelelikazi**	**stewardess**	ndi-	I
Molweni	good day / hello (pl.)	*-ng-*	***am***
*ma***nene**	**gentlemen** (direct address)	*u***Thandi**	**Thandi**
na*ma***nenekazi**	and **ladies**	-**vuya**	**glad**
namkelek*ile*	you (pl.) are **welcome**	ndiya**vuya**	I am **glad**
*ku*flight	*on (board)* flight	uku-	to
*o***ya** *e***Kapa**	*which* is **going** *to* **Cape Town**	*-kw-*	*you* (s.) (object)
		-**azi**	**know**
molo	hello (to one person)	uku*kw***azi**	to **know** *you*
sisi (< *u***sisi**)	**sister** (direct address)	wena	as for you (s.)
ù-	you (s.) (subject)	-**phila**	**be well**, **alive**
njani?	**how**?	hayi	no
ù**njani**?	**how** are you?	si**phil***ile*	we are **well**
namhlanje	today	enkosi	thank you
ewe	yes	nam	me too, I also
si-	we	-**hlala**	stay, live (also sit)
-**khona**	(be) present / here	*e***Pinelands**	*in* **Pinelands**
si**khona**	we are **here** i.e. well	ndawoni kanye?	whereabouts exactly?
-si-	it (referring to *isi***Xhosa**)	ngase*e*-	near / in the vicinity
-**thetha**	**speak**	*u***xolo**	excuse me (lit. peace)
kakuhle	well	**qhobosha***ni*	**fasten** (pl.)
*isi***Xhosa**	**Xhosa**	*ama***bhanti**	(seat) **belts**

siza ku**fika**	we will **arrive**	**hamba***ni*	**go** (pl.)
kamsinya(ne)	shortly, soon	**hamba**	**go** (s.)
ngoku**khetha**	for **choosing**	beku**mnandi**	it was **nice**
-themba	**hope**	kakhulu	very
so**bonana**	we'll **see each other**	**na***we*	**with** *you*
kwakhona	again	uku**dibana**	to **meet**

Try to memorize

Namkelekile!	Welcome! (pl.)
Ndiyavuya uku*kw***azi**	I am glad to know *you* (s.)
Ndawoni?	Whereabouts exactly?
Sobonana	We shall see each other
Bekumnandi ukudibana nawe	It was nice to meet (with) you (s.)
Bekumnandi ukuthetha nawe	It was nice to talk with you (s.)

How to ...

Exchange greetings

With **one person**:

Mol<u>o</u> **sisi**!
Mol<u>o</u> ***n*kosikazi**!

With ***more than*** **one person**:

Mol<u>weni</u> *ma***nene n***ama***nenekazi**!

Insight

When greeting one person you say **Molo!** which comes from the Afrikaans 'Môre!' = *Good morning/day!*
When greeting more than one person you say **Molweni!**
Molo/Molweni are used to greet at any time of day or night.

CD 1, tr 2, 02:02

MOLWENI NONKE!

Molweni nonke, niphila njani?	*Hello all of you, how are you?*
Sisaphil' enkosi,	*We are still well thank you,*
Kunjani kuwe?	*How are you?*

A guide to help you greet appropriately in Xhosa

1 An older man of your father's generation:

Molo tata! (affectionate)	Hello father!
Molo bawo! (more respectful)	Hello my father!
Molo mnumzana!	Hello sir! (lit. owner of homestead/s = *um***zi** / *imi***zi**)
Molo mhlekazi! (formal)	Hello sir! (lit. handsome big one)

2 An older man of your grandfather's generation:

Molo tat'omkhulu!	Hello grandfather!

3 A woman of your mother's generation:

Molo mama!	Hello mother!

4 A woman of your grandmother's generation:

Molo makhulu!	Hello grandmother!

5 A married woman of your age or younger:

Molo nkosikazi!	Hello madam! (cf. Afrikaans *mevrou*, French *madame*)

6 An unmarried lady or a young girl:

Molo nkosazana!	Hello miss! (cf. Afrikaans *mejuffrou*, French *mademoiselle*)

(The literal meaning of *in***kosazana** is a little chieftainess i.e. princess.)

7 A person of approximately the same age as yourself:

Molo mfondini!	Hello my fellow!

(< *um***fo** = fellow) + *-ndini* is used as a term of affection between male equals)

Molo bhuti!	Hello brother!
Molo sisi!	Hello sister!
Molo mhlobo wam/mhlob' am!	Hello my friend!

8 A young man:

Molo mfana!	Hello young man!

(A young man after circumcision is referred to as *um***fana**.)

9 A young girl (also daughter):

Molo ntombi!	Hello young lady!

10 A little girl:

Molo ntombazana!	Hello little girl!

11 A little boy:

Molo nkwenkwe!	Hello little boy!
Molo nkwenkwana!	Hello little boy!
Molo kwedini!	Hello little chap!

(**kwedini** < i*n***kwenkwe** + *-ndini* expresses affection, intimacy between an older and younger man / boy)

12 A child:

Molo mntwan'am!	Hello my child!

→ See Cultural background.

Sign at Cape Town International Airport

Welcome a group

Namkelek*ile* (lit. You [pl.] are **welcome**)
Note: W**amkelek***ile* (lit. You [s.] are **welcome**)

Ask how someone is

Singular	**Plural**
Ùnjani?	**Ninjani**?
Ùphila njani?	**Niphila njani**?

Respond to being asked how you are

Singular	**Plural**
Hayi, ndi**phil***ile*.	Hayi, si**phil***ile*.
Ndi**khona**.	Si**khona**.

Insight

In Xhosa, unlike in English, there is a distinction in form between the second person singular and plural *you* (cf. Afrikaans *jy; julle*, French *tu; vous*). It is common practice in Xhosa to use the plural form **Ni-** instead of the singular form **Ù-** when enquiring after someone's health thereby showing an interest in the well-being not only of the person being directly addressed, but also in that of the immediate family. Similarly, the response more often than not will be in the plural form **Si-** (= *We*) even though only one person is responding.

Xhosa speakers often preface **Hayi** (= *No*) when responding positively to the question, *How are you*?:

Hayi, si**phil***ile*. *No, we are well.*

(cf. Afrikaans **Nee**, dit gaan goed. *No, it's going well.*)

A positive response will often also be qualified by a complaint of sorts, e.g. about the weather, work, fatigue, etc.:

Ndiphilile **ngaphandle k**obu bushushu. *I'm fine except for this heat.*

→ See Unit 7 for other ways of asking after someone's health and responding.

Introduce yourself

Ndi*ngu***Jenny Murray**
Ndi*ngu***Nkosikazi Thamsanqa**

Note:	*in***kosikazi**	= lady, madam
	*uN***kosikazi** + surname	= Mrs

Respond to an introduction

Ndiyav**uya** uku*kw***azi**.

Insight

You will have noticed that Xhosa is an agglutinative language, i.e. it laces words together. For example:

I am Mrs Thamsanqa.	Four words
Ndi*ngu***Nkosikazi** Thamsanqa	Two words
I am **pleased** to **know** you.	Six words
Ndiyav**uya** uku*kw***azi**.	Two words

Ask where someone lives

Singular
Ùhlala phi?

Plural
Ni**hlala phi**?

Respond to being asked where you live

Singular
Ndi**hlala** *e***Kapa**.

Plural
Si**hlala** *e***Kapa**.

Say goodbye

Singular
Hamba kakuhle!

Plural
Hamba*ni* kakuhle!

So**bonana**!

Note: Sala kakuhle! (s.) **Sala***ni* kakuhle! (pl.) = '**Stay well**!' is said by the party who is leaving to the party who is staying.

Cultural background

> '**Greetings** are the key to almost everything among Xhosa speakers in particular, and among Africans in general. We do not only get surprised but also are somewhat disturbed when someone walks past without saying hello.'
> (Chapole, S. *Course Notes in Conversational Xhosa.* [Summer School] Department of Adult Education and Extra-Mural Studies University of Cape Town, 1988.)

The various stages from babyhood to old age are of great importance in Xhosa society. This is mirrored in how people of various age groups address each other. It is important for us, as learners of Xhosa, to be aware of this etiquette when greeting Xhosa speakers.

Molo/Molweni is used to greet at any time of day. It is followed by the name or title of the person/s being addressed and is the usual way of initiating a conversation with anyone, irrespective of age. Usually the person who is arriving greets first. However, a younger person should always be the first to address an older person, whatever the circumstances. The greeting includes questions about state of health, current affairs, the weather, etc.

In an article in the *Sunday Independent* (23/11/1997, p.10) entitled *Urban Youth don't know what it means to be African*, journalist **Lungile Madywabe** describes the puzzlement of his 23-year-old nephew when he discovers that his urban way of greeting an older man meets with indignation. 'He is used to meeting and greeting a lot of people in Johannesburg, but no one has told him before that merely saying "*Molo, kunjani ndikhona*" (*Hi, how are you, I am fine)* is inadequate, at least in the subtle terms of traditional Xhosa etiquette.' The young man didn't realise that 'greeting in an African culture is more than just uttering the words.' A detailed explanation of who he was and where he came from had been expected.

Madywabe goes on to reflect on 'how important a role the rural setting plays in the development of our minds. Those of us who grew up in urban areas when the influence of Western cultures was still minimal, and where elderly people counselled us a lot, are fortunate to have had access to the experiences and insight that have made us understand certain indigenous practices. Although certain things may not have made sense then because we were young, it is somehow strangely ironic how they now fit into place as we travel through adulthood.'

How it works

1 The Xhosa equivalent of English pronouns 'I,' 'we', 'you' (s. & pl.)

Ndi-	I
Si-	We
Ù-	You (s.)
Ni-	You (pl.)

The Xhosa equivalents of English pronouns **never stand alone**. They are therefore known as **subject concords** (SC):

Ndiyavuya	**I** am glad
Siyavuya	**We** are glad
Ùyavuya?	**You** (s.) are glad?
Niyavuya?	**You** (pl.) are glad?

2 Proper names

You will have noticed **proper names** are **prefixed** by *u*- which is omitted in direct address:

*u***Jenny** *u***Thandi**	**Molo Jenny / Thandi**

Xhosa first names ending in **-a** or **-e** are not necessarily feminine and those ending in **-o** are not necessarily masculine as is the case in many Romance languages:

*u***Themba** (promise)	*u***Sipho** (gift)	masculine
*u***Thembeka** (reliable)	*u***Nomvuyo** (mother of joy)	feminine

3 Giving instructions

Giving instructions in Xhosa is easy. When instructing one person simply use the verb stem.* To give instructions to more than one person simply suffix '*-ni*':

Singular	**Plural**
Hamba kakuhle!	**Hamba***ni* kakuhle!
Sala kakuhle!	**Sala***ni* kakuhle!
Thetha *isi***Xhosa**!	**Thetha***ni* *isi***Xhosa**!
Hlala phantsi!	**Hlala***ni* phantsi! (Sit down!)
Qhobosha *i***bhanti**!	**Qhobosha***ni* *ama***bhanti**!

*Verb stems prefix 'uku-' = 'to', and thereby form the **infinitive**. In **Xhosa** the infinitive is also a noun and as such is listed in dictionaries under the stem.

4 Making statements

The Xhosa statements that you have come across so far have a similar pattern to their English equivalent:

Ndi*ngu***Jenny**.	I *am* **Jenny**.
Si**hlala** *e***Pinelands**.	We **live** *in* **Pinelands**.

5 Asking questions

As in English, there are two types of question: The first type requires a 'yes'/'no' answer. In Xhosa only **intonation** distinguishes statements and questions:

Ù**thetha** *isi***Xhosa** kakuhle.	You **speak** Xhosa well.
Ù**thetha** *isi***Xhosa** kakuhle (na)?	Do you **speak** Xhosa well?

To make this distinction clearer, **na** is often added.

The second type of question requires **specific answers. Question words** (interrogatives) usually follow **the verb** (or **predicate**) and **do not occur at the beginning of a question** as is the case in English:

Ùphila **njani**?	**How** are you? (lit. You are alive **how**?)
Ùhlala **phi**?	**Where** do you **stay**?

→ See **Unit 2** and **Unit 8** for more about **interrogatives**.

Insight

Remember that **ph** is pronounced like the English **p** and NOT like the English **f**:

Ù**phila** njani?
[oo-**p**ee-lah njah-nee]
th is not pronounced like English **th**, but like the English **t.**

6 Some Xhosa equivalents of English prepositions

In Xhosa, there are several ways in which the equivalent of English prepositions (*in, on*, *at, to, from*, etc.) can be expressed, two of which are illustrated in this unit:

Ukw**azana** <u>*kwi*</u>-**eropleni**.	Getting **acquainted** <u>*on*</u> the **aeroplane**.
Ùhlala <u>*e*</u>**Kapa**?	Do you **stay** <u>*in*</u> **Cape Town**?
Namkelek*ile* <u>*e*</u>**Kapa**!	**Welcome** <u>*to*</u> **Cape Town**!

Note: The **context** denotes translation of the preposition.

→ See **Unit 4** for more examples.

Cultural background

In Xhosa society a great deal of significance is attached to the name given to a new-born baby. The name often reflects the hopes, aspirations, emotions, special qualities, historical events and even family circumstances at the time of birth, e.g. a boy called **Kwanele** (< *ukw***anela** = to become enough) indicates that the family now considers itself complete!

Natural occurrences at the time of the birth also influence a choice of name: a girl named **Nomakhwezi** (< *ama***khwezi** = stars) was probably born on a clear night while a girl named **Nomvula** (< *im***vula** = rain) was probably born when it was raining!

No- meaning '**mother of**' is often prefixed to a masculine name to form the feminine equivalent while *-kazi* / *-wa* / *-eka* are feminine suffixes. The suffix *-iwe* indicates either a girl's or boy's name.

Boys	Girls	Meaning	Derivation
Sipho	**Sipho***kazi*	**gift**	(< *isi***pho** = a **gift**)
Siph*iwe*	*Nozi***pho**		
Vuyo	**Vuyo***kazi*	**gladness**, **joy**	(< *uku***vuya** = *to* be **glad**)
Vuyani	*No*m**vuyo**		
Mandla	*No***mandla**	**strength**	(< *ama***ndla** = **strength**)
Khaya	*No***khaya**	**home**	(< *i***khaya** = **home**)
Mpumelelo	*No***mpumelelo**	**success**	(< *uku***phumelela** = *to* **succeed**)
Mbulelo	**Bulel***wa*	**gratitude**	(< *uku***bulela** = *to* **thank**)
Xola	**Xolis***wa*	**pacifier**	(< *uku***xola** = *to* **calm down**)
Bongani	**Bong***iwe*	**praise**, *be* **prais***ed*	(< *uku***bonga** = *to* **praise**)
Linda	**Lind***iwe*	**wait**, ***a*****wait***ed*	(< *uku***linda** = *to* **wait**)
Thando	**Thand***iwe*	**love**, **lov***ed*	(< *uku***thanda** = *to* **love**)
	Thand*eka*	**love***able*	
Themba	**Themb***eka*	**trust**, **trust***worthy*	(< *uku***themba** = *to* **hope**)

How to apply it

1 Greetings and introductions

(a) How would you greet Thandi?
(b) How would you greet an older lady?
(c) How would you greet an older gentleman?
(d) How would you greet a female friend?
(e) How would you greet a male friend?
(f) How would you greet a married lady?
(g) How would you greet a gentleman?
(h) How would you greet an unmarried lady?
(i) How would you greet a child?
(j) How would an air hostess greet passengers?
(k) How would you introduce yourself?
(l) How would you respond to an introduction?

2 Ask one person

(a) How are you?
(b) Do you live in Cape Town?
(c) Whereabouts exactly?

3 Say

(a) Welcome to Cape Town
ladies and gentlemen!
(b) I am well, thank you.
(c) I am glad to meet you.
(d) I live in Cape Town.
(e) It was nice to talk with you!
(f) It was nice to meet you!
(g) We shall see each other soon again!
(h) Goodbye when leaving a friend.
(i) Goodbye when leaving a group.
(j) Goodbye when a friend is leaving.
(k) Goodbye when a group is leaving.

4 What questions would you ask to obtain the following answers?

(a) Sikhona.
(b) Ndihlala eKapa.
(c) NgaseForest Drive.

5 Re-write the following putting in the appropriate word breaks

NamndiyavuyaukukwaziJenny.

6 Do you recognize the following Xhosa words which are in everyday use?

fundi	ingozi	zama
indaba	ithuba	

7 Listen to the following Xhosa words adopted from English and write down their meanings in the order in which you hear them.

CD 1, tr 2, 02:48

(a) _______	(h) _______	(o) _______
(b) _______	(i) _______	(p) _______
(c) _______	(j) _______	(q) _______
(d) _______	(k) _______	(r) _______
(e) _______	(l) _______	(s) _______
(f) _______	(m) _______	(t) _______
(g) _______	(n) _______	

Test yourself

1 How do you greet a lady of approximately the same age as yourself?

2 How do you welcome one person and how do you welcome a group of people?

3 How do you introduce yourself?

4 What are the equivalents to English pronouns known as? Why? How do you use them? Give examples by asking somebody how he/she is.

5 Could you also ask the question **Niphila njani?** or **Ninjani?** speaking to one person only?

6 How do you say that you are well?

7 How do you ask where somebody lives, and what is the correct word order in this question?

8 How do you make it clear that **Úthetha isiXhosa kakuhle?** is meant as a question, not a statement?

9 What is the difference between **Hamba kakuhle** and **Sala kakuhle** when saying *Goodbye*?

10 What does one say to a group of people from whom one takes leave?

If you have done all exercises and answered the questions above correctly, then you are well prepared to proceed to the next unit.

2 Ukudibana kwakhona kwaMurray

Meeting again at the Murrays' house

In this unit you will learn how to:

- invite guests into your home
- express pleasure at meeting
- make introductions (using kinship terms)
- ask what someone's name is
- offer refreshments
- ask someone what they want to do
- ask someone what they prefer to do
- suggest doing something
- offer help

Incoko

CD 1, tr 3

Thandi and Themba Thamsanqa visit Jenny and Peter Murray.

UJenny	Molweni! **Ngena***ni*!
UThandi	Ewe, ni**njani**?
UJenny	Hayi, si**khona**. Kumnandi kakhulu uku*ni***bona**!
UThandi	***Ngum*****yeni** wam, *u***Themba** lo.
UJenny	Molo Themba, ndiya**vuya** kakhulu uku*kw***azi**. Lo ***ngum*****yeni** wam, *u***Peter**.
UThemba	Ndiya**vuya** uku*n***azi**.
UPeter	**Na***thi* siya**vuya** uku*n***azi**. **Namkelek***ile* *e***khay***eni* lethu!

David, Jenny and Peter's son, comes in.

	Lo ***ngu*****nyana** wethu.
UThandi	Molo *m***ntwan**'am. *Ng***ubani** *i***gama** lakho?
UDavid	Ndi***ngu*****David**.

UThemba	Ùya**funda**,* David?
UDavid	Ewe, ndi**funda** *e***Grove**.
UThandi	Ù**funda phi** uku**thetha** *isi***Xhosa**?
UDavid	Ndi*si***funda** *esi***kol***weni*, **Nkosikazi**.

Peter asks about Themba and Thandi's children.

UPeter	Nina, ni**na***ba***ntwana**?
UThemba	Ewe si**na***bo*, *u***nyana** ne**ntombazana**.
UPeter	Baya**funda**?*
UThemba	Ewe, baya**funda**. Ba**funda** *e***Westerford**.
UJenny	**Kunjani** ngoku**phunga**? Ni**khetha** *i***ti** okanye *i***kofu** okanye *in***to** *e***banda***yo* yoku**sela**?
OoThamsanqa	Nokuba yintoni. Ewe, nokuba yintoni.
UPeter	Ni**funa** *uku***hlala** ngaphakathi okanye ngaphandle?
UThandi	Masi**hlal***eni* ngaphandle. Li**hle** namhlanje! Ndinga*ku*-**ncedisa**, Jenny?
UJenny	Enkosi **sisi**. **Peter** no**Themba,** ninga**ncokola**!
UPeter	Ku**lung***ile*!

*Lit. Are you learning? i.e. Are you at school? Are they learning? i.e. Are they at school?

Isigama

kwa-	*at the home of*
ngena*ni*!	**come in** (pl.)
ni-	you (subject) (pl.)
ku**mnandi**	it's **nice**
-ni-	*you* (object) (pl.)
-**bona**	**see**
*um***yeni** wam	my **husband**
lo	this
-n- (< *-ni-*)	*you* (object) (pl.)
na*thi*	**and** *us*
*e***khaya***eni* lethu	*to* our **home**
*u***nyana** wethu	our **son**
*m***ntwan**'am (< *um***ntwana** wam)	my **child**
*ng***ubani** *i***gama** lakho?	**what** *is* your **name**?
-funda	**learn/study/read**
phi?	**where**?
*esi***kol***weni* (< *isi***kolo**)	*at* **school**
uku**thetha**	to **speak**
nina	as for you (pl.)
nin*aba***ntwana**?	do you have **children**?
*aba***ntwana**	**children**
si**na***bo*	we **have** *them*
ne**ntombazana**	and a **daughter**
ba-	they
kunjani ngoku-	how about
-phunga	**drink** (hot liquid)
-khetha	**prefer**
*i***ti**	**tea**
okanye	or
*i***kofu**	**coffee**
*in***to** *e***banda***yo*	something **cold**
yoku**sela**	(of) to **drink**
*oo***Thamsanqa**	the **Thamsanqa**s
nokuba yintoni	whatever
-funa	**want**
ngaphakathi	inside
ngaphandle	outside
masi**hlal***eni*	let's **sit**
li**hle**	it's **beautiful**
-nga-	may/can
-ncedisa	**help** someone **with**
-ncokola	**chat**
kulungile	it's all right / fine

Try to memorize	
Namkelekile ekhayeni lethu!	Welcome to our home!
Kunjani ngokuphunga?	How about something warm to drink?
Nikhetha into yokusela?	Do you prefer something cold to drink?
Nokuba yintoni	Whatever
Masihlaleni ngaphakathi / ngaphandle	Let's sit inside / outside
Lihle namhlanje!	It is beautiful (weather) today!

How to ...

Invite guests into your home

Singular | **Plural**
Ngena! | **Ngena***ni*!

Express pleasure at meeting (again)

Ku**mnandi** kakhulu uku*ku***bona** (kwakhona) (to one person)
Ku**mnandi** kakhulu uku*ni***bona** (kwakhona) (to more than one person)

Make introductions

Jenny noPeter, lo ***ngum*****yeni** wam, *u***Themba**
Ndinga*n***azisa** *um***yeni** wam, *u***Themba**

Ask what someone's name and surname is

*N***gubani** *i***gama** lakho?
*N***gubani** *i***fani** yakho? (*i***fani** < Afrikaans *van*) (What is your surname?)

Insight

There is a difference when asking:

What is your **name**? — Ngubani *i***gama** *l***akho**?

and

What is your **surname**? — Ngubani *i***fani** *y***akho**?

The reason for this difference will be explained later in this unit.

Note: When you can't recall the name of someone whom you've met before you might say: Ndiza kuthi u*ng***ubani** kanene? (lit. I am going to say who are you, by the way, i.e. just remind me)

Offer refreshments

Ku**njani** ngoku**phunga**/ngoku**sela**?

Singular	**Plural**
Ù**funa** *in***to** yoku**phunga**?	Ni**funa** *in***to** yoku**phunga**?
Ù**funa** *in***to** yoku**sela**?	Ni**funa** *in***to** yoku**sela**?

Insight

There are two words for *to* **drink** in Xhosa.

*uku***sela** = *to* **drink** something **cold**

*uku***phunga** = *to* **drink** something **hot**

In Xhosa tradition one always accepts refreshment that is offered. Not to do so could cause offence. Hence the saying:

Awungeni emzini ungatyi! ***You do not enter a home and not eat!***

Ask what someone wants/prefers to do

Ù**funa** uku**hlala** ngaphakathi okanye ngaphandle?
Ù**khetha** uku**hlala** ngaphakathi okanye ngaphandle?

Suggest doing something

Masi**ncokole**! Masi**phunge** *i***kofu**! Masi**hlale** ngaphandle!

Note: These forms already incorporate a plural marker, i.e. '-si-' = 'us'. However, the addition of the plural suffix '-**ni**' can be heard in everyday speech when addressing a group.

Masi**hlal**e*ni* phantsi! Masi**theth**e*ni* *isi***Xhosa**! Masi**hamb**e*ni*!

Offer to help with a specific activity

Ndinga*ku***ncedisa**?

cf. uku**nceda** = to **help someone by doing something for them** not together with them.

Insight

Apart from a surname, every Xhosa person has a **clan name** = *isi***duko.** When Xhosa speakers meet for the first time, it is customary to find out each other's **clan names** by saying:

'**Ùngumni**?' (lit. You are of what kind?) (to a **male**);
'**Ùngumamni**?' (to a **female**) or: **Khawu***zi***bonge**!/**Khawu***zi***thuthe**! Please praise *yourself!*
A **clan** is a conceptual kinship group. Members trace their kinship to a common male ancestor. The name of this male ancestor is the **clan name** – *isi***duko** – and members are usually called by this name. Mentioning the **clan** name(s) of someone you wish to thank or sing the praises (*izi***bongo**) of, starting with the main clan name and then continuing with the sub-**clan names**, is the ultimate way of showing respect among family and friends. For example, if you wish to praise or extol someone of the **Tolo** clan you would say: ***Tolo, Zulu, Mchenge, Mabhanekazi*** etc., and the response would be: ***Utsho kum kanye!*** (lit. You say so to me exactly) or ***Ndim kanye lowo!*** (lit. It is me exactly that one!)
A man and woman of the same **clan name** never marry as they are considered to be related to one another. A woman always keeps her **clan name** which is prefixed by *Ma-*. Children take their father's **clan name**.
A few other clan names are ***Dlamini, Gambu, Jwarha, Jili, Mbanjwa, Mnguni, Mpinga*** *and* ***Tshawe*** (**royal** *clan name*). Do you know which famous South African has the **clan name *Madiba***? Find out the **clan names** of your Xhosa friends and acquaintances by asking:
'**Ùngumni**?'/'**Ùngumamni**?' or by saying:
Khawu*zi***bonge**!/**Khawu***zi***thuthe**! Please praise *yourself*!

How it works

1 The Xhosa equivalent of English 3rd person pronouns 'he', 'she', 'they'

You have already learned how to say **'I'**, **'we'** and **'you'** (s. & pl.) in Xhosa. In English, the pronouns for the **3rd** person **'he'** / **'she'** / **'it'** tell us whether the noun we are referring to is masculine, feminine or neuter. This gender distinction does not exist in Xhosa. Instead, **subject concords** are used. These subject concords are **derived** from **noun prefixes** and are **attached** to the **verbal form**, e.g.:

*Um***ntwana** úya*kw***azi** uku**thetha** *isi***Xhosa**?	Does the **child** (he / she) **speak** Xhosa? (lit. He / she **knows how** to **speak** Xhosa?)
*Aba***ntwana** ba**funda** *isi***Xhosa**.	The **children** (they) **learn** Xhosa.

Note: The use of both noun and subject concord in Xhosa explains why some Xhosa speakers, when speaking English, will say, for example:

The **children** **they** are learning.

Similarly, the fact that 'ú-' = 'he' / 'she' explains why some Xhosa speakers are inclined to use 'he' / 'she' interchangeably in English.

'ú-' = 'he' / 'she' has a **higher tone** while 'ù-' = 'you' (s.) is pronounced with a **low tone**.

To ensure that you are not misunderstood, you can use the so-called **emphatic pronoun** '*we***na**' = **'as for** *you*' (cf. French *'toi'*), as well as the **subject concord** 'ù-':*

*We***na**, ù**phila njani**?

→ *See **Unit 3** for a complete list of noun classes and their corresponding **subject concords**.

2 The present tense – positive

In the present tense (as well as in all other tenses) verb endings are the same for all persons, masculine and feminine, singular and plural.

In the **present tense** the verb ends in -**a**. The subject concord (SC) is the only indicator of person and number.

Ndiyafund**a**	**I** am learning
Siyafund**a**	**We** are learning

Ùyafund**a**	**You** are learning
Niyafund**a**	**You** are learning
Úyafund**a**	**He/she** is learning
Bayafund**a**	**They** are learning

The **infix -ya-**, inserted between SC and verb, only occurs in the **present tense positive** and simply denotes the **long form** of this tense.

However, if an **object** (noun) or an **adverb** (e.g. 'kakhulu' = 'a lot/much') follows the verb, -**ya**- is usually **omitted**. This is known as the **short form** of the present tense:

Ndifund**a** **kakhulu**.	I read **a lot**.
Ùfund**a** *e***yunivesithi**?	Do you study *at* **the university**?
Úfund**a** *esi***kol***weni*.	He/she learns *at* **school**.
Sifund**a** **namhlanje**.	We are studying **today**.
Nifund**a** **phi** ukuthetha isiXhosa?*	**Where** are you learning to speak Xhosa?
Bafund**a** *e***khaya**.	They are studying *at* **home**.

Note: * '-ya-' is **never** used in a sentence **with a question word**:

*Aba***ntwana** ba**ya**fund**a**.
Bafund**a** **phi**? Bafund**a** *esi***kol***weni*. Bafund**a** **kakhulu**.

3 '-nga-' = 'may', 'can' and '-sa-' = 'still'

Unlike '-**ya**-', '-**nga**-' and '-**sa**-' have a specific meaning:

Ndi**nga***ku*nceda?	**May** I help *you*?
Ni**nga**ncokola.	You **may** chat.
Ndi**nga**ngena?	**May** I come in?
Si**sa**phila (often shortened to 'Si**sa**phil') enkosi.	We are **still** well, thanks.

4 The infinitive

Nearly all **verbs** in the **infinitive**, like the forms in the present tense positive, also end in '-**a**':

uku**thetha**	uku**phunga**	uku**sela**
uku**fika**	uku**dibana**	uku**hlala**

There are only **three exceptions**:

uk*w***azi****	to **know**	Ndiya**zi**.	I **know**.
uku**thi**	to **say**	Ù**thi**ni?	What do you **say**?
uku**tsho**	to **say so**	Ú**tsho**.	He / she **says so**.

Note: '-**thi**' and '-**tsho**' never occur with '-ya-'.

* As it is not possible to have two different vowels following one another in the same word in Xhosa, **sound changes** must take place, i.e. **u** > **w**: uk**u**- + -**azi** > ukwazi.

5 The Xhosa equivalent of English 'am', 'is', 'are' (known as copulatives)

With **nouns beginning with** '*u*-' and '*um*-'

Ndi*ngu***Jenny**.	I ***am*** Jenny.
Lo ***ngu*nyana** wam.	This ***is*** my son.
Lo ***ngum*yeni** wam.	This ***is*** my husband.
Lo ***ngum*ntwana** wam.	This ***is*** my child.

Note: The idiomatic expression:

*N*g**ubani** *i***gama** lakho? (Lit. It is **who** name of your?) '**What** is your name?'

Where '***am***', '***is***', '***are***' is understood

Ù**njani**?	**How** (**are**) you?
Ndi**khona**.	I (am) **well**. (lit. I am **here**.)
Si**khona**.	We (are) **well**. (lit. We are **here**.)

6 The Xhosa equivalent of English 'me', 'us', 'you' (s. & pl.) called object concords

-ndi-	*me*	*-si-*	*us*
-ku-	*you* (s.)	*-ni-*	*you* (pl.)

The form of the **object concord** is **identical** to that of the **subject concord** except where the subject concord is a vowel only:

ù- (SC) > *ku*- (OC)

In this case -*k*- is inserted to separate two vowels.

Object concords are always placed **directly before the verb**:

Ndiya*ku***thanda**. I **love** *you*. (lit. I *you* **love**.)

Position of subject and object concord

Ndiya**bona**.	**I see**.	Uya*ndi***bona**?	Do you **see** *me*?
Siya**bona**.	**We see**.	Uya*si***bona**?	Do you **see** *us*?
Ndiya**fundisa.**	**I teach**.	Ndiya*ku***fundisa**.	I **teach** *you*.
Siya**fundisa**.	**We teach**.	Siya*ni***fundisa**.	We **teach** *you*.

The '*-i-*' of *-ndi-*, *-si-*, *-ni-* is dropped before a vowel verb:

Ùya*nd***azi**?	Do you **know** *me*?
Niya*s***azi**?	Do you **know** *us*?
Ndiya**vuya** uku*n***azi**.	I am **glad** to **know**, i.e. meet *you*.

Note: In the present tense positive -ya- is usually omitted when some other word follows the verb (predicate), e.g.:

Ndiya**funda**.	BUT	Ndi**funda** *isi***Xhosa**.

This is also the case when there is an object concord involved:

Ndiya*si***funda**.*	BUT	Ndi*si***funda** *esi***kol***weni*.

*-*si*- = '*it*' refers to *isi***Xhosa**.

7 Interrogatives

You are already familiar with the interrogative -**phi**? = '**where**?':

Uhlala **phi**?	**Where** do you live/stay?
Ufunda **phi** isiXhosa?	**Where** do you learn Xhosa?

You have also come across **njani**? = '**how**?':

Uphila **njani**?	**How** are you?
Ku**njani** ngokuphunga?	**How** about (something hot) to drink?

Another important question word is -**bani**? = '**who**?':

*Ng***ubani**?	**Who** is it?
*Ng***ubani** igama lakho?	**What** is your name? (lit. It is **who** name of your?)

8 Na = *'and', 'with'* as well as *'have', 'has'*

Before a noun '**na**-' = '**and**' (as well as '**with**', '**also**', '**even**'):

na- + *a*- = **na**-

Manene **na**manenekazi, namkelekile eKapa!

na- + *i-* = **ne-**

Sinabo abantwana, unyana **n**e̲ntombazana.

na- + *u-* = **no-**

Ndifuna ukudibana **no**Peter **no**Themba. (i.e. **with** Peter **and** Themba)

When two dissimilar vowels follow one another in the same word, to avoid an inharmonious sound, yet another **sound change** occurs.

Between a subject concord and a noun '-**na**-' = '**have**', '**has**':

	Ni**na***ba*ntwana?	(Do you **have** children?)	(lit. You **with** children?)
	Ewe, si**na***ba*ntwana.	(Yes, we **have** children.)	(lit. We **with** children.)
or:	Ewe, si**na***bo*.*	(Yes, we **have** *them*.)	(lit. Yes, we **with** *them*.)

* *-bo* shortened form of emphatic pronoun '*bo***na**' 'as for *them*'.

9 Possessive adjectives – 'my', 'our', 'your' (s. & pl.)

In Xhosa, unlike in English, **possessive adjectives** e.g.'**my**'; '**our**'; '**your**' follow the noun. From the examples below you can see that Xhosa **possessive adjectives** consist of **two parts**. The **first part**, e.g. '*wa-*' '*la-*' = '*of*', **changes** according to the noun in question. The **second part** represents the possessive stem:

-**m** = my	-**ithu** = our
-**kho** = your (s)	-**inu** = your (pl.)
Lo ***ngum*ntwana** *wa***m**.	This ***is*** **my** child. (lit. This is child *of* **my**)
Lo ***ngum*ntwana** *w***akho**?	***Is*** this **your** (s.) child?
Lo ***ngu*nyana** *w***ethu**. (*wa-* + -**ithu** > **wethu**)	This ***is*** **our** son.
Lo ***ngu*nyana** *w***enu**? (*wa-* + **inu** > *w***enu**)	This is **your** son?
N*gubani** *igama** *la***kho**?	What ***is*** **your** name?
I*gama** *lam** ***ngu***David.	**My** name is David.

→ See **Unit 14**, for more **possessive adjectives**.

Some kinship terms and relationships

- **Parents – *Aba*zali**

mother	*u***mama**	father	*u***tata**

- **Children – *Aba*ntwana**

daughter	*in***tombi**	son	*u***nyana**

- **Grandparents – *Oo*mawokhulu**

grandmother	*u***makhulu**	grandfather	*u***tat'omkhulu**

- **Grandchild(ren) – *Um*zukulwana** (*aba-*)
- **Aunts**

maternal	*u***makazi**	paternal	*u***dad'obawo**

- **Uncles**

maternal	*u***malume**	paternal	*u***tat'omkhulu** (older) *u***tat'omncinci** (younger)

- **Cousins – *Aba*zala**

parents are **brother** and **sister**	*um***za** / *um***zala**
fathers are **brothers**	*u***kayise**
mothers are **sisters**	*u***kanina**

- **Nieces and Nephews – *Aba*tshana**
- **Kinship terms between siblings**

*um***nta***kwethu*	*my / our* **brother**
*u***dade***wethu*	*my / our* **sister**
*u***mafungwashe**	*eldest* **sister** (lit. by whom one takes an oath)
*aba***nta***kwethu*	*my / our* **siblings** (lit. *of our* ***home***)
*aba***nta***kwenu*	*your* (s./pl.) **siblings** (lit. *of your* ***home***)
*aba***nta***kwabo*	*his / her / their* **siblings** (lit. *of their* ***home***)
*oo***dadewethu**	*my / our* **sisters**

Brothers refer to one another as:

*um***khuluwa** = **older brother**

*um***ninawa** = **younger brother**

When talking **<u>about</u>** a **third person's <u>brother</u>** or **<u>sister</u>**:

*um***na***kwabo* (*his / her / their* **brother**)

*u***dade***wabo* (*his / her / their* **sister**)

When talking **<u>to</u>** a second person about a:

<u>sister</u>	*u***dade***wenu*	*your* (s./pl.) **sister**
<u>brother</u>	*um***na***kwenu*	*your* **brother**

How to apply it

1 Ask the appropriate question for the following answers

(a) NdinguDavid.
(b) Hayi, sikhona.
(c) Ewe, ndifunda eGrove.
(d) Ndisifunda esikolweni.

2 Complete appropriately

UThandi: Uphi umyeni __________, Jenny?
UJenny: Lo ngumyeni __________, uPeter.
UThandi: Lo ngumntwana ________, Jenny?
UJenny: Ewe, lo ngunyana _______, uDavid.

3 Being hospitable

(a) Invite someone into your home: __________
(b) Express pleasure at meeting: __________
(c) Ask him / her to sit down (phantsi): __________
(d) Offer refreshment: __________
(e) Say goodbye (to someone leaving): __________

4 Ask a guest what he/she wants

(a) Do you want coffee?
(b) Do you want tea?
(c) Do you want to meet (with) Peter?
(d) Do you want to speak with Themba?
(e) Do you want to speak Xhosa?
(f) Do you want to sit outside?
(g) Do you want to sit inside?
(h) Do you want go now (ngoku)?

5 Ask guests what they want

(a) Do you want to drink coffee?
(b) Do you want to drink tea?
(c) Do you want to meet (with) Peter?
(d) Do you want to speak with Themba?
(e) Do you want to speak Xhosa?
(f) Do you want to sit outside?

(g) Do you want to sit inside?
(h) Do you want go now?

6 Ask what your guest prefers

(a) Do you prefer tea or coffee?
(b) Do you prefer to sit inside or outside?
(c) Do you prefer to speak Xhosa or English (isiNgesi)?

7 Suggest to your friend

(a) Let's go in!
(b) Let's sit down
(c) Let's speak Xhosa!
(d) Let's drink coffee!
(e) Let's drink tea!
(f) Let's drink something cold!
(g) Let's sit outside!
(h) Let's chat!
(i) Let's stay!
(j) Let's go!

8 Ask where and give the answer

(a) ____hlala phi uThandi noThemba?
(b) ____funda phi ukusithetha isiXhosa, uDavid?
(c) ____funda phi ukusithetha isiXhosa, David?
(d) ____hlala phi ooThamsanqa nooMurray?

9 Complete the questions and answer them

(a) Ngu_______ igama lakho?
(b) Ùhlala ________?
(c) Ùphila _________ namhlanje?

10 Listen to the dialogue and say whether the statements are correct or not

CD 1, tr 3, 02:05

(a)	Thandi visits Jenny.	yes	no
(b)	Thandi wants a cool drink.	yes	no
(c)	Thandi wants to sit inside .	yes	no
(d)	Jenny accepts Thandi's help.	yes	no

Test yourself

1 Ask someone what their name is and what their surname is.

2 How do you know, in spoken language, whether the subject concord '**u**-' in '**u**philile' refers to the 2nd person or the 3rd person?

3 Is there gender distinction in Xhosa?

4 Do you use the same word for 'drink' for all beverages? How would you say that you like to drink tea but your child prefers to drink something cold?

5 How many forms are there of the **present tense**? Give examples.

6 If 'Ndi**ya**funda' means 'I am studying', what does 'Ndi**sa**funda' mean? If 'Ndi**ya**hamba' means 'I am going' what does 'Ndi**nga**hamba' mean?

7 Translate the following sentences which incorporate the object concord:

He teaches *me*. She teaches *us*.

8 How would you suggest to guests that you all sit down?

9 Give the different meanings of -**na**-.

10 Besides a first name and a surname, what other name do Xhosa speakers have?

If you have done all exercises and answered the questions above correctly, then you are well prepared to proceed to the next unit.

3 Ukwazi ukuthetha isiXhosa
Knowing how to speak Xhosa

In this unit you will learn how to:

- discuss your ability with regard to speaking and understanding Xhosa
- make comparisons
- make polite requests

Incoko

CD 1, tr 4

Peter and Themba continue with their conversation.

UThemba	*We***na** Peter, ù*si***thetha** kakuhle *isi***Xhosa**! *Ndi***xelele**, wa**funda phi** uku*si***thetha** kakuhle kangaka?
UPeter	Nda**khulela** *e***fama** ngas*e***Rhini**. Nda**qhuba** ke ngoku*si*-**funda** *esi***kol***weni*. Ngelishwa ndi**libele** *in***to** *e***ninzi**. *E***nye** *in***to**, ndiy**azi** ukuba ndisa**phazama** kakhulu kodwa ndiya**zama** noko!
UThemba	Ayinamsebenzi loo *n***to** yoku**phazama**. *In***to** *e***balulekile***yo* kukuba ù**zame** uku*si***thetha** yonke *imi***hla**!
UPeter	Ù**nyanis***ile*. Ku**funeka** ù*ndi***xelele** xa ndi**phazama**.
UThemba	Kulungile, kodwa ke ùya**landela**.
UPeter	Ewe, ukuba *um***ntu** úya**cothisisa**!
UThemba	Heke, **na***m* ndiza ku**zama** uku**zekelela**.
UPeter	Enkosi kuba *a*ndi**theth***i* kakuhle njengoJenny. **Na***ye* wa**khulela** *e***fama** *eM***puma-Koloni**. *Ye***na** wa*si***funda** *esi***kol***weni* nas*e***yunivesithi**. Ú*si***thetha** njengo*m***Xhosa** kangangokuba uya*si***fundisa** ngoku!
UThemba	Intle loo *n***to**! Uy**azi** ba**thi** *aba***ntu** bas*e***Holani**: *'So veel tale as jij kan, so veel male is jij man'* (lit. As many languages as you can, so much more are you a person!).
UPeter	Y*in***yaniso** leyo!

Isigama

*Ndi***xelele**	**tell** *me*	xa	whenever
wa**funda**	you **learned**	**-landela**	**follow**
kangaka	so	ukuba	if
nda**khulela**	I **grew up**	*um***ntu**	a **person**
*e***fama**	*on* a **farm**	**-cothisisa**	**speak slowly**
nga*se***Rhini**	near **Grahamstown**	heke	well then
nda**qhuba**	I **continued**	**na***m*	I **too**
ke	then	ndiza ku**zama**	I will **try**
ngelishwa	unfortunately	uku**zekelela**	to **speak slowly**
-libele	forgotten	*a*ndi**theth***i*	I **do***n't* **speak**
*in***to** *e***ninzi**	a lot	njengoJenny	as Jenny
*e***nye** *in***to**	another **thing**	**na***ye*	she **also**
ukuba	that	*eM***puma-Koloni**	**Eastern Cape**
ndisa**phazama**	I still **make mistakes**	*ye***na**	as for her
kodwa	but	wa*si***funda**	she **studied** *it*
ndiya**zama**	I am **trying**	na*se***yunivesithi**	and *at* **university**
noko*	in a small way	njengo*m***Xhosa**	like a **Xhosa**
ayinamsebenzi	it doesn't matter	kangangokuba	so much so
loo *n***to**	that (thing)	**-fundisa**	**teach**
yoku**phazama**	of **making mistakes**	ngoku	now
*in***to**	the **thing**	intle loo *n***to**!	that's lovely!
*e***balulekile***yo*	which is important	*aba***ntu**	Dutch (lit. the people
kukuba	is that	ba*se***Holani**	of Holland)
yonke *imi***hla**	every **day**	y*in***yaniso** leyo	that's the **truth**
ùnyanis*ile*	you are **right**		
ku**funeka**	you must (lit. it's **necessary**)		

*There is no exact equivalent in English for '**noko**'. It is a kind of pleading for the listener's sympathy and understanding (cf. Afrikaans 'maar').

Try to memorize

Ngelishwa ndilibele into eninzi	Unfortunately I've forgotten a lot
Ayinamsebenzi loo nto	It doesn't matter
Into ebalulekileyo kukuba uzame	The important thing is that you try
Unyanisile	You are right
Intle loo nto!	That's lovely!
Yinyaniso leyo	That's the truth

How to …

Discuss your ability with regard to speaking and understanding Xhosa

Ndiya*kw***azi** uku**thetha** *isi***Xhosa**.	I know (how) to **speak** Xhosa.
*Andikw***azi**.	I do *not* **know** (how).
*U***xolo**, *a*ndis*i***theth***i* kakuhle.	I'm sorry, I do*n't* **speak** *it* well.
Ndi*si***thetha** kancinci nje.	I **speak** *it* just a little.
Ndisa**funda**.	I am still **learning**.
Ndiya**zama** noko.	I am **trying** in a small way.
Ùya**qonda**?	Do you **understand**?
Ùya*ndi***va**?	Do you **understand** *me*? (lit. Do you **hear** *me*?)
Ùya*ndi***landela**?	Do you **follow** *me*?
Ndiya**qonda**.	I **understand**.
*Andi***qond***i*.	I do*n't* **understand**.
Ndi**qonda** kancinci nje.	I **understand** a little.
*Andi***landel***i* kakuhle.	I do*n't* **follow** well.
*U***xolo**, ù**thini**?	**Pardon**, **what** do you **say**?
*U***xolo**, ù**theni**?	**Pardon**, **what** did you **say**?
Zekelela! / Nceda ù**zekelele**!	**Speak slowly**!/Please **speak slowly**!
Cothisisa! / Nceda ù**cothisise**!	**Speak slowly**!/Please **speak slowly**!
Phinda kwakhona.	**Repeat** (again)!
Nceda ù**phinde** kwakhona.	Please **repeat** (again).
Nceda ù*ndi***xelele** xa ndi**phazama**.	Please **tell** *me* when I make mistakes.
*Yi***ntoni** le nge*si***Xhosa**?	**What** is this in Xhosa?
*Yi***ntoni** '…' nge*si***Xhosa**?	**What** is '...' in Xhosa?
Ithetha **ntoni** le nto nge*si***Xhosa**?	**What** does this (thing) mean in Xhosa?

Make comparisons

*Andi***theth***i* kakuhle **njengo**Jenny.
Yena u*si***thetha** *isi***Xhosa njengo**mXhosa.

How it works

1 Summary of nouns of Units 1–3

To help you understand how **nouns** are **grouped** into classes according to their **prefix**:

um-:	*um***ntu**, *um***ntwana**, *um***yeni**, *um***hlobo**, *um***fana**, *um***ququzelelikazi**, *um***Xhosa**, *um***numzana**, *um***hlekazi**
u-:	*u***mama**, *u***tata**, *u***nyana**, *u***bawo**, *u***sisi**, *u***bhuti**, *u***makhulu**, *u***tatomkhulu**, *u***Nkosikazi Thamsanqa**, *u***Thandi**, *u***Jenny**, *u***Peter**, *u***Themba**, *u***David**
aba-:	*aba***ntu**, *aba***ntwana**, *aba***hlobo**, *aba***fana**
um-:	*um***sebenzi**
imi-:	*imi***hla**
i(li)-:	*i***gama**, *i***khaya**
ama-:	*ama***nene**, *ama***nenekazi**, *ama***Xhosa**, *ama***bhanti**
isi-:	*isi***Xhosa**, *isi***Ngesi**, *isi***Bhulu**, *isi***Zulu**, *isi***Phutukezi**, *isi***kolo**, *isi***gama**
in- / i-:	*in***coko**, *in***kosikazi**, *in***kosazana**, *in***kwenkwe**, *in***tombazana**, *i***kofu**, *i***Kapa**, *i***-eropleni**, *in***qwelo-moya**, *i***ti**, *in***to**, *i***fama**, *i***yunivesithi**
uku- / ukw-:	*uku***vuya**, *uku***phila**, *uku***funa**, *uku***khetha**, *uku***hamba**, *uku***sala**, *uku***dibana**, *uku***bona**, *uku***thanda**, *uku***phunga**, *uku***ngena**, *uku***funda**, *uku***ncokola**, *uku***ncedisa**, *uku***sela**, *uku***qonda**, *uku***themba**, *uku***xelela**, *uku***zekelela**, *uku***zama**, *uku***thetha**, *ukw***amkela**, *ukw***azi**, *ukw***azisa**, *ukw***azana**

Noun classes and their subject concords (SC)

Class	Prefix	Stem	SC	Translation
1	*um-*	**ntu**	*ú-*	the person *(he/she)*
2	*aba-*	**ntu**	*ba-*	the people *(they)*
1a	*u-* *u-* *u-* *u-* *u-*	**Themba** **Thamsanqa** **mama** **nyana** **loliwe**	*ú-*	Themba *(he)* Thamsanqa *(he)* the mother *(she)* the son *(he)* the train *(it)*
2a	*oo-* *oo-* *oo-* *oo-* *oo-*	**Sipho** **Thamsanqa** **mama** **nyana** **loliwe**	*ba-*	Sipho and co. *(they)* the Thamsanqas *(they)* the mothers *(they)* the sons *(they)* the trains *(they)*
3	*um-*	**hla**	*u-*	the day / date *(it)*
4	*imi-*	**hla**	*i-*	the days *(they)*
5	*ili-* *i-*	**zwe** (one syllable) **gama** (two syllables)	*li-* *li-*	the country *(it)* the name *(it)*
6	*ama-* *ama-*	**zwe** **gama**	*a-* *a-*	the countries *(they)* the names *(they)*
7	*isi-*	**kolo**	*si-*	the school *(it)*
8	*izi-*	**kolo**	*zi-*	the schools *(they)*
9	*in-* *in-* *i-*	**to** **coko** **fama**	*i-*	the thing *(it)* the conversation *(it)* the farm *(it)*
10	*izin-* *iin-* *ii-*	**to** (one syllable) **coko** (two syllables) **fama**	*zi-*	the things *(they)* the conversations *(they)* the farms *(they)*
11	*ulu-* *u-*	**thi** (one syllable) **lwimi** (two syllables)	*lu-* *lu-*	the stick *(it)* the tongue / language *(it)*
10	*izin-* *ii-*	**ti** (no **'h'**) **lwimi**	*zi-* *zi-*	the sticks *(they)* the tongues/languages *(they)*
14	*ubu-* *ubu-*	**sika** **ntu** *	*bu-* *bu-*	the winter *(it)* human decency *(it)*
15	*uku-* *ukw-* *uk-*	**hamba** **azi** **oja**	*ku-*	to walk / walking *(it)* to know / knowledge *(it)* to roast / roasting *(it)*

* See Insight box

From these tables you will see that all **nouns** are grouped into **classes according** to their **prefix**.

- The noun classes are **numbered 1–15**.
- Classes **1**, **3**, **5**, **7**, **9** and **11** are **singular** nouns.
- Classes **2**, **4**, **6**, **8** and **10** are the corresponding **plural** nouns.
- Classes **14** and **15** have **no plural**.
- Classes **12** and **13** **are no longer active** in Xhosa.

There are no hard and fast rules to enable one to classify a particular noun into a specific class or group. However, a few principles apply. Nouns of:

- **Classes 1** and **2**: only refer to **people** (but not all nouns referring to people are in this class).
- **Classes 1**a and **2**a: include all **proper names**, **kinship terms**, (e.g. mother/s, father/s, uncle/s, aunt/s, sister/s, brother/s), some **professions** (e.g. doctor/s, social worker/s, teacher/s) and **personifications** (e.g. train/s, radio/s, machine/s).
- **Classes 3** and **4**: many trees and rivers; some parts of the body (e.g. leg/s, mouth/s, finger/s), as well as some abstract nouns (e.g. miracle/s, anger, contribution/s, organisation/s, law/s, marriage/s).
- **Classes 5** and **6**: some parts of the body (e.g. eye/s, breast/s, knee/s, ankle/s, bone/s), nouns describing personal characteristics (e.g. brave person/s, eloquent speaker/s, skilful person/s, liar/s) and some adopted from English/Afrikaans (e.g. police, card, wheel, kitchen).

  Note: Some nouns of **Classes 1 and 9** have their plural in **Class 6**, e.g.:

  *um***Xhosa** *in***doda** (man) *in***kosikazi** *in***kwenkwe** *in***tombazana**
  *ama***Xhosa** *ama***doda** *ama***khhosikazi** *ama***khhwenkwe** *ama***ntombazana**.

- **Classes 7** and **8**: all **languages**, **ordinal numbers** 2–10 (2nd, 3rd, 4th etc.), many **implements**, words adopted from English or Afrikaans beginning with '**sc**-', **st**-', '**sp**-' (e.g. *isi***kolo** < **sc**hool, *isi***tovu** < **st**ove, *isi***pili** < **sp**ieël [mirror]), as well as many **grammatical terms**.
- **Classes 9** and **10**: many **animals**, nouns adopted from English and Afrikaans (e.g. bus/es, car/s, money, bicycle/s, window/s, phone/s).
- **Class 11**: many **abstract nouns**. Plural: prefix of Class 10 where applicable.
- **Class 14**: mainly abstract nouns but also others (e.g. face, beer, honey, winter, night). **No plural**.
- **Class 15**: all **infinitives** which can also function as nouns.

Insight

Nouns that prefix *ubu*- are mainly abstract nouns, e.g. *ubu***ntu** = common human decency.

Professor Daniel Ncayiyana, the editor of the *S.A. Medical Journal*, writes in an editorial that '*ubu***ntu**, the deeper meaning of which cannot be explained in one or two sentences, encompasses all the attributes of caring for one's fellow human being.' The concept of *ubu***ntu** is also closely related to the proverb:

'Umntu ngumntu ngabantu.'

Lit. A person is a person through other people.

Professor Ncayiyana explains the meaning of this proverb as 'attaining the totality of being a fully adjusted member of society only through the support, counselling, love, assistance, shelter, example, etc., of one's fellow human beings.'

→ See **Unit 10** for more about proverbs and idioms.

2 Emphatic pronouns

Similar to the French '*moi*', *toi*', '*lui*', '*m***na**', '*we***na**', '*ye***na**' is used for **emphasis** and **contrast**, and can be used as well as, but **never instead of**, the **subject concord**:

*M***na**, **ndi**yahamba ngoku.	**As for** *me*, **I** am going now.
*Thi***na**, **si**yahamba ngoku.*	**As for** *us*, **we** are going now.
*We***na**, **ù**phila njani?	**As for** *you*, how are **you**?
*Ni***na**, nina*bo aba***ntwana**?	**As for** *you*, do **you** have children?
*Ye***na**, uPeter wa*si***funda** *isi***Xhosa** *esi***kol***weni*.	**As for** *him*, Peter, **he** learned Xhosa *at* **school**.
*Ye***na**, *u***Jenny** wakhulela *e***fama**.	**As for** *her*, Jenny **she** grew up *on* a **farm**.
*Bo***na**, *aba***ntwana** bakhulela *e***Kapa**.	**As for** *them*, the children, **they** grew up *in* **Cape Town**.

You will surely recognise '**thina**' from the refrain of '**NKOSI SIKELEL' IAFRIKA'**

*→ see Cultural background.

Insight

You have not yet come across a **one syllable word** in Xhosa. (Remember that m**na** = *as for me* is pronounced with two syllables as **m** is syllabic.) As Xhosa has an aversion to monosyllabic words, **na**- is suffixed to emphatic pronouns and has no specific meaning. However, when **na**- precedes an emphatic pronoun it means '**and**'/ '**with**'/ '**also**':

na_m_	**and** *me* / **with** *me* / *I* **too, also**
na_we_	**and** *you* / **with** *you* / *you* **too, also**
na_thi_	**and** *us* / **with** *us* / *we* **also**
na_ye_	**and** *he /she* / **with** *him, her* / *he, she* **too, also**

Na_m_, ndiyavuya ukukwazi.	*Me* **too**, I'm pleased to know you.
Bekumnandi ukuthetha **na**_we_.	It was nice to talk with you.
Na_thi_, siyavuya ukunazi.	*We* **also,** we are pleased to meet you.

3 Present tense negative

The negative of the present tense is formed by prefixing '*a*-' before the subject concord and changing the final vowel of the verb '-a' to '-*i*'. If a noun (object) follows the verb, the initial vowel of the prefix of all subsequent nouns is dropped e.g.:

Andi**phung**_i_ kofu.	I do*n't* **drink** coffee.
Andi**fun**_i_ kuphunga kofu.	I do*n't* **want** to drink coffee.

Positive	**Negative**	
Ndiya**phunga**.	_Andi_**phung**_i_.	
Siya**phunga**.	_Asi_**phung**_i_.	
Ùya**phunga**?	_Aku_**phung**_i_?	(kofu)
Niya**phunga**?	_Ani_**phung**_i_?	
Úya**phunga**.	_Aka_**phung**_i_.	
Baya**phunga**.	_Aba_**phung**_i_.	

As you can see, when the subject concord consists of a vowel only, e.g. ù- / ú; -**k**- (or -**w**- in spoken language), is inserted:

a- + ù- > *aku*- / awu-; **a**- + ú- > *aka*-.

Note: The negative form of: 'Ndiya**phila**' / 'Ndi**phil**_ile_' is _Andi_**phil**_anga_. → See **Unit 7**.

Insight

-ya- only occurs in the present tense positive when no object follows the verb and there is no emphasis on the verb:

Ndi**ya**funda. BUT Ndi**funda** *isi***Xhosa**.

-ya- is also inserted in a sentence with an **object concord**:

Ndi**ya***si*funda (*isi***Xhosa**).

-sa- = 'still' in a positive sentence BUT 'no longer' in a negative sentence:

Ndi**sa**funda. = I am **still** studying.	Andi**sa**fundi. = I am **no longer** studying.

4 Remote past tense

One of the past tenses used when talking about past events and actions is the remote or narrative past tense. The subject concord indicates the tense. It is characterised by a long '-**a**-' with a falling tone:

Ndakhulela efama.	**I** grew up on a farm.
Sakhulela efama.	**We** grew up on a farm.
Wakhulela* efama.	**You** (s.) grew up on a farm.
Nakhulela efama.	**You** (pl.) grew up on a farm.
Wakhulela* efama.	**He/she** grew up on a farm.
Bakhulela efama.	**They** grew up on a farm.

* ù- + **a** = **wa**- and ú- – + **a** = **wa**-.

5 Polite requests

The **tone** used when giving a one-word instruction in Xhosa largely indicates the 'softness' or 'severity' of such an instruction, e.g.:

Hlala phantsi! (s.)	**Hlala***ni* phantsi! (pl.)

However, this can easily be changed into a **polite request** by saying:

Ndi**cela** u**hlal**<u>e</u> phantsi.	(lit. I **beg** you [s.] sit down.)
Ndi**cela** ni**hlal**<u>e</u> phantsi.	

When asking for something, it is polite to introduce your request with: 'Ndi**cela . . .** ':

Ndi**cela** *ama***nzi**.	(lit. I **beg** for water.)
Ndi**cela** *i***kofu**.	(lit. I **beg** for coffee.)
Ndi**cela** *in***to** yoku**sela**.	(lit. I **beg** for something to drink.)

'**Nceda**' (lit. help) is the equivalent of the English '**please**' and can also introduce a polite request:

Nceda uhlale phantsi.
Nceda*ni* ni**hlale** phantsi.

Note: The verb following 'Ndi**cela**' and '**Nceda**' ends in -**e**.
→ See also **Unit 4**.

Ndi**cela** ù**thethe** *isi***Ngesi**.	**Please** (you) speak English. (lit. I **beg** [that] you speak English.)
Nceda ù**thethe** *isi***Xhosa**.	**Please** (you) **speak** Xhosa.
Nceda ù**zame** uku**thetha** *isi***Xhosa**.	**Please** (you) **try** to speak Xhosa.
Nceda ù**cothisise**.	**Please** (you) **speak** slowly.
Nceda ù**khumbule**.	**Please** (you) **remember**.
Nceda*ni* ni**thethe** *isi***Xhosa**.	**Please** (you all) **speak** Xhosa.

6 Impersonal ku-: *the equivalent of English 'it'*

Kunjani?	How is **it**? (lit. **It** is how?)
Kufuneka ndihambe.	**It** is necessary (that) I go (i.e. I must go)
Kulungile.	**It** is all right.
Kushushu.	**It** is hot.
Kuthethwa *isi***Ngesi** apha.	**It** is spoken (English here).

7 More interrogatives

In **Units 1** and **2** you were introduced to the question words '**phi**?'; '**njani**?' and '**bani**?'. Two other interrogatives which you will need are '**nini**?' = '**when**?' and '**ntoni**?' = '**what**?':

Wazalwa **nini**?	**When** were you born?
Ufuna **ntoni**?	**What** do you want?
Uth**ini**?	**What** do you say?

Note: with the verb '-**thi**' = '**say**', the shortened form '-**ni**?' (< **ntoni**?) must be used.

8 Conjunctions 'because', 'but', 'if', 'that', 'when'

Like English, Xhosa has **conjunctions to join clauses**:

Ndilandela kakuhle **kuba** uyacothisisa.	I follow well **because** you are speaking slowly.

Ndiyazama ukuthetha isiXhosa, **kodwa** kunzima. — I am trying to speak Xhosa, **but** it is difficult.

Ndiyaqonda **ukuba** umntu úyacothisisa. — I understand **if** a person speaks slowly.

Ndiyazi **ukuba** ndiyaphazama kakhulu. — I know **that** I make a lot of mistakes.

Nceda *ndi***lungis**<u>e</u> **xa** ndiphazama. — Please **correct** *me* **when** I make a mistake.

Insight

The verb after the conjunctions **kodwa** = *but*; **kuba** = *because*; **ukuba** = *if* or *that,* insert **-ya-** in the present tense positive, but **-ya-** is **NEVER** inserted after the conjunction **xa** = *when, whenever*.

Nceda *ndi***lungis**<u>e</u> **xa** <u>ndiphazama</u>. — Please **correct** *me* **when** I make a mistake.

→ See **Unit 12**.

Cultural background

The national anthem

The first verse of **NKOSI SIKELEL' I-AFRIKA** opens South Africa's multilingual national anthem.

Nkosi sikelel' iAfrika,
Maluphakanyisw' uphondo lwayo,
Yiva imithandazo yethu,
Nkosi, sikelela, **thina**,
Lusapho lwayo,
Nkosi, sikelela, **thina**,
Lusapho lwayo.

God bless Africa,
Let its horn (i.e. spirit) rise,
Hear also our prayers,
God bless us,
Its (Africa's) family,
God bless us,
Its family.

Enoch Sontonga

Photo courtesy of Anthropology Collection of the Amathole Museum, King William's Town

In 1995 President Mandela appointed an Anthem Committee to work out the choral and instrumental combined Xhosa, Sotho, Afrikaans and English version which is sung today.

The first verse of **NKOSI SIKELEL' I-AFRIKA** was composed in 1897 by **Enoch Sontonga**, a school teacher from Kliptown, to be sung by school children and church choirs. It was completed by **Samuel E. Mqhayi** (→ see **Unit 16** for more about **Mqhayi**) and later, it was adopted by the African National Congress as the closing hymn at meetings. Other organizations followed this practice and the song became recognized as the people's national anthem. As its dissemination was largely oral, there are a number of versions which often vary from place to place and from occasion to occasion. It is often sung in a combination of Xhosa, Zulu and Sotho, and versions of it are also used as the national anthems in Zambia, Zimbabwe and Tanzania.

How to apply it

1 Say (Yithi)

(a) I want to speak Xhosa.
(b) May I speak English?
(c) I like to speak Xhosa.
(d) I try to speak Xhosa.
(e) I speak only a little Xhosa.
(f) I am still learning.
(g) I still make a lot of mistakes when I speak Xhosa.
(h) Please correct me.

2 What would you say when you don't understand what someone says?

(a) ______________________________
(b) ______________________________
(c) ______________________________
(d) ______________________________

3 Answer the following questions in the negative

(a) Uyakwazi ukuthetha isiNgesi?	Hayi, ______________
(b) Uthetha kakuhle isiXhosa?	Hayi, ______________
(c) Uyaqonda?	Hayi, ______________
(d) Uyaphila? / Uphilile?	Hayi, ______________

(e) Uyakhumbula? Hayi, ______________

(f) Ufuna ikofu? Hayi, ______________

(g) Ufuna amanzi? Hayi, ______________

4 Convert these instructions into polite requests

(a) Thetha isiXhosa.

(b) Zekelela.

(c) Phinda kwakhona.

(d) Zama kwakhona.

(e) Ndixelele.

5 Try to get the gist of the following dialogue

These are the sorts of questions you will find useful should you want to know someone's biographical details:

(a) Wazalwa nini *u***Nelson Rolihlahla* Mandela** owayesakuba ng*um***ongameli**?

(b) Wazalwa nge18 Julayi ngo-1918.

(a) Wakhulela phi?

(b) Wakhulela *e***Qunu** *e***Mpuma-Koloni** (Eastern Cape Province).

(a) Wafunda phi?

(b) Waya kwisikolo sama**Wesile** (Wesleyan). Emva koko (after that) waya kufunda eyunivesithi yase**Fort Hare**.

(a) Emva koko wenza ntoni?

(b) Wasebenza njengepolisa lasemgodini (as a mines policeman) kodwa waqhuba ngokufundela (study for) ubugqwetha (legal profession).

*President Mandela's Xhosa name, Rolihlahla, meaning '*pulling a branch from a tree*' with the colloquial meaning '*troublemaker*', written without 'h' following 'R' is the old orthography.

NELSON ROLIHLAHLA MANDELA, born in 1918 in the village of Mvezo from where his mother moved to Qunu, south of Umtata, became South Africa's first democratically elected President on 10 May 1994 after spending 27 years in prison. On 11 February 2000, ten years to the day that he stepped out of prison, Nelson Mandela opened a museum dedicated to his life-long struggle for freedom. At Mvezo a simple structure of concrete, brick and gum poles has been built. An open-air display, it also features everyday objects of rural Xhosa life – reed mats, mealie stampers and corn-grinding stones. A proposed Youth and Heritage Centre is to be built at Qunu a few hundred metres from the former President's home. The local museum in Umtata houses some of the gifts and awards he has received from all over the world. A multi-media exhibition, housed in the museum and based on his autobiography *Long Walk to Freedom*, celebrates and contextualises his role in South Africa's liberation.

Nelson Mandela Museum, Mvezo (Courtesy of Daily Dispatch)

Nelson Mandela Museum, Umtata

Besides English, *isi***Ngesi**, and Afrikaans, *isi***Bhulu**, South Africa has nine official languages: **Nguni** group: *isi***Xhosa**, *isi***Zulu**, *isi***Swati**, *isi***Ndebele**; **Sotho** group: *isi***Suthu**, *isi***Pedi** (North Sotho), *isi***Tswana**. Other groups: *isi***Venda**, *isi***Tsonga** (or Shangaan).

All languages prefix *isi-*: *isi***Jamani**, *isi***Frentshi**, *isi***Phutukezi**, etc.

6 Use the map opposite to answer the questions.

(a) Kuthethwa eziphi iilwimi kakhulu *eN***tshona-Koloni**?
(b) Kuthethwa eziphi iilwimi kakhulu *eM***puma-Koloni**?
(c) Kuthethwa eziphi iilwimi kakhulu *eM***ntla-Koloni**?
(d) Kuthethwa eziphi iilwimi kakhulu *e***Freyistata**?
(e) Kuthethwa eziphi iilwimi kakhulu *e***Gauteng**?
(f) Kuthethwa eziphi iilwimi kakhulu *eM***pumalanga**?
(g) Kuthethwa eziphi iilwimi kakhulu *kwa***Zulu-Natal**?
(h) Kuthethwa eziphi iilwimi kakhulu *eM***ntla-Ntshona**?
(i) Kuthethwa eziphi iilwimi kakhulu *e***Limpopo**?
(j) Kuthethwa *isi***Xhosa** kakhulu ndawoni *eM***zantsi Afrika**?
(k) Kuthethwa *isi***Zulu** kakhulu ndawoni *eM***zantsi Afrika**?
(l) Kuthethwa *isi***Tswana** kakhulu ndawoni *eM***zantsi Afrika**?
(m) Kuthethwa *isi***Suthu** kakhulu ndawoni *eM***zantsi Afrika**?

7 Complete according to the example

*Um***Xhosa** uthetha *isi***Xhosa** — *Ama***Xhosa** athetha *isi***Xhosa**.

(a) *Um***Zulu**____________. *Ama***Zulu** ____________.
(b) *Um***Swati**____________. *Ama***Swati** ____________.
(c) *Um***Ndebele**__________. *Ama***Ndebele** _______.
(d) ***I*****Bhulu**____________. *Ama***Bhulu** _________.
(e) *Um***Venda**__________. *Ama***Venda** _____________.
(f) ***I*****Ngesi**____________. *Ama***Ngesi** ______________.
(g) *Um***Tswana**__________. *Abe***Tswana*** _____________.
(h) *Um***Suthu**____________. *Abe***Suthu*** ______________.

*__Note__: The plural prefix is *abe-* instead of *aba-*

QV

kuthethwa	it is spoken	nase-	and *in*
*u***lwimi**	language (lit. tongue)	*eziphi ii***lwimi**?	which languages?
*ii***lwimi**	languages	zonke *ii***lwimi**	all languages

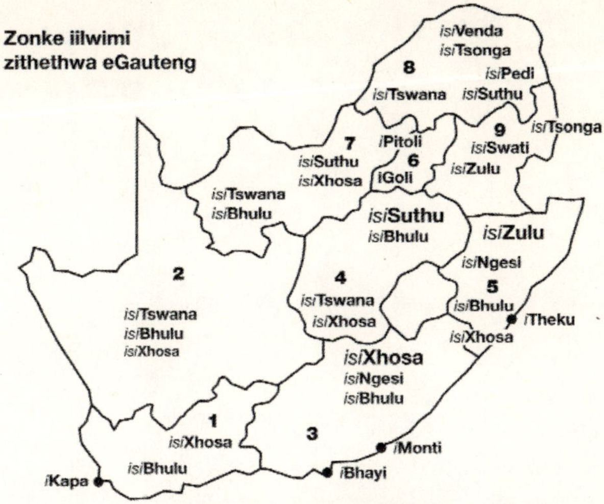

Provinces of South Africa

1. *iN***tshona-Koloni** (Western Cape)
2. *uM***ntla-Koloni** (Northern Cape)
3. *iM***puma-Koloni** (Eastern Cape)
4. *i***Freyistata** (Free State)
5. *Kwa***Zulu-Natal**
6. *i***Gauteng** (Sotho for 'gold')
7. *uM***ntla-Ntshona** (North Western Province)
8. *i***Limpopo** (< Limpopo River)
9. *iM***pumalanga** (Lit. coming out of the sun i.e. the east)

Test yourself

1 Do all Xhosa nouns have singular and plural classes?
2 Which word have you come across that occurs in the plural only?
3 What distinguishes the Classes 5 and 11 from the other classes?
4 There are a few nouns which prefix '*um-*' in the singular where the plural form is '*ama-*' not the regular '*aba-*'. Give three examples.
5 What is the plural *um***Suthu** and what is the singular of *ama***Ngesi** and *ama***Bhulu**?
6 *Ama***k<u>h</u>wenkwe** = *boys* is the plural of '*in***kwenkwe**' = *boy.* Why is the consonant 'k' not aspirated in the singular?
7 Can you use the emphatic pronoun instead of the subject concord?
8 Which proverb is closely related to the concept of *ubu***ntu**?
9 How do you recognize that a verb is in the remote past tense?
10 How can you make an instruction, e.g. 'Hlalaphantsi.', polite?

If you have done all exercises and answered the questions above correctly, then you are well prepared to proceed to the next unit.

4 Ukuthetha ngomsebenzi
Speaking about work

In this unit you will learn how to:

- ask what someone does for a living
- say what your occupation is
- ask where someone works
- respond to being asked where you work
- comment on someone's work

Incoko

CD 1, tr 5

Peter and Themba discuss work while waiting for Jenny and Thandi to join them with the coffee, cake and sandwiches.

UPeter	Ndixelele Themba, wenza ntoni ngokomsebenzi?
UThemba	Ndisebenzela inkampani yeenqwelo-moya njengomphathi-basebenzi.
UPeter	Oo, ipersonnel manager ngesiNgesi na?
UThemba	*Uchan' ucwethe*!*
UPeter	Uya*kw*azi ke ukusebenza nokuthetha kakuhle nabantu!
UThemba	Ewe, ndiyakuthanda kakhulu ukusebenza nabantu. Uyazi isaci sesiXhosa sithi: *Umntu ngumntu ngabantu*!
UPeter	Unyanisile!
UThemba	Wena, yintoni umsebenzi wakho, Peter?
UPeter	Mna, ndiyingcaphephe yezityalo eKirstenbosch.
UThemba	Mm, yinto enomdla leyo!
UPeter	Ewe, ngumsebenzi onomdla. Kananjalo laa ndawo yindawo entle yokusebenza! UThandi naye uyasebenza?
UThemba	Ewc, naye uthanda ukusebenza nabantu. Ungugqirha. Usebenza kwisibhedlele sabantwana i**Red Cross**. Uya khona kusasa kuphela. Emva kwemini usebenza kwikliniki

	yePrimary Health Care.
UPeter	Naye usebenza kakhulu!
UThemba	UJenny, ufundisa kwesiphi isikolo?
UPeter	Akafundisi sikolweni. Ufundisa abantu abadala abafuna ukufunda ukuthetha isiXhosa. Uyazi, baninzi kakhulu abantu abafuna ukufunda ukuthetha isiXhosa ngoku ngakumbi oosomashishini nabasebenzi beenkampani, abanikazi-khaya, oogqirha nabongikazi, njalo njalo.
UThemba	Heke, bathini kanene ngesiNgesi? '*Better late than never!*'
UPeter	Ithini loo ntetho ngesiXhosa?
UThemba	Andazi. Lunjalo kaloku ulwimi. Akusoloko kulula ukutolika ngakumbi wakufika kwizaci.

Isigama

wenza	you do
ntoni?	what?
ngokomsebenzi	as far as work goes
-sebenza	work (verb)
-sebenzela	work for
inkampani	company
umphathi-basebenzi	personnel manager
umsebenzi	worker
abasebenzi	workers, staff
**uchan' ucwethe!*	*you're spot on!* (lit. you've aimed at [and hit] the shrew)
-thanda	like, love
isaci sesiXhosa	Xhosa idiom
sithi	saying
yintoni?	it is what?
mna	as for me
ingcaphephe yezityalo	horticulturist
umdla	interest
-nomdla	interesting
leyo	that
kananjalo	also
laa ndawo	that place
yindawo entle yokusebenza	it's a lovely place to work
ugqirha	doctor
isibhedele	hospital
sabantwana	of children
khona	there
kusasa	in the morning
kuphela	only
emva kwemini	in the afternoon
kwikliniki ye	at a clinic of
kwesiphi isikolo?	at which school?
akafundisi	she doesn't teach
abantu abadala	adults
abafuna	who want
baninzi	they are many
ngakumbi	especially
oosomashishini	business people
abanikazi-khaya	housewives
abongikazi	nurses
njalo, njalo	etc. etc.
ngesiNgesi	in English
ithini	what is it?
loo ntetho	that saying
kanene	indeed
ngesiXhosa	in Xhosa
lunjalo kaloku	it's like that
ulwimi	language
akusoloko kulula ukutolika wakufika kwizaci	it isn't always easy to translate when it comes to idioms

How to ...

Ask what someone does for a living

Wenza **ntoni** ngokom**sebenzi**?
*Y***intoni** *um***sebenzi** wakho?

Say what your occupation is

Ndi*ngu***gqirha**
Ndi*ngu***somashishini**
Ndi*ngum***phathi-basebenzi**
Ndi*ngum***ongikazi**
Ndi*ngum***nikazi-khaya**
Ndi*li***gqwetha**
Ndi*yin***gcaphephe yezityalo** (lit. an expert in plants)
Ndi*yi***personnel manager**
Ndi**sebenza** njengo*m***phathi weshishini**
Ndi**sebenzela** *in***kampani**

Ask where someone works

U**sebenza** phi?
U**phangela** phi?

Respond to being asked where you work

Ndi**sebenza**
*e***doloph***ini*
*e***yunivesithi**
*esi***bhedlele**
*esi***kol***weni*
e-**ofis***ini*
*e***Kirstenbosch**
*kwi***shishini** le**encwadi** (publishing house)
*kwi***shishini** le**mpahla** (clothing factory)

Comment on someone's work

*Ngum***sebenzi** *onom***dla**
*Yin***dawo** *en***tle** yoku**sebenza**

How it works

1 More about the Xhosa equivalent of English 'am', 'is', 'are' (known as copulatives) followed by nouns

You already know that '*-ng-*' prefixed to **nouns beginning with** '*um-*' and '*u-*', (Classes 1, 1a and 3 **nouns**) expresses ***'am'***, ***'is'*** (→ see **Unit 2**):

Ndi***ngu*Jenny**.	I ***am*** Jenny.
Lo ***ngu*nyana** wam.	This ***is*** my **son**.
UThandi ***ngu*gqirha**.	Thandi ***is*** a **doctor**.
Ndi***ngum*yeni** wakhe.	I ***am*** her **husband**.
UDavid ***ngum*fundi**.	David ***is*** a **pupil / student**.
UThemba ***ngum*phathi**.	Themba ***is*** a **manager**.
***Ngum*sebenzi** onomdla.	It ***is*** interesting **work**.

Similarly, '***ng-***' / '***-ng-***' prefixed to **nouns** beginning with '*aba-*', '*oo-*' and '*ama-*' (Classes 2, 2a, and 6 **nouns** → see **Unit 3**):

*Aba***ntwana** *ngaba***fundi**.	The **children** ***are*** **pupils**.
*Ngoo***Thamsanqa** aba.	These ***are*** the **Thamsanqas**.
*Ngoo***Murray** aba.	These ***are*** the **Murrays**.
Ba*ngama***gqwetha**.	They ***are*** **lawyers**.

< *uku***gqwetha** = to turn upside down, to be back to front, i.e. everything is the opposite of what it should be.

To express ***'am'***, ***'is'***, ***'are'*** with **Class 5 nouns** prefix '*-l-*':

Ndi*li***gqwetha**.	I ***am*** a **lawyer**.
Ú*li***gqirha**.	He ***is*** a **traditional healer**.
Ú*li***xhwele**.	She ***is*** a **herbalist**.

To express ***'am'***, ***'is'***, ***'are'*** with **Classes 7** and **8 nouns** prefix '*-s-*' and '*-z-*' respectively:

U*sisi***thethi** sepalamente.	She ***is*** the **speaker** of parliament.
Ba*zizi***thethi** zepalamente.	They ***are*** **speakers** of parliament.

To express ***'am'***, ***'is'***, ***'are'*** with **Class 9 nouns** prefix '*-y-*':

Ndiy*in***gcaphephe yezityalo**.	I ***am*** a **horticulturist**.
Ndi*yi***personnel manager**.	I ***am*** a personnel manager.

Note: Ndifuna ukuba ***ngum*phathi / *li*gqwetha / y*in*gcaphephe yezityalo** means I want to ***become*** a manager / lawyer / horticulturist.

2 Some occupations

Those derived from verbs prefix *um-* and change the final vowel -**a** to -**e**:

uku**phatha**	to **handle**	>	*um***phathi**	manager
uku**funda**	to **study**	>	*um***fundi**	student
uk**ongamela**	to **rule over**	>	*um***ongameli**	president
uku**pheka**	to **cook**	>	*um***pheki**	cook
uku**qhuba**	to **drive**	>	*um***qhubi**	driver
uku**thunga**	to **sew**	>	*um***thungi(kazi)**	tailor (seamstress)
uku**sebenza**	to **work**	>	*um***sébenzi**	worker

(cf. *um*sêbenz**i** Class 3 = work)

Note: uku**thetha** to speak > *isi***thethi** speaker

Those adopted from **English** or **Afrikaans** prefix '*u-*' / '*i-*' or '*in-*':

*u***titshala** / *oo***titshala**(kazi) — teacher/s
*i***titshala** / *ii***titshala**(kazi) — teacher/s
*u***profesa** / *oo***profesa** — professor/s
*u***njingalwazi** / *oo***njingalwazi**
*i***njingalwazi** / *ii***njingalwazi**
(< -**jinga** = **wave around**
+ *ulw***azi** = **knowledge**)
*u***mantyi** / *oo***mantyi** — magistrate/s
*i***joni** / *ama***joni** (< English Johnny) — soldier/s
*i***polisa** / *ama***polisa** — policeman/men
*i***toliki** / *ii***toliki** (< Afrikaans vertolk) — interpreter/s
*in***tatheli** / *iin***tatheli** (< -thathela = to take to) — journalist/s
*im***balisi** / *iim***balisi** (< -balisa = relate) — historian/s

Those incorporating '-**no**-', a contraction of '*u*nina wo-' = 'mother of' or the male equivalent '-**so**-', a contraction of 'uyise wo-' = 'father of':

*u***no**bhala / *oo***no**bhala (lit. **mother of** writing) — secretary/ies
*u***no**gadi / *oo***no**gadi (lit. **mother of** guards) — guard/s
*u***no**ncwadi / *oo***no**ncwadi (lit. **mother of** books) — librarian/s
*u***no**ndyebo / *oo***no**ndyebo (lit. **mother of** abundance) — treasurer/s
*u***no**ngendi / *oo***no**ngendi (lit. **mother of** not marrying) — nun/s
*u***no**ntlalo-ntle / oo**no**ntlalo-ntle (lit. **mother of** good living) — social worker/s

*u***no**posi / *oo***no**posi (lit. **mother of** post)	postman/men
u**no**silarha / *oo***no**silarha (lit. **mother of** slaughtering)	butcher/s
u**no**venkile / *oo***no**venkile (lit. **mother of** a shop)	shopkeeper/s

Insight

The male equivalent of '**-no-**' is '**-so-**' meaning the male who is associated with, or has the quality of, the object mentioned:

*u***so**mashishini/*oo***so**mashishini	businessman/men (lit. **father/s of** factories)
*u***so**mizi-mveliso/*oo*somizi-mveliso	captain/s of industry (lit. **father/s of** homesteads of production)
*u***so**mpempe/*oo***so**mpempe	referee/s (lit. **father/s of** the whistle)
u**So**bantu	**Father of** the people
u**So**mandla	**Father of** strength, i.e. The Almighty

3 Suffixing '-kazi' *to a noun*

Can make it feminine

inkosi	chief	inkosi**kazi**	chief's wife, lady, wife, madam
utitshala	teacher	utitshala**kazi**	
umongi	nurse	umongi**kazi**	
umnini	owner	umni**kazi**	

Can indicate greatness of size

ilizwe	country	ilizwe**kazi**	continent
umthi	tree	umthi**kazi**	**big** tree
umlambo	river	umlambo**kazi**	**large** river
intaba	mountain	intaba**kazi**	**high** mountain

Insight

Umhle**kazi** (lit. The **big** beautiful one) **means His/Her Excellency** and is used as a form of address:

Mhle**kazi** = Your Excellency, Majesty, Highness

In Xhosa folktales (iintsomi), it is often used when talking to a dominant male animal as a sign of respect:

'Uphila njani u**Mhlekazi**, namhla?' Ingonyama yavuyiswa kukubizwa ngokuthi 'Mhlekazi' yaza ke ngoko ayanqwanqwa ukumphendula uDyakalashe.

('How is His Highness today?' The lion was pleased to be called 'Your Highness', so he deigned to answer Jackal.)

Can express relationship

uma**kazi**	my mother's sister, i.e. maternal aunt
ubawo**kazi**	my father's brother, i.e. paternal uncle
indoda**kazi**	sister-in-law

4 Omission of the initial vowel of the noun

In direct address

If you look again at the explanation in **Unit 2** of how to greet appropriately, you will see that all nouns following 'Molo / Molweni' have lost their initial vowel:

*u***tata** / *u***bawo** / *um***numzana**
> Molo tata, bawo, *m*numzana
*in***kosikazi** / *in***kosazana** / *in***tombi** / *in***tombazana** / *in***kwenkwe**
> Molo *n*kosikazi / *n*kosazana / *n*tombi / *n*tombazana / *n*kwenkwe

After negative forms

*Andi***thand***i* **kofu**.	I don't like coffee.
UJenny *aka***fundis***i* *ba***ntwana**.	Jenny doesn't teach children.

After emphatic pronouns

Thina, bafundi, sifunda isiXhosa.	We, the students, are learning Xhosa.
'Nkosi sikelela, thina, lusapho lwayo'	God bless us, 'its (Africa's) family'

After demonstratives

*Ayi*namsebenzi **loo** ***n*****to**.
Intle **loo** ***n*****to**.

→ See **Unit 9.5** for more about **demonstratives**.

5 When verbs end in '-e' instead of '-a' (subjunctive)

In instructions preceded by an object concord

*Ndi***xelele**.	**Tell** *me*.
*Si***bonise**.	**Show** *us*.

After the expressions **kufuneka** (ukuba) = it is **necessary** (that) / **must**, **kubalulek***ile* (ukuba) = it is **important** (that)

Kufuneka ukuba uzam**e** ukuthetha isiXhosa yonke imihla!	You **must try** to speak Xhosa every day!
Kubalulek*ile* ukuba **uzame** ukuthetha isiXhosa yonke imihla.	**It is important** that you **try** to speak Xhosa every day.

After ma- *'let'*

Masithethe isiXhosa.	**Let**'s **speak** Xhosa.
Masihlale ngaphandle.	**Let**'s **sit** outside.

After -cela *'ask', 'request', 'beg'*

Ndi**cela uthethe** isiXhosa!	I **request** you to **speak** Xhosa.

→ cf. **Unit 3**.

6 Verbal extensions '-ela', '-isa', '-ana'

Another interesting feature of Xhosa is the extension of verbs thereby adding an implicit preposition or even a change of meaning.

'-ela' *translates 'for', 'to'*

UNomsa u**funda** eyunivesithi.	Nomsa **studies** at the university.
U**fundela ntoni**?	**What** is she **studying for**?
Ndi**sebenza** njengomphathi.	I **work** as a manager.
Ndi**sebenzela** inkampani.	I **work for** a company.
Xela igama lakho!	**Tell** your name!
*Ndi***xelele**.	**Tell** (**for**) *me*.

'-isa' *translates 'cause to', 'make'*

UPeter u**funda** isiXhosa.	Peter **learns** Xhosa.
UJenny u**fundisa** isiXhosa.	Jenny **teaches** (lit. causes to learn) Xhosa.
Ndiya**bona**.	I **see**.
*Ndi***bonise**.	**Show** *me* (lit. **make** *me* **see**).
Hamba!	**Go**!
Hambisa!	**Continue**! (lit. **make go**)
*Ndi***xelele** xa ndi**phazama**.	**Tell** *me* when I **make a mistake**.
Uxolo ngoku*ku***phazamisa**.	Sorry for **disturbing / interrupting** *you*.

Note: When '-**isa**' is doubled = '-**isisa**' it intensifies the meaning:

Fundisisa	=	**Read carefully**
Cingisisa	=	**Think carefully**
Cothisisa	=	**Speak very slowly**
Qhuqhisisa	=	**Beat very well** (See **Unit 5**)
Xubisisa	=	**Mix very well** (See **Unit 5**)

'-ana' *usually indicates reciprocity, 'each other'*

Siza ku**bona**.	We'll **see**.
Siza ku**bonana** > So**bonana**	We'll **see each other**.

More than one extension can be used in the same verb: uku**bon / is / an /a** to discuss something (lit. show **each other**):

Masi**bonisane** ngale nto!	**Let**'s **discuss** that!

7 *Various meanings of* 'nga-'

Indicating place = 'in the vicinity of', 'towards', 'near'

ngaseRhini	**near** Grahamstown
ngaseForest Drive	**in the vicinity of** Forest Drive

In connection with 'phandle', 'phakathi'

Nifuna ukuhlala **nga**phakathi okanye **nga**phandle?	Do you want to sit inside or outside?

Indicating time = 'at', 'in'

ngeli xesha	**at** this time
ngamanye amaxesha	sometimes (lit. **at** some times)
ngokuhlwa	**in** the evening

Translating 'by (means of)', 'with'

ukuhamba **nge**-eropleni	to go **by** plane
ukuhamba **nge**bhasi / **nge**moto	to go **by** bus / car
ukuhlawula **nge**khadi	to pay **by** card

Translating 'about', 'concerning', 'as'

W**enza** ntoni **ngoko***m*sebenzi?	What's your line of work? (lit. What **do** you do **as far as** work is concerned?)
Kunjani **ngo**kuphunga?	How **about** (something hot) to drink?

Forming an adverb

ngelishwa (*ili***shwa** = 'misfortune')	unfortunate**ly**
ngethamsanqa (*i***thamsanqa** = 'luck')	lucki**ly**

With a language translating 'in'

Yintoni leyo **nge**siNgesi?	What is this **in** English?
Uthini **nge**siXhosa?	What do you say **in** Xhosa?

After* 'enkosi' *= 'thanks'*; '*u*xolo' *= 'sorry' translating 'for'

Enkosi **nge**nto yonke.	Thanks **for** everything.
Uxolo **ngo**ku*ni***lindisa** ixesha elide.	Sorry **for making** *you* **wait** so long.

nga- + a- = nga-   nga-+ i- = nge-   nga- + u- = ngo-
(cf. na- + a- / i- / u- etc. → see **Unit 2**).

8 *More about the equivalent of English prepositions (known as locatives in Xhosa)*

You already know that to express the English prepositions '*at*', '*in*', '*to*', '*from*' with **place names**, you change the **initial vowel** of the prefix to '*e-*':

Uhlala phi?	Ndi**hlala** <u>*e*</u>**Kapa**, <u>*e*</u>**Pinelands**.
	Ndi**hlala** <u>*e*</u>**fama**.
	Ndi**hlala** <u>*e*</u>**Mzantsi Afrika**.
Uvela phi?	Ndi**vela** <u>*e*</u>**Monti** / <u>*e*</u>**Goli** / <u>*e*</u>**Pitoli** / <u>*e*</u>**Bhayi**.
	Ndi**vela** <u>*e*</u>**Mpuma-Koloni** / <u>*e*</u>**Ntshona-Koloni**.

Another verb which is always followed by the locative form of the noun is 'uku**ya**' = 'to **go** <u>**to**</u>':

Uya phi?	**Where** are you **going to**?
Ndi**ya** *e***yunivesithi**.	I am **going** *to* **university**.
Ndi**ya** *esi***bhedlele**.	I am **going** *to* **hospital**.
Ndi**ya** *e***khaya**.	I am **going** (*to*) **home**.

Insight

The verb '*uku***ya**' = '*to* **go** <u>**to**</u>' is used when a destination or direction is mentioned.
'*uku***hamba**' = '*to* **go**' in the sense of leave, depart (also walk) **IS NOT USED** when a **destination** is mentioned:

Ndiya**hamba**. I am **going.** BUT
Ndi**ya** *e***dolophi***ni*. I am **going** <u>*to*</u> **town.**

You have also come across '*ku-*' expressing '*at*', '*in*', '*on*', '*to*', '*from*':

Namkelekile <u>*ku*</u>**flight** 301 oya eKapa.
Usebenza <u>*kwi*</u>**kliniki** yePrimary Health.
Ukwazana <u>*kwi-*</u>**eropleni**.

ku- + *i-* = *kwi-* (< *ku-* + *i***kliniki**), (< *ku-* + *i-***eropleni**).

Note: '*ku-*' is normally used when the noun is followed by a qualifying phrase.

Insight

Kwa- is always prefixed to proper names and translates as '*at* **the place of,** *at* **the residence of**':

UKUDIBANA KWAKHONA *kwa*MURRAY
Meeting again ***at the home of*** the Murrays

*Kwa***Langa** = *In, at* Langa, a suburb of Cape Town named after the Xhosa chief *u***Langa**.

*Kwa***Zulu-Natal** - *At* the place of the Zulu nation (one of the nine provinces of South Africa – see map in **Unit 3**).

By far the commonest way of expressing prepositions in Xhosa is by changing the **initial vowel** of the noun to '*e*-' and the **final vowel** of the noun as follows:

-a >	*-eni*:	*i***khaya**	>	*e***khay***eni** lethu	*at / in / from / to* our **home**
-e >	*-eni*:	*ili***zwe**	>	*eli***zw***eni*	*in / from / to t*he **country**
-i >	*-ini*:	*um***sebenzi**	>	*em***sebenz***ini*	*at / to / from* **work**
-o >	*-weni*:	*isi***kolo**	>	*esi***kol***weni*	*at / in / from / to* **school**
-u >	*-wini:*	*i***Theku**	>	*e***Thek***wini*	*in / to / from* **Durban**

But -u > *-ini* after:

f:	*i***kofu**	> *e***kof***ini*	*in* the coffee
ph:	*i***dolophu**	> *e***doloph***ini*	*at* / *in* / *from* / *to* **town**

Note: **e***khaya** = *at* home BUT *e***khay***eni* lam = *at* my home when followed by a possessive.

How to apply it

1 Complete the dialogue

UDavid	Uyafunda, Bongani?
UBongani	Ewe, ndifunda eWesterford. Wena?
UDavid	Ndifunda eGrove. Uya*ba*thanda* (a) __titshala bakho?
UBongani	Abanye (some) (b) ____lungile kakhulu, abanye hayi.
UDavid	Udadewenu wenza (c) ________?
UBongani	(d) ____umfundi eyunivesithi.
UDavid	Ufundela (e) ________?

UBongani	Ufundela ubugqwetha. Benza ntoni abazali (f) __________?
UDavid	Utata (g) ____ingcaphephe yezityalo. Usebenza eKirstenbosch. Umama (h) _____utitshalakazi.
UBongani	Ufundisa (i) ________?
UDavid	Ufundisa (j) ____Xhosa (k) n ____Ngesi. Benza ntoni (l) _____zali bakho, bona?
UBongani	Utata (m) ___umphathi, umama (n) ____ugqirha. Nam ndifuna ukuba ngugqirha. Wena?
UDavid	Andazi. Mhlawumbi ndiza kuba yinjineli. (engineer)

* *-ba-* = them.

2 Derive the appropriate occupations from the verbs

-akha	build
-bhala	write
-coca	clean
-cula	sing
-fota	to take photos
-guqula	translate
-lawula	direct
-lima	farm
-phatha	manage
-qeqesha	train
-sasaza	broadcast
-thengisa	sell ('**-thenga**' = '**buy**')
-thwala	carry*
-zoba	paint, draw

* What is the English translation of this occupation?

3 You are introduced to a number of people by name and occupation. Write in English who does what

CD 1, tr 5, 02:30

(a) ________ ________ (f) ________ ________
(b) ________ ________ (g) ________ ________
(c) ________ ________ (h) ________ ________
(d) ________ ________ (i) ________ ________
(e) ________ ________ (j) ________ ________

4 You are already able to introduce your husband, son and friend (Ngumyeni wam lo; ngunyana wam; ngumhlobo wam, uThandi, etc.). Now introduce other members of your family (usapho lwakho)

your parents	Ngabazali bam
your children	___abantwana bam
your grandchildren	___abazukulwana bam
your wife	Yinkosikazi yam
your daughter	___intombi yam, uLindi.

Use the list of greetings in **Unit 1** to introduce:

your father
your mother
your grandfather
your grandmother

5 You are introduced to someone's relatives. Write down who they are

CD 1, tr 5, 03:50

(a) ______________________ (e)
________________________.
(b) ______________________ (f)
________________________.
(c) ______________________ (g)
________________________.
(d) ______________________ (h)
________________________.

6 Answer the questions

(a) Uvela phi uPeter?
(b) Uhlala phi ngoku?
(c) Uya phi yonke imihla?
(d) Uvela phi uJenny?
(e) Ufundisa bani?
(f) Usebenza phi uThandi kusasa?
(g) Uya phi emva kwemini?
(h) Usebenzela bani uThemba?

7 Say in Xhosa

(a) Where you come from
(b) Where you live now
(c) What your occupation is
(d) Where you work

8 Fill in the verbal extension for a meaningful answer

(a) Wena uyasebenza?
Ewe, ndisebenz__a inkampani yekhomphyutha.
(b) Intombi yakho uyakwazi ukupheka?
Ewe, iphek__a usapho.
(c) Uyasifunda isiXhosa?
Ewe, uJenny uyandifund__a.
(d) UNomsa ufunda eyunivesithi?
Ewe, ufund__a ubugqwetha.
(e) OoThamsanqa bathanda ooMurray?
Ewe, bayathand__a!

9 Say to a friend

(a) Let's teach each other!
(b) Let's meet!
(c) Let's help each other!
(d) Let's pull together!
(i.e. Let's build one another!)

10 Say that you must

(a) go now	Kufuneka ndi__________________.
(b) go to work	Kufuneka ndi __________________.
(c) work now	Kufuneka ndi __________________.
(d) go to the hospital	Kufuneka ndi __________________.
(e) go home (-goduka)	Kufuneka ndi __________________.
(f) speak Xhosa every day	Kufuneka ndi __________________.
(g) pay by card	Kufuneka ndi __________________.

11 Complete appropriately

(a) Ndiya eBhayi ngomso.
Uhamba __bhasi? Hayi, ndihamba __eropleni.
(b) Uthanda ukuhamba ___eropleni?
Hayi, ndikhetha ukuhamba ___moto.

(c) Wenza ntoni ___komsebenzi? Ndi___umphathi.
(d) Usebenza __shishini lempahla? Hayi, ndisebenza __-ofisi___.
(e) Usebenza na___kuhlwa? Ewe, ___manye amaxesha.
(f) Hamba kakuhle. Sala kakuhle. Enkosi ___nto yonke.

12 Complete the idioms using the correct form of 'is', 'are'

Ba___umthi nexolo.	They <u>are</u> great friends. (lit. They <u>are</u> tree and resin.)
Ba___inyoka nesele.	They <u>are</u> great enemies. (lit. They <u>are</u> snake and frog.)
U___inyoka.	He/she <u>is</u> a treacherous person.
U___umkhombe.	He/she <u>is</u> a very angry person. (lit. He/she <u>is</u> a rhino.)
U___indlovu.	He/she <u>is</u> a very strong person. (lit. He/she <u>is</u> an elephant.)

13 Listen to the dialogue and answer the questions

umsebenzi omkhulu	huge job	kanjalo	as well
umsebenzi onzima	a hard job	-phumelela	succeed, manage
ndigqibile	I have finished		

QV

CD 1, tr 5, 04:53

(a) **Who** are talking to one another?
(b) **What** are they talking about?
(c) **Where** are they talking?

Test yourself

1 To translate the equivalent of English 'am', 'is', 'are', simply prefix **ng-** (the **copulative**) to nouns of Classes **1/1a** and **3**, e.g.:

Ndi**ngu**John.	I **am** John.
UThemba **ng**umfundi.	Themba **is** a student.
Ngumsebenzi onomdla.	It **is** interesting work.

To nouns of which other classes do you prefix the copulative 'ng-'? Give examples.

2 What are the copulatives for **Classes 5, 7** and **8**? How would you say:

I am a lawyer — South Africa is a country

She is the speaker of parliament — They are speakers of parliament?

3 What does the suffix '**-kazi**' indicate?

4 What happens to the initial vowel of the prefix of the noun when you greet someone by name?

5 If '*uku***funda**' = *to* **learn**, what does '*uku*fund**isa**' mean? What is its literal meaning?

6 If **-isa** and **-ana**- are combined in *uku*fund**isan**a, what is the meaning?

7 What does the verbal extension **-ela** in 'Ùfund**ela** ntoni?' mean?

8 How do you say the following in Xhosa?

I live in the vicinity of the university

Do you go by car?

Yes, but sometimes I go by bus

9 What is the final vowel of the verb when an instruction is preceded by an object concord, e.g. 'Help me'?

10 Which other idiomatic expression do you know besides '**Umntu ngumntu ngabantu**'?

If you have done all exercises and answered the questions above correctly, then you are well prepared to proceed to the next unit.

5 Uyithanda njani ikofu yakho?

How do you like your coffee?

In this unit you will learn how to:

- apologize
- say you are thirsty / hungry
- ask guests how they take their coffee
- offer refreshments
- accept and decline
- express appreciation
- remark on a change in the weather

Incoko

CD 1, tr 6

Jenny and Thandi arrive with refreshments.

UPeter	Ekugqibeleni. Masiqabuleni unxano!
UJenny	Uxolo ngokunilindisa ixesha elide. Besincokola! Ndiqinisekile ukuba ninxaniwe.
UPeter	Ewe, sinxanwe kakhulu! Silambile kananjalo.
UThemba	Hayi, kulungile, nathi besincokola!
UJenny	Thandi, uyithanda njani ikofu yakho? Ufuna ubisi neswekile?
UThandi	Ubisi *qha*, enkosi sisi.
UJenny	Wena, Themba ufuna ikofu enobisi?
UThemba	Ewe, enkosi neetispuni ezimbini zeswekile.
UJenny	Nantsi iswekile. Zincede.
UPeter	Kunjani ngekeyiki neesengwitshi, Thandi?
UThandi	Enkosi Peter. Ndingafumana isilayi esincinci sekeyiki? Ijongeka intle!
UPeter	Inene, imnandi kakhulu. Nasi isilayi.
UThandi	Enkosi. Mmm! inencasa le keyiki. Jenny, ndingafumana iresiphi?

UJenny	Ngokuqinisekileyo, sisi. Undikhumbuze. Themba, ndingakupha isilayi sekeyiki, nawe?
UThemba	Enkosi, Jenny. Mna, ndizithanda kakhulu izinto ezimnandi!
UJenny	Peter, nceda ugqithisele uThemba ikeyiki ngoku ndigalela ikofu yakho.
UPeter	Kulungile. Thandi, kunjani ngenye ikomityi yekofu?
UThandi	Hayi enkosi. Ikomityi enye yekofu yanele kum!
UPeter	Yho! ilanga lithe *shwaka*. Kuyaphola ngoku. Sifanele ukungena ngaphakathi?
UJenny	Ewe, ngesaquphe kuyabanda. Mna, ndiyagodola. Nina?
UThandi	Ewe, kancinci.
UJenny	Kulungile, masingeneni! Peter, nceda uvale ucango!

After coffee Thandi reminds Jenny about the recipe.

UThandi	Jenny, ungalibali ukundinika iresiphi yekeyiki.
UJenny	Andilibalanga, sisi. Nantsi.

Ukuba ukhetha i chocolate icing, unganyibilikisa icephe lecocoa powder kwicephe lamanzi abilayo, uqhuqhisise kwi-icing.

QUICK VOCAB

Isigama

ekugqibeleni	at last	imnandi	it's nice
-qabula	quench	nasi (isilayi)	here it is
unxano	thirst	inencasa	it's delicious
-lindisa	cause to wait	iresiphi	recipe
ixesha elide	a long time	ngokuqinisekileyo	certainly
besincokola	we were chatting	-khumbuza	remind
-qinisekile	(be) certain / sure	-pha	give
-nxaniwe	thirsty	isilayi sekeyiki	a slice of cake
-nxanwe kakhulu	very thirsty	izinto ezimnandi	sweet things
-lambile	hungry	-gqithisela	pass to someone
kananjalo	also	-galela	put in, pour
ubisi	milk	enye ikomityi yekofu	another cup of coffee
iswekile	sugar		
qha	*only*	ikomityi enye yanele kum	one cup is enough for me
enobisi	which has milk		
neetispuni ezimbini	and 2 teaspoons	ilanga lithe *shwaka*	the sun's disappeared
zeswekile	of sugar	kuyaphola	it's getting cool
zincede	help yourself	-fanele	ought
ikeyiki	cake	kuyabanda	it's cold
iisengwitshi	sandwiches	ngesaquphe	suddenly
-fumana	get, obtain	-godola	(be) cold (humans)
isilayi esincinci	a small slice	-vala	close
ijongeka intle	it looks lovely	ucango	door
inene	indeed	-nika	give

Ikeyiki enye eneencasa
EZININZI

IZITHAKO:

4 amaqanda
310ml (1 ¼ yekomityi) yecastor sugar
*500ml (2 iikomityi) ye**SNOWFLAKE Cake Flour***
15ml (3 iitispuni) yebaking-powder
250ml (ikomityi) yobisi
90g yemagarini OKANYE ibhotolo
7ml (1 ½ yetispuni yevanilla essence

INDLELA YOKWENZA:

Ionti yenze shushu kwangaphambili ifike kwi-180°C. Qhuqha amaqanda neswekile ndawonye de aqine abe nombala olubhelu. Sefa i**SNOWFLAKE Cake Flour** ndawonye nebaking powder, kuxube umxube weqanda. Yenza shushu ubisi nemagarini ndawonye kodwa **ungalubilisi**. Umxube wobisi nevanilla essence wuzamisele entlameni, galela ngecephe kwiitin zekeyiki ezingqukuva neziyi-23cm, bhaka ama-25 ukuya kuma-30 emizuzu.

I-icing Engundoqo

Qhuqha i-500g (ipakethi) yeicing sugar ne-250g yemagarini okanye ibhotolo ethambileyo de ibe khaphukhaphu. Yisebenzise phakathi koomaleko nakumphezulu wekeyiki.

QUICK VOCAB

icephe (ama-)	spoon	uxube kumxube weqanda	fold into egg mixture
-qhuqhisisa	beat well	unga*lu*bilisi	you shouldn't boil *it*
izithako	ingredients	*wu*zamisele entlameni	stir it into the batter
amaqanda	eggs	*ez*ingqukuva	*which* are round
indlela yokwenza	method (lit. way of making / doing)	i-icing engundoqo	basic icing
i-onti	oven	*e*thambileyo	*which* is soft
yenze	make *it*	khaphukhaphu	light and fluffy
shushu	hot	*yis*ebenzise	use *it*
kwangaphambili ifike kwi-180ºC	pre-heat to 180ºC	phakathi koomaleko	between layers
qhuqha ndawonye	beat together	nakumphezulu	and on top
de aqine abe nombala olubhelu	until thick and yellow in colour		

Try to memorize

Uxolo ngokunilindisa ixesha elide	Sorry for keeping *you* waiting such a long time
Zincede!	Help yourself!
Ikomityi enye yekofu yanele kum!	One cup of coffee is enough for me!
Ilanga lithe *shwaka*!	The sun has *disappeared!*
Ungalibali!	Don't forget!
Andilibalanga!	I haven't forgotten!

How to ...

Apologize

*U*xolo! (ngoku*ku*lindisa *i*xesha *eli*de)
*U*xolo! (ngoku*ni*lindisa *i*xesha *eli*de)

Say you are thirsty / hungry

Nd**inxan***iwe*. Nd**inxan***we* kakhulu.
Ndi**lamb***ile*. Ndi**lamb***e* kakhulu.

Ask how someone takes their coffee / tea

U*yi***thanda njani** *i***kofu** / *i***ti** yakho?
U**funa** *u***bisi** ne**swekile** *e***kof***ini* / *e***t***ini*?
U**funa** *i***kofu** *e***nobisi**?
U**funa** *i***kofu** *e***neswekile**?

Offer something to eat

Kunjani ngekeyiki?
Kunjani ngeesengwitshi?
*Zi***ncede**!
Ndinga*ku***pha** *isi***layi** se**keyiki**?
Ndinga*ku***pha** *i***sengwitshi**?
Remember the saying (p. 17): **'Awungeni emizini ungatayi'**
You do not enter a home and not eat.

Offer liquid refreshments

Kunjani ngekofu / nge**ti**?

Insight

*U***tywala,** beer made according to Xhosa custom, nowadays also refers to beer or any type of liquor.
The brewing of beer is the exclusive domain of womenfolk. There are a number of different types of traditional brews and no social event or ritually important occasion is complete without a plentiful supply of *um***qombothi**.
*Um***qombothi** is made from mealie (maize) meal, sprouts, crushed mealie (maize) malt, crushed sorghum malt and water and involves an intricate brewing process. It is the custom to cook the initial porridge (*isi***dudu**) outside in a pot and cool it outside (not in a fridge) before fermentation. It is said to be good for diabetes and high blood pressure.
*Ama***rhewu** is **non-alcoholic** maize meal liquid. A small amount is mixed with **flour** and **sugar** (optional). It is then put into the main porridge container until ready.
*U***blayi** is a m**aize porridge** made in a three-legged pot. It is cooked until the bottom of the pot is scalded. This scalded part is then scraped off, mixed with the porridge and allowed to ferment.

Kunjani ngenye *i***komityi** ye**kofu** / ye**ti**?
Kunjani ngokusela *in***to** *e***banda***yo*?
Kunjani ngewayini? (wine)
Kunjani ngotywala? (beer / alcohol)

Accept and decline

Ewe, enkosi.
Hayi, enkosi.
Ndinga**fumana** *isi***layi** *esi***ncinci** *qha*?
*I***komityi** *e***nye** ye**kofu** **yanele ku***m* enkosi.

Express appreciation

Ku**mnandi**!
Ine**ncasa** gqitha!
Imnandi kakhulu!
Ijongeka *in***tle** le **keyiki**!

Remark on a change in the weather

Li**njani** *i***zulu**? / **Injani** *im***ozulu**? (lit. **How** is the **weather**?)
Ingathi *i***langa** li**the** *shwaka.*
*I***langa** li**tshon***ile* (the sun has gone down).
Liya**phola** ngoku.
Kuya**banda** ngesaquphe.

Insight

Ideophones (*izi***fanekisozwi**) are a characteristic and distinctive feature of the Xhosa language, two examples of which you have come across in the '**Incoko**' of this unit:

'qha', shwaka

Ideophones are often onomatopoeic, i.e. suggesting the action by their sound, e.g. '*dyumpu*', similar to the English 'plop', but they mostly describe manner and are used where English uses adverbs, e.g.:

Hamba *ngqo*!'	**Go** *straight along!*

Ideophones are often introduced by '*uku***thi**' which indicates the tense, mood, person and class, but they can also be used with other verbs, e.g.:

Si**phile** *qete!*'	We are *completely* **well**!

However, because **ideophones** are interjectional in nature, they are often more effective when standing alone, e.g.:

*Nkqi i***vili**!	The wheel is *stuck fast!*

Ideophones are also used to emphasize the intensity of some colours:

Le **ntyatyambo** i**bomvu** *krwe*(*e*).	This flower is *blood* **red**.
*Imi***thi iluhlaza** *yaka.*	The trees are *grass* **green**.
*Ii***nwele** zakhe zi**mnyama** *khaca* (*thsu*).	Her hair is *pitch* **black**.
*Ii***nwele** zakhe zi**mhlophe** *qhwa.*	Her hair is *snow* **white**.

→ See also **Unit 14**.

How it works

1 More object concords

In English, the pronouns '*him*' and '*her*' are the same irrespective of whether you are referring to a student, lawyer or engineer, etc. This is not so in Xhosa where '*him*' and '*her*' are represented by different forms which change according to the *noun* to which they refer. These are known as **object concords** and are derived from the noun prefixes:

Jenny **teaches** *him/her* (the **student**).	UJenny uya*m***fundisa** (*um***fundi**).
She **teaches** *him/her* (the **lawyer**).	Uya*li***fundisa** (*i***gqwetha**).
She **teaches** *him/her* (the **engineer**).	Uya*yi***fundisa** (*in***jineli**).

The plural form '*them*' also has different forms in Xhosa:

She **teaches** *them* (**workers**).	Uya*ba***fundisa** (*aba***sebenzi**).
She **teaches** *them* (**doctors**).	Uya*ba***fundisa** (*oo***gqirha**).
She **teaches** *them* (**lawyers**).	Uya*wa***fundisa** (*ama***gqwetha**).
She **teaches** *them* (**engineers**).	Uya*zi***fundisa** (*iin***jineli**).

Similarly, there are several Xhosa equivalents for the English pronoun '*it*' and its plural '*them*', which also depend on the noun referred to:

I **ask** for *it* (**work**).	Ndiya*wu***cela** (*um***sebenzi**).
I **like** *them* (**illustrations**).	Ndiya*yi***thanda** (*imi***zobo**).
I **like** *it* (the **name**).	Ndiya*li***thanda** (*i***gama**).
I **like** *them* (the **names**).	Ndiya*wa***thanda** (*ama***gama**).
I **like** *it* (the **Xhosa language**).	Ndiya*si***thanda** (*isi***Xhosa**).
How do you **like** *it* (**coffee**)?	U*yi***thanda** njani (*i***kofu**)?
How do you **like** *them* (**sandwiches**)?	U*zi***thanda** njani (*ii***sengwitshi**)?
Do*n't* you **like** *it* (the **milk**)?	*Akulu***thandi** (*u***bisi**)?
I do*n't* **like** *it* (**winter**).	*Andibu***thandi** (*ubu***sika**).
I **like** *it* (**travelling**).	Ndiya*ku***thanda** (*uku***hamba**).

Insight

In the table that follows, you will notice that **object concords** have the **same form as subject concords** except where the subject concord is a vowel only. In these cases the subject concord incorporates a consonant to form the **object concord**, e.g.:

Ndiya + u + **thanda** > Ndiya*ku***thanda** = I **love** *you*.

Ndiya + u + **cela** (*um***sebenzi**)	> Ndiya<u>*wu*</u>**cela**	=	I **ask** for *it*. (work)
Ndiya + i + **thanda** (*imi***zobo**)	> Ndiya<u>*yi*</u>**thanda**	=	I **like** *them.* (the illustrations)
Ndiya + a + **thanda** (*ama***gama**)	> Ndiya<u>*wa*</u>**thanda**	=	I like *them*. (the names)

Subject concords / **at a glance** / **Object concords**

Subject concords		Object concords	
ndi-	I	*-ndi-*	*me*
si-	we	*-si-*	*us*
<u>ù</u>-	you (s.)	*-<u>k</u>u-*	*you* (s.)
ni-	you (pl.)	*-ni-*	*you* (pl.)
<u>ú</u>-	he / she	*-<u>m</u>-*	*him / her*
ba-	they	*-ba-*	*them*
<u>u</u>-	it	*-<u>w</u>u-*	*it*
<u>i</u>-	they	*-<u>y</u>i-*	*them*
li-	it / he / she	*-li-*	*it / him / her*
<u>a</u>-	it	*-<u>w</u>a-*	*them*
si-	it	*-si-*	*them*
zi-	them	*-zi-*	*them*
<u>i</u>-	it / he / she	*-<u>y</u>i-*	*it / him / her*
zi-	them	*-zi-*	*them*
lu-	it	*-lu-*	*it*
bu-	it	*-bu-*	*it*
ku-	it	*-ku-*	*it*

2 Possessives

In English, possessive relationship can be expressed by '*'s*' or '*of*', e.g. 'the **boy**'<u>*s*</u> **name**' or 'the **name** <u>*of*</u> the **boy**'.

In Xhosa, only the '*of*' construction exists. The two nouns ('name' and 'boy') are **linked** by a **possessive concord** which is characterized by the possessive '*-a*'.

This **link** (representing '*of*') between the two nouns **changes** according to the prefix of the first noun (possessee) and influences the prefix of the second noun (possessor) resulting in a **sound change**:

*um***sebenzi** *wa*-	+ *i***nkampani**	> *we***nkampani** (employee *of* a company)
*u***somashini** *wa*-	+ *i***nkampani**	> w*e***nkampani** (businessman *of* a company)
*aba***sebenzi** *ba*-	+ *ii***nkampani**	> *bee***nkampani*** (staff *of* a company)
*oo***somashini** *ba*-	+ *ii***nkampani**	> *bee***nkampani*** (businessmen *of* a company)
*um***xube** *wa*-	+ *i***qanda**	> *we***qanda** (mixture *of* egg)
*imi***zobo** *ya*-	+ *aba***ntwana**	> *yaba***ntwana** (paintings *of* the children)
*i***xesha** *la*-	+ *i***ti**	> *le***ti** (time *of* tea i.e. teatime)
*ama***gama** *a*-	+ *aba***ntwana**	> *aba***ntwana** (names *of* the children)
*isi***celo** *sa*-	+ *um***sebenzi**	> *som***sebenzi** (application *of* a job)
*izi***celo** *za*-	+ *um***sebenzi**	> *zom***sebenzi** (applications *of* jobs)
*i***komityi** *ya*-	+ *i***kofu**	> *ye***kofu** (cup *of* coffee)
*ii***tispuni** *za*-	+ *i***swekile**	> *ze***swekile** (teaspoons *of* sugar)
*ulu***hlu** *lwa*-	+ *izi***thako**	> *lwezi***thako** (list *of* ingredients)
*ubu***ntu** *ba*-	+ *aba***ntu**	> *baba***ntu** (the humanity *of* the people)
*uku***bhakwa** *kwa*-	+ *ii***keyiki**	> *kwee***keyiki*** (the baking *of* cakes)
*ukw***enziwa** *kwa*-	+ *ubu***si**	> *kobu***si**† (the making *of* honey)

ii- > -ee-*. †For ease of pronunciation 'w**' is omitted before '**o**'.

3 How to express 'am', 'is', 'are'

With interrogative '-phi?' where *'am', 'is', 'are'* are understood

Uphi uDavid?	**Where** (is) David?
Siphi isibhedlele?	**Where** (is) the hospital?
Iphi i-ofisi yakho?	**Where** (is) your office?

→ cf. **Unjani**? = lit. You **how**? (see **Unit 2**).

With the adverb 'apha' = *'here'*

I-ofisi i*l***apha** *e***Kapa**.	The office *is* here *in* **Cape Town**.

With forms such as '*esikolweni*', '*e-ofisini*', '*emsebenzini*', *esi*bhedlele, *e*Kapa, etc. (known as the locative form)

Ndis*e***khaya**.	I ***am*** *at* **home**.
Us*e*-**ofis***ini*.	He ***is*** *in* the **office**.
Bas*esi***kol***weni*.	They ***are*** *at* **school**.

Note: The locative -**s**- also separates the two vowels in:

ngas*e*-: ngas*e***Rhini**	**near Grahamstown**
nas*e*-: nas*e***yunivesithi**	**and** *at* the **university**
bas*e*-: *aba***ntu** bas*e***Holani**	the **people of** (in) **Holland**

4 How to express 'here is', 'here are' (known as adverbial demonstratives)

Once again the noun class system in Xhosa necessitates the use of several different forms where only two are used in English, namely: Here is …/Here are …:

Nanku *u***Jenny**.	**Here is Jenny**.
Naba *aba***ntwana**.	**Here are** the **children**.
Nanku (or **nangu**) *um***nxeba**.	**Here is** the **phone**.
Nantsi *imi***qamelo**.	**Here are** the **pillows**.
Nali *i***cephe**.	**Here is** the **spoon**.
Nanga *ama***cephe**.	**Here are** the **spoons**.
Nasi *isi***layi** **sekeyiki**.	**Here is** a **slice** of **cake**.
Nazi *ezi***nye** *izi***layi**.	**Here are** some **more slices**.
Nantsi *i***kofu**.	**Here is** the **coffee**.
Nazi (or nanzi) *ii***tispuni**.	**Here are** the **teaspoons**.
Nalu *u***bisi**.	**Here is** the **milk**.
Nabu* *ubu***si**.	**Here is** the **honey**.
Naku *uku***tya**.	**Here is** the **food**.

* **Nabu** is seldom used as nouns belonging to Class 14 are nearly all abstract.

5 The equivalent of English 'myself', 'yourself', etc.

At last, here is a case where there is only one form in Xhosa where English has more than one form!

Like the object concord, '*-zi-*' = '*myself*', '*yourself*', '*ourselves*', etc., is placed immediately before the verb:

Ndiya*zi***dla**. (lit. I am eating *myself*)	I am **proud** of *myself*.
Baya*zi***dla**.	They are **proud** of *themselves*.
*Zi***ncede**.	**Help** *yourself*.

6 *Expressions in Xhosa ending in '-ile'*

These expressions often refer to a **physical state**. They are verbal forms in Xhosa, but correspond to adjectives in English:

Ndi**phil**_ile_.	I am **well**.	**Namkelek**_ile_!	You're **welcome**!
Ndi**lamb**_ile_.	I am **hungry**.	**Uxakek**_ile_?	Are you **busy**?
Ndi**qinisek**_ile_.	I'm **sure**.	Ndi**ngxam**_ile_.	I'm in a **hurry**.
Utshat_ile_?	Are you **married**?	**Unyanis**_ile_.	You're **right**.
Ukhululek_ile_?	Are you **comfortable**?	Ndi**gug**_ile!_	I'm worn out, i.e. very **old**!
Kubalulek_ile_.	It's **important**.		
Kulung_ile_.	It is **all right**.		
Kuphol_ile_.	It is **cool**.		

Note: Two frequently used stative verbs end in *-iwe*, not *-ile*:

Ndi**nxan**_iwe_.	I am **thirsty**.	Ndi**din**_iwe_.	I am **tired**.

7 *'Xhosalized' words*

In Units 1-5 you have come across a number of '**xhosalized**' nouns, i.e. those nouns adopted from **English** and / or **Afrikaans**:

from English		*from Afrikaans*	
_i_**bhotolo**	butter	_i_**bhanti** (*ama-*)	band
_i_**fama**	farm	_i_**dolophu**	dorp
_in_**kampani**	company	_i_**komityi**	koppie
_i_**keyiki**	cake	_i_**swekile**	suiker
_i_**kliniki**	clinic		
_i_**kofu**	coffee		
_i_**majarini**	margarine		
_i-_**ofisi**	office		
_i_**resiphi**	recipe		
_i_**sengwitshi**	sandwich		
_i_**ti**	tea		
_i_**tispuni**	teaspoon		
_i_**yunivesithi**	university		

As you can see, most of these 'adopted words' belong to Classes 9 /10 prefixing *i-/ii-*. However, when the adopted English or Afrikaans word begins with an '**s**' followed by a consonant, e.g. '**sc**hool', '**sl**ice', these nouns usually belong to the '*isi-*' class:

isi**kolo**	school	_isi_**layi**	slice

Although the majority of nouns adopted from English or Afrikaans belong to Classes 9 and 10, there are a number of nouns besides '*i***bhanti**' which belong to Classes 5 and 6 and **not** to Classes 9 and 10:

*i***khitshi**	*ama***khitshi** (kitchen/s)	*i***khadi**	*ama***khadi** (card/s)
*i***phepha**	*ama***phepha** (paper/s)	*i***polisa**	*ama***polisa** (police)
*i***tikiti**	*ama***tikiti** (ticket/s)	*i***vili**	*ama***vili** (wheel/s)

Adopted words are often used in everyday speech while the original Xhosa words are preferred in the written language, especially in literature, e.g.:

*i-***eropleni**	*in***qwelo-moya** (lit. wagon [of the] air)
*i***khitshi**	*i***gumbi** lo*ku***phekela** (lit. room of / for cooking)
*i***flawa**	*um***gubo** (flour)
*i***fowuni**	*um***nxeba** (phone) (lit. a rope) (→ See also **Unit 6**)

Note: When English words are used in written or spoken Xhosa they must have a prefix which is usually '*i-*' (Class 9):

*i***personnel manager**
*i***Red Cross Hospital**
*i***Primary Health Care**

How to apply it

1 Ask

(a) Where is the sugar?
(b) Where is the milk?
(c) Where is the cake?
(d) Where is a spoon?
(e) Where is the coffee?
(f) Where is the tea?
(g) Where is a teaspoon?

2 Answer

(a) Here is the sugar.
(b) Here is the milk.
(c) Here is the cake.
(d) Here is a spoon.
(e) Here is the coffee.
(f) Here is the tea.
(g) Here is a teaspoon.

3 Say that you like *'it'*

(a) Ndi___thanda (ikeyiki).
(b) Ndi___thanda (amaqanda).
(c) Ndi___thanda (izinto ezimnandi).
(d) Ndi___thanda (iisengwitshi).
(e) Ndi___thanda (ikofu) enganaswekile. (without sugar) (lit. not having sugar)

4 Give the instructions replacing the word in brackets with the appropriate object concord

(a) _____zalise (iketile – fill the kettle).
(b) _____bilise (amanzi).
(c) _____zise (ubisi).
(d) _____gqithise (iswekile).
(e) _____ncede (yourself).
(f) _____vale (ucango).

5 Ask (using *-njani*)

(a) How are you today?
(b) How are the children?
(c) How is your husband?
(d) How is your wife?
(e) How are your parents?
(f) How is work?
(g) How is the weather?
(h) How is the cake?
(i) How are the sandwiches?

6 Look at the recipe Jenny gives Thandi

(a) Circle the object concords and the noun to which they refer. (You should find three.)

__________ __________ __________

(b) Circle the possessives.

7 Write a list in Xhosa of the things Thandi asks Lindiwe to buy for her

UThandi 'Lindiwe, ndifuna ukubhaka ikeyiki ngomso kusasa kodwa andinaxesha lokuthenga izithako ezifunekayo. Ndicela uye esuphamakete uzithenge. Nalu uluhlu:'

eggs	__________
flour	__________
butter	__________
sugar	__________
milk	__________
margarine	__________
icing sugar	__________

ULindiwe Kulungile. Ndiza kukwenzela loo nto.

8 Complete the text by filling in

Use 'amanzi', 'ikofu' and 'ubisi'.

A Ngena sisi, uphumle umzuzwana. Ujongeka udiniwe! Hlala phantsi. Lixesha leti okanye ukhetha _______?
B Enkosi. Nokuba yintoni.
A David, layita iketile ubilise _________.
D Kulungile, mama.
A Nantsi _______. Ungathanda ______ neswekile?
B Galela _______ qha, enkosi.
A David, nceda uzise ________.
D Luphi _______, mama? Lusefrijini? Andiluboni *tu*!
A Oo, ndilibele ukuluthenga _______!

QV

-phumla	rest, relax	iketile	kettle
umzuzwana	a little while	-bilisa	boil
-layita	switch on	-zisa	fetch

9 Fill in the missing forms, using:

(a) ndilambile, (b) kubalulekile, (c) wamkelekile, (d) ndiphilile, (e) ndingxamile, (f) utshatile, (g) ndinxanwe and (h) kupholile

Molo, (1) ______________________ ekhayeni lam!
Unjani namhlanje? (2) ____________________ enkosi.

Ufuna into yokusela? Ewe, (3) ndi __________________kakhulu!
Ufuna into yokutya kananjalo? Ewe, (4) __________________.
Ndicela uze apha. Ungandincedisa? Hayi, ndilusizi,
(5) ________________.
Nceda uzise ijezi yam. Ndiyagodola. (6) _______________ngoku.
(7) ___________________ufowune uThandi.
(8) _______________________uThemba? Ewe, uThandi yinkosikazi yakhe.

Test yourself

1 What is the meaning of '*zi*' in '*Zi***ncede**' and 'Ndiya*zi*thanda izinto ezimnandi'?
2 Which **'loan' words** from English and Afrikaans are in the '**Incoko**'? Which one does not belong to Class 9/10?
3 Some '**loan' words** from English which prefix '**i-'** do not belong to Class 9/10. To which class do they belong and what is their plural form?
4 The forms of the subject and object concords are identical except for which person and classes?
5 Combine '*aba***sebenzi'** and '*iin***kampani'** to form a possessive relationship.
6 You know that '*uku***khumbula**' means '*to* **remember**'. What does '*uku***khumbuza**' mean?
7 Illustrate how you use the **locative '-l-**' and the **locative '-s-**' when saying:
'I am here.' 'I am at school.'
8 What is the difference in meaning between '*uku***hamba**' and '*uku***ya**'?
9 When asking 'Where are you?' do you translate 'are'?
10 Do you know another interrogative where 'are' is understood?

If you have done all exercises and answered the questions above correctly, then you are well prepared to proceed to the next unit.

6 Nifudumele ngokwaneleyo?
Are you warm enough?

In this unit you will learn how to:

- ask whether someone is warm enough
- discuss the weather
- express likes / dislikes
- refer to the days of the week / months / seasons

Incoko

CD 1, tr 7

The Murrays and the Thamsanqas move inside and discuss the variable weather.

UPeter	Nifudumele ngokwaneleyo okanye ndilayite isifudumezi?
UThemba	Hayi enkosi, asifuni sifudumezi. Akubandi kangako.
UJenny	Linjalo izulu laseKapa. Umzuzu ilanga liyakhanya, kolandelayo kuyana!
UThandi	Hayi, maan, musa ukubaxa! Yaye ungakhalazi ngezulu laseKapa! Imvula ibhetele kunembalela! Ibe siyayifuna imvula eMzantsi Afrika. Inqabile.
UPeter	Jenny, ufana nabantu abavela eGauteng! Bona, kaloku, abalithandi izulu lethu! Ebusika bakhalaza ngemvula; ehlotyeni ngokuvuthuza komoya!
UThemba	Kodwa masiyivumeni inyani, lihle izulu laseGauteng ebusika. Lomile, alini.
UThandi	Kodwa iindudumo nemibane phaya ehlotyeni!
UJenny	Hayi, masivumeni yonke indawo inezinto ezilungileyo nezinto ezingalunganga!
UThandi	Unyanisile! Umzekelo, eThekwini kumnandi ebusika kodwa ukufuma apho ehlotyeni, *kugqithe emgceni*!!
UJenny	Ewe, kunjalo kanye sisi.

UPeter	Ndiyathemba ukuba liza kuba lihle* ngempela-veki ezayo kuba kukho ukhuphiswano olukhulu lweqakamba eNewlands. Uyakuthanda ukubukela iqakamba, Themba?
UThemba	Kakhulu! Utsho no**Makhaya Ntini** kwiTV: *'I don't like cricket. I love it!'*
UPeter	Heke, ndiza kuya noDavid emdlalweni ngoMgqibelo. Uyafuna ukusikhapha nonyana wakho?
UThemba	Ewe, singavuya kakhulu.
UPeter	Kulungile, ndiza kukufowunela ngoLwesihlanu ukuze sithethe ngexesha nendawo yokudibana.

*In 'liza kuba lihle' 'li-' = 'it' refers to Class 5 noun '*i***zulu**' = weather.

Isigama

QUICK VOCAB

-fudumele	be warm	masiyivumeni inyani	let's admit the truth
ngokwaneleyo	enough	-omile	be dry
-layita	switch on	alini	it doesn't rain
isifudumezi	heater	iindudumo	thunder
kangako	so	imibane	lightning
-njalo	like that	phaya	over there
izulu	weather	yonke indawo	every place
laseKapa	of the Cape	inezinto ezilungileyo	has good things
umzuzu	minute	ezingalunganga	not good (things)
-khanya	shine	umzekelo	for example
kolandelayo	at the next	eThekwini	in Durban
-na	rain (verb)	ukufuma	humidity
musa	don't	apho	there
-baxa	exaggerate	*kugqithe emgceni*	intolerable
yaye	and		lit. beyond the line
ungakhalazi	don't complain	kunjalo kanye	it's exactly like that
imvula	rain (noun)	liza kuba lihle	it will be fine
-bhetele	better	impela-veki ezayo	coming weekend
kunembalela	than drought	ukhuphiswano olukhulu lweqakamba	big match of cricket
imbalela	drought		
ibe	moreover	iqakamba	cricket
-nqabile	be scarce	-bukela	watch
-fana na-	be like	-tsho	say so
abavela	who come	emdlalweni	to the game
bona, kaloku	as for them	ngoMgqibelo	on Saturday
ebusika	winter	-khapha	accompany
-khalaza nga-	complain about	-fowunela	phone (for)
ehlotyeni	in summer	ngoLwesihlanu	on Friday
-vuthuza komoya	blowing of wind	ukuze	so that

How to ...

Ask whether someone is warm enough/cold

U**fudumele** ngokw**anele***yo*?
Uya**godola**?

Note: '-**godola**' = 'be **cold**' refers to **humans** while '-**banda**' = 'be **cold**' refers only to **inanimate** objects.

Comment on warm/hot/pleasant weather

Ku**shushu**!	It's **hot**!
Ku**fudumele**.	It is **warm**.
Ndi**fudumele**.	I am **warm.**
Ilanga liya**khanya**.	The **sun** is **shining**.
Ilanga liya**qaqamba** (lit. throbbing).	The **sun** is **shining**.
Ilanga liya**tshisa**!	The **sun** is **burning**!
Ilanga li**balele**.	It is **intensely hot**. There is a **drought**.
*Yi***mini** *en***tle**!	***It is*** a **beautiful day**!

Insight

A number of idioms and idiomatic expressions vividly characterize different weather conditions:

**Likhupha intlanzi emanzini!*	It is so hot that it takes the fish out of the water!
**Ligqatse ubhobhoyi!*	It is so hot that it scorches the African hoopoe bird!
**Limathumb' antaka!*	It is rather unsettled! (lit. It is like the intestines of a bird!)

* *Li-* = 'It' refers to the Class 5 noun '*i***zulu**' = weather
→ See **Unit 10** for more about idioms and proverbs.

Comment on cool/cold/less pleasant weather

Kuya**phola**.	It is becoming **cool**.
Ku**phol***ile.*	It is **cool**.
Kuya**banda** (phandle)!	It is **cold** (outside)!

Ku**jongeka** ngathi *i***mini** iza kuba *m***bi**!	It **looks as if** it is going to be a **terrible day**!
*I***hlobo** *ali***funi** kufika.	**Summer** doesn't want to come.
*I***hlobo** *ali***vumi** ukude lingene.	**Summer** is late. (lit. summer does*n't* **agree** [yet] to **come in**.)
*I***hlobo** li**phel***ile*.	**Summer** *has* **come to an end**.
Beku**banda** izolo.	It was **cold** yesterday.
*Yi***mini** *em***bi**!	It is a **terrible day**!
*Ubu***sika** *abu***funi** ku**mka**.	**Winter** does*n't* **want** to **go away**.
*Andizi***thand***i tu iin***yanga** zo*bu***sika**!	I do*n't* **like** the **winter months** *at all*!

Comment on rainy weather

*I***zulu** liye**zisa**.	**Rain** is imminent. (lit. the weather is **bringing** rain.)
Kuya**na**.	It's **raining**.
Ndi**cinga** ukuba kuza ku**netha**!	I think it is going **to rain**!
Ngathi kuza ku**netha**.	It looks like it is going **to rain**.
Ndi**themba** ukuba iza ku**yeka** kamsinya *uku***netha**!	I **hope** that it **stops raining** soon!
Si**fumene** *im***vula** eninzi kutshanje.	We've **had** a lot of **rain** recently.
Nantsi *im***vula**!	Here's the **rain**!
Iya**galela** *im***vula**!	It's **pouring** with **rain**!
*Im***vula** iya**dyudyuza**!	It's **pouring** with **rain**!

Insight

*im***vula** = rain is derived from the verb *uku***vula** = *to* **open** i.e. rain **opens** the ground for ploughing.

Comment on windy/misty/overcast/dry weather

*U***moya** uya**vuthuza**.	It's **very windy**. (lit. it is **blowing**.)
*U***moya** uya**bhudla**.	The wind is **blowing hard**.
Kukho *in***kungu**.	It's **misty**.
Kusibekele.	It's **overcast**.
Kom*ile*.	It's **dry**.
Kufum*ile*.	It's **humid**.
Kuzol*ile*.	It's **calm**.

Insight

*in***kungu** ne**langa**' – lit. **mist** and **sun,** is an idiomatic way of describing 'a multitude of people':

'Bekukho *in***kungu** ne**langa**.' = There was a huge crowd.

Comment on thunder/lightning/hail

Mamela *iin***dudumo**!	**Listen** to the **thunder**!
Jonga *um***bane**!	**Look** at the **lightning**!
Jonga *isi***chotho**!	**Look** at the **hail**!

Ask what the temperature is

*Y***intoni** *i***qondo** l*obu***shushu** namhlanje?	**What**'s the **temperature** today? (lit. degree of heat)

Cultural background

Seasons of the year

(*Ama***xesha** Lo**nyaka**) (lit. times of the year)

summer	*i***hlobo** (Class 5)	(< *um***hlobo** = friend (i.e. the friendly season)
spring	*in***tlakohlaza** (Class 9)	(lit. the points of the green grass)
	*in***twasahlobo** (Class 9)	(< -**thwasa** = become visible, appear (lit. the appearance of summer)
autumn	*u***kwindla** (Class 15)	(< -**dla** = eat, i.e. the season of eating) (Class 14!)
winter	*ubu***sika** (Class 14)	(< -**sika** = cut, i.e. the cutting season)

Months of the year

(*Iin***yanga** Zo**nyaka**)

January	uJanuwari	eyom**Qungu**	(month of the **Tambuki grass**)
February	uFebruwari	eyom**Dumba**	(month of the **swelling grain**)
March	uMatshi	eyo**Kwindla**	(month of the **first fruits**)
April	uApril	eka**Tshaz'iimpuzi**	(month of the **withering pumpkins**)
May	uMeyi	eka**Canzibe**	(month of the **Canopus**)*
June	uJuni	eye**Silimela**	(month of the **Pleiades**)

July	uJulayi	eye**Khala**	(month of the **aloes**)
August	uAgasti	eye**Thupha**	(month of the **buds**)
September	uSeptemba	eyom**Sintsi**	(month of the **coast coral tree**)
October	uOktobha	eye**Dwarha**	(month of the **ragwort**)
November	uNovemba	eye**Nkanga**	(month of the **broad-leaved ragwort**)†
December	uDisemba	eyom**Nga**	(month of the **mimosa thorn tree**)

*Bright star seen before dawn in May. †Tall and smaller yellow daisies respectively.

Insight

Xhosa months (as can be seen from the explanation in brackets) were named after flowers or plants flowering in that particular month. The original names of the months are very often used in literature while the Anglicized versions seem to be used in everyday speech especially by the younger generation.

Poem and songs

CD 1, tr 7, 02:28

Imbalela	**Drought**
'Yoo! Yoo!	Oh! Oh!
Siyalila,	We are weeping,
Iinkomo zethu zifile,	Our cattle are dead,
Iintlanti zikhedamile,	The cattle *kraals* are bereft,
Amasimi axwebile.	The fields are cracked like dry skin.
Imimango ibharile,	The hillsides are parched,
Izityalo zibunile.	The plants are withered.
Izilwana ziziimpanza,	The small wild animals are like a broken up, dispersed army,
Amacebo aphelile.'	We don't know what to do. (lit. Plans have come to an end.)

(From a poem by **G. Soya Mama**)

🔊 **CD 1, tr 7, 03:01**

Imvula	**Rain**
Imvula, imvula,	Rain, rain,
Chapha, chapha, chapha,	*Splash, splash, splash,*
Imanz' ilokhwe yam,	My dress is wet,
imanz' ilokhwe yam,	My dress is wet,
Gqum, gqum, kuyaduduma,	*Boom, boom,* it is thundering.
Gqum, gqum, kuyaduduma.	*Boom, boom,* it is thundering.
Imanz' ilokhwe yam,	My dress is wet,
Imanz' ilokhwe yam.	My dress is wet.

🔊 **CD 1, tr 7, 03:56**

Umoya	**Wind**
Khanibone nank ' umoya!	Please see here is the wind!
Wu! Wu! Wu!	*Wu! Wu! Wu!*
Ungen' efestileni,	It comes through the window,
Ucim' isibane sam.	It puts out my light.
Uyaphuma ndiyasala,	It goes out and I stay,
Undishiya emnyameni.	It leaves me in the dark.
Zuhambe zuhambe (uze uhambe).	It should go, it should go.
Wu! Wu! Wu!	*Wu! Wu! Wu!*

How it works

1 The equivalent of English 'every', 'all', 'the whole' = '-onke' (known as quantative pronouns)

From the following list you can see that '-onke' is preceded by the consonant associated with the noun to which it refers and can precede or follow a noun depending on emphasis:

wonke *um***ntu**	*every* **person, everyone**
bonke *aba***ntu**	*all* **persons, everybody**
wonke *um***sebenzi**	*all* **work**
yonke *imi***hla**	*every* **day** (lit. all days)
lonke *ili***zwe**	the *whole* **country**
lonke *i***xesha**	*all* the **time**

onke *ama***zwe**	*all* **countries**
onke *ama***xesha**	*all* **times**
sonke *isi***kolo**	the *whole* **school**
zonke *izi***kolo**	*all* **schools**
yonke *in***to**	*every***thing**
zonke *izin***to**	*all* **things**
lonke *ulu***ntu**	*all* **mankind**
bonke *ubu***sika**	the *whole* **winter**
konke *u***kwindla**	the *whole* **autumn**

Remember: in the case of nouns prefixing '*um-*' the associated consonant is 'w-' and in the case of nouns prefixing '*imi-*' / '*i-*' / '*in-*' / '*im-*' the associated consonant is 'y-'.

Note: No concord in Class 6 (*ama-*).

'-onke' can also be used with 'si-' = 'we' and 'ni-' = 'you' (pl.):

Yizani apha *n*onke.	*All of you* come here.

2 Adjectives

There are only a few so-called adjectives in Xhosa, several of which you have already come across, but they are frequently used. They include the numerals 1–6 as well as the following adjectival stems:

-nye	=	one	**-ne**	=	four
-bini	=	two	**-hlanu**	=	five
-thathu	=	three	**-thandathu**	=	six
-hle	=	beautiful	**-bi**	=	bad, ugly
-de	=	long, tall, far	**-futshane**	=	short
-fuphi	=	near	**-tsha**	=	young, fresh
-dala	=	old, stale	**-ninzi**	=	many
-ngaphi?	=	how many?	**-ncinane**	=	little
-khulu	=	big	**-ncinci**	=	small

In Xhosa, adjectives follow nouns and to mark the relationship between noun and adjective, an **adjectival concord** (corresponding to 'that', 'which', 'who') is used e.g.:

*um***sebenzi** *om***khulu**	a **big** job	(lit. a **job** *that* is **big**)
*isi***layi** *esi***ncinci**	a **small** slice	(lit. a **slice** *that* is **small**)
*i***komityi** *e***nye**	**one** cup	(lit. a **cup** *that* is **one**)

(cf. enye ikomityi yekofu = **another** cup of coffee)

om-	*um***ntwana**	*om***nye**	**one** child
aba-	*aba***ntu**	*aba***dala**	**adults** (lit. old people)
om-	*um***sebenzi**	*om***khulu**	**big/much** work
emi-	*imi***hla**	*emi***de**	**long** days
eli-	*i***zulu**	*eli***hle**	**fine** weather
ama-	*ama***cephe**	*ama***khulu**	**big** spoons
esi-	*isi***layi**	*esi***ncinci**	a **small** slice
izi-	*izi***kolo**	*ezi***ninzi**	**many** schools
en-	*i***keyiki**	*e*n**tle*****	a **beautiful** cake
en-	*in***to**	*e*n**kulu**†	a **great** thing
ezin- / ezim-	*ii***tispuni**	*ezim***bini**[a]	**two** teaspoons
olu-	*u***bisi**	*olu***tsha**	**fresh** milk
obu-	*ubu***sika**	*obu***bi**	a **bad** winter
oku-	*uku***tya**	*oku***dala**	**stale** food

* **-hle** > **-tle** before an **n**: *in***to** *e***ntle**; *i***keyiki** *e***ntle**.

† A consonant after **n** is **never aspirated**. [a] **n** > **m** before **b**, **p**, **f**, **v**.

A larger group includes those referred to in Xhosa grammar books as '**relative adjectives**', e.g.:

-mnandi	sweet, nice	**-muncu**	sour
-lula	easy, light	**-nzima**	difficult, heavy
-lusizi	sad, sorry	**-bomvu**	red
-mhlophe	white	**-mnyama**	black
-ntsundu	brown	**-blowu**	blue
-luhlaza	green / blue	**-lubhelu**	yellow

Insight

'**-luhlaza**' can mean **green** or **blue**. In order to differentiate add:

okwe**ngca** = as **grass** (green)

okwesi**bhakabhaka** = as the **sky** (blue)

→ See **Unit 8** for more **relative stems.**

Other equivalents of English adjectives are **derived from verbs** and often suffix *–yo:*

-balulekile*yo*	important
K**ubalulek***ile*.	It's **important**.

Ng*um***buzo** *o***balulekile***yo* *lo*.
That is an **important** question. (lit. *which* is **important**)

-**phelile***yo*	past

Kunyaka *o***phelile***yo* ibikho imbalela enkulu emZantsi Afrika.
Last year there was a big drought in South Africa.

-**za***yo*	coming

Ngempela-veki *e***za***yo* kuza kuba ikhonsethi enkulu eKirstenbosch.
In the coming weekend there will be a big concert at Kirstenbosch.

-**landela***yo*	following

Phendula imibuzo *e***landela***yo:*
Answer the **following** questions:

-**lungile***yo*	good

Licebo *eli***lungile***yo* elo!
That is a good idea/plan!

-thandeka*yo*	dear, beloved

Sipho *o***thandeka***yo* . . .
Dear Sipho . . .

Yet another group uses -**na**- = 'have' / 'has' / 'with' together with an **abstract noun** to form the equivalent of English adjectives:

-**no***m***dla** (interesting): *um***sebenzi** *o***no***m***dla** (lit. **work** that **has interest**)
-**na***ma***ndla** (strong): *in***doda** *e***na***ma***ndla** (lit. a **man** who **has strength**)

The **difference** between **adjectives** and **other descriptives** is in their **concord** or **link** to the noun they qualify in the following noun classes only:

		Adjectives	**Relatives**	
Class 1	*um***ntu**	*om***hle**	*um***ntu**	*o***nomdla**
Class 3	*um***sebenzi**	*om***hle**	*um***sebenzi**	*o***nomdla**
Class 4	*imi***hla**	*emi***hle**	*imi***hla**	*e***mnandi**
Class 6	*ama***zwe**	*ama***hle**	*ama***zwe**	*a***mnandi**
Class 9	*in***to**	*en***tle**	*in***to**	*e***mnandi**
Class 10	*izin***to**	*ezin***tle**	*izin***to**	*ezi***mnandi**

Note: A **relative concord** prefixed to a **verb** forms a **relative clause**:

Ufana nabantu *aba***vela** eGauteng.	You are like people *who* **come from** Gauteng.

3 The present tense in the negative

There is no word in Xhosa corresponding to the English '**not**'.

Instead, the **negative** form of the subject concord is used and the verb ending changes (cf. **Unit 3**). Compare the subject concords of the 3rd person:

Positive	Negative	
ú-	*aka-*	*U***Thandi** *aka***thand***i* *n***dudumo** namibane.
ba-	*aba-*	*Aba***ntu** baseGauteng *abali***thand***i* *i***zulu** laseKapa.
u-	*awu-*	*Um***oya** *awu***band***i* namhlanje.
i-	*ayi-*	*Imi***sebenzi** *ayi***phel***i*. (The tasks have not ended.)
li-	*ali-*	*I***langa** *ali***khany***i* namhlanje.
a-	*aka-*	*Ama***nzi** *aka***band***i*.
si-	*asi-*	*Isi***fudumezi** *asi***sebenz***i* kakuhle.
zi-	*azi-*	*Izi***fudumezi** *azi***sebenz***i* kakuhle.
i-	*ayi-*	*Im***vula** *ayi***fun***i* kuma namhlanje.
zi-	*azi-*	*Iim***vula** *azi***fun***i* kuma namhlanje.
lu-	*alu-*	*U***lwandle** (the sea) *alu***band***i* namhlanje.
bu-	*abu-*	*Ubu***sika** *abu***band***i*.
ku-	*aku-*	*Uku***tya** *aku***band***i*.

4 The future tense

In **Unit 1** you came across an example of the **future tense**:

Si**za ku**fika eKapa kamsinya.	We **will** arrive in Cape Town soon.

As you can see the future tense is formed in the following way:
SC + '**-za ku-**' (or '**-ya ku-**') + verb stem:

Ndi**za ku**zama.	I'**ll try**.
Ndi**za ku***ku***fowunela**.	I'**ll** phone *you*.
Ndicinga ukuba li**za ku**na.	I think it **will** rain.

Note: the position of the object concord.

The **short** (**contracted**) **form** of the **future tense** is often heard in colloquial speech but can also be found in written texts:

Nd**o**bona, s**o**bona, w**o**bona, n**o**bona, etc.	I'**ll** see, you'**ll** see, he'**ll** / she'**ll** see, you'**ll** see, etc.
Remember: S**o**bonana.	We'**ll** see each other.

The **negative form**: '-**zi ku**-' (or '-yi ku-'):

*Andi***zi kuk***w***enzakalisa**. I **will** *not* **hurt** *you*.

→ See **Unit 8**.

5 Instruct not to do something

It is very easy to instruct someone **not to do** something. Simply use '**Musa**' followed by the infinitive when instructing one person and '**Musa***ni*' when instructing more than one person:

One person		**More than one person**
Musa ukubaxa.	**Don't** exaggerate.	**Musa***ni* ukubaxa.
Musa ukukhalaza.	**Don't** complain.	**Musa***ni* ukukhalaza.
Musa ukulibala.	**Don't** forget.	**Musa***ni* ukulibala.
Musa uku*zi*khathaza.	**Don't** worry (*yourself*).	**Musa***ni* uku*zi*khathaza.

In spoken language the shortened forms are preferred:

Sukubaxa.	**Sanuku**baxa.
Sukukhalaza.	**Sanuku**khalaza.
Sukulibala.	**Sanuku**libala.
Suku*zi*khathaza.	**Sanuku***zi*khathaza.

If you want to express yourself more 'elegantly' you can say:

U**nga**khalaz**i**.	Ni**nga**khalaz**i**.	You should**n't** complain.
U**nga**libal**i**.	Ni**nga**libal**i**.	You should**n't** forget.
U**nga***zi*khathaz**i**.	Ni**nga***zi*khathaz**i**.	You should**n't** worry.

→ See **Unit 15**.

6 Different ways of expressing 'can'

The English translations show that these different ways of expressing '**can**' are not always interchangeable:

U**nakho** ukuza/U**noku**za?	**Can** you (are you able to) come?
Ewe, ndin**akho** ukuza/ndin**oku**za.	Yes, I **can** come.
Hayi, andi**nakho** kuza/*a*ndi**naku**za.	No, I **ca***n't* come.
U**nga***ndi***nceda**?	**Can** you **help** *me*?
Ndi**nga**ngena?	**Can** (may) I come in?
Uya*kw***azi** *uku***thetha** isiXhosa?	**Can** you (do you know how to) **speak** Xhosa?

7 *More Xhosa equivalents of the English prepositions 'in', 'at'*

Times of the day **(***ama***xesha osuku) (usuku =** ***24-hour day*****)**

*e***mini**	*in* **daytime**
*e***mini** e*ma*qanda	*at* **midday**
*ema***langa** / emva kwe**mini**	*in* the **afternoon**
*ebu***suku**	*at* **night**
*ezin***zul***wini* zobu**suku**	*at* **midnight**
ngorhatya (< *u***rhatya**)	**at** dusk
ngokuhlwa (< *uku***hlwa**)	**in** the evening

'**Nga**-' is also used with **days** of the **week** – *iin***tsuku zeveki**:

Monday	*uM***vulo** (< -**vula** = open)
on Monday	**ngo***M***vulo**
Tuesday	uLwesi**bini*****
on Tuesday	**ngo**Lwesi**bini**
Wednesday	uLwesi**thathu*****
on Wednesday	**ngo**Lwesi**thathu**
Thursday	uLwesi**ne*****
on Thursday	**ngo**Lwesi**ne**
Friday	uLwesi**hlanu*****
on Friday	**ngo**Lwesi**hlanu**
Saturday	*uM***gqibelo** (< -**gqibela** = finish)
on Saturday	**ngo***M***gqibelo**
Sunday	*i***Cawa** (cf. *i***cawa** = church)
on Sunday	**ngeCawa**

*cf. '**Adjectival stems**' above.

'**Nga**-' is used also with **months** of the **year** – *iin***yanga zonyaka**:

in which **month**?		**nge**yiphi *in***yanga**?	
in January	**ngo**Janyuwari	**in** July	**ngo**Julayi
in February	**ngo**Febhuwari	**in** August	**ngo**Agasti
in March	**ngo**Matshi	**in** September	**ngo**Septemba
in April	**ngo**Apreli	**in** October	**ngo**Oktobha
in May	**ngo**Meyi	**in** November	**ngo**Novemba
in June	**ngoJ**uni	**in** December	**ngo**Disemba

Seasons – *ama***xesha** *o***nyaka**:

in summer	*e***hlo***tyeni* *	(< *i***hlobo**)
in autumn	*e***kwindla**	(< *u***kwindla**) (Class 14 *ubu-*)
in winter	*ebu***sika**	(< *ubu***sika**)
in spring	*en***tlakohlaza**	(< *in***tlakohlaza**)

* 'b' followed directly by 'w' is not easily pronounceable in Xhosa, therefore '**b**' > '***ty***' before *-eni*.

8 Adverbs

You have already come across some adverbs of time and place:

namhlanje	today	apha	here
ngomso	tomorrow	apho	there
lonke ixesha	always	onke amaxesha	always
phaya	over there	futhi	often

Adverbs can be formed with **ka**-:

kakuhle	well	**ka**kubi	badly
kakhulu	much	**ka**ncinci	a little
kangaka	so much	**ka**njalo	like this
kamnandi	nicely	**ka**msinya(ne)	soon
kanye	once, exactly	**ka**bini	twice
kaninzi	often		

Note: **Ka**hle! = Hold on!

Adverbs can be formed with **ku**-:

kudala	long ago	**ku**phela	only
kunge**ku**dala	shortly (lit. **it** is **not** long ago)		

And adverbs can be formed with **nga**-:

ngethamsanqa	luckily	**nge**saquphe	suddenly
ngelishwa	unfortunately	**nga**kumbi	especially
ngokukhawuleza	quickly	**nga**phakathi	inside
ngokwaneleyo	sufficiently	**nga**phandle	outside
ngamanye amaxesha	sometimes		

Others include:

kwakhona	again	*qha*	only
ekugqibeleni	at last	*qho*	always

How to apply it

1 Find the contrasting word / expression

Choose from: (a) Ilanga libalele, (b) Liyabanda kakhulu, (c) Lomile, (d) Kusibekele, (e) Umoya uyavuthuza and (f) Masihlale elangeni.

1 Likhupha intlanzi emanzini.
2 Ilanga liyakhanya.
3 Iyagalela imvula.
4 Kuzolile. / Akukho moya.
5 Lifumile.
6 Masihlale emthunzini. (shade)

2 Yithi

(a)	I am cold.	It is cold.
	____________________	____________________
(b)	I am warm.	It is warm.
	____________________	____________________
(c)	It becomes cool.	It is cool.
	____________________	____________________
(d)	It will rain tomorrow.	It won't rain today.
	____________________	____________________

3 Yithi

(a)	It's a nice day.	Yimini ________________
(b)	It's an awful day.	Yimini ________________
(c)	It's a cool day.	Yimini ________________
(d)	It's hot day.	Yimini ________________
(e)	It's a cool night.	Bubusuku ________________

4 Complete the dialogue with the appropriate subject concord

A (a) ____za kuya eRobben Island ngoLwesihlanu, mna nabantwana. (b) ____ngathanda uku*si*khapha, wena nabantwana? (c) ___namanye amatikiti amathathu.

B Mna (d) ____ngathanda ukunikhapha, kodwa (e) ___xhomekeke kwimozulu. Ukuba umoya (f) ____vuthuza gqitha, ulwandle
(g) ___za kulwa. (h) ____oyika ukuba ndingagula ngenxa yokudlokova kwenqanawa!

A Hayi, (i) ____zi kuya ukuba (j) ____vuthuza gqitha.
B (k) ____za kuya ukuba (l) ____yanetha?
A Ewe, mna, (m) ___oyiki mvula.
B (n) ____za kuya ukuba (o) ____shushu gqitha?
A Ewe, (p) ____khathazeki bubushushu.

ulwandle	sea	-gula	be sick
-xhomekeke ku-	depend on	ngenxa ya-	because of
-lwa	fight i.e. rough	-dlokova kwenqanawa	rolling of the ship
-oyika	be afraid of	-khathazeka	mind, worry

5 Listen to the weather reports and say which refers to the weather in summer and which to the weather in winter

CD 1, tr 7, 05:08

(a) ____________________ (b) ____________________

6 Use the appropriate expression in Xhosa for 'can'

(a)	Can you speak Xhosa?	No, I can only speak a little Zulu.
(b)	Can you speak English?	Yes, I am learning it at school.
(c)	Can you please help me?	Of course (kakade), I'll help you.
(d)	Can you come on Friday?	I'm sorry, I can't help you.
(e)	Can I phone you tomorrow?	I'm sorry. I can't come. I am too busy.
(f)	Can I pour you another cup of coffee?	No thanks, one cup is enough.
(g)	Can I come in?	Yes, please come in.

7 Say what you prefer

(a) Someone says: Ndithanda izinto ezimuncu (sour).
Say you prefer sweet things.

(b) Someone says: Ndithanda ikofu engenabisi* naswekile. (*See **Selected Summaries, 2**)
Say you prefer coffee with milk and sugar.

(c) Somebody says: Ndithanda ikeyiki.
Say you prefer sandwiches.

(d) Somebody says: Ndithanda ibhotolo.
Say you prefer margarine.

(e) Somebody says: Ndithanda iwayini ebomvu.
Say you prefer white wine.

8 The South African flag (indwe yoMzantsi Afrika). Colour in appropriately and number the colours

imnyama
ilubhelu
iluhlaza
(okwengca)

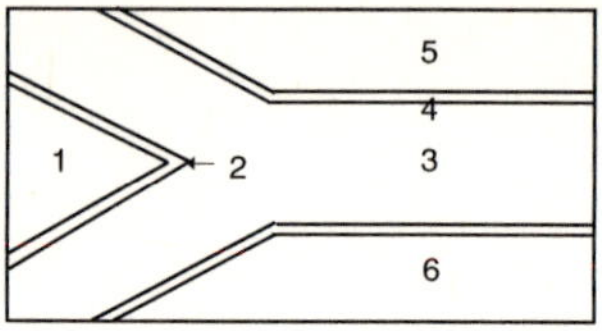

ibomvu
imhlophe
iluhlaza
(okwesibhakabhaka)

9 Read this excerpt from a poem by Minazana Dana

From which climatic region is the poet writing? How do you know? Complete the missing lines of the translation.

Ihlobo	**Summer**
'Ewe, kambe ihlobo lifikile	Yes, no doubt summer has arrived
Ngubo yehlwempu, mhlaziyi-lizwe	Blanket of the poor, renewer [...]
Kaloku nje sinethemba lempilo,	Now we have hope for health
Kaloku nje sinethemba loxolo	....
Kaloku nje sinethemba lokonwaba	....
Ngokufika kweemvula zehlobo	....
Zithembis' isivuno soxolo harvest	They promise a peaceful
Kuba kambe ihlobo lifikile.'	....

Test yourself

1. What is the difference between *uku***godola** and *uku***banda** both meaning 'to be cold'? How do you say: 'It is cold today!' How do you ask: 'Are you cold'?
2. What is the difference between kuya**phola** and ku**pholile**?
3. Name the four seasons of the year. To which classes do they belong?
4. Why do you say '**w**onke *um***ntu**' (every person) but '**y**onke *imi***hla**' (every day) (lit. all days)?
5. Is the position of an adjective in relation to a noun the same in Xhosa and English? Illustrate your answer by saying: 'Many people are learning to speak Xhosa.'
6. The function of an adjective and a relative adjective is the same, i.e. to qualify a noun. What differentiates them?

7 Nouns can also be qualified by using '**-na-**' (= has/have) + an **abstract noun**. How do you say:
   'It is interesting work.'   'They are strong men!'?
8 Change 'Ndithanda ukupheka' into the negative.
9 How do you give an negative instruction? Say: '**Don't** forget' (s. & pl.)
10 'Can' may be translated in three different ways. To illustrate the difference, how would you say:
   Can (may) I come in? **Can** you speak Xhosa? **Can** you come?

If you have done all exercises and answered the questions above correctly, then you are well prepared to proceed to the next unit.

7 UJenny emsebenzini – 'Masithethe isiXhosa'

Jenny at work – 'Let's speak Xhosa'

In this unit you will learn how to:

- ask how you may help someone
- ask how someone is in different ways
- respond in different ways
- know what to say when at the garage
- thank someone in different ways
- know what to say when giving someone a tip
- congratulate and express good wishes

Incoko

CD 1, tr 8

One of Jenny's groups has come to the end of its module. Jenny puts her students through their paces to see whether they are proficient enough to proceed to the next level.

UJenny	Molweni bafundi! Namhlanje nina niza kuthetha isiXhosa, mna ndiza kuphulaphula! Ngoobani abafuna ukuqala?
UMark noPaul	Siza kuqala Jenny.
UMark	Mna, ndiza kuba ngumthengisi-petroli. Yena, uPaul uza kuba ngumqhubi-wemoto.
UJenny	Kulungile, bafundi, thethani!

Egaraji.

Umthengisi-petroli	Molo mhlekazi. Kunjani? Ndingakunceda ngantoni namhlanje?
Umqhubi wemoto	Molo, mnumzana. Kunjani?
Umthengisi-petroli	Hayi, akukho nto. Ndihamba nazo! Wena?
Umqhubi wemoto	Nam, ndiphilile enkosi.

Umthengisi-petroli	Ndiyizalise itanki namhlanje?
Umqhubi wemoto	Hayi, ndiphe nge-fifty rand *qha* namhlanje.
Umthengisi-petroli	Kulungile mhlekazi. Anjani amavili?
Umqhubi-wemoto	Ingathi ivili lasekunene ngaphambili lifuna umoya. Khawukhangele onke jikelele.
Umthengisi-petroli	Kulungile, mhlekazi. Umoya ungakanani?
Umqhubi wemoto	Wampompe aye ku-210 jikelele. Ndicela ungalibali ukukhangela namanzi ne-oyile.
Umthengisi-petroli	*Utsho endodeni*!

After a few moments

	Heke, zonke izinto zilungile ngaphambili. Ndisule neefestile?
Umqhubi wemoto	Ungaba undincedile!
Umthengisi-petroli	Heke, ndigqibile, mhlekazi.
Umqhubi-wemoto	Ndiyabulela. Undincedile. Nantsi imali yepetroli. Nali ke icuba.
Umthengisi-petroli	Enkosi. Uhambe kakuhle, mhlekazi.
Umqhubi wemoto	Usale kakuhle, mnumzana. Sobonana!
UJenny	Mark noPaul nenze kakuhle! *Huntshu*!
UJenny	Heke, Val noSally, masiveni eyenu incoko!
OoVal	Kulungile.

Isigama

-phulaphula	listen
umthengisi-petroli	petrol attendant
umqhubi wemoto	motorist
ndihamba nazo	I'm fine
ndiyizalise itanki?	should I fill the tank?
amavili	tyres, wheels
ivili lasekunene	the right wheel
ngaphambili	in front
umoya	air
khawukhangele	please check
-khangela	check, look at
onke jikelele	all round
-ngakanani	how much?
-mpompa	pump up
aye ku-	up to
i-oyile	oil
utsho endodeni	*no sooner said than done* (lit. you've said so to a man!)
-sula	wipe
ifestile	window
ungaba undincedile	that would be helpful
nantsi imali yepetroli	here is money for the petrol
nali ke icuba	here then is (money) for tobacco
-bulela	to be grateful
huntshu!	*well done!*
masiveni eyenu incoko	let's hear your conversation

Incoko

CD 1, tr 8, 02:18

Val accidently bumps into a lady with her trolley while waiting in the checkout queue and a conversation ensues.

UVal	Uxolo Nkosikazi! Ndikwenzakalisile?
Inkosikazi	Hayi, akukho nto. Oo! uyasithetha isiXhosa?
UVal	Ndiyazama noko!
Inkosikazi	Hayi, akuzami! Uyasithetha! Usazela phi isiXhosa?
UVal	Uxolo, andiva kakuhle. Khawuphinde.
Inkosikazi	Ndithe usifunde phi?
UVal	Heke, ndiyaqonda ngoku! Ndisifunda eklasini yesiXhosa.
Inkosikazi	Ufundiswa ngubani?
UVal	NguNkosikazi Murray. Yena wakhulela emaXhoseni.
Inkosikazi	Nam, ndivela emaXhoseni.
UVal	Liphi ikhaya lakho?
Inkosikazi	LiseCacadu.
UVal	Oo YiLady Frere ngesiNgesi leyo?
Inkosikazi	Yho! Unyanisile. Uyasazi isiXhosa inene!
UVal	Uhlala phi, Nkosikazi?
Inkosikazi	EClaremont. Wena uhlala phi?
UVal	EKenilworth kodwa ndisebenza apha eClaremont.
Inkosikazi	Nam ndisebenza apha eClaremont. Ndinerestyu eFir Avenue ebizwa ngegama elithi '*Ningene*'.
UVal	Inene! Mhlawumbi ndiza kukutyelela apho! Yhoo, ndiphantse ndalibala, igama lam nguVal Todd.
Inkosikazi	Ndiyavuya ukukwazi Val. Mna ndinguXoliswa Silinga.
UVal	Nam ndiyavuya ukukwazi, Xoliswa. Bekumnandi kakhulu ukuthetha nawe. Ndiyathemba ukuba siza kubonana kwakhona. Ndiza kuxelela utitshalakazi wam neklasi yam ngerestyu yakho. Mhlawumbi sonke siza kutyelela irestyu yakho kamsinyane!
UXoliswa	Ingantle loo nto, Val. Uhambe kakuhle.
UVal	Uhambe kakuhle nawe, Xoliswa. Sobonana kwakhona apho erestyu!
UJenny	Nani nenze kakuhle, Val noSally! Ndonwabile! Ndonwabe gqitha ngokuqhubela phambili kwenu! Ndiyavuyisana nani! Ngoku mandininqwenclele iholide emnandi!

Isigama

ndikwenzakalisile?	did I hurt you?	-tyelela	visit
usazela phi?	where do you know it from?	ndiphantse	I nearly
		ingantle loo nto!	that would be lovely!
iklasi	class	ndonwabile	I'm happy
ufundiswa ngubani?	by whom are you taught?	ndonwabe gqitha	I'm very happy
		ngokuqhubela phambili kwenu	with your progress
leyo	that		
irestyu	restaurant	-vuyisana na-	rejoice with, i.e. congratulations
ebizwa	which is called		
ngegama elithi	by the name	mandininqwenelele	let me wish you
mhlawumbi	perhaps	iholide	holiday

How to ...

Ask how you may help someone

Ndinga*ku***nceda** ngantoni?

Ask how someone is in different ways

Uphila / Niphila njani?
Uphil*ile* **/ Niphil***ile*?
Usaphila / Nisaphila?
Unjani / Kunjani? **/ Ninjani**?

Respond to being asked how you are in different ways

Ndiya**phila**. / **Siphila** kakuhle enkosi.
Ndi**phil***ile*. / **Siphil***ile*.
Ndisa**phila**. / Sisa**phila**.
Ndi**khona**. / Si**khona**.

Insight

There are many idiomatic expressions in Xhosa when enquiring after someone's health and well-being:

U**vuka njani** / Ni**vuka njani**?	(lit. How do you **wake up**?)
U**vuk***ile* / Ni**vuk***ile*?	(lit. Have you **woken up**?)
Usa**hleli** / Nisa**hleli**?	(Are you still **seated**? – implication being that those who are not well would not be sitting up!)

Many responses can be even more descriptive:

Ndi**hleli**.	I am **seated**.
Si**hleli**.	We are **seated**.
Ndi**hamba na***zo*.	I am **going along with** *them*.
Si**hamba na***zo*.	We are **going along with** *them*.
('*-zo*' refers to '*iin***gxaki** =. **problems**)	
Ndi**khohlela** ndihamba.	I am '**coughing** along'.
Si**khohlela** sihamba.	We are '**coughing** along'.
Ndiya**cothoza**.	I am **going along slowly**.
Siya**cothoza**.	We are **going along slowly**.
Ndi**qhwalela** ndisiya.	I am **limping** going along.
Si**qhwalela** sisiya.	We are **limping** going along.
Ndisa**totoba**.	I am still **tottering along**.
Sisa**totoba**.	We are still **tottering along**.
Nd**onwab***ile*.	I am **happy**.
Sonwab*ile* (ekhaya).	We are **happy** (at home).
*Aku***kho** *n***to** (*im***bi**). (Shortened to: *A***kho**'*n***to**)	**There is nothing bad**.
Ku**nceda** ntoni *uku***khalaza**?	What does it **help** *to* **complain**?
Aku**ncedi** *uku***khalaza**!	It doesn't **help** *to* **complain**!

Know what to say at the garage

Ndinga**fumana** *i***petroli**.
Nceda, **zalisa** *i***tanki**.
Nceda *yi***zalise**.

Galela nge-50 rand *qha*.
Unga**khangela** *i*-**oyile**, *ama***nzi** n*ama***vili**.
Mpompa amavili ngo-1.8.
*Wa***mpompe** ngo-1.8.
Ingathi *i***vili** ngaphambili / ngasemva li**hl***ile* kakhulu.

Thank in different ways

Enkosi kakhulu (nge*n***to** yonke).
U*ndi***nced***ile.*
Ungaba u*ndi***nced***ile.*
Ndiya**bulela**.

Insight

There are several idiomatic ways of saying '**thank you**' in Xhosa which you may come across:

'*Nangamso*' or the full saying '*Ungadinwa nangomso*' (lit. 'you should not be tired [to do the same] tomorrow') was coined by one of the greatest Xhosa teachers, scholars and writers of our time **AC Jordan** whose novel ***Ingqumbo Yeminyanya - The Wrath of the Ancestors*** is considered one of the finest Xhosa novels.

Maz' enethole (lit. a female animal and its young, usually cow and calf) is another, the explanation being as follows: as a mother always does things for her young, especially when still suckling, the recipient of a kind gesture feels the kindness that has been bestowed is equivalent only to that which a mother usually bestows on her young.

Ukwanda kwaliwa ngumthakathi: lit. Increase (of prosperity) is opposed by the witch, i.e. there is only one 'person' (the witch) who rejects the kindness, help, etc. shown by one person to another which has led to an increase in happiness and prosperity of the person on whom this kindness has been bestowed.

Ndibamba ngazibini / ngazo zombini (lit. I hold with two / both hands) is usually said when one person receives something concrete from another.

Know what to say when giving someone a tip

Nali *i***cuba**.	(lit. Here is **tobacco**.)
Nazi *ii***lekese**.	(lit. Here are **sweets**.)
Ina **tshaya**.	(lit. Take for something to **smoke**.)

Congratulate and express good wishes

Huntshu! / Halala!	*Hurray*!
Nantso ke!	*That's it*!
Ndiya**vuyisana na***we*!	Congratulations! (lit. I **rejoice with** *you*)
Ngxatsho ke!	*Well spoken*!
*Maqobokazana phambili!**	Young ladies, well done!
Siya**vuyisana na***we* ngo*ku***nyuselwa** kwakho!	Congratulations on your **promotion**!
Zonwabise! / **Zonwabise***ni*!	**Enjoy** *yourself / yourselves*!
Ndi*ku***nqwenelela** *im***pumelelo**!	Good luck! (lit. I **wish** *you* **success**)
U**bhale** / Ni**bhale** kakuhle!	Good luck for the exams! (lit. **Write** well)
Mini *E***mnandi** (yoku**zalwa**) **ku***we*!	Happy Birthday **to** *you*!
/**Kresmesi** *e***myoli** / *e***mnandi**!	Happy Christmas!
Nyak' *om***tsha** *o***mnandi!** (*o***zele** ng*ama***thamsanqa**!)	Happy New Year! (**filled** with **good luck**)
*N***dlela** *n***tle**!	Have a **good trip**!
Ube / Nibe ne**mini** *e***mnandi**!	Have a **nice day**!
Ube / **Nibe** ne*m***pela-veki** *e***mnandi**!	Have a **nice weekend**!
Ube / **Nibe** neholide emnandi!	Have a **nice holiday**!
Njalo **naku***we*!	And the same to *you*! (lit. **and** it is like that to *you*)

* '*Ama***qobokazana** anga**lal'** emzini alahlekile.' lit. Girls who do not sleep at the village get lost. This saying is used to thank young girls for completing a task efficiently.

Insight

The influence of the 19th-century missionaries is manifested in the celebration of Christmas (*i***Kresmesi**) and Easter (*i***Pasika)** and the secular New Year (*U***nyaka** *Om***tsha**).

This influence can often be seen in names given to babies born at Christmas or Easter:

Kresmesi (m) No**kresmesi**(f) **Pasika** (m) No**pasika** (f)

How it works

1 Verb stems beginning with a vowel

You will have observed that most verb stems in Xhosa begin with a consonant. There are, however, a number of verb stems that begin with vowels.

-**amkela** (welcome)		
Ni- + **amkelek***ile*!	> N**amkelek***ile*!	(ni- > n-)
-**azi** (know)		
Ndiyavuya uku*ku* + **azi**	> Ndiyavuya uku*kw***azi**	(*-ku-* > *-kw-*)
-**enza** (do, make)		
U + **enza** ntoni?	> W**enza** ntoni?	(u- > w-)

A verb beginning with a vowel influences a preceding vowel in one of two ways, yet another example of a **sound change** occurring.

2 Verb stems with a latent 'i-'

There are also a few very frequently used **one-syllable verbs** in Xhosa containing a so-called latent **i**-. This latent **i**- influences a preceding **'a'** which changes to **'e'** in the **present tense and past tenses**, **positive:**

-(**i**)**va** (hear, feel)	Ndiy*a* + (**i**)**va**	> Ndiy**e**va	I **hear, understand**
	Nd*a* + (**i**)**va**	> Nd**e**va	I **heard**
-(**i**)**za** (come)	Ndiy*a* + (**i**)**za**	> Ndiy**eza**	I am **coming**
	Nd*a* + (**i**)**za**	> Nd**eza**	I **came**
-(**i**)**ma** (stand, stop)	Ndiy*a* + (**i**)**ma**	> Ndiy**ema**	I am **stopping**
	Nd*a* + (**i**)**ma**	> Nd**ema**	I **stopped**
-(**i**)**mba** (dig)	Ndiy*a* + (**i**)**mba**	> Ndiy**emba**	I am **digging**
	Nd*a* + (**i**)**mba**	> Nd**emba**	I **dug**

In the negative this sound change only occurs in Classes 1, 2 & 6:

Umfundi ak*e*va	The student doesn't hear/understand
Abafundi ab*e*va	The students don't hear/understand
Amantombazana ak*e*va	The girls don't hear/understand

Note: When using vowel and one-syllable verbs to give instructions, prefix ' *y- / yi-*' respectively:

*Y***enza** ikofu, nceda!	**Make** coffee, please!
*Yi***z**' apha	**Come** here!
*Yi***ma**!	**Stop**!
*Yi***mba**!	**Dig**!
*Y***omba**!	**Dig**! (often used in spoken Xhosa)
*Yi***tsho uphinde**!	You can **say** that **again**!

3 Tenses denoting past actions and events

The main ways of describing **past actions** and **events** are:

- The **recent** past tense
- The **remote** past tense
- The **continuous** *recent* past tense (see **Unit 12**)
- The **continuous** *remote* past tense (see **Unit 12**).

The recent past tense

Like the present tense, the **recent past** tense has two forms which correspond to the long and short form of the present tense (cf. **Unit 2**).

The **long form** is characterized by suffixing '*-ile*' to the verb when no other word follows, while the **short form** is characterized by suffixing *-e* when another word follows the verb:

U**gqib***ile*?	*Have* you **finish***ed*?
U**gqib***e* nini?	When *did* you **finish**?
Abafundi ba**phum***ile*.	The students *have* **left**.
Ba**phum***e* ngokukhawuleza.	They **left** in a hurry.

Insight

There are a number of frequently used verbs that don't follow this rule in that they have **only one written form** with **tone** and **length distinguishing between long and short forms**:

-libala (forget)	>-libele:	**Ndilibèlè.** I have **forgotten** Ndilibelé i-adelesi yakho. (I have **forgotten** your address.)
-lala (sleep)	>-lele	Ulèlè **Did** you **sleep**? Ulelé kakuhle? (Did you **sleep** well?)
-fumana (get, find)	>-fumene:	Ufumené incwadi? (Did you **get** the letter / book?)
-dibana (meet)	>-dibene:	Udibené nini noThandi? (When did you **meet** [with] Thandi?)
-phatha (bring)	>-phethe	U*yi*phethé imali? (Did you **bring** [*it*] the money?)

Remember there are a number of expressions incorporating '*-ile*' (cf. **Unit 5**). These expressions, often referring to one's **physical state**, are **present tense in meaning**, even though they have a **past tense form** and are referred to as **stative verbs** in Xhosa grammar books:

Si**thabhathek***ile.*	We *are* **impressed**.
Ndonwab*ile.*	I *am* **happy**.
Ú**dum***ile.*	He /she is **famous.**

To form the **negative** of the **recent past tense** (and **stative** verbs) prefix the **negative SC** and suffix '*-anga*':

Abafundi *aba***phum***anga.*	The students **have** *not* gone out. (**recent past**)
*Andi***phil***anga.*	I am *not* **well**. (**stative**)

→ See **Unit 12** for the **past tense** of **stative** verbs.

The remote past

This tense characterized by the long '**-a**' of the subject concord (cf. **Unit 3**) is used in the narration of events and actions which have taken place in the relatively distant past. An illustration of the use of the remote past tense is seen in the folktale 'Imbangi Yokuba Imbila Iswele Umsila' (→ See **Unit 16**).

ndi-	> **Nda**zalwa ngo-1975.	**I was** born in 1975.
si-	> **Sa**zalwa ngo-1975 nathi.	**We were** also born in 1975.
ù-	> **Wa**zalwa nini?	When **were you born**?
ni-	> **Na**zalwa nini?	When **were you** (pl.) **born**?
ú-	> **Wa**zalwa ngo-l975.	**He/she was born** in 1975.
ba-	> **Ba**zalwa ngo-1975 nabo.	**They were born** in 1975 too.

REMOTE SUBJECT CONCORDS FOR CLASSES 3–15

u-> **wa**-:	*Um***thi wa**tyalwa kudala.	The tree **was planted** long ago.
i- > **ya**-	*Imi***thi ya**tyalwa kudala.	The trees **were planted** long ago.
li-> **la**-	*I*xhego **la**zalwa ngo1918.	The old man **was born** in 1918.
a-> **a**-	*Ama***xhego a**zalelwa phi?	Where **were** the old men **born**?
si- > **sa**-	*Isi***kolo s**akhwa kudala.	The school **was built** long ago.
zi- > **za**-	*Izi***kolo z**akhwa kudala	The schools **were built** long ago.
i- > **ya**-	*In*tombi **ya**zalwa nini?	When **was** the girl **born**?
zi- > **za**-	*Iin***tombi za**zalwa nini?	When **were** the girls **born**?
lu- > **lwa**-	*U***donga lw**akhwa kudala.	The wall **was built** long ago.
bu- > **ba**-	*Ub***omi ba**nzima ngemfazwe.	Life **was** difficult during the war.
ku- > **kwa**-	*Ukw***azisana kwa**nzima ngexesha lobandlululo.	Getting to know one another **was** difficult during apartheid.

To form the **negative** of the **remote past tense** use '*-anga*' of the recent past tense:

*Andi***hamb***anga.* I didn't go.

*Aka***hamb***anga*. He/she didn't go.

or the auxiliary verb -**zange**:

*Andi***zange** ndahamb**a** often shortened to: **Zange** ndahamb**a**.
(lit. I **never** went.)

*Aka***zange wa**hamb**a** often shortened to: **Zange wa**hamba.
(lit. He/she **never** went.)

4 Kha- = *'(would you) please'*

Khawu**linde** umzuzwana.	Would you **please** wait a moment.
Khani**linde** umzuzwana.	Would you (pl.) **please** wait a moment.

Kha-+ u- > **kha**wu-.

→ cf. **Unit 4** verb form ending in '-**e**'.

How to apply it

1 Say sorry when

(a) you think you may have hurt someone by accident.
(b) you have to interrupt someone.
(c) you are late.
(d) you have forgotten something.
(e) you've kept someone waiting.
(f) you don't speak Xhosa well.

2 Match verb and noun to give the appropriate instruction

Use: (a) iifestile, (b) i-oyile namanzi, (c) ipetroli, (d) itanki and (e) amavili.

1 Galela
2 Sula
3 Mpompa
4 Khangela
5 Zalisa

3 Give instructions and responses

(a)	Come here.	OK, I'm coming.
(b)	Stop!	OK, I'm stopping.
(c)	Make the tea now.	OK, I'll make it now.

4 Complete the dialogue between a petrol attendant and a customer

Umthengisi-petroli	Molo nkosikazi. Ndingakunceda?
Umqhubi	________________________________
Umthengisi-petroli	Ufuna eyiphi ipetroli? Uthatha u-95 okanye u-97?
Umqhubi	________________________________
Umthengisi-petroli	Ndiyizalise *qhu* itanki?
Umqhubi	Hayi, ____________________________
Umthengisi-petroli	Kulungile. Ungandipha izitshixo (keys)?
Umqhubi	________________________________
Umthengisi-petroli	Enkosi. Ndingakhangela i-oyile?
Umqhubi	Hayi, ____________________________
Umthengisi-petroli	Kulungile. Umoya ungakanani?
Umqhubi	______________________________

Umthengisi-petroli	Amavili ngaphambili ahlile kakhulu. Ndiwampompe ngo-210. Ndisule neefestile?
Umqhubi	Ewe.
	______________________________
Umthengisi-petroli	Hayi, amanzi alungile. Ndigqibile nkosikazi.
Umqhubi	______________________________
Umthengisi-petroli	Enkosi. Hamba kakuhle.

5 Complete the dialogue

Xoliswa and Val meet again. Complete their chat by filling in the missing subject concords:

UVal	Ndiyakhumbula, uthe uvela eCacadu. (a) __zalelwa khona?
UXoliswa	Hayi, (b) ___zalelwa kuKomani, kodwa abazali bam (c) __fudukela eCacadu ndisemncinci. (d) __khulela khona.
UVal	Oo, ndiyabona.
UXoliswa	Wena (e) __zalelwa eKapa?
UVal	Ewe, (f) ___zalelwa eFish Hoek, kodwa (g) ___hlala eminye iminyaka eGoli. (h) __tshatile, Xoliswa?
UXoliswa	Ewe, (i) __sebenza erestyu, mna nomyeni wam. (j) __tshatile wena?
UVal	Hayi, andisatshatanga. Sahlukene.
UXoliswa	Torho! Unabantwana?
UVal	Ewe, (k) __neentombi ezimbini. Wena (l) __ nabantwana?
UXoliswa	Ewe, (m)___nabantwana abathathu, oonyana ababini nentombi. Intombi (n) __sencinci.
UVal	(o)__funeka ndihambe ngoku. (p)___leyithi. (q)____mnandi ukuthetha nawe. Hamba kakuhle, wethu.
UXoliswa	Sobonana.

QV

-fudukela	move to
torho!	shame!
ndisemncinci	while I was still young
andisatshatanga	I am no longer married
sahlukene	we are divorced (lit. we are separated from each other)

6 Wish someone

(a) A nice weekend in Grahamstown.
(b) A good holiday.
(c) Good luck (success) at work.
(d) Good luck for exams.
(e) Happy Christmas and a happy New Year.
(f) Listen to the songs on tape. Can you guess the special occasions on which they are sung?

CD 1, tr 8, 04:55

Min' Emnandi Kuwe
Min' emnandi kuwe,
Min' emnandi kuwe,
Min' emnandi kuwe, Thandi,
Min' emnandi kuwe.

Thina Sobabini Sovumelana
Mna nawe,
Thina sobabini sovumelana
Sovumelana nawe
Sovumelana
(-vumelana = be in harmony)

7 Match the English sentence with the correct Xhosa sentence

(a) Please sit down (lit. perch) and make yourself comfortable.
(b) Please repeat, I'm listening (lit. hearing).
(c) Please come in and sit down.
(d) Please talk, I'm listening.
(e) Please help me here.
(f) Please advise (me).
(g) Please check the oil and the battery.
(h) Please give me your phone number.
(i) Please wait a few minutes.
(j) Please give me your address.

1 Khawulinde nje imizuzu embalwa.
2 Khawundinike idilesi yakho.
3 Khawuphinde ndive.
4 Khawundinike inombolo yefowuni yakho.
5 Khawukhangele i-oyile nebhetri.
6 Khawuthethe ndive.
7 Khawungene uhlale phantsi.
8 Khawundincede apha.
9 Khawundicebise.
10 Khawuchophe apha ukhululeke.

8 The poet Soya Mama

How would you translate 'igama' in the context in which it is found in the notes on the poet Soya Mama whose poem *Imbalela* appears in **Unit 6**?

USoya Mama u*li*bone ilanga kwilali yaseNew Brighton eBhayi ngomhla we-11 kweyeNkanga ngonyaka we-1919. Uqale ukuy*i*bonakalisa imibongo kwamanye amaphepha-ndaba. Emva koko wapapasha ingqokelela yemibongo phantsi kwegama elithi *AmaQunube*.

QV

ilali (< Afrikaans 'laager')	settlement	imibongo	poems
-bonakalisa	make appear	ingqokelela	collection
-papasha	publish	amaphepha-ndaba	newspapers
		amaqunube (ama-)	berries

Test yourself

1. Explain why you say 'Ndiy**e**za.' = 'I'm coming.' even though the infinitive of the verb is *uku***za**?
2. There are several ways of expressing thanks in Xhosa. Name three which are the most commonly used.
3. Give the literal translation of:
   (a) Ùndincedile (c) Sikuncedile (e) Nindincedile
   (b) Ùsincedile (d) Sinincedile (f) Nisincedile
4. Most verb stems in Xhosa begin with a consonant. Give an example of a verb stem that begins with:
   'a-' **'e-'** **'o-'**
5. If 'ù-' = 'you' (s.) and 'ni-' = 'you' (pl.), explain why you say: '<u>W</u>enza ntoni?' (What are you (s.) doing? '<u>N</u>amkelekile'. (You (pl.) are welcome.)
6. How do you form the imperative of vowel verbs (e.g. –enza) latent (i) verbs (e.g. –ma) and monosyllabic verbs (e.g. –tsho)?
7. Which tense is used at the beginning of this folktale:
   Ngenye imini uFudwazana wagqiba ukuba aye edolophini. Wahamba ke esiya kuthenga ingxowa yetyuwa. Wayifumana wayibopha leyo ngentambo ende wayithatha egxeni wagoduka. …
   (lit. One day a little tortoise decided to go to town. It went then going to buy a bag of salt. It got it and tied the bag with a long rope, carried it over its shoulder and went home. …)

8 How do you make an instruction more polite?
9 How do you ask: 'Have you finished?' 'When did you finish?'
10 Name five verbs which have only one written form for the recent past tense.

If you have done all exercises and answered the questions above correctly, then you are well prepared to proceed to the next unit.

8 UThandi emsebenzini – 'Ndingugqirha Thamsanqa'

Thandi at work – 'I am Dr Thamsanqa'

In this unit you will learn how to:

- comfort / reassure by telling someone not to worry
- ask what is wrong with someone
- say what is wrong with you
- ask someone's age
- characterize pain

Incoko

CD 1, tr 9

A mother brings her small child who complains of a headache to the hospital.

UThandi	Molo Nkosikazi. Molo mntwan 'am. Khaningene. Ndingugqirha Thamsanqa. Hlalani phantsi. Nasi isitulo. Ngubani igama lakho, Nkosikazi?
UMama	NdinguNonceba Majola.
UThandi	Wena, mntwan'am, ngubani igama lakho?
Umntwana	NguLindiwe.
UThandi	Hayi, sukulila mntwan'am. Ungazikhathazi! Andizi kukwenzakalisa! Nanku unopopi. Ufuna ukumphatha? Heke, Nkosikazi, ndixelele, nize kusibona ngantoni apha esibhedlele?
UMama	Hayi, yile ntwazana, gqirha.
UThandi	Itheni?
UMama	Iphethwe yintloko, gqirha. Enye into iyakhohlela. Ikhohlela kakhulu.
UThandi	Mingaphi iminyaka yakhe?
UMama	Mihlanu, gqirha.
UThandi	Uliphethe ikhadi le**Ndlela eya eMpilweni**?
UMama	Ewe, nali.

UThandi	Kulungile. Heke, sana lwam, ndibonise, intloko ibuhlungu phi kanye? Ungandikhombisa na apho ibuhlungu khona intloko?
ULindiwe	Ibuhlungu apha, gqirha.
UThandi	Ubuhlungu umqala?
ULindiwe	Hayi.
UThandi	Zibuhlungu iindlebe?
ULindiwe	Ewe.
UThandi	Uvuza ezindlebeni umntwana wakho, Nkosikazi?
UMama	Ewe, gqirha.
UThandi	Uqale nini ukugula umntwana wakho, Nkosikazi?
UMama	Lusuku lwesithathu olu.
UThandi	Ndixelele, ukhe wamnika into yokudambisa iintlungu?
UMama	Ewe, ndimnike iiPanado kodwa azincedi *tu*.
UThandi	Wakhe wenzakala entloko ngaphambili, umntwana lo?
UMama	Hayi, gqirha.
UThandi	Wakhe wagula kakhulu ngaphambili?
UMama	Hayi, gqirha.
UThandi	Ingaba unazo ezinye iingxaki, lo mntwana?
UMama	Ewe gqirha, akakucacelanga ukutya.
UThandi	Kulungile, Nkosikazi. Ngoku, ndifuna ukumxilonga. Khawumkhulule umlalise apha ebhedini.

Isigama

QUICK VOCAB

isitulo	chair	mihlanu	they are five
sukulila	don't cry	uliphethe	did you bring it
ungazikhathazi	don't worry	ikhadi	card
andizi kukwenzakalisa	I won't hurt *you*	**Indlela eya eMpilweni**	**Road to Health**
unopopi	doll		
-phatha	hold	(u)sana lwam	my baby
nize	you have come	-buhlungu	sore, painful
kusibona	to see us	-khombisa	point
ngantoni?	about what?	apho … khona	where
yile ntwazana	it is this little one	umqala	throat
itheni?	what is it?	-vuza	discharge
-phethwe yintloko	have a headache	iindlebe	ears
-khohlela	cough	-qala	begin
mingaphi iminyaka yakhe	how old is she? (lit. they are how many her years?)	ukhe	did you ever
		wa*m*nika	give *her*
		-dambisa	alleviate

QV

iintlungu	pain	wakhe wagula?	was she ever ill?
azincedi *tu*!	they didn't help *at all*!	ezinye iingxaki	other problems
		-cacela ukutya	have interest in food
wakhe wenzakala entloko?	did she ever hurt (her) head?	akakucacelanga	she has no appetite
		-xilonga	examine
ngaphambili	before	-khulula	undress
lo	this	-lalisa	let someone lie down

How to ...

Reassure someone

Musa ukuz*i***khathaza**, (andizi ku*kw***enzakalisa**).
Sukuz*i***khathaza**, (andizi ku*kw***enzakalisa**).
U**nga***zi***khathaz***i*, (andizi ku*kw***enzakalisa**).

Ask what's wrong with someone

U**nantoni** na?
U**phethwe** *y***intoni**?
U**gula** *y***intoni**?
U**khala** nga**ntoni** ke?

Say what is wrong with you

Ndiya**khohlela**.
Andi*ku***cacel***anga uku***tya**.
Ndiya**bhitya** (I'm **getting thin**).

Wonke *um***zimba** wam ubuhlungu		My whole **body** is sore.
Ndine*n***tloko**.	I have a **head**ache.	(lit. I have a **head**)
Ndine*n***tamo**.	I have a sore **neck**.	(lit. I have a **neck**)
Ndine*n***dlebe**.	I have a sore **ear**.	(lit. I have an **ear**)
Ndino*m***qala**.	I have a sore **throat**.	(lit. I have a **throat**)
Ndino*m***qolo**.	I have a sore **back**.	(lit. I have a **spine**)
Ndine*li***so**.	I have a sore **eye**.	(lit. I have an **eye**)
Ndin*ame***hlo**.	I have sore **eyes**.	(lit. I have **eyes**)
Ndine**zinyo**.	I have **tooth**ache.	(lit. I have a **tooth**)
Ndine*si***su**.	I have a sore **stomach**.	(lit. I have a **stomach**)
Ndine*si***fuba**.	I have **chest** pain.	(lit. I have a **chest**)
Ndine*n***galo**.	I have a sore **arm**.	(lit. I have an **arm**)

Ndine**gxalaba**.	I have a sore **shoulder**.	(lit. I have a **shoulder**)
Ndino*m***nwe**.	I have a sore **finger**.	(lit. I have a **finger**)
Ndine*s***andla**.	I have a sore **hand**.	(lit. I have a **hand**)
Ndino*m***lenze**.	I have a sore **leg**.	(lit. I have a **leg**)
Ndino**nyawo**.	I have a sore **foot**.	(lit. I have a **foot**)
Ndino**zwane**.	I have a sore **toe**.	(lit. I have a **toe**)
Ndine*n***gqiniba**.	I have a sore **elbow**.	(lit. I have an **elbow**)

Insight

Many idiomatic expressions incorporate **na-** = 'with' and parts of the body:

Une*si***bindi**	He/she is **brave**	(lit. to be with a **liver**)
Une*n***tliziyo**	He/she is **kind**	(lit. to be with a **heart**)
Uno**lwimi**	He/she is a **gossiper**	(lit. to be with a **tongue**)
Une*s***andla**	He/she is **skilful**	(lit. to be with a **hand**)
Uno*m***lomo**	He/she is a **big talker**	(lit. to be with a **mouth**)
Une*mi***nwe** *emi***de**	He/she is a **thief**	(lit. to be with long **fingers**)
Uno*m***qolo**	He/she is **reliable**	(lit. to be with a **backbone**)
*Ndi***ph***eni* *iin***dlebe**	Listen carefully	(lit. Give *me* your **ears**)
*Ndi***cela** *iz***andla**	I need help	(lit. I ask for **hands**)
*Is***andla** si**hlamba** *esi***nye**	help each other	(lit. One **hand** washes the other)

Ask how old someone is

Une*mi***nyaka** *emi***ngaphi** (*ubu***dala** = **age**)?
*Mi***ngaphi** *imi***nyaka** yakho?
Wazalwa nini?

Say how old you are

Ndineminyaka eyi25 | Ndazalwa ngo-1990

Characterize pain

Kuya**tshisa**.	It is **burning**.
Kuya**luma**.	It is **colicky**. (lit. it **bites**)
Kuya**qaqamba**.	It is **throbbing**.
Kuya**hlaba**.	It is **stabbing**.

Song

🔊 CD 1, tr 9, 02:42

Thula thul' thula bhabha
Hush hush hush baby
(originally a Zulu song)

Thula thu' thula bhabha,	Hush, hush, hush baby,
thula sana,	Hush baby,
Thul' umam' uzobuya	Hush mother will come back
ekuseni,	in the morning,
Thula thu' thula bhabha,	Hush, hush, hush,
thula sana,	Hush baby,
Uzodlul' entaben'	She will cross the mountain
emathafeni,	and hills,
Kukhw'inkanyezi ekhokhel'	There is a star that leads
ubaba	the father
Emkhanyisela indlel' eziy' ekhaya.	Lighting his path coming home.
Sobe sikhona xa bonke	It will be there when they all
betshoyo,	say so,
Bethi buyela ubuyel'	Saying return, return,
uzekhaya.	and come home.
Thula, thu', thula bhabha	Be quiet, be quiet, be quiet, baby
Ungakhali, thula sana,	Don't cry, be quiet, baby,
Thula, thu' thula, thul' mntwana.	Be quiet, be quiet, be quiet, child
Thula bhabha, thula sana.	Be quiet baby, be quiet baby.

How it works

1 Relatives and adjectives used as predicates

Relatives

The most commonly used relative stems are those conveying ideas of taste, degrees of warmth, heaviness, etc., and include the colours (cf. **Unit 6**):

Some opposites

easy	**-lula**	difficult	**-nzima**
light	**-lula**	heavy	**-nzima**
expensive	**-dulu**	cheap	**-tshiphu**
bitter	**-krakra**	sweet	**-mnandi**
blunt/rounded	**-ngqukuva**	pointed	**-tsolo**
wide	**-banzi**	narrow	**-mxinwa**

Miscellaneous

better	**-bhetele / -ngcono**	dark	**-mdaka**
deep	**-nzulu**	hot	**-shushu**
innocent	**-msulwa**	lukewarm	**-dikidiki**
nice	**-mnandi**	painful	**-buhlungu**
sad	**-lusizi**	sharp	**-bukhali**

It is very easy to use relatives as predicates. Simply prefix the relevant subject concord to the relative stem:

Ndi**lusizi**.	I am **sorry**. (lit. I **sorry**.)
Ulusizi?	Are you **sad**?
Ibuhlungu intloko?	Is (your) head **sore**?

Adjectives

When adjectives are used as **predicates**, the adjectival concord **minus its initial vowel** is prefixed to the adjectival stem except in Class 9 nouns where the adjectival concord '<u>*e*</u>*n*-' > '<u>*i*</u>*n*-':

AC	***AC* minus initial vowel**	
om-	***M*hle *um*ntwana.**	The child *is* **beautiful**.
aba-	***Ba*hle *aba*ntwana.**	The children *are* **beautiful**.
om-	***M*khulu *um*sebenzi.**	The task *is* **huge**.
emi-	***Mi*khulu *imi*sebenzi.**	The tasks *are* **huge**.
eli-	***Li*hle *i*zulu.**	The weather *is* **beautiful**.
ama-	***Ma*hle *ama*zinyo.**	The teeth *are* **beautiful**.
esi-	***Si*ncinci *is*andla.**	The hand *is* **small**.
ezi-	***Zi*ncinci *iz*andla.**	The hands *are* **small**.
<u>*e*</u>*n-*	**<u>*I*</u>*n*kulu *i*pilisi.**	The pill *is* **big**.
ezin-	***Zin*kulu *ii*pilisi.**	The pills *are* **big**.
olu-	***Lu*khulu *u*sana.**	The baby *is* **big**.
obu-	***Bu*de *ubu*sika.**	The winter *is* **long**.
oku-	***Ku*tsha *uku*tya.**	The food *is* **fresh**.

Note: When adjectives are used predicatively the preferred word order seems to be adjective followed by noun.

With the **1st** and **2nd persons** (s.) and (pl.) (I, we, you), the adjectival concords '*-m-*' and '*-ba-*' are placed between the subject concord and the adjectival stem:

Ndi*m***dala**.	I am **old**.	U*m***tsha**	You are **young**.
Si*ba***dala**.	We are **old**.	Ni*ba***tsha**.	You are **young**.

→ See **Unit 15** for **negative** of adjectives and relatives.

Insight

In order to express 'still' with adjectives and relative adjectives '-**se**-' as opposed to '-sa-' (which is used with verbs) is placed between the subject and adjectival concords:

U**se***m***tsha**.	You are still **young.**
Lu**se***lu***ncinci** usana.	The baby is still **small.**
Ba**se***ba***hle** abafazi.	The women are still **beautiful.**
Ubisi lu**se***lu***tsha**.	The milk is still **fresh.**

'-**se**-' can also be used with other non-verbs:

U**se***sesi***bhedlele** umntwana.	The child is still in hospital.
U**se****khona** ugqirha.	The doctor is still here.

In the **negative** '-**se**-' means '**no longer**':

Hayi, ugqirha aka**se**kho.	No, the doctor is **no longer** here.

2 Equivalent of 'and' between verbs

In **Unit 2** you learned that **nouns** are connected by '**na**-':

*aba*zali **na***ba*ntwana:	parents **and** children

However, when **two verbal forms** follow one another, the second verb ends in '-**e**' to indicate a sequence of actions:

*M***khulule** u*m***lalise** *e***bhed***ini*.	Undress her **and** lie her down *on* the **bed**.
*Iin***tlungu** zi**fika** zimke?	Does the **pain** come **and** go?

Note: *iin***tlungu** = physical pain(s) always in the plural form.

3 *Equivalent of the English adverbs 'already', 'always', 'ever', 'never', 'nearly', 'usually'*

These English adverbs are expressed in Xhosa by so-called **auxiliary** (helping) **verbs**:

'-khe' = '*ever*'

Wakhe we**nzakala** intloko ngaphambili?	Did she **ever** hurt her head before?
Wakhe wa**gula** kakhulu ngaphambili?	Was she **ever** very sick before?
Wakhe wa*m***bona** ngaphambili?	Have you **ever** seen *him* before?

'-phantse' = '*nearly*'

Yhu, ndi**phantse** ndawa!	Oops, I **nearly** fell!

'-zange'= '*never*' (mostly with remote past tense)

*Andi***zange** ndatsho.	I **never** said so.
*Aka***zange** wagula.	She has **never** been sick. (cf. **Unit 7**)

'Zange' can also be used without the negative subject concord:

Zange sabonana.	We've **never** met.

'khange' = *never*' (mostly with recent past tense)

Khange ndi*ku***bon***e* ixesha elide.	I haven't seen *you* for a long time.

'-sele(-)', *often shortened to* '-sel / se-'= '*already*'

Sekwan**ele**!	It's all over! (lit. It's **already enough**!)

'-soloko' = '*always*'

Intloko i**soloko** ibuhlungu?	Is your head **always** sore?

'-soze'= '*shall*' / '*will never*'

Uxolo, andi**soze** ndi**phinde**.	Sorry, I'**ll never** do it again.
Soze ndisele kwakhona.	I'**ll never** drink (alcohol) again.

'-dla ngoku-' = '*usually*', '*frequently*'

U**dla ngoku**gula ebusika.	He/she is **frequently** ill in winter.

4 *Different ways of asking 'why?'*

When Thandi asked Mrs Majola **why** she had come to hospital she said:

'Nize kusibona **ngantoni** apha esibhedlele?'
(lit. You have come to see us **for what** here at the hospital?).

Here are three of the several other ways of expressing '**why**?' in Xhosa:

'Kutheni'

Unlike other interrogatives '**kutheni**' *introduces* a question:

Kutheni unga*ndi***xelel***anga*?	**Why** did*n't* you **tell** *me*?
Kutheni ufunda isiXhosa?	**Why** are you **learning** Xhosa?

→ See also **Unit 12**.

'-elani' / '-eleni' ***(lit. 'what for?')***

U*si***fundelani** isiXhosa?	**Why** do you learn Xhosa?
U*si***fundeleni** isiXhosa?	**Why** did you learn Xhosa?

'ngo(ku)ba'

Ufunda isiXhosa **ngoba**?	**Why** are you learning Xhosa?

5 *Another interrogative:* '-phi?' = *'which?'*

You are already familiar with '-**phi**?' = '**where**?' which is prefixed by the subject concord:

U**phi** *um***ntwana**?	**Where** (is) the **child**?
Ba**phi** *aba***ntwana**?	**Where** (are) the **children**?

However, '-**phi**?' can also mean '**which**?':

*Wu***phi** *um***ntwana**?	*Which* **child**?
*Ba***phi** *aba***ntwana**?	*Which* **children**?

In the so-called '**strong**' classes, i.e. where the subject concord consists of a consonant and a vowel (ba-, li-, si-, zi-, lu-, bu-, ku-) **only tone distinguishes the two interrogatives**:

'**where**?' = **high** tone	'**which**?' = **low** tone

Where the subject concord consists of a vowel only (in the so-called '**weak**' classes), 'w-' or '-y-' is prefixed to the subject concord:

U**phi** *um***andlalo**?	**Where** is the **bed**?
*Wu***phi** *um***andlalo**?	*Which* **bed**?

Iphi *im*andlalo?	**Where** are the **beds**?
*Yi*phi *im*andlalo?	*Which* **beds**?
Aphi *ama*yeza?	**Where** are the **medicines**?
*Wa*phi *ama*yeza?	*Which* **medicines**?
Iphi *in*cwadi?	**Where** is the **book**?
*Yi*phi *in*cwadi?	*Which* **book**?

Besides this **basic form** there is also a longer, more specific form (prefixing o- / a- / e-), with the meaning '**which** *particular*'. It seems to be preferred in everyday speech, possibly to distinguish between the meaning 'where?' and 'which?':

*Wu*phi *um*ntwana?	*Which* **child**?
*Owu*phi *um*ntwana?	*Which* ***particular*** **child**?
*Ba*phi *aba*ntwana?	*Which* **children**?
*Aba*phi *aba*ntwana?	*Which* **children**?
*Wu*phi *um*andlalo?	*Which* **bed**?
*Owu*phi *um*andlalo?	*Which* **bed**?
*Yi*phi *im*andlalo?	*Which* **beds**?
*Eyi*phi *im*andlalo?	*Which* **beds**?
*Li*phi *i*khadi?	*Which* **card**?
*Eli*phi *i*khadi?	*Which* **card**?
*Wa*phi *ama*yeza?	*Which* **medicines**?
*Awa*phi *ama*yeza?	*Which* **medicines**?
*Si*phi *isi*bhedlele?	*Which* **hospital**?
*Esi*phi *isi*bhedlele?	*Which* **hospital**?
*Zi*phi *izi*kolo?	*Which* **schools**?
*Ezi*phi *izi*kolo?	*Which* **schools**?
*Yi*phi *i*pilisi?	*Which* **pill**?
*Eyi*phi *i*pilisi?	*Which* **pill**?
*Zi*phi *iin*cwadi?	*Which* **books**?
*Ezi*phi *iin*cwadi?	*Which* **books**?
*Lu*phi *u*siba?	*Which* **pen**?
*Olu*phi *u*siba?	*Which* **pen**?
*Ku*phi *uku*tya?	*Which* **food**?
*Oku*phi *uku*tya?	*Which* **food**?

When **nga-** / **ku-** / **na-** are prefixed to this form it makes the 'string' even longer.

Wazalwa **ng***owu*phi *u*nyaka?
Uya **kw***esi*phi *isi*bhedlele?
Ufuna ukuthetha **n***owu*phi *u*gqirha?

How to apply it

1 Give the plurals

iliso	umlenze
indlebe	unyawo
ingalo	uzwane
isandla	izinyo
umnwe	idolo (knee)

2 Questions and responses

You meet a friend whose child has been ill. In order to complete the conversation, translate your questions and responses into Xhosa:

(a) *How is your child? Is she still in hospital?*
Hayi, ubhetele kancinci, akasekho sibhedlele.

(b) *I am sorry that she is only a little better, but I am glad that she is at home again.*
Ndikhathazeka kakhulu kuba akakucacelanga ukutya. Ubhityile.

(c) *What did the doctor say?*
Undinike iyeza, kodwa ngelishwa alisebenzi.

(d) *Let's hope she will soon be well again.*
Hayi, sithemba njalo.

3 Read the dialogue and answer the questions

UZodwa	Molo, Nomsa.
UNomsa	Molo sisi. Uphila njani?
UZodwa	Hayi, akukho nto. Wena?
UNomsa	Awu, mna, andiphilanga.
UZodwa	Awu, ukhangeleka ugula ngenene. Ugula yintoni?
UNomsa	Ndineflu. Intloko ibuhlungu. Ndinefiva.
UZodwa	Kufuneka ugoduke uphumle ebhedini. Ubuyile kugqirha?
UNomsa	Ewe, undiphe amayeza. Ndiyathemba ukuba aza kusebenza ngokukhawuleza.
UZodwa	Nam, ndithemba njalo. Ngubani oza kukugcina ekhaya?
UNomsa	Usisi uza kundigcina.
UZodwa	Kulungile. Ndiyathemba ukuba uza kuphila kamsinyane kwakhona. Hamba kakuhle.
UNomsa	Enkosi. Kamnandi.

-buya	return	-gcina	look after

Which of the following Xhosa words can replace the 'Xhosalized' English words in the dialogue between Zodwa and Nomsa?

(a) umkhuhlane can replace ____________
(b) ubushushu can replace ____________
(c) umandlalo (lit. mat) can replace ____________
(d) udadewethu can replace ____________

Insight

There are many other Xhosalized English words which are often used instead of the original Xhosa:

i-eropleni	*in***qwelo-moya**	aeroplane	(lit. wagon of the air)
itreyini	*u***loliwe**	train	(< onomatopoeic 'railway')
ibhafrum	*i***gumbi lokuhlambela**	bathroom	(lit. room of washing for)
ikhitshi	*i***gumbi lokuphekela**	kitchen	(lit. room for cooking)
ishelefu	*i***thala**	shelf	(lit. the shelf in a traditional homestead)
iflawa	*um***gubo**	flour	
ifowuni	*um***nxeba**	phone	(lit. a rope)
irediyo	*u***nomathotholo**	radio	(lit. a traditonal healer's box from where voices are heard)

4 Read the dialogue

UNokhaya Hi Xoliswa.
UXoliswa Molo wethu. Ndiyakubona uphilile, Nokhaya. Banjani ekhaya?
UNokhaya Oo, umama yena akaphilanga *tu*.
UXoliswa Kwenzekeni?
UNokhaya Uwile ebesihla iziteps. Ugqirha umthumele esibhedlele kwangoko.
UXoliswa Oo, nkosi yam! Ndilusizi kakhulu.
UNokhaya Ewe, waphuka umlenze, usesibhedlele ndithetha nje (as I speak).

UXoliswa	Ndiyathemba ukuba uza kuchacha ngokukhawuleza. Khawundibulisele kumama wakho.
UXoliswa	Enkosi. Hamba kakuhle.

QV

-wa	fall	-aphuka	break
ebesihla	going down	-chacha	recover
iziteps	steps	-khawundibulisele	please greet from me
-thum<u>el</u>a	send <u>to</u>		

Imagine you are visiting Nokhaya's mother in hospital. How would you:

(a) greet her (you are younger)?
(b) ask her how she is today?
(c) say you are sorry that she is in hospital and ill?
(d) ask whether you can help her with something?
(e) ask whether she is in pain?
(f) wish her a speedy recovery?
(g) say goodbye?

5 Match the following appropriately

Use these phrases: (a) isifuba sibuhlungu phi kanye? (b) kuba utya kancinci gqitha (c) ulale apha ebhedini (d) xa ukhohlela? (e) andazi kukwenzakalisa (f) nasi isitulo.

1	Hlala phantsi	4	Khawukhulule
2	Isifuba sibuhlungu kakhulu	5	Ndicela undibonise
3	Wena uyabhitya	6	Ungazikhathazi

6 Put the sentences in the right sequence

(a) Lifuna ukubona ugqirha kuba linesisu.
(b) Emva koko uthi: Nanzi iipilisi. Zitye kathathu ngemimi emva kokutya.
(c) Ixhegokazi elithile liya ekliniki.
(d) Isisu sibuhlungu kakhulu.
(e) Heke gqirha, Ndiza kuzitya iipilisi, kodwa ngubani oza kundinika ukutya?
(f) Ugqirha uyalixilonga.

QV

kathathu	three times	-thile	certain
emva kokutya	after meals (lit. after eating / food)	ukutya iipilisi	take pills
ixhegokazi	old woman		

7 Say

(a) He is brave.
(b) She is very kind.
(c) They are very reliable.
(d) He is a big talker.
(e) She is very skilful.

8 Give the literal meaning for the idiomatic expressions

(a) Unesandla esibandayo
(He/she is stingy.) ______________________________
(b) Unesandla esishushu
(He/she is generous.) ______________________________
(c) Unika ngentliziyo entle
(He/she gives gladly.) ______________________________
(d) Unentliziyo emhlophe
(He/she has a kind heart.) ______________________________
(e) Unamadolo anzima?
(Are you exhausted?) ______________________________

9 Translate the following

(a) Intliziyo yam ibuhlungu. ___________________________
(b) Unentliziyo emdaka/emnyama. ___________________________
(c) Unentliziyo emsulwa. ___________________________

10 Complete the questions

(a) Wena, uthetha ___phi ulwimi ekhaya?
(b) Ufunde ___phi iilwimi esikolweni?
(c) Ufunde n___nye iilwimi eyunivesithi okanye kw___nye ilizwe?
(d) Ukhetha ukuthetha___phi ulwimi?
(e) Ndixelele, wazalwa ng___phi unyaka?
(f) Wazalwa ng___phi inyanga?
(g) Wazalwa ng___phi imini?
(h) Wazalelwa kw___phi ilizwe?
(i) Wazalelwa kw___phi idolophu?
(j) Ufunde kw___phi isikolo?
(k) Waphuma kw___phi ibanga (standard)?
(l) Ufunde kw___phi iyunivesithi?

Test yourself

1. What concord is used with **relative stems** to form a **predicate**? How do you say: 'I (am) sorry'?
2. Using the appropriate adjectival concord say: 'The weather is beautiful today!' (predicate) 'It is beautiful weather today.' (qualifier)
3. Nouns of which class do not follow the rule of dropping the initial vowel of the adjectival concord when used as a predicate?
4. How do you express 'still' with adjectives?
5. You know that **'na-'** joining **nouns** means **'and'**, e.g.: abazali **na**bantwana = parents **and** children. How do you express **'and'** in a sequence of **verbs**, e.g.: 'Does the pain come **and** go?'
6. Which auxiliary verbs are used to express **'ever'** and **'never'** when translating:
   'Have you **ever** been sick before?' 'No, I've **never** been sick before.'
7. There are several ways to translate **'why?'** in Xhosa. Name three.
8. You know that the interrogative -**phi**? means **'where**?', e.g. Ù**phi** = **Where** (are) you? In this unit you learned that '**-phi**' can also mean '**which**'? What distinguishes the two?
9. Which suffix changes '*i***xhego**' = 'old man' to 'old woman'?
10. How would you ask: 'How old is your child'?

If you have done all exercises and answered the questions above correctly, then you are well prepared to proceed to the next unit.

9 UPeter emsebenzini eKirstenbosch

Peter at work at Kirstenbosch

In this unit you will learn how to:

- introduce someone you work with
- point or single out
- say what a place is famous for
- encourage environmentally-friendly practices
- request that appropriate etiquette be observed in public places
- say what the best is

Incoko

CD 1, tr 10

Peter introduces his colleague Phumla Bongela to a group of school children who will tell them about two vital projects that Kirstenbosch is involved in.

UPeter Molweni bafundi. Namkelekile e***Kirstenbosch***! Igama lam nguPeter Murray. Lo nguNkosikazi Phumla Bongela, endisebenza naye. Sobabini siziingcaphephe zezityalo apha e***Kirstenbosch***.

UNkosikazi Bongela uza kunixelela ngeegadi ezinolondolozo-manzi ne*Outreach Gardening Project.* Le nkqubo yaqalwa ukuze sincede izikolo ukuseka iigadi ezifanelekileyo.

Kodwa kuqala ndiza kuthi *gqaba-gqaba* nge***Kirstenbosch***. UNkosikazi Bongela uza kunika umfundi ngamnye imaphu yase***Kirstenbosch***. Le gadi idume kulo lonke ihlabathi ngobuhle. Yasekwa ngo-1913. Ithandeka kakhulu ngenxa yenkitha yezityalo zaseMzantsi Afrika.

Jongani nje lo mfanekiso othathwe e*Chelsea Flower Show* yaseLondon apho i***Kirstenbosch*** yazuza izidanga ezininzi khona iminyaka ngeminyaka.

Isigama

endisebenza naye	with whom I work	idume kulo lonke ihlabathi	it is famous all over the world
sobabini	both of us	ubuhle	beauty
iigadi	gardens	yasekwa	it was established
ezinolondolozo-manzi	which save water	-thandeka	be popular
le nkqubo	this project	inkitha yezityalo	collection of plants
yaqalwa	was started	jongani nje	just look at
ukuseka	to establish	lo mfanekiso	this picture
ezifanelekileyo	suitable	othathwe	which was taken
kuqala	firstly	yazuza	it won
gqaba-gqaba	a bit about (lit. here and there)	izidanga	medals
umfundi ngamnye	each pupil	iminyaka ngeminyaka	year(s) after year(s)
imaphu	map		

Flower muti: Traditional healer, Elliott Ndlovu, from the Drakensberg foothills, brought a little magic to London's world-famous Chelsea Flower Show this week. South Africa's Syfrets-Kirstenbosch exhibit depicted a botanical representation of the R6-million conservatory at Kirstenbosch as well as a traditional healer's hut, with Ndlovu in his traditional attire (which impressed the Queen). The stand won a silver gilt medal for its efforts – its 22nd medal in its 22 years at the show.
(Courtesy *Cape Times*, 23/5/97)

Iindlela ezintandathu zokulondoloza amanzi

1 Tyala izityalo ezingafuni manzi maninzi *(Plant plants which do not require a lot of water)*	2 Wulungise umhlaba ngokufaka isivundiso ukuze ukwazi ukuwagcina amanzi *(Prepare the soil by putting in compost so that it is able to retain water)*
3 Wugqume umhlaba phakathi kwezityalo ngezinto ezigcina ukufuma emhlabeni – umzekelo umgquba *(Cover the soil between plants with material that will keep the moisture in the soil – for example, compost)*	4 Zahlule izityalo ngokweemfuno zazo zamanzi *(Group plants according to their watering needs)*
5 Yityale ingca kuphela apho kuyimfuneko khona *(Plant grass only where needed)*	6 Nkcenkceshela ngokufanelekileyo kunjalo nje xa kuyimfuneko *(Water appropriately according to need only)*

Phumla gives each pupil a map of Kirstenbosch and takes them on the tour of the gardens starting with the waterwise garden. She asks them to read the information boards that explain how to establish an environmentally friendly waterwise garden.

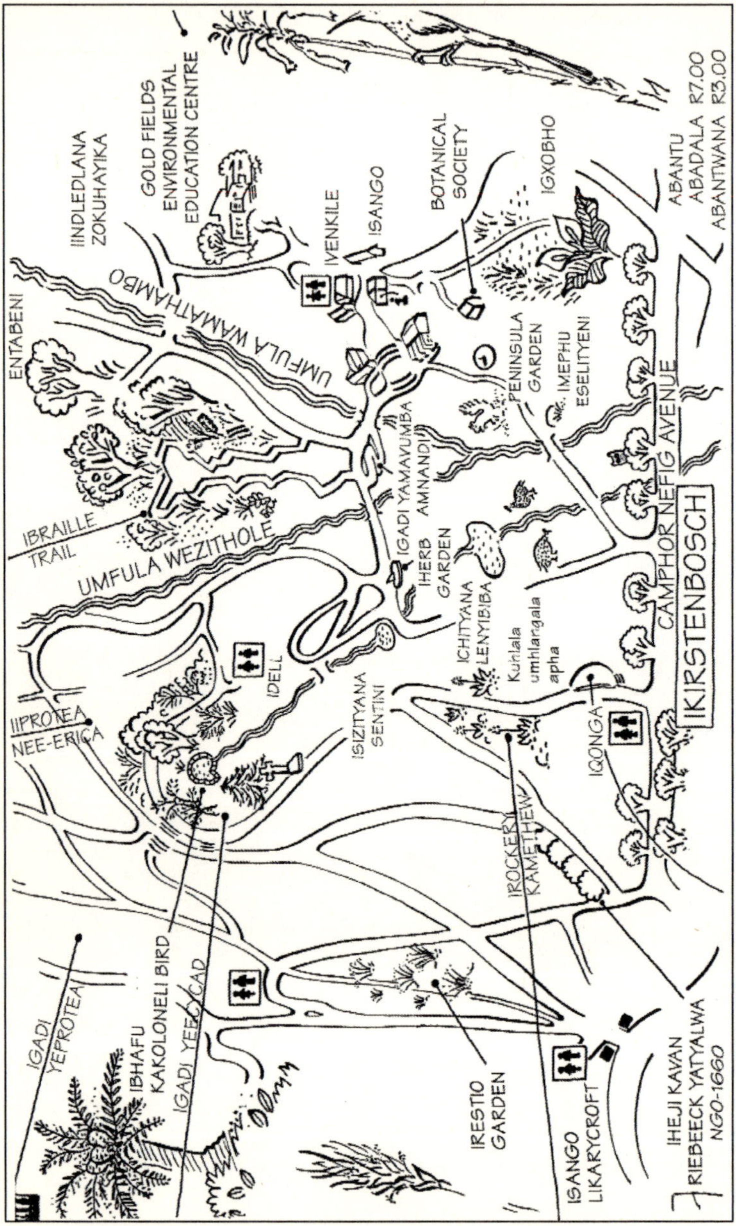
IINDLEDLANA ZOKUHAYIKA
GOLD FIELDS ENVIRONMENTAL EDUCATION CENTRE
IVENKILE
ISANGO
BOTANICAL SOCIETY
IGXOBHO
ABANTU ABADALA R7.00
ABANTWANA R3.00
ENTABENI
UMFULA WAMATHAMBO
PENINSULA GARDEN
IMEPHU ESELITYENI
CAMPHOR NEFIG AVENUE
IKIRSTENBOSCH
IGADI YAMAVUMBA AMNANDI
IBRAILLE TRAIL
UMFULA WEZITHOLE
IHERB GARDEN
ICHITYANA LENYIBIBA
Kuhlala umhlangala apha
IDELL
ISIZITYANA SENTINI
IIPROTEA NEE-ERICA
IQONGA
IROCKERY KAMETHEW
IGADI YEPROTEA
IBHAFU KAKOLONELI BIRD
IGADI YEECYCAD
IRESTIO GARDEN
ISANGO LIKARYCROFT
IHEJI KAVAN RIEBEECK YATYALWA NGO-1660

The Kirstenbosch Outreach Bus sponsored by the Anglo-American and De Beers Chairman's Fund. (Photographs courtesy National Botanical Gardens, Kirstenbosch)

They go on a tour of the gardens after which Phumla tells the pupils that she will be coming to their school shortly to help them establish their own waterwise garden.

UPhumla Heke, bafundi, ndiza kunityelela esikolweni ukuze siqale igadi enolondolozo-manzi. Mna, ndiza kuzisa izityalo nezixhobo zegadi, kodwa ndifuna ukuba nina nithabathe inxaxheba kulo msebenzi ngokuzama ukulungisa umhlaba esikolweni.

Abafundi Siyenza njani, loo nto, Nkosikazi?

UPhumla Eyona ndlela ilungileyo kukuqala ngokwenza umgquba. Ningaqala ngokuqokelela inkunkuma yekhitshi. Umzekelo, amaxolo emifuno, amaqokobhe amaqanda, amagqabi, amathambo kunye nengca esikiweyo neentyatyambo ezifileyo neentsiba nothuthu lweenkuni. Kodwa ningazifaki iitoti, iiplastiki okanye amaphepha.

Ndiza kutyelela esikolweni senu kwiveki ezayo. Siza kukhetha indawo efanelekileyo senze umgquba kuyo. De kube ngoko, ningafaka yonke into eniyiqokeleleyo kwezi ngxowa.

Heke, bafundi, ndiyanibulela ngokumamela ngenyameko engaka. Nibe nepikiniki emnandi ke ngoku, kodwa ndicela niyigcine icocekile igadi. Ningalibali ukuchola onke amaphepha phambi kokuba nihambe niwafake emigqomeni yenkunkuma. Hambani kakuhle. Sobonana kwiveki ezayo.

Isigama

-zisa	bring	-faka	put in
izixhobo zegadi	garden implements	iitoti	tins
-thabatha inxaxheba	take part	amaphepha	papers
kulo msebenzi	in this work	kuyo	in it
-lungisa	prepare	de kube ngoko	until then
umhlaba	soil	ezi ngxowa	these bags
eyona ndlela ilungileyo	the best way	eniyiqokeleleyo	which you've collected
umgquba	compost	-mamela	listen
-qokelela	collect	ngenyameko	with such
inkunkuma	waste, garbage	engaka	attention
amaxolo emifuno	vegetable peelings	nibe nepikiniki emnandi	have a nice picnic
amaqokobhe amaqanda	egg shells		
amagqabi	leaves	-gcina	keep
amathambo	bones	-cocekile	clean
kunye na-	together with	-chola	pick up
ingca esikiweyo	grass cuttings	phambi kokuba	before
iintyatyambo ezifileyo	dead flowers	nihambe	you leave
iintsiba	feathers	imigqomo	rubbish
uthuthu lweenkuni	ash (of wood)	yenkunkuma	bins

A traditional healer or herbalist – (ixhwele) (Courtesy *Weekend Argus*, 10/11/94)

Insight

Many indigenous plants have medicinal properties and are used in traditional practice:

*Isi***cakathi** *agapanthus*

Used in ante-natal and post-natal medicine.

*um***hlaba** *bitter aloe*

Used as a laxative but also for arthritis, eczema, conjunctivitis, hypertension and stress.

*um***hlonyane** *African wormwood*

One of the most widely used traditional medicines in South Africa. Used for treating coughs, colds and influenza, fever, loss of appetite, colic, headache, earache, malaria and intestinal worms.

*im***phewula** *pig's ear*

Another widely used plant to treat corns, warts, earache and toothache.

*in***cwadi** *bushman poison bulb*

Used as a dressing after circumcision and for treating boils and septic wounds, also corns, warts, earache and toothache.

*im***pepho** *everlastings*

Used for wound dressings, coughs, colds, fever, infections, headache and menstrual pain.

*ubu***vuma** *winter cherry*

Mainly used for wound healing, abscesses, haemorrhoids and rheumatism.

*um***hlabavuthwa** *thornapple*

Used prolifically to relieve asthma and reduce pain.

Herbalist/s	*i*xhwele/*ama*xhwele
Traditional practitioner/s	*i*gqirha*/*ama*gqirha
Western practitioner:	*u*gqirha/*oo*gqirha

*Remember the **Click Song** made famous by the late Miriam Makeba: 'Igqirha lendlela nguqongqothwane . . .' (The witchdoctor of the road is a black beetle . . .)

How to ...

Introduce someone you work with

Lo nguNkosikazi __________ / **Lo** nguMnumzana ___________ *e*ndi**sebenza** naye. / Si**sebenza** ku**nye**.
Ndinga*kw***azisa** uNkosikazi ________ / Mnumzana ___________ *e*ndi**sebenza na***ye*.
Mandi*kw***azise** uNkosikazi __________ / Mnumzana __________ endi**sebenza na***ye*.
Nd**ingathanda udibane** noNkosikazi ____ noMnumzana ______ *e*ndi**sebenza na***bo*.

Point out / single out

Lo nguNkosikazi Bongela.
Le *n*k**qubo** ya**qalwa** ukuze si**ncede** *izi***kolo**.
Le gadi **idume** kulo lonke *i***hlabathi**.
Lo *m***fanekiso** wa**thathwa** eChelsea Flower Show yaseLondon.

Say what a place is renowned for

Le gadi idume ngo*bu***hle**.
Le gadi idume ngenxa yen**kitha** ye*zi***tyalo** *e***na***zo*.
Le gadi idume nge*mi***boniso** ye*zi***tyalo**.

Encourage environmentally-friendly practices

Tyala *izi***tyalo** *ez*inga**fun***i* *ma***nzi** *ma***ninzi**.
*Wu***lungise** *um***hlaba** ngoku**faka** *isi***vundiso** ukuze ukw**azi** uku*wa***gcina**
*ama***nzi**.
*Wu***gqume** *um***hlaba** phakathi kwe*zi***tyalo** nge*zin***to** *ezi***gcina** uku**fuma** *em***hlab***eni*.

Zahlule *izi***tyalo** ngoku**funa** kwazo *ama***nzi**.
*Yi***tyale** *in***gca** kuphela apho ku*yim***funeko** khona.
Nkcenkceshela ngoku**fanelekile***yo* kunjalo nje xa ku*yim***funeko**.
*W***enze** *um***gquba** ngoku**qokelela** *in***kunkuma** *e***khitsh***ini*.

Say what the best is

*E***yona** *n***dlela** **ilungile***yo* kuku**qala** ngokwenza umgquba.
*E***yona** *n***dawo** **ilungile***yo* loku**tyala** esi sityalo iselangeni.
*E***lona** **xesha** li**lungile***yo* loku**tyala** esi sityalo lisekwindla

Request that appropriate etiquette is observed in a public place

Ndi**cela** ni**gcine** *i***gadi** **icocek***ile*.
Ni**ngalibali** uku**chola** onke *ama***phepha** phambi kokuba ni**hambe** ni*wa***fake** *emi***gqom***eni* ye*n***kunkuma**.

How it works

1 Possessives of Class 1a

In **Unit 5**, you learned that **possessive relationship** in Xhosa is expressed by means of a **possessive concord** (equivalent to English *'s* or *of*) for Classes 1–15, e.g.:

*um***sebenzi** *we***ngcaphephe** ye*zi***tyalo**
(< *um***sebenzi** *wa*- + *in***gcaphephe**)

However, with nouns of **Class 1a**, i.e. proper names and kinship terms, relationships, '**ka**-' is used:

*um***sebenzi** **ka**Peter   Peter**'s** job

If you look at the map of Kirstenbosch in this Unit you will find the following examples:

*I***BHAFU** **KA**KOLONELI BIRD
(Colonel Bird**'s** bath)
*I***HEJI** **KA**VAN RIEBEECK
(van Riebeeck**'s** hedge)

Colonel Bird's bath

'*I***bhafu**' and '*i***heji**' (possessees) are Class 9 nouns. Like nouns of Classes 1, 3, 4 and 6 (*um-*, *imi-*, *ama* -) they are **weak class** nouns.

However, when the noun possessed belongs to a strong class, its subject concord is prefixed to '**ka-**'. You will also see an example of this construction on the map:

*I*SANGO *LI*KARYCROFT (Rycroft's entrance/gate)

'*I***sango**' is a strong Class 5 noun.

2 The equivalent of English 'each'

This is formed by '**nga-**' + *adjectival concord** + '**-nye**' (one):

*um***fundi nga***m***nye**	**each** student
*um***thi nga***m***nye**	**each** tree
*isi***tyalo nga***si***nye**	**each** plant
*in***tyatyambo nganye**	**each** flower
*ulu***dwe nga***lu***nye**	**each** list
*ubu***sika nga***bu***nye**	**each** winter

→ *cf. **Unit 8**.

3 Emphatic pronouns referring to the 3rd person

You are already familiar with the **emphatic pronouns** referring to the 1st and 2nd persons, i.e., '*m***na**,' '*thi***na**,' '*we***na**,' '*ni***na**', (→ **Unit 3**).

The pronouns for the **3rd person** (Classes 1-15) usually follow the noun they emphasize:

*u***Peter**	*ye***na**	**Peter**, as for him
*aba***fundi**	*bo***na**	the **pupils**, as for them
*um***sebenzi**	*wo***na**	the **job**, as for it
*imi***sebenzi**	*yo***na**	the **jobs**, as for them,
*i***gqwetha**	*lo***na**	the **lawyer**, as for him / her
*ama***gqwetha**	*wo***na**	the **lawyers**, as for them
*isi***thethi**	*so***na**	the **speaker**, as for him / her
*izi***thethi**	*zo***na**	the **speakers**, as for them
*in***tatheli**	*yo***na**	the **journalist**, as for him / her
*iin***tatheli**	*zo***na**	the **journalists**, as for them
*u***ndwendwe**	*lo***na**	the **guest**, as for him / her
*ii***ndwendwe**	*zo***na**	the **guests**, as for them
*ubu***sika**	*bo***na**	**winter**, as for it
*uku***tya**	*ko***na**	the **food**, as for it

When the **emphatic pronoun** is used with '**na**-'= 'have' / 'with', the shortened form (i.e. without '-**na**') is used:

U**na***ye* *um***ncedisi**?	Do you **have** an **assistant**?
Ewe, ndi**na***ye*.	Yes, I **have** one.
Hayi, andi**na***ye*.	No, I don't **have** one.

U**na***bo*	*aba***ncedisi**?	Ewe, ndi**na***bo*.	Hayi, andi**na***bo*.
U**na**wo	*um***hlakulo**?	Ewe, ndi**na***wo*.	Hayi, andi**na***wo*.
U**na**yo	*imi***hlakulo**?	Ewe, ndi**na***yo*.	Hayi, andi**na***yo*.
U**na***lo*	*i***xesha**?	Ewe, ndi**na***lo*.	Hayi, andi**na***lo*.
U**na***wo*	*ama***nzi**?	Ewe, ndi**na***wo*.	Hayi, andi**na***wo*.
U**na***so*	*isi***tyalo**?	Ewe, ndi**na***so*.	Hayi, andi**na***so*.
U**na***zo*	*izi***tyalo**?	Ewe, ndi**na***zo*.	Hayi, andi**na***zo*.
U**na***yo*	*i***gadi**?	Ewe, ndi**na***yo*.	Hayi, andi**na***yo*.
U**na***zo*	*iin***tyatyambo**?	Ewe, ndi**na***zo*.	Hayi, andi**na***zo*.
U**na***lo*	*ulu***dwe**? (list)	Ewe, ndi**na***lo*.	Hayi, andi**na***lo*.
U**na***ko*	*uku***tya**?	Ewe, ndi**na***ko*.	Hayi, andi**na***ko*.

The **emphatic pronoun** can also be used with prepositions '**ku**-' / '**nga**-'

Kulungile **ku***we*?	Ewe, kulungile **ku***m*.
*Ndi***xelele** **nga***we*.	
Kuku*we*! (It is up **to** *you*!)	

4 *Superlative pronouns* + '-lungileyo' = *'the best'*

Superlative pronouns are formed by prefixing the relative elements'*o*-', '*e*-', or '*a*-' (cf. **Unit 6**) to the emphatic pronoun:

*o***yena**	*m***ntu**	*u***lungile***yo*	the **best** person
*a***bona**	*ba***ntu**	*ba***lungile***yo*	the **best** people
*o***wona**	*m***thi**	*u***lungile***yo*	the **best** tree
*e***yona**	*mi***thi**	*i***lungile***yo*	the **best** trees
*e***lona**	**xesha**	*li***lungile***yo*	the **best** time
*a***wona**	*ma***nzi**	*a***lungile***yo*	the **best** water
*e***sona**	*si***tyalo**	*si***lungile**yo	the **best** plant
*e***zona**	*zi***tyalo**	*zi***lungile***yo*	the **best** plants
*e***yona**	*n***to** / *n***dawo**	*i***lungile***yo*	the **best** thing / place
*e***zona**	*n***tyatyambo**	*zi***lungile***yo*	the **best** flowers
*o***kona**	*ku***tya**	*ku***lungile***yo*	the **best** food

From the above you can also see that**:**

the **initial vowel of the prefix** of the noun is **omitted** and the **qualificative '–lungile***yo*' takes the same form as the **subject concord**

COMPARE:

Ung*um***ntu** *o***lungile***yo*.	He / she is a **good** person.
*O***yena** *m***ntu** *u***lungile***yo* ng*u*Sipho	The **very best** person is Sipho.

This rule also applies to **demonstratives**.

Y*i***gadi** *e*n**tle**!	*It is* a **beautiful** garden!
Le **gadi** *i*n**tle** iseKapa.	*This* **beautiful** garden is in Cape Town.

Superlative pronouns can be used with other adjectives or relative adjectives to form the equivalent of the **English superlative**:

*O***yena** *m***bhali** *u***dumil**e*yo* wamaXhosa nguAC Jordan.	The **most famous** Xhosa author is AC Jordan.
*E***yona gadi** *i***ntle** yaseKapa yiKirstenbosch.	The **most beautiful** garden of the Cape is Kirstenbosch.
*A***bona** *ba***sebenzi-gadi** *ba***nolwazi** basebenza eKirstenbosch.	The **most knowledgable** gardeners work at Kirstenbosch.
*O***wona** *m***boniso** *m***khulu** wezityalo ehlabatini yiChelsea Flower Show yaseLondon.	The **greatest** flower show in the world is the Chelsea Flower Show in London.
*E***yona** *n***dlela** *i***lula** ukuya eKirstenbosch kukuhamba ngemoto.	The **easiest** way to get to Kirstenbosch is to go by car.
Ngamanye amaxesha *eyona mi***buzo** *i***nzima** ibuzwa ngabantwana.	Sometimes the **most difficult** questions are asked by children.

To express 'it *is* / they *are*' before a **superlative**, prefix the copulative (cf. **Unit 4**):

*Ii***Cycad** *ze***zona** *zi***tyalo** *zi***dala** egadini yaseKirstenbosch.	Cycads **are** the **oldest plants** in Kirstenbosch gardens.

5 Demonstratives

As is the case in English, when pointing out people or objects, there are **three sets** of **demonstratives** in Xhosa corresponding to '*this*' / '*these*'; '*that*' / '*those*'; '*that over there*' / '*those over there*'.

Nouns preceded by a **demonstrative lose** their **initial vowel**:

Ngubani *lo m***ntu**?	Who is *this* **person**?
Ngubani *loo m***ntu**?	Who is *that* **person**?
Ngubani *laa m***ntu**?	Who is *that* **person** (*over there*)?

As usual, each noun class has its corresponding form. It is interesting to note that the form of the **first set** of **demonstratives** '*this*' / '*these*' corresponds to the relative concords in the 'strong' classes (cf. **Unit 6**) with '***l***' added in the 'weak' classes.

First set of demonstratives

*'**Weak**' classes*

lo	*m***ntu**	*this* **person**
lo	*m***thi**	*this* **tree**
le	*mi***thi**	*these* **trees**
la	*ma***gqabi**	*these* **leaves**
le	*n***to**	*this* **thing**

*'**Strong**' classes*

aba	*ba***ntu**	*these* **people**
eli	**sango**	*this* **gate**
esi	*si***tyalo**	*this* **plant**
ezi	*zi***tyalo**	*these* **plants**
ezi	*zin***to**	*these* **things**
olu	**londolozo-manzi**	*this* **water conservation**
obu	*bu***tyebi**	*this* **resource**
oku	*ku***londoloza amanzi**	*this* **saving** (of) **water**

These **demonstratives** can be used:

before the noun, e.g.:

Idum*ile le* gadi! (initial vowel of the prefix of the noun omitted);

after the noun for **emphasis**, e.g.:

Idum*ile i*gadi *le*! (initial vowel of the prefix of the noun retained);

without a noun, e.g.:

Idum*ile le!*

Second set of demonstratives

*'**Weak**' classes*

	*m***ntu**	*that* **person**
	*m***thi**	*that* **tree**
loo	*mi***thi**	*those* **trees**
	*ma***nzi**	*that* **water**
	*n***to**	*that* **thing**

Note: The full forms of the demonstratives of these nouns are *lowo* (Classes 1 and 3); *leyo* (Classes 4 and 9) and *lawo* (Class 6). They are normally used **after the noun** for emphasis:

Yinto enomdla *leyo*	It is an interesting thing *that*

*'**Strong**' classes*

abo	*ba***ntu**	*those* **people**
elo	**xesha**	*that* **time**
eso	*si***tyalo**	*that* **plant**
ezo	*zi***tyalo**	*those* **plants**
ezo	*zi***nto**	*those* **things**
olo	**hlobo**	*that* **way**
obo	*bu***tyebi**	*that* **resource**
oko	*ku***tya**	*that* **food**

(cf. Apho = there)

Third set of demonstratives

*'**Weak**' classes*

	*m***ntu**	*that* **person** *over there*
	*m***thi**	*that* **tree** *over there*
laa	*mi***thi**	*those* **trees** *over there*
	*ma***phepha**	*those* **papers** *over there*
	*n***dawo**	*that* **place** *over there*

Note: As is the case with the second set of demonstratives in the weak classes, there is a full form: ***lowa*** (Classes 1 and 3); ***leya*** (Classes 4 and 9) and ***lawa*** (Class 6). Like those of the second set they are normally used **after the noun** for emphasis.

*'**Strong**' classes*

abaa	*ba***ntu**	*those* **people** *over there*
elaa	**sango**	*that* **gate** *over there*
esaa	*si***tyalo**	*that* **plant** *over there*

ezaa	*zi***tyalo**	*those* **plants** *over there*
ezaa	*zin***to**	*those* **things** *over there*
olaa	*lu***dwe**	*that* **list** *over there*
obaa	*bu***si**	*that* **honey** *over there*
okwaa	*ku***tya**	*that* **food** *over there*

Note: The strong classes of the third position also have full forms: *abaya* (Class 2), *eliya* (Class 5), *esiya* (Class 7), *eziya* (Classes 8 and 10), *oluya* (Class 11), *obuya* (Class 14) and *okuya* (Class 15). (Cf. 'phaya' = over there).

6 Another conjunction – 'ukuze' 'in order to'

'**Ukuze**' is a **conjunction** that must be followed by a verb ending in *-e* (subjunctive) (cf. **Unit 4** and **Unit 8**):

Le nkqubo yaqalwa **ukuze** si**ncedise** izikolo ukuseka iigadi.	This project was started **to help** (lit. in order that we **help**) the schools to establish gardens.
Qokelela inkunkuma yekhitshi **ukuze** we**nze** umgquba.	Collect kitchen waste **to make** (lit. in order that you **make**) compost.

As you can see from the translations, Xhosa uses this construction where English simply uses the infinitive. However, it is interesting to note that now and again one comes across examples where the infinitive is used where one would expect the subjunctive:

'Kubaluleke kakhulu **ukunkcenkceshela** ngendlela efanelekileyo.'

It is very important **to water** in an appropriate manner.

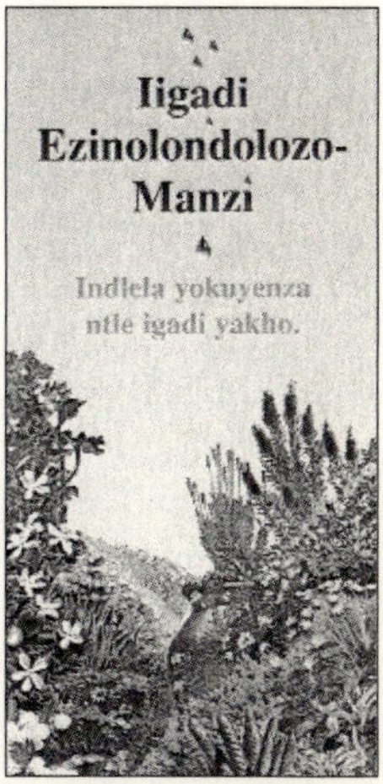

This sentence is taken from Iigadi Ezinolondolozo-manzi ('Waterwise Gardening'), a brochure published by the Department of Water Affairs, Pretoria.

The brochure and others can be obtained, free of charge, from Kirstenbosch, where you will also have many opportunities to test your knowledge of Xhosa by trying to read the plant information boards.

How to apply it

1 Complete the questions by filling in the appropriate link

(a) Iphi i-ofisi ______Nkosikazi Bongela?
(b) Liphi isango ______Rycroft?
(c) Abafundi ______Peter bafika nini?
(d) Umsebenzi ______Peter unomdla na?
(e) Inkqubo ______Phumla inempumelelo (success) na?

2 Give the literal translation of this idiomatic expression used to express 'hoping in vain'

Kukuza kukaNxele' ________________________________

Insight

Nxele Makanda was a Xhosa chief who is considered to be South Africa's first 'freedom fighter'. His attempt to destroy the new British settlement of Grahamstown in 1819 led to his imprisonment on **Robben Island**. In 1820, when trying to escape, he drowned but many of his followers did not believe that he was dead and waited in vain for his return. One of the boats taking visitors to **Robben Island** is named the **Makanda**.

3 Reading and understanding

Here is some information about *Abalimi Bezekhaya*, a community-based greening and food gardening project. Consult the Xhosa–English vocabulary list for help in understanding this extract.

Abalimi Bezekhaya yisenta yegadi yabantu. Lo mbutho wasekwa ngo-1982. Injongo yawo (its) kukwazisa, ukunceda nokucebisa abantu ngezinto zonke malunga nokulima – indlela yokulima imifuno, indlela yokutyala imithi nemithana ngokufanelekileyo. Abantu baseCape Flats banokuthenga zonke izinto zegadi ngexabiso eliphantsi kakhulu kulo mbutho. Umzekelo______ , ________, ________ ______ . Ungabona impumelelo yomsebenzi lo ezigadini ezininzi.

4 Ask where each garden implement is and answer appropriately

IZIXHOBO ZEGADI: QUICK VOCAB

ingobozi (iin-)	basket	isikere sokuthena	pruning shears
isarha	saw	ithumbu lamanzi	hose
iharika / ireki	rake	ikani yokunkcenkceshela	watering can
ifolokhwe	fork	umhlakulo	spade
igaba	hoe	ikiriva	wheelbarrow
imbiza (iim-)	pot	i-emele	bucket
ipeki	pick	umatshini wokucheba ingca	lawn mower

Uphi umtya? Where's the string?	Unawo? Do you have it?	Ewe, nangu! Yes, here it is!
(a) ___phi umhlakulo?	Una_____?	Ewe, _______
(b) ___phi iimbiza?	Una_____?	Ewe, _______
(c) ___phi ikiriva?	Una_____?	Ewe, _______
(d) ___phi ithumbu lamanzi?	Una_____?	Ewe,_______
(e) ___phi isikere sokuthena?	Una_____?	Ewe,_______
(f) ___phi i-emele?	Una_____?	Ewe,_______
(g) ___phi igaba?	Una_____?	Ewe,_______
(h) ___phi iharika?	Una_____?	Ewe, _______
(i) ___phi ifolokhwe?	Una_____?	Ewe, _______
(j) ___phi umatshini wokucheba ingca?	Una_____?	Ewe, _______

5 Match the instructions

Use the following words and phrases: (a) amanzi, (b) inkunkuma yekhitshi, (c) ingca, (d) umhlaba ngezinto ezigcina ukufuma emhlabeni, (e) inkunkuma kwimigqomo yenkunkuma, (f) umhlaba, (g) umthi and (h) amagqabi.

1 Lungisa	5 Harika
2 Tyala	6 Londoloza
3 Gquma	7 Qokelela
4 Cheba	8 Faka

6 Complete the instructions

Fill in the missing demonstratives to complete the instructions:

(a) Beka (these things) _______ ________ emgqubeni.
(b) Landa (fetch) (that wheelbarrow) ______ _______.
(c) Tyala (these trees) _______ ___________ elangeni.
(d) Tyala (those trees) ________ ___________ emthunzini.
(e) Nkcenkceshela (those seedlings [izithole] over there) ____ ____.
(f) Cheba (that hedge over there) ________ ___________.

7 Complete the questions

Fill in the missing demonstratives to complete questions which you might ask when walking through Kirstenbosch:

(a) Ibizwa (called) njani ______ ntyatyambo?
(b) Ubizwa njani _____ mthi?
(c) Ubizwa njani _____ mthana (shrub)?
(d) Ibizwa njani ______ heji?
(e) Sibizwa njani _____ sityalo?
(f) Ubizwa njani _____ mfula (stream)?
(g) Ibizwa njani ______ ntaka (bird)?
(h) Ibizwa njani ______ ndlela?

8 Complete the information using the superlative form

(a) _________ ntyatyambo idumileyo yaseMzantsi Afrika yiProtea.

(b) _________heji indala yaseKapa yatyalwa nguvan Riebeeck ngo-1660.

(c) ___________ gadi idumileyo yaseMzantsiAfrika yiKirstenbosch.

(d) ___________ ndawo ilungileyo yokwenza ipikiniki isemthunzini walo mthi.

(e) ___________xesha lilungileyo lokutyelela iKirstenbosch lisentlakohlaza.

(f) Ndiza kunicacisela _________ ndlela ilungileyo yokulondoloza amanzi.

9 Use the correct verb forms

Phumla goes to a school to show the pupils how to make compost and how to water in a waterwise way. Complete the information she gives them by filling in the correct verb forms. Consult the Xhosa–English vocabulary for verbs you have not yet come across:

Heke, bafundi ndiyabona ukuba (a) beni__________ (have been collecting) izinto ezininzi ukuze siqale ukwenza umgquba! Masiwenzeni ke! Kuqala (b)__________ (separate) umhlaba ngefolokhwe. (c)_________ (Put) uhlaza nokutya okudala nje emgqubeni. Kufuneka ezi zinto (d) zi_______ (decay). Ukuba (e) ni*zi*______ (keep) zifumile, uza kubola ngokukhawuleza umgquba. Ukubola kuza (f) ku_______ (take) malunga neeveki ezintandathu. Kufuneka (g) ni*wu*___________ (water) kakuhle *rhoqo*.

Ngoku ndifuna ukunibonisa indlela efanelekileyo yokutyala imbewu. Nantsi imbewu yemifuno. (h) Masi*yi*______ (plant). Nanzi iibhokisi ezincinci. (i) *Zi*________ (fill) ngalo mhlaba. (j) *Yi*________ (plant) imbewu ezibhokisini ngolu hlobo (in this way). (k) *Zi*_________ (keep) iibhokisi ngaphandle okanye izityalo ziza kuba buthakathaka (weak) (l) zi____ (die). Ngoku ndifuna uku*ni*bonisa indlela yokunkcenkceshela izityalo ngokufanelekileyo.

(m) ____________ (Remember) bafundi, amanzi (n)________ (scarce) kakhulu eMzantsi Afrika. Kufuneka sonke sisoloko (o) si _________ (try) (p) uku*wa*__________ (save) amanzi ngakumbi ezigadini zethu. Ngoku, (q)________________ (water) ezi zithole ngononophelo. Musani (r) uku________________ (water) amagqabi, (s)___________ (water) umhlaba kuphela. (t)_________ (be careful) (u) ningazi_______ (damage) izithole. (v)____________ (surround) izityalo ngomgquba ukuze (w)_______ (keep) ukufuma emhlabeni.

-thatha	nkcenkceshelani	Lumkani	Jikelezani
-moshi	khumbulani	-nkcenkceshela	-tyaleni
-zaliseni	yahlukanisani	-gcine	Fakani
-zama	anqabe	-bole	-qokelela
-nkcenkceshele	-fe	-tyaleni	-gcineni
ugcine	nkcenkceshelani	-londoloza	

QV

Test yourself

1 What are the different meanings of the following expressions incorporating '**nga**-'?
(a) umfundi **ngamanye** (b) igadi idume **ngobuhle**
(c) iminyaka **ngeminyaka**

2 When the possessor is a noun belonging to class 1a, e.g. 'uPeter', what links the possessee (the thing possessed), e.g. '*um***sebenzi** (work) belonging to a so-called 'weak' class, to the possessor? What happens when the possessee belongs to a so-called 'strong' class, e.g. *ubu***chule** (expertise)?

3 You know the **emphatic pronouns** for the 1st and 2nd persons (s. & pl.): mna, wena, thina, nina. What is the easiest way to formulate the emphatic pronouns corresponding to the noun classes (3rd person)? Which class is the exception?

4 The **subject concord** + '-**na**-' = 'have' + **noun**, e.g.: **Unabantwana**? = 'You have children?' is often used with the shortened emphatic pronoun for emphasis: U**nabo** abantwana? Ewe, ndi**nabo**. How do you ask: 'Do you have water?' Give the answer.

5 Emphatic pronouns can also be used with the prepositions **ku**- and **nga**-. How do you say:
'It's fine **for me.**' 'Tell me **about** yourself.'

6 After a superlative pronoun, the initial vowel of the noun is omitted and the concord of the relative adjective changes. With this in mind, how would you say: 'You ask a most difficult question'?

7 Point out a tree to someone by saying:
This tree That tree That tree over there

8 Can the demonstrative be placed after the noun?

9 In the phrase '**olo hlobo**' = 'that way', to which class does '*u***hlobo**' belong? What is its plural?

10 '**ukuze**' (in order that/so that) is a **conjunction**. Name four other conjunctions.

If you have done all exercises and answered the questions above correctly, then you are well prepared to proceed to the next unit.

10 UThemba emsebenzini – udliwano-ndlebe

Themba at work – an interview

In this unit you will learn how to:

- put an interviewee at ease
- ask questions as an employer
- talk about your education, training, previous experience
- ask for further information

Incoko

CD 2, tr 1

Themba interviews an applicant for a position in his company.

UThemba	Molo, Nkosazana Green. Khawungene uhlale phantsi. Ndiyavuya ukukubona. Kunjani?
UNksz Green	Molo Mnumzana Thamsanqa. Enkosi. Hayi ndiphilile ngaphandle *kokuba nentaka*!
UThemba	Hayi, nkosazana, sukuxhala! Khululeka! Ubonakala ukwazi ukusithetha kakuhle isiXhosa! Ndixelele, usazela phi?
UNksz Green	Ndaqala ukusithetha ndisemncinci kuba abazali bam babesebenza esibhedlele kufuphi nakuQoboqobo.
UThemba	Oo, uyasazi ke isiXhosa esithethwa ngamaNgqika omgquba!* Uyakwazi nokusibhala?
UNksz Green	Ewe Mnumzana Thamsanqa, ndasifunda isiXhosa esikolweni kwanaseyunivesithi.
UThemba	Uyakwazi ukuthetha nezinye iilwimi?
UNksz Green	Ewe, ndiyakwazi ukuthetha isiBhulu nesiFrentshi kancinci kodwa ke sona.
UThemba	Heke, Nkosazana, khawuthi *gqaba-gqaba* ngawe.
UNksz Green	Ndazalwa ngo-1969 eKapa. Abazali bam bafudukela kuQoboqobo ndisemncinci ngoko ke amabanga aphantsi, ukususela ku-Sub A ukuya kuStd 5, ndawenza ngakuQoboQobo.

*See *Only got ten minutes*?

UThemba	Amabanga aphakamileyo wawenza phi?
UNksz Green	Esinaleni ngaseMonti, iMatriki ndayiphumelela ngo-1986. Emva koko ndafundela iqondo leBA eyunivesithi yaseRhodes, eRhini.
UThemba	Wathatha ziphi izifundo eziyintloko?
UNksz Green	Ndathatha isiNgesi nesiXhosa.
UThemba	Wawufundiswa ngubani isiXhosa?
UNksz	Nguprofesa Majola. Ingaba uyamazi?
UThemba	Oo, kakhulu! Sasifunda kunye, ekrelekrele.
UNksz Green	Onjani utitshala! Wandinceda kakhulu. Ndazuza isidanga sam se-BA ngo-1989. Ndaqala ukusebenza njengotitshalakazi. Ngo-1994 ndanyuselwa ndaba lisekela-inqununu.
UThemba	Khawutsho, kutheni ufuna ukutshintsha umsebenzi?
UNksz Green	Ndinoloyiko kuza kuncitshiswa inani leetitshala. Enye into, ndingumntu wabantu. Ndithanda kakhulu ukusebenza neentlobo-ngeentlobo zabantu. Yaye ndicinga ukuba ndinganegalelo kwinkampani yakho.
UThemba	Heke, Nkosazana. Wena, unayo imibuzo?
UNksz Green	Ewe, Mnumzana Thamsanqa. Ucinga ukuba ndinethuba lokuwufumana lo msebenzi?
UThemba	Ewe, ndicinga ukuba unethuba elilungileyo kakhulu!
UNksz Green	Ndingalindela ukwaziswa nini ukuba ndiphumelele?
UThemba	Siza kukwazisa ekupheleni kweveki ezayo.
UNksz Green	Enkosi kakhulu. Ndiyabulela, Mnumzana.
UThemba	Kulungile Nkosazana Green. Bekumnandi kakhulu ukudibana nawe. Uhambe kakuhle.
UNksz Green	Kamnandi, MnumzanaThamsanqa.

Isigama

kokuba nentaka	*to be nervous* (lit. be with a bird)	-fudukela	move home
		amabanga	standards
-xhala	be anxious	ukususela ku-	from
khululeka	relax i.e. be free	ukuya ku-	until
-bonakala	seem / appear	-phantsi	low(er)
-azela	know from	-phakamileyo	high(er)
kufuphi na-	near	isinala	boarding school
kuQoboqobo	to Keiskammahoek	-phumelela	succeed
kwanase-	even at	iqondo	degree
kodwa ke sona	the latter less	izifundo eziyintloko	majors

sasifunda	we studied	-tshintsha	change
kunye	together	uloyiko	fear
ekrelekrele	he being very bright	-ncitshiswa	be cut back, reduced
onjani	what	inani	the number
utitshala!	a teacher!	ngeentlobo-ntlobo	different
-zuza	graduate	igalelo	contribution
isidanga	degree (lit. necklace)	ithuba	chance
-nyuselwa	be promoted	ekupheleni kwa-	at the end of
ndaba lisekela-inqununu	I became vice-principal		

How to ...

Put an interviewee at ease

*Suku***xhala / Khululeka**, Nkosikazi (Nkosazana, Mnumzana)

Ask questions as an employee

Wafunda phi?
Kw*esi***phi** *isi***kolo**?
Kw*eyi***phi** *i***yunivesithi**?
Kutheni ufuna uku**tshintsha** *um***sebenzi**?
Wafundiswa *ng***ubani**?
Waqeqeshwa *ng***ubani**?
Wathatha *ezi***phi** *izi***fundo** njeng*ezi***fundo** *eziyin***tloko**?
Una*wo* *ama***va**?
Una*yo* *imi***buzo**?

Talk about your education, training, experience

Nda*w***enza** *ama***banga** *a***phantsi** e________
Nda*w***enza** *ama***banga** *a***phakamile***yo* e_________
Nda**phumelela** ngo-19____ iMatriki
Nda**fundela** *i***qondo** leBA ngo_____
Nda**fundiswa** ngu_________
Nda**qeqeshwa** ngu_________
Nda**zuza** *isi***danga** sam se-BA
Nda**sebenza njeng**______
Nda**nyuselwa** ndaba ____________

Ndin*ama*va *eku***fundis***eni* / *eku***thengis***eni* / *eku***sebenz***eni* nge**khompyutha**

Ask for further information

Uya*kw***azi** *uku***thetha** *isi***Ngesi** / *isi***Xhosa** / *isi***Bhulu** / *ezi***nye** *ii***lwimi**?
Uya*kw***azi** *uku***qhuba**?
Una*lo* *i***phepha** loku**qhuba**?
Una*yo* *i***referensi** / *in***cwadi** e*ku***ncoma***yo*. (lit. a letter praising *you*)
Wakhe wa*w***enza** lo *m***sebenzi** ngaphambili?
Wakhe wa**sebenza** njeng _____ ngaphambili?
Uya*kw***azi** *uku***sebenza** nge**khompyutha**?

How it works

1 The passive

The **passive** voice is a grammatical term that means exactly what it says – something is done to somebody or something without necessarily mentioning who is performing the action. The **passive** form is used more extensively in everyday Xhosa speech than it is in English.

Uya**fundisa**.	He / she **teaches**.	(active)
Uya**fundiswa**.	He / she is **being taught**.	(passive)
Uya**qeqesha**.	He / she **is training**.	(active)
Uya**qeqeshwa**.	He / she is **being trained**.	(passive)

As you can see, the **passive is formed** simply by **inserting** '-**w**-' before the **final -a** (cf. verbal extensions **Unit 4**):

Uprofesa u**fundisa** abafundi.	The professor **is teaching** the students.	(active)
Abafundi ba**fundiswa** ***ngu*****profesa**.	The students **are taught** **by** the professor.	(passive)
Umqeqeshi u**qeqesha** abafundi.	The trainer **is training** the apprentices.	(active)
Abafundi ba**qeqeshwa** ***ngum*****qeqeshi**.	The apprentices are **being trained by** the trainer.	(passive)

When the agent, i.e. 'the doer of the action', is mentioned, it is prefixed by the copulative.

In the examples above, the copulative '***ng-***' is prefixed to the agents '*u***profesa**' and '*um***qeqeshi**' to express '***by***' because these nouns belong to the '*u-*' and '*um-*' noun classes (Classes 1a & 1 respectively, cf. **Unit 4** for the copulatives of the other noun classes). As is the case in the active voice, there is **no '-ya-'** when another word follows the verb (cf. **Unit 2**).

Noteworthy features of the passive

Some verbs which are **only used in the passive:**

*uku***kholwa**	*to* **believe**
*uku***dinwa**	*to* **become tired**
*uku***nxanwa**	*to* **become thirsty**

Like the present tense, the recent past tense of the passive also has a **long** and **short** form:

*Aba***fundi** baqeqeshiwe.	The students **have been trained**.
*Aba***fundi** baqeqeshwe ***ngum*****qeqeshi**.	The students **have been trained** ***by*** the trainer.
Ndi**diniwe**.	I am **tired**.
Ndi**dinwe** kakhulu.	I am very **tired**.
Ndi**nxaniwe**.	I am **thirsty**.
Ndi**nxanwe** kakhulu.	I am very **thirsty**.

→ cf. **Unit 7 long** and **short** form of the **recent past tense** '*-ile*' / '*-e*'.

The passive '**-w-**' can also be used in combination with other verbal extensions:

Nda**nyus*el*wa**.	I was **promoted**. (lit. I **was made** to go up *for*)
Kuya ku**thethw*an*a** ngo*m***vuzo**.	**Salary** is **negotiable**. (lit. It will **be talked** about with *each other* about the salary.)

Insight

Some expressions incorporating the **passive** are virtually untranslatable into English, e.g.

Kuya**nxanwa**	(-**nxanwa** = become thirsty)
Kuyagodukwa*	(-**goduka** = go home)

*However, it is interesting to note that this construction exists in some other languages, e.g. German:

'Jetzt wird aber nach Hause gegangen.'

The negative form of the passive

Other than the **negative subject concord,** there is no indicator for the **negative of the passive voice,** i.e. no final -i as in the active voice:

Akaqeqesh**wa.**	He is **not** train**ed**.
Akaqeqeshwanga.	He was **not** train**ed.**

In the infinitive -**nga**- is inserted:

Kumnandi ukufun**wa**.	It is nice to **be** need**ed**.
Akumnandi uku**nga**fun**wa**.	It is not nice **not to be** need**ed**.

In colloquial speech, -**anga** is often suffixed to an adjective and relative adjectives:

Akumnand**anga** uku**nga**fun**wa**.	It is not nice **not to be** need**ed**.

→ See **Unit 15**

The negative passive is often used in notices of **restriction**, **restraint** or **forbiddance**:

*Aku***ngenwa**	*No* **entry**	(lit. It is **not** enter**ed**)
*Aku***tshaywa**	*No* **smoking**	(lit. It is **not** smok**ed**)
*Aku***miswa**	*No* **stopping**	(lit. It is **not** stopp**ed**)
*Aku***pakwa**	*No* **parking**	(lit. It is **not** park**ed**)
*Aku***hlalwa** engceni	*No* **sitting** on the grass	(lit. It is **not** seat**ed**)
*Aku***tyiwa** elayibhri	*No* **eating** in the library	(lit. It is **not** eat**en**)
*Aku***dadwa**	*No* **swimming**	(lit. It is **not** swum)

The **passive** form is reflected in some **nouns**:

*isi*thand**wa**	beloved (lit. the loved one)
*um*qesh**wa**	employee (lit. hired one)
*um*phathis**wa**	cabinet minister
*u*dliwano-ndlebe	interview
< *uku***dlana** *iin***dlebe**	'*to* **interview**'(lit. *to* **eat each other's ears**)

Note: **Consonant verbs of one syllable**, e.g. -dla > dl**iwa**; -tya > -ty**iwa** (be eaten) and **vowel verbs of two syllables**, e.g. -enz**iwa** = (been done, etc.) have **only one form** irrespective of whether they are followed by an agent or another word.

The **passive** form is also reflected in many **proper names** which are predominantly **girls' names**:

uBulel**wa**	(the one who is thanked for)
uVuyel**wa**	(the one who has been rejoiced for)
uVuyis**wa**	(the one who has been made to be joyful)
uXolis**wa**	(the one who is made satisfied)
uZolis**wa**	(the one who has calmed)
uBong**iwe**	(the one praise has been given for)
uLind**iwe**	(the one who has been waited for)
uLiz**iwe**	(the one who has been given as a gift)
uSiph**iwe**	(the one who has been given as a gift)
uSind**iwe**	(the one who has transcended)
uThand**iwe**	(the one who is loved)

Remember the omission of 'u-' when addressing someone directly:
Biza uLindiwe! = Call Lindiwe! BUT Molo Lindiwe! = Hello Lindiwe!

Some frequently used **idiomatic expressions** with the **passive** include:

Uphethwe ***yi*ntoni**?	**What**'s wrong with you? (lit. You **are ruled *by* what**?)
Ungenwe ***yi*ntoni**?	**What**'s got into you?
Ukhathazwa ***yi*ntoni**?	**What** worries you?
Ndiphelelwe ***li*themba**.	I've lost hope. (lit. **deprived *of***)
Ndiphelelwe ***ngum*sebenzi**.	I am unemployed.
Ndibonwa ***yi*ntoni**?	How lucky can I be? (lit. ***By* what** am I **seen**?)

Insight

Quoting **proverbs** (*ama***qhalo**) and **idioms** (*iz***aci**) in Xhosa, which are often drawn from animal life or related to fables (*iint***somi),** (see **Unit 16**) is a quintessential and much favoured way of epitomizing a situation and driving home a point. Their meaning may be varied to suit the occasion but their application to a specific situation is rarely in doubt.

'Akulula ukuba ufumane umXhosa eyigqiba intetho yakhe engakhange asebenzise isaci.'
(It is not easy to find a Xhosa person finishing his/her speech without using an idiom.)
(Professor SC Satyo (Igrama Noncwadi LwesiXhosa ibanga le-9 nele-10, Pretoria, Via Afrika Ltd, 1992, p. 215).

Many **proverbs** and **idioms** incorporate the **passive:**

'*In***dlovu** *ayi***sindwa** *ngom***boko** wa*yo.*'
(lit. The elephant **is not weighed down** by its trunk.)
i.e. No one ever finds his natural responsibilities too burdensome.

(This could very well be said when commiserating with someone who has a lot on their plate.)

'*In***yathi** *i***buzwa** *kwaba***phambili**'
(lit. The buffalo is asked [among the] first)
i.e. from the horse's mouth

'*Uku***zalwa** *wedwa ngum***lu** *wa***nyama**.'
(lit. *to* **be born** alone is to be a strip of meat)
i.e. one must have family/kinship

Some euphemistic idiomatic expressions incorporating the passive have to do with death:

*uku***fihlwa**	lit. *to* **be hidden**
*uku***goduswa**	lit. *to* **be taken home**
*uku***siwa**	lit. *to* **be taken** (to the fathers, i.e. ancestors)

When -**w**- follows certain consonants and consonant combinations, **sound (phonetic) changes** known as **palatalization** take place:

*uku***ngcwaba** = *to* **bury** > *uku***ngcwatywa** = *to* **be** buri**ed**

Some frequently used verbs which undergo this **sound change** are:

b > ty	**-gqiba**	**-gqitywa**	**be** finish**ed**
	-sebenzisa	**-setyenziswa**	**be** used
bh > j	**-bhubhela**	**-bhujelwa**	**be** bereav**ed** (lit. **be died for**)
m > ny	**-fumana**	**-funyanwa**	**be found**
	-phuma	**-phunywa**	lit. **be gone out**: kuphunywa apha 'exit'
mb > nj	**-hamba**	**-hanjwa**	lit. **be gone**: **kuhanjwa** ngoku
	-khumbula	**-khunjulwa**	**be** remember**ed**
ph > tsh	**-khupha**	**-khutshwa**	**be** take**n** out

Note: This **sound change** also occurs in **locatives** (cf. **Unit 4** and **Unit 6**): *i***hlobo** > *e***hlotyeni**

The same sound change occurs with **diminutive** forms which suffix **-ana**. Look at the map of Kirstenbosch in **Unit 9** where you will find diminutives of:

*isizi***ba** (pool) > *isizi***tyana** (**small** pool)
*i***chiba** (pond) > *i***chityana** (**small** pond)

2 How to express 'alone' / 'by itself' / 'special' / 'exclusive' = '-odwa'

Andihambi nd**edwa**/nd**odwa.**	I'm not going **alone**.
Asihambi **sedwa/sodwa**.	We are not going **alone**.
Uhamba **wedwa/wodwa**?	Are you going **alone**?
Nihamba **nedwa/nodwa**?	Are you (pl.) going **alone**?

To express I **am alone**, we **are alone** etc., simply prefix the appropriate subject concord:

Ndi**ndedwa**/Ndi**ndodwa** ekhaya.	I am **alone** at home.
Si**sedwa**/Si**sodwa** ekhaya.	We are **alone** at home.
U**wedwa** kowenu?	Are you **alone** at (your) home?
Ni**nedwa** / Ni**nodwa** kowenu?	Are you **alone** at (your) home?

In the 3rd person, '**-odwa**' is preceded by the consonant associated with the noun to which it refers, except for Class 1:

U**yedwa** kowabo.	He / she is **alone** at his / her home.
Ba**bodwa** *aba***ntwana** ekhaya.	The children are **alone** at home.

'**-odwa**' can also be used as a relative adjective, in which case it means '**special, exclusive**', and is therefore prefixed by the relative concord:

*um***sebenzi**	*ow***odwa**	a **special** activity
*imi***sebenzi**	*ey***odwa**	**special** activities
*i***yeza**	*elil***odwa**	**special** medicine
*ama***lungelo**	*aw***odwa**	**exclusive** rights
*isi***zathu**	*esis***odwa**	**special** reason
*izi***zathu**	*eziz***odwa**	**special** reasons
*in***jongo**	*ey***odwa**	**special** purpose
*u***dliwano**-*n***dlebe**	*olul***odwa**	**exclusive** interview
*ubu***chule**	*obub***odwa**	**special** skills
*uku***tya**	*okuk***odwa**	**special** food

Remember: In the case of nouns prefixing '*um-*' (Class 3) the associated consonant is '*w-*' and in the case of nouns prefixing '*imi-*' / *i-*' / '*in-*' /
'*im-*' the associated consonant is '*y-*'.

Note: No concord in Class 6 (*ama-*): *ama***Xhosa odwa**, but '-*w*-' is inserted between a relative concord and '**odwa**': *ama***lungelo** *awo***dwa**.

3 *The use of* 'ukuba' = '*to be*'

In the infinitive

Sonke sithanda uku**ba ne**thamsanqa.	We all like *to* **be** lucky. (lit. We all like to **be with** luck.)

In the future

Uza ku**ba ne**thuba *eli***lungile***yo*.	You **will have** a good chance. (lit. You will **be with** a good chance.)

In the remote past

Nda**ba ne**thamsanqa.	I **was** lucky. (lit. I **was with** luck.)

In the subjunctive

Ndinqwenela ukuba ndi**be ne**thamsanqa.	I wish that I **were** lucky. (lit. I wish that I **be with** luck.)
U**be ne**thamsanqa!	Good luck! (lit. You **be with** luck!)

Insight

The subject concord of **Class 1/1a nouns** '**ú**-' = '**he**'/'**she**' changes to '**a**-' after the **subjunctive:**

Ndinqwenela ukuba **a**be nethamsanqa.	= I wish him/her luck. (lit. I wish that **he/she** has luck.)
Kufuneka **a**be namava.	= **He/she** must have experience.
Khange **a**tsho.	= **He/she** never said so.
Soze **a**sele kwakhona.	= **He/she** will never drink again.

This change of subject concord of **Class 1/1a nouns** also occurs with '**-nga-**' = '**can**'/ '**may**':

Angandifowunela ngomso.	= He/she **can/may** phone me tomorrow (→ See **Unit 11**)

In the imperative (instructions)

*Yi*__ba ne__thamsanqa! — Good luck! (lit. __Be__ **with** luck!)

Note: When an adjective or relative adjective follows '*uku***ba**' = '*to* **be**', it is **not** preceded by a concord:

Ndiyathemba ukuba uza ku__ba__ __bhethele__ kamsinya.
I hope that you'll be better soon.

When a locative follows 'uku**ba**', the locative prefixes 's-':

Ndisenoku**ba** __s__emsebenzini — I could still **be** at work

4 How to express 'who'/'whom' in relative clauses

A **relative clause** is introduced by the **relative concord** of the noun concerned and is prefixed to the verb**.** This is well illustrated in the first four lines of a poem by Samuel Edward Krune Mqhayi **'Umfo Endimthandayo'** 'A Fellow Whom I Like', in the anthology *Indyebo Yesihobe*:

Ndithand' umf' ***o*hlamba** futhi,	I like a fellow ***who*** washes often,
Ndithand' umf' ***o*funda** futhi,	I like a fellow ***who*** studies often,
Ndithand' umf' ***o*lima** futhi,	I like a fellow ***who*** cultivates often,
Ndithand' umf' ***o*guqa** futhi,	I like a fellow ***who*** kneels often,

Now compare the fifth line of this verse:

Nanko k'umf' *__e__*ndi*__m__*thanda*yo*.' — That's the fellow ***__whom__*** I like (*him*)

In the **first four lines** '*um***fo** *__o__*- ...' = a fellow ***who*** ... , the **relative concord *o*-** connects the noun '*um***fo**' to the predicate '-**hlamba**' etc., of the **relative clause**.

In the **fifth line** '*um***f'** *e*ndi*m***thanda***yo*' = ***whom*** **I like** *him,* the **relative concord *e*-** is prefixed to '-ndi-' = '***whom*** I'* and introduces the *indirect* **relative clause** which is completed by the *object concord* '-*m*-' = '*him*'
*In the same way: *e*si- ***whom*** we / ***that*** we *e*ni- ***whom*** you / ***that*** you (pl.)

Some more examples of direct relative clauses

Abanye bafuna ukwazi iindawo *ezi***thandwa** ngabakhenkethi.	Some want to know places **which** are popular with tourists. (See exercise 5.1)
Ndithanda ukubhala ngezinto *ez***enzeka** imihla ngemihla.	I like to write about what happens every day. (lit.… about the things which happen – see exercise 5.3)

Some more examples of indirect relative clauses

Ningafaka yonke *in***to** *e*ni*yi***qokele***leyo* kwezi ngxowa.	You can put everything ***that*** you have **collected** (*it*) into these bags. (→ See **Unit 9**)
Kukho enye *in***to** ***o****yi***nqwenela***yo*?	Is there something else ***that*** you **want** (*it*)? (→ See **Unit 14**, exercise 4)

In the **negative -nga-** follows the subject concord:

*In***to** *e*ndi**nga***yi***thandi***yo* kukusebenza iiyure ezininzi.	The thing ***that*** I do **not like** (*it*) is to work many hours. (See exercise 5.2)

If the verb is followed by **'na-'**/ **'nga-'** or **'ku-'**, the **shortened emphatic pronoun** is added and there is **no object concord**:

Nd**amkela** *iin***dwendw**e xa zifika ndi*zi***bonise** *in***dlela** eziza ku**hlala** **nga***yo* ehotele	I welcome the guests on their arrival and show them their accommodation (lit. the way in which they will stay) in the hotel. (See exercise 5.1)
Thumela ii**referensi** *ezin*tathu zabantu *esi*nokuqhakamshelana **na***bo* ku ...	Send three references of people *with* **whom** *we* can get in touch, to … (lit. ***who*** we can get in touch *with* **them**, to…) (See exercise 6b)
Lo nguPhumla *endi*sebenza **na***ye*.	This is Phumla *with* **whom** ***I*** work (*with* **her**). (→ See **Unit 9**)

Note: The **suffix -yo** is added in relative clauses when the verb is in the final position or is stressed.

How to apply it

1 Match the public signs

The English equivalents are: (a) No Littering (b) Silence (c) No Dogs Allowed and (d) No Swimming Allowed.

1 Akuvunyelwa ukungena nezinja apha!
2 Akuthethwa
3 Akuvunyelwa ukuqubha!
4 Akungcoliswa

2 What is the literal meaning of the idioms and proverbs

(a) *Intlama idliwe yinja.* Things have gone wrong.
Lit.:____

(b) *Umhlaba ubethwe lilanga.* The soil is very dry.
Lit.:____

(c) *Abantwana bangenwe yintaka.* The children are frightened.
Lit.:____

(d) *Kuhanjwa ngesiko.* It's done according to custom.
Lit.:____

(e) *Le nto yaphelelwa lixesha.* This is old fashioned.
Lit.:____

(f) *Ubunzulu besiziba* (deep pool in river)
buviwa ngodondolo (stick)! Look before you leap!
Lit.:____

3 Give the English equivalent of newspaper / magazine columns

Okuxelwa ziinkwenkwezi (What is told by the stars)____________
Abakhunjulwayo (Who are remembered) ____________________

4 Reading, understanding and answering questions

Read the conversation between Themba and Mary at work and answer the questions that follow:

UThemba	Molo Mary, uphila njani namhlanje?
UMary	Ewe Themba. Sikhona. Wena?
UThemba	Hayi, nam ndisaphila ngaphandle komsebenzi. Kanene, uzifihle phi? *(Where have you hidden yourself?)* Andikubonanga ixesha elide.
UMary	Bendinekhefu elimnandi *(I had a nice holiday)* nosapho lwam.
UThemba	Unethamsanqa! Ndixelele ngekhefu lakho. Masiye ekhefi siphunge.
UMary	Kulungile. Andi<u>ka</u>lifumani ixesha lokuphunga. *(I have not <u>yet</u> found the time)* Masiye ke.
UThemba	Unjani umsebenzi wakho? Usawuvuyela? Kanene unyuselwe, ndiyavuyisana nawe! Usebenzile!
UMary	Enkosi, kodwa kunzima ngamanye amaxesha. Linqabile ixesha. Ndisoloko ndixakekile.
UThemba	Ndim lowo *(same here)*. Lunjani usapho?

UMary	Sonke siphilile. Banjani abantwana nenkosikazi yakho?
UThemba	Basaphila nabo. Yho! Jonga ixesha! Mandikhawulezise *(Let me hurry)* okanye ndiza kuphoswa yintlanganiso. *(lit. I will be missed by the meeting.)*
UMary	Ewe, kufuneka nam ndihambe. Sobabini sishiywe lixesha.
UThemba	Bekumnandi ukuphunga nawe. Sobonana kwakhona.
UMary	Kulungile. Sebenza kakuhle. Undibulisele kuThandi nabantwana.
UThemba	Enkosi. Ube nempela-veki emnandi.

(a) UThemba noMary bancokola phi?
(b) Baphila njani?
(c) Baya phi ukuze bancokole kancinci?
(d) UThemba uvuyisana noMary. Kutheni?
(e) UThemba uza kuya phi?

5 Who's who?

Three people describe what their work entails. They are:

(a)	a chef (cook)	umpheki
(b)	a journalist	intatheli
(c)	a receptionist in a hotel	ireceptionist yehoteli

Match the job description with the job:

1 Ininzi into ekufuneka ndiyenze! Mandinichazele ngomsebenzi wam. Ndisebenza eFront-Office. Ndamkela iindwendwe xa zifika ndizibonise indlela eziza kuhlala ngayo ehotele. Ndisebenza noosomashishini beli lizwe nabamanye amazwe ngokunjalo nabakhenkethi. Lo msebenzi unobunzima gqitha ngamanye amaxesha. Abanye abatyeleli bakhalaza kakhulu, kufuneka ukuba ndizisombulule kwaye zonke izikhalazo. Abanye bafuna ukwazi iindawo ezithandwa ngabakhenkethi, imeko yelizwe njalo, njalo. Kufuneka ukuba ndibanike iingcombolo ezichanekileyo. Ndisenokuba semsebenzini xa abanye abantu belele okanye bezonwabisa.

QUICK VOCAB

-chazela	explain (to)	imeko (ii-)	situation
undwendwe (iin-)	guest	ingcombolo (iin-)	information
-sombulula	solve	-chanekileyo	precise
kwaye	and	*xa ... belele	when ... are asleep
isikhalazo (izi-)	complaints		

* → See **Unit 12**

Ndi __________ .

2 Kuqala ndasebenza kwikhitshi lenkampani enkulu, kodwa ngoku ndisebenza ehotele enkulu. Ndilungisa imenyu. Ndi-odola ukutya ndiqeqeshe ndiphathe abasebenzi basekhitshini. Ndinomdla ebantwini nasekulungiseni izidlo. Ndithanda ukusebenza kwindawo enomdla, kodwa into endingayithandiyo ngamanye amaxesha kukusebenza iiyure ezininzi neeshifti. Ezo zinto zindenza ndizive ndicinezelekile

-odola	order	iiyure	hours	QV
isidlo (izi-)	meal	ezo zinto	those things	
into endingayithandiyo	*what I do not like	-cinezelekile	be stressed	

* → See **Unit 16**

Ndi ____________ .

3 Ndithanda ukudibana nabantu nokuthetha nabo nokubaphulaphula. Ndithanda ukubhala amanqaku ngabantu nangezinto ezenzeka imihla ngemihla. Ndenza uphando ngebali lam ndilibhale kwikhompyutha yam. Ndisebenza yonke imihla iiyure ezininzi kwanangempela-veki.

-phulaphula	listen	inqaku (ama-)	article	QV
uphando	research			

Ndi ____________ .

6 Read and understand

With the help of the vocabulary you should be able to understand the following advertisements (*iz***aziso**):

(a) ***KUFUNWA UNONTLALO-NTLE***

Umbutho wenu ufuna inkonzo yomntu ozondelelayo onokusebenza nzima ekukhuseleni abantwana.
Izinto ezifunekayo kanye ngamava ekugcineni abantwana, iphepha lokuqhuba nokukwazi ukuthetha isiXhosa.
Ukukwazi ukuthetha nesiNgesi nesiBhulu kakuhle kuyanceda kakhulu.
Kuya kuthethwana ngomvuzo ngokwamava awo omsebenzi. Uthumele iCV neereferensi ezintathu zabantu esinokuqhagamshelana nabo, nencwadi yokucela umsebenzi ku_______. Umhla wokuvala isicelo ngu____.

QV			
umbutho (imi-)	organization	umvuzo (imi-)	salary
inkonzo	service	-qhagamshelana na-	contact
-zondelelayo	energetic	umhla wokuvala	closing date
-thumela	send to	isicelo	application
-khusela	protect		

Note: The **non-anglicized expression** for '*i***referensi**':

*in***cwadi** e***ndi*****ncoma***yo* = letter that praises *me,* i.e. my **reference**
*in***cwadi** e***ku*****ncoma***yo* = letter that praises *you,* i.e. your **reference**

(b) ***KUFUNWA IRECEPTIONIST / UNOBHALA***

Indawo enkulu ebalulekileyo ethengisa ikhande iimoto ifuna ireceptionist / unobhala okhutheleyo.
Kufuneka umceli-msebenzi abe nobuchule obulandelayo:*

- *bokusebenza ngekhompyutha*
- *bokubhala nokuthumela iincwadi zetyala*
- *bokubhala nokusabela zonke iincwadi*
- *bokuthetha nabantu*
- *bokwazi ukuthetha isiXhosa nesiNgesi nesiBhulu.*

Kufuneka kanjalo abe namava ekusebenzeni njengereceptionist.*
Umsebenzi umzekelo ngulo:

- *ukusabela ifowuni nemibuzo*
- *ukwamkela abaveleli*
- *ukubhala nokuthumela iincwadi*
- *ukugcina zonke izinto zokubhala namaphepha*
- *ukulungiselela iintlanganiso*

Thumela ngefaksi iCV neereferensi ezintathu zabantu esinokuqhagamshelana nabo ku__________.

QUICK VOCAB			
-khanda	repair	-sabela	answer
-khutheleyo	diligent	umveleli	visitor
kufuneka abe* na-	she must have	izinto zokubhala namaphepha	stationery
ubuchule	skill(s)		
iincwadi zetyala	accounts		
*See Unit 10.3			

7 Translate the expressions that characterize people

(a) umntu olungileyo ___________
(b) umntu ombi ___________
(c) umntu onomdla ___________
(d) umntu onesibindi ___________ (cf. **Unit 8**, first Insight box)
(e) umntu othandayo ___________
(f) umntu ozondelelayo ___________
(g) umntu onolwazi ___________
(h) umntu onobubele ___________
(i) umntu oyedwa ___________
(j) umntu onamava ___________
(k) umntu ozolileyo ___________
(l) umntu okhutheleyo ___________
(m) umntu odumileyo ___________
(n) umntu oxakekileyo ___________

Test yourself

1. How do you say: 'We need a chef' and 'A chef is needed'?
2. What is the sound change that occurs when '**-w-**' comes into proximity with certain consonants and consonant combinations in the passive voice?
3. What is the passive form of monosyllabic verbs and vowel verbs, e.g. -**tya**, -**enza**?
4. 'Exit' = 'Kuphunywa apha'. What is the infinitive of '-phunywa'?
5. How do you say:
   'The students asked many questions.'
   'Many questions were asked by the students.'
6. Tell someone: 'I am unemployed.'
7. Give the English equivalent of the following notices of restriction or forbiddance:
   Akungenwa Akutshaywa Akupakwa Akudadwa
8. How do you say: 'I prefer to go **alone**.' '**I am alone** at home.'
9. How do you say: 'I am lucky' and 'I was lucky'.
10. How do you wish someone good luck?

If you have done all exercises and answered the questions above correctly, then you are well prepared to proceed to the next unit.

11 Ndingathetha noMnumzana Thamsanqa?

May I speak to Mr Thamsanqa?

In this unit you will learn how to:

- communicate on the telephone
- make arrangements to meet, including place and time

Incoko

CD 2, tr 2

Peter phones Themba to make arrangements to meet at the cricket.

UPeter	Hello, ndingathetha noMnumzana Thamsanqa? Ingaba ukhona?
UNobhala	Ndingabuza ukuba ngubani ofuna ukuthetha naye?
UPeter	Ewe, nguPeter Murray lo uthethayo.
UNobhala	Khawubambe njalo, Mnumzana Murray. Ndiza kubona ukuba ukhona na phaya e-ofisini yakhe.
UPeter	Kulungile.

After a few minutes …

UNobhala	Mnumzana Murray, ndilusizi, uMnumzana Thamsanqa akakho okwangoku. Usaphumile.
UPeter	Uyazi ukuba uza kufika nini na?
UNobhala	Ndilusizi, khange atsho. Ungathanda ukushiya umyalezo?
UPeter	Ewe, uze umxelele ukuba ndifuna ukuqhakamshelana naye malunga neqakamba yangomso. Mhlawumbi angandifowunela ekhaya ngokuhlwa.
UNobhala	Kulungile Mnumzana Murray. Ndiza kumxelela. Ngubani inombolo yefowuni yakho?
UPeter	Ngu 531–3767.
UNobhala	Kulungile, Mnumzana Murray.
UPeter	Ndiyabulela. Bye.
UNobhala	Bye, Mnumzana Murray.

Themba returns Peter's call that evening. David answers the phone.

UDavid	David Murray speaking.
UThemba	Hello, David. Kunjani, mfondini?
UDavid	Oo, molo Mnumzana Thamsanqa. Ndiphilile, enkosi. Wena?
UThemba	Hayi, sikhona. Ingaba utata ukhona?
UDavid	Ewe. Yima kancinci. Ndiza kumbiza.

After exchanging pleasantries, Peter and Themba continue their conversation.

UThemba	Molo Peter. NguThemba kweli cala. Enkosi ngokufowuna. Ngelishwa bendisentlanganisweni imini yonke! Ndiwufumene umyalezo wakho sekuhlwile.
UPeter	Ayinamsebenzi loo nto. Ndiyazi ukuba uxakekile!
UThemba	Siza kudibana ngabani ixesha ngomso?
UPeter	Kunjani ngo-9.30?
UThemba	Kulungile. Phi?
UPeter	Phambi kwesango elikhulu.
UThemba	Kulungile, siza kuba lapho ngo-9.30. Sobonana!
UPeter	Sobonana!

The next morning Thandi phones Jenny.

UJenny	Hello!
UThandi	Hello, ndingathetha noNkosikazi Murray?
UJenny	Molo Thandi, ndim!
UThandi	Oo uxolo sithandwa sam, khange ndilichane ilizwi lakho! Unantoni na?
UJenny	Awu, ndinomkhuhlane kancinci phofu!
UThandi	Oo, ndiluzisi. Ndikufowunela kuba mna noThemba siya kwirestyu entsha yezakwaNtu ngokuhlwa ngoMgqibelo. Sifuna ukunimema wena noPeter. Ningeza? Ucinga ukuba uza kuba sele ubhetele?
UJenny	Oo, ingantle loo nto. Bendifunda ngaloo restyu kwiphephandaba ngempela-veki ephelileyo. Ndatsho *ndavuz' izinkcwe*! Ukutya kwayo kwandikhumbuza ubuntwana bam. Sasizitya zonke ezo zinto zakwaNtu efama!
UThandi	Heke, mandikulande ukuze sidibane noPeter noThemba erestyu emva komdlalo weqakamba.
UJenny	Ungaba undincedile, sithandwa. Sobonana!

QUICK VOCAB

Isigama

okwangoku	at the moment	sithandwa sam	my dear
-bamba	hold on	-chana	recognize
-shiya	leave		(lit. be accurate)
umyalezo	message	ilizwi	voice
uze	you should	phofu	though
-qhakamshelana na-	get in touch with	zakwaNtu	traditional
malunga na-	about	-mema	invite
ngokuhlwa	in the evening	bendifunda	I was reading
inombolo	number	*ndavuz' izinkcwe*	*it made my mouth water*
kweli cala	on this side	-khumbuza	remind
bendisentlanganisweni	I was at a meeting	ubuntwana	childhood
sekuhlwile	already evening	-landa	fetch
isango	gate		

CULTURE SHOCK Parliament was recently treated to a scene seldom seen in Cape Town when the Masizakhe Cultural Group of Lady Grey in the Eastern Cape, resplendent in their traditional dress, took a tour of the legislature. But the pastoral illusion was rudely shattered when this lady's cellular phone rang.

(Courtesy *Cape Times* 8/5/1996. Photo: Benny Gool)

How to ...

Communicate on the telephone when you are *making* the call

*Ng*u __________ *o***theth***ayo*.
*Ng*u____________ kw*eli* **cala**.
Nding**athetha noMnumzana** _________ / no*N***kosikazi**________, nceda.
Ndi**cela** uku**thetha noMnumzana** _________ / no*N***kosikazi**
__________.
Oo, *u***xolo**, **khange** ndi*li***chane** *ili***zwi** lakho!
Ukhona *uM***numzana** _____________?
Ukhona *u***Nkosikazi** _______________?
U*m***lindele nini**?
Ung**anceda** u*ndi***fake** kwi-**ofisi** ka*M***numzana** ___________?
Nding*awu***shiya** *um***yalezo**?
Ndiza ku*m***fowunela** kwa**khona**.

Communicate on the telephone when you are *answering* the call

Ndi**thetha nabani**?
Nding**abuza**, ***ng*ubani** *o***theth***ayo*?
Nding*am***xelela *ng*ubani** *o***funa** uku**thetha na***ye*?
Khawubambe njalo.
*Yi***ma** kancinci, ndiza ku*m***biza**.
*Yi***ma** kancinci, ndiza ku**khangela** ukuba u**khona** na.
Ndi**lusizi** *aka***kho** okwangoku.
Usa**phum***ile*.
Us*en***tlanganis***weni*.
U**xakek***ile* komnye *um***nxeba**. Unga**thanda** uku**bamba**?
Nding**athatha** *um***yalezo**?
Ukhona *um***yalezo**?
Unga*wu***shiya** *um***yalezo**?

Make arrangements to meet

Siza ku**dibana ngabani** *i***xesha**? **Phi**?
Kunjani ngo-9?
Ndiza ku**dibana na***we* phambi kwe**sango** *eli***khulu**.

Ndiza ku**dibana na***we* phambi kwe**restyu**.
Ndiza ku*ku***landa** ngo-7.
Uze u**ncede** u**fike** nge**xesha**.
Unga**fiki***i* emva kwe**xesha**!

Insight

There are a number of **idioms** related to **time**:

Ixesha lixhatshwe yinja*	It's late.	(lit. Time has been lapped up by the do
Xa kumpondo zankomo	Very early in the morning.	(lit. When the horns of the cattle are just visible)
Xa libantu bahle	In the early evening/ twilight.	(lit. When people are beautiful, i.e. blemishes are less obvious!)
Ngolwemivundla	In the early evening/ dusk.	(lit. At the time that rabbits come out of their warrens)

*< -xhapha = lap up

Ask whether you may use someone's phone

Nding**asebenzisa** *i***fowuni** yakho, *N***kosikazi** / *M***numzana**?

Ask where the nearest public phone is

Iphi *i***fowuni** ka**wonke-wonke** *e***kufutshane**?

Ask to borrow a telephone directory

Ndi**funa** *i***nombolo**. Nding**aboleka** *i***directory** yakho ye**fowuni**?

How it works

1 More expressions incorporating 'ng-' (copulative)

'It *is* **who** *who*'... ? = '*N***g**u**bani** *o*- ...'?:

*N***g**u**bani** o**thetha***yo*?
*N***g**u**bani** o**funa** uku**thetha na***ye*?
*N***g**uPeter Murray o**thetha***yo*?

'*Ng*ubani' with other expressions, translating '**What** *is*?':

Ng*ubani** *ixesha**?	**What** *is* the **time**?
Ng*ubani** *igama** lakho?	**What** *is* your **name**?
Ng*ubani** *ifani** yakho?	**What** *is* your **surname**?

2 Copulatives with emphatic pronouns

ndim	It ***is*** *me*	***ng**uye*	(*um***ncedisi**)	It ***is*** *him / her*
sithi	It ***is*** *us*	***ng**abo*	(*aba***ncedisi**)	It ***is*** *them*
***ng**uwe*	It ***is*** *you* (s.)	***ng**uwo*	(*um***sebenzi**)	It ***is*** *it*
nini	It ***is*** *you* (pl.)	***y**iyo*	(*i***fowuni**)	It ***is*** *it*, etc.

3 '-khona' = 'there' (be present)

Like '**apha**' / '**apho**' = '**here**' / '**there**' (cf. **Unit 5**), '**khona**' can be used as an adverb:

Usebenza **khona**.	She works **there**/at that place.
Siza kuba **khona** ngo-9.30.	We'll be **there** at 9.30.

It can also be used **with a subject concord**:

Ukhona *u***Themba**?	Is Themba **there**?
Ewe, **ukhona**.	Yes, he (is) **there**.
Ikhona *i***fowuni**?	Is **there** a **phone**?
Ewe, **ikhona**.	Yes, it (is) **there**.
Lukhona *u***siba**?	Is **there** a **pen**?
Ewe, lu**khona**.	Yes, it (is) **there**.
Ikhona *i***pensile**?	Is **there** a **pencil**?
Ewe, **ikhona**.	Yes, it (is) **there**.

'**-kho**' (without -na) is used in impersonal expressions – '**Ku**kho...':

Kukho iphepha?	Is **there** paper?
Ewe, ku**kho** iphepha etafileni.	Yes, **there** is paper on the table.
Kukho imiyalezo?	Are **there** messages?
Ewe, ku**kho** imiyalezo.	Yes, **there** are messages.

In the negative '**-khona**' > '**-kho**':

Ukhona *u***Themba**?	Hayi, *aka***kho**.
Ukhona *um***sebenzi**?	Hayi, *awu***kho**.
Ikhona *i***fowuni**?	Hayi, *ayi***kho**.
Ikhona *i***pensile**?	Hayi, *ayi***kho**.
Lu**khona** *u***siba**?	Hayi, *alu***kho**.

4 *More about adverbs and equivalents of English prepositions*

As already mentioned, there are **simple adverbs** like **apha** (here), **apho** (there), **phaya** (over there).

Some adverbs are also formed by prefixing:
ka-: **ka**kuhle (well) **ku**-: **ku**dala (long ago) **nga:**- **nga**kumbi (especially) (cf. **Unit 4** and **Unit 6**)

Adverbs with (nga) **pha**-	Followed by **kwa-** function as **Prepositions**
phambili = **in front**, **forward**	**phambi** kwa- = in front **of** / before
Hamba **phambili**! (Walk **in front**!) Wakhe wambona **ngaphambili?** (Have you ever seen him **before?**) (cf. **Unit 8**)	Dibana nam **phambi kwe**restyu. (Meet me **in front of** the restaurant.) Masitye **phambi ko**kuba siye efilimu. (Let's eat **before** we go to the film.)
phantsi = **down**, below	**phantsi kwa**- = under
Jonga **phantsi**! (Look **down**!) Thethela **phantsi**! (Speak softly! i.e. keep your voice **down**.)	Khangela **phantsi kw**etafile. (Look **under** the table.)
phezulu = **up**, above, on top	**phezu kwa- =** on top **of**
Jonga **phezulu**! (Look **up**!) **Ingaphezulu** incwadi? (Is the book on top?) Hayi, i**ngaphantsi.** (No, it's **underneath**.)	Khangela **phezu kwe**khabhathini. (Look **on top of** the cupboard.)
ngaphakathi = inside	**phakathi kwa**- = between/among
Yiya **ngaphakathi**! (Go **inside**!)	**Phakathi kwa**m nawe . . . (**Between** you and me …) Uyinkwenkwe yedwa **phakathi kwa**mantombazana! (He is the only boy **among** the girls.)

ngaphandle = outside

Kuyabanda **ngaphandle**.
(It's cold **outside**.)

ngaphandle kwa- = outside of/besides/without

Ndilindele **ngaphandle kwe**restyu.
(Wait for me **outside** the restaurant.)
Ngaphandle kokuthetha isiXhosa, uthetha nesiSuthu.
(**Besides** speaking Xhosa he/she also speaks Sotho.)
Akunakho ukuloba **ngaphandle kwe**mvume. (You cannot fish **without** a permit.)

Other prepositions followed by **kwa-:**

emva kwa- = after/behind

Masidibane **emva ko**mdlalo. (Let us meet **after** the game.)
Masidibane **emva kwe**filimu. (Let us meet **after** the film.)
Jonga **emva kwe**milengalenga. (**Look** behind the curtain.)

ecaleni kwa- = at the side **of**, next to

Yiza uhlale **ecaleni kwam**. (Come and sit **next to** me.)

phesheya = overseas

Ndiza kuhambela **phesheya** kunyaka ozayo.
(I am going **overseas** next year.)

phesheya kwa- = across, on the other side

Umhlobo wam uvela **phesheya kwe**Nciba.
(My friend comes **from** Transkei)
(lit. across the Kei River)

5 Numerals

You are already familiar with the numerals 1–6 (cf. **Unit 6**):

*um***ntwana**	*om***nye**	*in***cwadi**	*e***nye**
*aba***ntwana**	*aba***bini**	*iin***cwadi**	*ezim***bini***
*aba***ntwana**	*aba***thathu**	*iin***cwadi**	*ezin***tathu**†
*aba***ntwana**	*aba***ne**	*iin***cwadi**	*ezi***ne**
*aba***ntwana**	*aba***hlanu**	*iin***cwadi**	*ezin***tlanu**
*aba***ntwana**	*aba***thandathu**	*iin***cwadi**	*ezin***tandathu**

The **sound changes** caused by 'n' in the **adjectival concord** '*ezin*'-:
*b influences a preceding 'n': n + b > **mb**, † n + th > **nt**, n + hl > **ntl**, n + **n** > **n**. (→ See Summary of Sound Changes in **Unit 16**)

Numerals 6–10 are **nouns** (not adjectival stems like 1–6):

isi**xhenxe**:	_aba_**ntwana**	_abasi_**xhenxe**	7	(lit. which are **7**)
isi**bhozo**:	_aba_**ntwana**	_abasi_**bhozo**	8	(lit. which are **8**)
_i_**thoba**:	_aba_**ntwana**	_abali_**thoba**	9	(lit. which are **9**)
_i_**shumi**:	_aba_**ntwana**	_abali_**shumi**	10	(lit. which are **10**)

Numerals from 11 onwards are more complex than their English equivalents, but luckily for learners, even Xhosa speakers often use the English numerals above 10.

You might like to know:

100	=	_i_**khulu** (_ama-_)
1,000	=	_i_**waka** (_ama-_)
1,000,000	=	_isi_**gidi**

Can you work out what '_u_**sozigidi**' (_oo-_) means?

Ordinal numbers 1–10:

-_oku_**qala**	_um_**ntwana** _woku_**qala**	1st
isi**bini**	_um_**ntwana** _wesi_**bini**	2nd
isi**thathu**	_um_**ntwana** _wesi_**thathu**	3rd
isi**ne**	_um_**ntwana** _wesi_**ne**	4th
isi**hlanu**	_um_**ntwana** _wesi_**hlanu**	5th
isi**thandathu**	_um_**ntwana** _wesi_**thandathu**	6th
isi**xhenxe**	_um_**ntwana** _wesi_**xhenxe**	7th
isi**bhozo**	_um_**ntwana** _wesi_**bhozo**	8th
isi**thoba**	_um_**ntwana** _wesi_**thoba**	9th
isi**shumi**	_um_**ntwana** _wesi_**shumi**	10th

Insight

Expressing the time in Xhosa is difficult. Even mother-tongue speakers often express the time using English numerals, especially in informal conversation. However, the time is given on Xhosa radio using Xhosa numerals, mainly at news time.

To ask what ***is*** the **time,** you say:

_Ngu_bani _i_xesha?	(lit. **Who** is the **time**?) or
L_i_thini _i_xesha?	(lit. It says **what** the **time**?)

To reply using **English numerals** for on the hour, you say:

Ngu-1 / 2 / 3 / 4 / 5	It's 1 / 2 / 3 / 4 / 5 **o'clock**, etc

To reply using **Xhosa numerals** for on the hour, you say:
*Yin***tsimbi** yo*ku***qala**/ye*si***bini**/ye*si***thathu**/ye*si***ne**/ye*si***hlanu**.
It's the **1st/2nd/3rd/4th bell**.
To ask **at** what **time**, you say:

Ngabani *i***xesha**? **At** what time?

To reply using **English numerals** for on the hour, you say:

Ngo-1/2/3/4/5 **At** 1 / 2 / 3 / 4 / 5 **o'clock**, etc.
Ukususela **ngo-**1 ukuya kutsho **ngo**-3. From 1–3 o'clock.

To reply using **Xhosa numerals** for on the hour, you say:

Nge*n***tsimbi** yo*ku***qala**/ye*si***bini**/ ye*si***thathu**/ye*si***ne**/ e*si***hlanu.**	**At** the **1st/2nd**/**3rd**/ **fourth bell.**

When it comes to expressing the time **other than on the hour**, English numerals are used – even in more formal situations, e.g.:

'*Y*ikota past **6**' is easier and quicker to say than:
'***Yimi*zuzu** *eli***shumi** *eli*na**ntlanu** emva kwe*n***tsimbi** ye*si***thandathu**' (lit. It is **minutes** *which **are*** **ten which** have **five** after the **bell** of **six**)

And

'**Nge**haf past **2**' is easier and quicker to say than: '**Ngecala** emva kwe*n***tsimbi** ye*si***bini** (lit. **At** past the **side** after the **bell** of **two**).

6 Expressions such as 'irestyu yezakwaNtu'

There are many expressions like this in Xhosa, i.e. incorporating a **double possessive**, for example 'irestyu **yeza**kwaNtu', the full form of which is irestyu **ya** + **i**zinto + **za** + kwaNtu = irestyu **ye**zinto **za**kwaNtu (a restaurant **of** things **of** tradition). However, this full form is contracted to irestyu **ya** + '**i**' of **i**zinto + **za** + kwaNtu = irestyu y**eza**kwaNtu.

Here are some other examples you may come across:

Umhleli w**eze**midlalo	sports editor
Umhleli w**ezo**politiko	political editor
Umcebisi w**ezo**mthetho	legal adviser
Umphathiswa w**eza**ngaphandle	minister of foreign affairs
Umphathiswa w**eze**mfundo	minister of education
Umphathiswa w**ezo**limo	minister of agriculture
Abalimi b**eze**khaya	home gardeners (lit. cultivators of the home)

7 '-ni?' = '*what*', *shortened form of* 'ntoni?'

When the shortened form of '**ntoni**?' = '-**ni**?' is used it must be suffixed to the verb:

Ufuna **ntoni**?	**What** do you want?
Ufuna**ni**?	**What** do you want?
Wenza **ntoni**?	**What** are you doing?
Wenza**ni**?	**What** are you doing?
Kwenzeke **ntoni**?	**What** happened?
Kwenzeke**ni**?	**What** happened?

Insight

Some idiomatic expressions incorporating the verb '-**thi**' = '**say**':

Lithi**ni** ixesha?	**What** is the time?
Ndingathi**ni**?	**How** do I go about this?
Bekuthe**ni**?	**What** happened?
Uthe**ni** na wena?	**What**'s the matter with you?

How to apply it

1 Answer the questions

(a) UThemba ukhona? Hayi, ________________.

(b) Uza kuba khona ngo-4? Hayi, ________________.

(c) Uza kubuya kamsinya? Hayi, __________namhlanje.

(d) UPeter use-ofisini? Hayi, ______, _____ekhaya.

(e) Ukhona umyalezo? Hayi, ________________.

(f) Ikhona ifowuni kawonke-wonke ekufutshane? Hayi, ________________.

2 Complete the dialogue

Hello, (a) ______________ (*can I speak*) noMnumzana Thamsanqa?

(b) _________________, (*I'm sorry*) uxakekile komnye umnxeba. Khawubambe njalo.

After some minutes.

UMnu Thamsanqa (c) ____________ (*is still busy*). Ungathanda ukubamba okanye ungathanda (d) __________________ (*leave a message*)?

Ewe, (e) ______________________________(*tell him that I will try to phone him again in the afternoon*).
Enkosi. Kamnandi.

3 Give the dialogue a title

UDavid	Hullo, nguDavid kweli cala. Ndingathetha noVuyo?
Ilizwi	Eh, uVuyo? Akukho Vuyo apha. Ufuna eyiphi inombolo?
UDavid	Ndifuna i-633-4253.
Ilizwi	Hayi, ndilusizi, lo ngu-633-4352.
UDavid	Khawuphinde. Yintoni inombolo yefowuni yakho?
Ilizwi	Ngu-633-4352.
UDavid	Owu, uxolo, yinombolo ewrongo.

4 Read, understand and answer the questions

See how well you have understood the dialogue by answering the questions that follow:

Bongile is looking for a job during the holidays.

UMncedisi	Molo, kukwaBizo's Takeaway. Ndingakunceda?
UBongile	Ngaba ndingamfumana uNksk. Bizo?
UMncedisi	Akakho. Usaphumile okwangoku. Ungashiya umyalezo?
UBongile	Kulungile. Ndive ukuba ufuna umntu oza kuncedisa kwishishini lakhe. Ndifuna ukwenza isicelo. Ubuya nini?
UMncedisi	Andiqinisekanga.
UBongile	Ndingaphinda ndifowune nini?
UMncedisi	Zama ukufowuna ngentsimbi yesithandathu. Khawushiye igama lakho nenombolo.
UBongile	Igama lam nguBongile Thamsanqa. Unokunditsalela kule nombolo ithi 770555.
UMncedisi	Mandiliphinde igama. UnguBongile Thamsanqa. Inombolo ithi 770555.
UBongile	Kulungile. Enkosi. Usale kakuhle.
UMncedisi	Kamnandi.

(a) UBongile ufuna ukuthetha nabani?
(b) UNksk. Bizo ukhona?
(c) UBongile ushiya owuphi umyalezo?
(d) Uza kuzama ukufowuna ngeyiphi intsimbi?

5 Read the conversation

UVal	Molo Xoliswa.
UXoliswa	Molo sisi. Nisaphila phofu?
UVal	Hayi, siphilile sonke. Ndiyakufowunela kuba ndingathanda ukubuza ukuba sinokudibana na kwakhona. Kunjani ngokuya kubukela ifilimu?
UXoliswa	Eyiphi ifilimu?
UVal	Singabukela 'u*Jump the Gun*'.
UXoliswa	Ngeyiphi imini?
UVal	NgoLwesine?
UXoliswa	Hayi, andizi kuba kho ngoLwesine. Kunjani ngo-Mgqibelo?
UVal	Hayi, uMgqibelo akalungi kum. Uza kuphumelela ngeCawa?
UXoliswa	Kulungile.
UVal	Ufuna ndikuphuthume ngabani ixesha?
UXoliswa	Ngentsimbi yesihlanu.
UVal	Kulungile. Siza kubonana ke ngeCawa. Sala kakuhle.
UXoliswa	Kamnandi.

Imagine that Xoliwsa tells another friend about her chat with Val:

(a) I spoke to Val today.

__________________________________.

(b) We are going to see a film on Sunday.

______________________.

(c) Can you come with us? __________________________________.

(d) Val is going to fetch me at 5 o'clock.

______________________.

6 Say you have

(a) three children, two daughters and a son
(b) four messages
(c) two telephone numbers
(d) five tickets
(e) six letters

7 Listen to the dialogue and say whether the statements are correct or not

CD 2, tr 2, 05:25

(a) Thandi is in a hurry.	yes	no
(b) She has to go shopping.	yes	no

(c)	She prepares a party for Friday.	yes	no
(d)	She only invites Nomsa and Sipho.	yes	no
(e)	Nomsa has to ask Sipho first.	yes	no

8 English equivalents of newspaper / magazine section headings

Use the headings: (a) For the Children (b) Health Matters (c) Business (d) Finance (e) Sport (f) Entertainment (g) For Teenagers and (h) Education.

1 Ezemidlalo
2 Ezempilo
3 Ezolutsha
4 Ezoshishino
5 Ezolonwabo
6 Ezabantwana
7 Ezemfundo
8 Ezemali

9 Complete the questions

(a) Ndithetha ________?
(b) _________ othethayo?
(c) Ufuna ______?
(d) Ufuna _______ inombolo?
(e) _______ igama lakho?
(f) _______ inombolo yakho yasekhaya?
(h) _______ inombolo yakho yasemsebenzini?
(i) _______ i-adelesi yakho?
(j) Ndingakwenzela _______?
(k) Ndingakunceda __________?
(l) ________ ingxaki?
(m) Kwenzeke ________?

10 Which verb fits?

Use these verbs to fit the spaces correctly (a) -bamba (b) -shiya (c) -cothisisa (d) -phinda and (e) -faka.

1 Uxolo, andiva kakuhle, unga_________ kwakhona?
2 Ungathanda uku________ umyalezo?
3 Ungandi________ kwi-ofisi kaMnu. Bizo?
4 Usaxakekile komnye umnxeba. Ungathanda uku_________?
5 Uthetha ngokukhawuleza kakhulu. Unga_______________?

Test yourself

1. What is the literal translation of '**Ngubani** *o***thethayo**?' What clause is characterized by the verbal suffix **-yo**?
2. There are **two** expressions that translate 'What's the time?' What are they?
3. What is the difference between '**Ngubani** ixesha' and '**Ngabani** ixesha'?
4. '**-khona'** can be used as an **adverb** like 'apha' and with a subject concord. Translate the following to show the difference: 'Themba works **here**.' 'Is Themba **here**?'
5. How do you say: 'No, he is **not here**'?
6. What is the difference in meaning between *om***nye** *um***ntwana** and *um***ntwana** *om***nye**?
7. Are **numerals 1-10** all adjectives?
8. Some adverbs function as prepositions when followed by **kwa**-. Tell someone to sit **down**. Tell someone that you found the key **under** the table.
9. There are many expressions (especially in newspaper headlines) with a double nominal possessive, e.g. '*um***hleli** we<u>z</u>e*mi***dlalo**' = 'sports editor', '*um***hleli** wez*o***politiko**' = 'political editor'. Which noun is represented by '-z-' in these compound nouns?
10. What is the shortened form of the question '**Ùfuna ntoni**?'

If you have done all exercises and answered the questions above correctly, then you are well prepared to proceed to the next unit.

12 Kumdlalo weqakamba
At the cricket

In this unit you will learn how to:

- ask about past sporting involvement and respond
- ask about present sporting involvement and respond
- ask what someone does to keep fit
- say what you do to keep fit
- ask whether someone has hobbies
- say what your hobbies are

Incoko

CD 2, tr 3

During the lunch break Peter and Themba walk around the cricket ground where several mini-cricket matches are on the go and, among other things, talk about the way cricket has become so popular throughout the whole country.

UThemba	Kuhle kakhulu ukubona umdla kangaka kwiqakamba kule mihla. Jonga bonke aba **Makhaya Ntini** basakhulayo bedlala iqakamba!
UPeter	Inene. Kule mihla naphina apho ujonga khona, kukho amakhwenkwe adlala iqakamba. Wena Themba, wawuyidlala iqakamba ngeentsuku zakho usesesikolweni?
UThemba	Ewe, ndandithanda kakhulu ukudlala iqakamba. Ndandingumgcini-pali. Ndingumbethi kanjalo. Inene, ndandivula amangeno!
UPeter	Nyhani!
UThemba	Wena, mfondini, wawudlala eyiphi imidlalo?
UPeter	Heke, ndandidlala intenetya nombhoxo ngeentsuku zam. Ngelishwa, yophuka ingalo yam ndisadlala kwi-under 15. Emva koko zange ndiphinde ndidlale mbhoxo kwakhona.
UThemba	Wawudlala ndawoni?

(Courtesy United Cricket Board of South Africa)

UPeter	Ndandisisikramhafu. Nangona ndandingadlali qakamba ndithanda kakhulu ukuyibukela ngakumbi xa sidlala namaqela aphesheya. Wena, wawuwudlala umbhoxo okanye ibhola ekhatywayo?
UThemba	Ndandidlala umbhoxo.
UPeter	Kweyiphi indawo?
UThemba	Ndandiyindoda yesibhozo.
UPeter	Kunjani ngebhola ekhatywayo? Wawuyidlala?
UThemba	Ewe, ndandi*yi*dlala kodwa ndandikhetha umbhoxo.
UPeter	Uyayibona phofu indlela umdlalo onamandla ngayo okumanya isizwe!
UThemba	Unyanisile. Khumbula ukuxhaswa kw*ama***Bhokobhoko** sisizwe sonke ngexesha lomdlalo wamanqam! Ngubani ongalibala ukuculwa kuka*Tshotsholoza* ngelizwi elinye ngumntu wonke!
UPeter	Inene, ndiqinisekile ukuba ukucula kwesihlwele kwawanika umoya ukuze aphumelele *ama***Bhokobhoko**!
UThemba	Yho! Ingubani ongalibala igugu ebusweni bukaMongameli Mandela enxiba ijezi kaNo. 6 ephethe indebe beyithe *qhiwu* phezulu noFrancois Pienaar.*
UPeter	Ne**Bafana Bafana** yafumana kwa enjalo inkxaso, yaphumelela kwiAfrican Cup of Nations. Kanene, wenza luthambo luni kule mihla ukuzigcina uphilile?

Bafana Bafana winning the World Cup of Nations in 1996
(*Bona*, March 1996. Photos by Jacob Morake and Southlight)

UThemba E-e ndiyazama ukubaleka kathathu ngeveki kwaye ndidllala isikhwashi *rhoqo*. Wena, mfondini?

UPeter Mna, ndithanda ukukhwela ibhayisekile kwaye ndiyazama nokunyuka intaba ngeeCawa. Kodwa ngamanye amaxesha kunzima ukufumana ithuba lokwenza loo nto kuba umsetyenzana wam wokuzonwabisa kukuchwela.

UThemba Owam kukufota, *qha* ke. Kodwa ke, liphi ixesha?

The cricketers come back on to the field after the lunch break.

UPeter Jonga, abadlali babuyile; isidlo sasemini siphelile. Umdlalo uza kuqala ngoku. Masibuyele kwizihlalo zethu!

*Although President Mandela never played rugby, his interest in the game goes back to his youth. He remembers the playing days of the former Transkei homeland leader KD Matanzima with a chuckle: ‘When he was tackled, the spectators would call out “help the son of a chief”’ (*Cape Times* 16/3/1998. Article by Roger Friedman and Benny Gool.)

Former President Mandela holding the soccer World Cup trophy after it was announced that South Africa would host the World Cup in 2010

QUICK VOCAB

Isigama

kuhle	it's lovely
iqakamba	cricket
basakhulayo	budding (lit. still growing)
bedlala	playing
naphina	everywhere
wawudlala ...?	did you play...?
iintsuku	days
usesesikolweni	you still being at school
ndandithanda	I loved, liked
umgcini-pali	wicketkeeper
umbethi	batsman
amangeno	innings
nyhani!	really!
intenetya	tennis
umbhoxo	rugby
-ophuka	be broken
zange ndiphinde	I never again
ndawoni?	what position?
isikramhafu	scrumhalf
nangona	although
ndandingadlali	I didn't play
amaqela aphesheya	overseas teams
ibhola ekha*ty*wayo	soccer (lit. ball which is kicked < -khaba = kick)
indoda yesibhozo	eighth man
phofu	in fact
-namandla	has the power
ngayo	by it
okumanya	of uniting
isizwe	nation
umdlalo wamanqam	final (game)
ukuxhaswa	support
isihlwele	crowd
kwawanika umoya	give them the impetus (lit. spirit)
igugu	pride
enxiba	wearing
ijezi	jersey
indebe (half split calabash)	trophy

beyithe *qhiwu*	*holding up high*	umsetyenzana wokuzonwabisa	hobby (lit. a little job of making oneself happy	QUICK VOCAB
kwa	also, even	owam	mine	
inkxaso	support	-fota	take photographs	
luthambo luni?	what sort of exercise?	*qha* ke	that's it	
-zigcina -philile	keep oneself fit	kodwa ke	but then	
-baleka	run	liphi ixesha?	where's the time?	
isikwashi	squash	-buya	return (<u>from</u>)	
rhoqo	regularly	isidlo sasemini	lunch	
-khwela	ride	-buy<u>e</u>la	return <u>to</u>	
ibhayisekike	bicycle	izihlalo	seats	
-nyuka	climb			
intaba	mountain			
-chwela	do woodwork			

(*Sunday Times* 23/11/1997, Picture Thomas Turck Courtesy Touchline Photo)

In 1997 a young man from **Mdingi**, a village 15 km from King William's Town, made cricketing history by being the first Xhosa-speaking cricketer to be selected to represent South Africa. In 1990 the skinny 14-year-old was first spotted by Border Cricket Development officer Raymond Maloyi.

Makhaya Ntini was'discovered' and has not looked back since.

He represented Border U-15a against a touring England team and was considered the best fast bowler the English team had faced. While at school at Dale College he was chosen for South Africa U19 to tour England where he played at the hallowed MCC! He also toured Australia with the Dale College touring team. He showed that he was not only a very talented fast bowler but that he was no slouch with the bat, scoring 102 to add to his bowling performance of five wickets for 50!

In 1998 in his debut for South Africa against New Zealand he took two wickets for 30 runs.

His interest in cricket was undoubtedly fostered by his late father who played at club cricket level while his uncle Lungile Makhulu still plays in the '***Amacala Egusha***' competition.

Cultural background

'The uncles greeted each other tumultuously. Apart from blood links they had other ties. They had taught at Lovedale together before I was born. In family albums I had poured over pictures of such things as the staff cricket team in which they had both played. All my life the men in my family were cricket mad; they 'rooted for South Africa' in Test Matches abroad and for provincial teams at home and followed their fortunes in newspapers and on radio despite the policy of apartheid in sport.' (**Noni Jabavu, *The Ochre People – Scenes from a South African Life*, John Murray, London, 1963**)

🔊 **CD 2, tr 3, 04:00**

Tshotsholoza

(onomatopoeic – the sound of a steam train)

'Tshotsholoza! Tshotsholoza!
Kwezo ntaba Stimela siphum' eRhodezhiya
Wen' uyabaleka kwezo ntaba
Wen' uyabaleka!
Stimela siphum' eRhodezhiya.'

[This is often sung by workers to give each other encouragement, hence its adoption as the unofficial anthem when ***AmaBhokobhoko*** needed that little extra something to win the rugby World Cup in 1995.]

'*Tshotsholoza*', a road menders' ditty or work-song, is a popular 'train song' of which there is a whole repertoire based on the theme of railway travel. It imitated the sound of a steam engine pulling out of a station […], and as it gathers speed and settles into a regular rhythm, the voices combine in four parts accompanied by tremendous thumps of feet stressing the beat: '*STIMela siphum' eRHODe-zhIYA*!' […] The voices blended together exhorting the engine in the vocative, '*WEN' uya baLEka*', inflections that praised the locomotive's magnificent performance on that two-thousand-mile journey across tawny *veld*, through *mopani* forest, gradations of plateaux, karoo, mountains, valleys until the coast is reached.'

(**Noni Jabavu, *The Ochre People***)

How to ...

Ask about someone's past sporting involvement

Wawudlala *eyi***phi** *imi***dlalo** ngeen**tsuku** zakho use*sesi***kolw***eni*?
Wawudlala *eyiphi imi***dlalo** ngee**ntsuku** zakho use*se***yunivesithi**?
Wawudlala ndawoni?

Respond to questions about your past sporting involvement

Ndandidlala:

*i***qakamba**
*in***tenetya**
*um***bhoxo**
*isi***kwashi**
*i***bhola** *e***kha***ty***wa***yo*
*i***hoki**
*i***bhola** yo*m***nyazi** (netball)

ngeen**tsuku** zam ndi*sesesi***kol***weni* / ndi*sese***yunivesithi**.

Ndandidlala *isi***kramhafu** / *in***doda** yesi**bhozo** / *i***phika** (wing).

Ask about present sporting involvement

Uya**dlala**?
Udlala ntoni?
Udlala phi?
Udlala kw*eli***phi** *i***qela**?
Uqeqesha phi?
Uqeqeshwa *ng***ubani**?

Respond to questions about your present sporting involvement

Ndi**dlala** *i***qakamba** / *in***tenetya** / *um***bhoxo** / *isi***kwashi** / *i***bhola** *e***kha***ty***wa***yo* / *i***hoki** / *i***bhola** yo*m***nyazi**.
*Andi***dlal***i* *m***dlalo**.
*Andi*sa**dlal***i* *m***dlalo**.
*Andi***na***lo* *i***xesha** loku**dlala** *imi***dlalo**.

Ask what someone does to keet fit

Wenza luthambo luni uku*zi***gcina** u**phil***ile*? (→ See **Unit 15**)

Say what you do to keep fit

Ndiya**baleka**.	I **run**.
Ndiya**qubha**.	I **swim**.
Ndiya**hamba-hamba**.	I **walk**.
Ndi**nyuka** intaba / entabeni.	I **do mountain climbing**.
Ndi**khwela** ibhayisekile.	I **cycle**.
Ndi**khwela** *ama***hashe**.	I **do horse riding**.
Ndiya**danisa**.	I **do ballroom dancing**.
Ndiya**xhentsa**.	I **do traditional dancing**.

Ask whether someone has hobbies

U**na***yo* *imi***se***ty***enzana** yoku*z***onwabisa**?

Say what your hobbies are

Ndiya**chwela**.	I do **woodwork**.
Ndiya**fota**.	I do **photography**.
Ndiya*ku***thanda** *uku***funda**.	I **like reading**.
Ndi**cula** *kwi***kwayari**.	I **sing** *in* a **choir**.
Ndiya**thunga**.	I **sew**.
Ndiya**nitha**.	I **knit**.
Ndiya**zoba**.	I **paint**.
Ndi**sebenza** *e***gad***ini*.	I **garden**.
Ndiya*ku***thanda** *uku***loba**.	I **like fishing**.
Nd**enza** *izi***tya** neem**biza** ngo**dongwe**.	I **do pottery**.
Ndi**qokelela** *izi***tampu**.	I **collect stamps**.
Ndiya**luka**.	I **do weaving**.

Cultural background

Ukuxhentsa

*Um***xhentso** is a traditional Xhosa dance consisting of rhythmic movements, stamping feet and various gestures accompanied by the singing and clapping of women and girls.

This dance is performed by women and men at beer drinking, by men at a wedding (*um***dudo**) and by a diviner while divining.

MULTI-CULTURAL COPS These South African Police Service members spend most of their spare time dancing the traditional way. They're trying to promote cultural diversity within their service.

(Courtesy *Cape Times* 17/5/96. Picture Alan Taylor)

Izinto zokuhambisa ixesha (*pastimes*)

uku**bukela** *u***mabona-kude** / *i***TV**
uku**phulaphula** *um***culo** (music) ngee**teyiphu** nangee**CD**
uku**phulaphula** *u***nomathotholo**

Insight

The word *u***nomathotholo** = 'radio' comes from the association between the disembodied voices and certain traditional healers who may have spirits manifest in themselves – voices, whistles, etc, (regarded as both rare and singular, and an honour from the ancestors)

***OO*NOMATHOTHOLO**

Oonomathotholo bayeza	The 'witchdoctors' are coming
kusasa bayeza.	early in morning they are coming.
Bayeza ekuseni	They are coming early in the morning
Bayeza!	They are coming!

How it works

1 The participial

The **participial** construction is similar to the English verbal '-**ing**' form (participle) but it is more extensively used in Xhosa. Like English, it usually denotes **two simultaneous actions** not necessarily carried out by the same person(s).

Except for nouns of Classes 1/1a; 2/2a and 6, the subject concords of the **participial** are the same as the present tense indicative.

The subject concord of **Class 1/1a nouns** changes from **u-** > '-**<u>e</u>**':

*Um***fundi** **<u>u</u>**sebenza erestyu **<u>e</u>**funda eyunivesithi.
The student works at a restaurant (while) studying at university.

The subject concord of **Class 2/2a nouns** changes from **ba**- > '-**<u>be</u>**':

*Aba***zali** **<u>ba</u>**ncokola *aba***ntwana** **<u>be</u>**dlala.
The parents chat (while) the children are playing.

The subject concord of **Class** 6 nouns changes from **a**- >'**<u>e</u>**-':

*Ama***doda** **<u>a</u>**ncokola **<u>e</u>**bukela iqakamba.
The men chat (while) watching cricket.

Monosyllabic verbs, e.g. '-**ya**' = '**go <u>to</u>**' insert '-*si*-' between the subject concord and the stem:

Ndiqhwalela ndi*si***ya**.	I am limping go**<u>ing</u>** along.

Vowel verbs e.g. '-**enza**' = **do**, **make**: '-*s*-' is inserted between the subject concord and the stem:

> Ungalibali ke **<u>e</u>*s*enza** iBA nje, ubambe imisebenzi emibini.
> Don't forget then, while do**<u>ing</u>** her BA, she holds down two jobs.

The **participial** is in the present tense even when the verb in the main clause is in a past tense:

Bancokole **be**bukela iqakamba.	They chatted (while) watching cricket.

The **participial** subject concords can also be prefixed to non-verbal predicates:

Waqala ukudlala ibhola ekhatywayo e*s*eneminyaka esibhozo.	He started to play soccer **from** the age of eight.
Ukhule enomdla kakhulu kumdlalo webhola ekhatywayo.	He grew up **with** a great interest in soccer.
Wazalwa ngo-1970 engumntwana wesithathu kusapho lwabantwana abahlanu.	He was born in 1970, (be**ing**) the third child in a family of five children.
Ufotwe ekunye nabanye abadlali beqela lakhe.	He was photographed (be**ing**) together with other players of his team.

The **participial** is also used:

after the **conjunction** '**xa**' = 'when' / 'whenever' / 'if':

Xa e*si***tsho** uthetha inyaniso.	Say**ing** so she tells the truth.

after the **interrogative** '**kutheni?**' = '**why**?' (→ cf. **Unit 8**):

Kutheni engandixelelanga?	**Why** did she not tell me?

after certain **auxiliary verbs**, e.g. '**se**- / **sel**- / **sele**-' = 'already':

Ukhona?	Is he/she there?
Hayi, **sel'**emkile.	No, he/she has **already** left.

after '-**soloko**' = 'always':

Wa**soloko** enqwenela ukudlala iqakamba njengomkhuluwa wakhe.	He **always** wanted to play cricket like his older brother.

after the adverb of time '**kudala**' = long ago:

Kudala esemtsha wayedlala *ama***nqindi**.	**Long ago** when he was still young, he used to box. (lit. used to play **fists**)

In the negative, '-**nga**-' (> '**-nge-**' with latent **i**-verbs) is inserted after the subject concord and the final vowel changes to **-i**:

Kudala ndi**nga**kuboni.	**It's a long time** since I've seen you.
Kutheni u**nge**zi?	**Why** don't you come?
Kutheni e**nge**zi?	**Why** doesn't he / she come?

Insight

As is the case with the passive construction, you should be familiar with the **participial** if you wish to read Xhosa texts. Many examples of the participial can be found in captions under photographs in newspapers and magazines. The following appeared in the October 1997, November 1997 and February 1998 editions of ***BONA*** magazine:

*Ekufikeni kwakhe **e**vela eLusuthu, **uPrince Charles** wamkelwa eMzantsi Afrika yiNkulumbuso yaseGauteng.*	On his arrival (com**ing**) from Lesotho Prince Charles was welcomed to South Africa by the Premier of Gauteng.
***UHarry noCharles noSekela Mongameli be**ngena kwibala lemidlalo.*	Harry and Charles and the Deputy President enter**ing** the stadium.
***UPrince Charles e**ncokola nosekela Mongameli nenkosikazi yakhe.*	Prince Charles chatt**ing** with the Deputy President and his wife.
***Usekela Mongameli, e**bulisa isihlwele ekufikeni kwakhe kwibala lemidlalo.*	The Deputy President greet**ing** the crowd on his arrival at the stadium.
*Xa **amaqhawe e**dibana ...*	**When** the celebrities met, …
***uNaomi Campbell** uthe kudibana nobaw' uMadiba kufana 'nokunyathelaku kukhanya kwelanga'.*	Naomi Campbell said that to meet with 'her father' Madiba was like stepping into the sunshine.
***Amadoda** axhentse imini yonke **e**nik' imbeko inkokeli yawo.*	The men danced the whole day giv**ing** respect to their leader.

2 The continuous recent past tense

This frequently used past tense usually covers any **continued action** or **state** during the *recent past* and is formed with '-**be**' + the **participial**:

Bendidlala (> Ndi**be** ndidlala) = I **was** playing.

Note: '-**be**' = '**was**' / '**were**' is the recent past tense of 'uku**ba**' = 'to **be**' (cf. **Unit 10**):

Subject concords of the continuous recent past tense	
Ubuphi izolo?	Where **were** you yesterday?
Beniphi izolo?	Where **were** you yesterday?
Bendidlala umbhoxo.	I **was** play**ing** rugby.
Besidlala umbhoxo.	We **were** play**ing** rugby.
Ubunjani umdlalo?	How **was** the game?
Ibinomdla imidlalo.	The games **were** interest**ing**.
Ebelapho* uThemba?	**Was** Themba there?
Bebelapho ooThemba?	**Were** Themba and co. there?
Belidlala njani iqela lakho?	How did your team play?
Ebedlala kakuhle amaqela omabini.	Both teams played well.
Besidlala njani isiskramhafu?	How did the scrumhalf play?
Bezidlala kakuhle iziskramhafu zozibini!	Both scrumhalves played well!
Beziziintshatsheli!	They **were** champions!
Belunzima ukhuphiswano olo!	It **was** a tough competition.
Bebukho ubuhlobo phakathi kwamaqela?	**Was** there camaraderie among the teams?
Ibinjani inxalenye yempela-veki?	How **was** the rest of your weekend?
Bekumnandi kakhulu!	It **was** very nice.
Bekuyimini enempumelelo kwiqela lethu.	It **was** a successful day for our team.

*You may hear '**ube**-' used instead of '**ebe**-' in colloquial speech.

From the above examples you can see that:

1 In the unshaded examples '**be**-' is simply prefixed to the subject concords. However, in the shaded examples where the **subject concords** consist of **a vowel only**, the subject concords and / or '**be**-' are slightly modified.

2 The **continuous recent past tense** is also used to describe an action or process taking place **at a certain point in time in the near past** where English would simply use the past tense:

Belidlala njani iqela lakho? — How **did** your team play (at the time)?

3 The **continuous recent past tense** is used not only with **verbs** but with **copulatives, interrogatives, locatives and qualificatives** including **stative verbs**:

Stative verbs present tense	**Stative verbs past tense**
Ndi**xakek***ile*. I **am** busy.	**Bendixakek***ile*. I **was** busy.
Si**thabathek***ile*. We **are** impressed.	**Besithabathek***ile*. We **were** impressed.
Ndi**ngxam***ile*. I **am** in a hurry.	**Bendingxam***ile*. I **was** in a hurry.
B**onwab***ile* abaxhasi! The supporters **are** happy!	**Bebonwab***ile* abaxhasi! The supporters **were** happy!

As is the case with the **participial**, '*-si-*' and '*-s-*' also occur in the **continuous recent past tense**.

'*-si-*' with **verbs of one syllable**:

Bebe*si*thini? — What **were** they saying?

'*-s-*' with **vowel verbs**:

Ubu*s*enza ntoni izolo? — What **were** you doing yesterday?

Formation of the **negative** of the **continuous recent past tense:**

Consonant verbs insert '**-nga**-' and change the final vowel to '**-i**':

Bendi**nga**sebenz**i**. — I **wasn't** working.

Vowel verbs insert '**-ng**-' and change the final vowel to '**-i**':

Bendi**ng**enz**i** nto izolo. — I **wasn't** doing anything yesterday.

Stative verbs insert '**-nga**-' and suffix '**-anga**':

Bendi**nga**xakek**anga**. — I **wasn't** busy.

Non-verbal predicates insert '**-nge**-':

Ebengekho uThemba?	**Wasn't** Themba there?
Belu**nge**nzima ukhuphiswano olo!	**Wasn't** that a difficult competition!
Bendi**nge**nathuba.	**I didn't** have a chance.

3 The continuous remote past tense

This past tense usually covers any continued action or state during the *remote past*. It is frequently used in biographies and reports of past events. (cf. **Units 3** and **7**).

It is formed with the subject concord of remote past tense + '-**be**' or '-**ye**' + the **participial**.

'-**be**' = '**was**' / '**were**' – the recent past tense of 'uku**ba**' = 'to **be**'
'-**ye**' = '**went**' – the recent past tense of 'uku**ya**' = 'to **go to**'

Ndabe ndidlala. I **used to** play (long ago) (lit. I **was** I play**ing**) shortened to: **Ndandi**dlala.

Waya edlala. He **was** play**ing** (long ago) shortened to: **Waye**dlala.

Note: As is the case with the continuous recent past tense, the full form is very rarely used in everyday speech.

This tense often has the connotation of '**used to**', which can be expressed explicitly by adding '-**kade**':

Ndandikade ndi**dlala**. = I used to play long ago (lit. I was **long ago** I playing).

Wawudlala ntoni ngelaa xesha?	What **were you** playing **at** that time?
Ndandidlala iqakamba.	**I was** playing cricket.
Ndanding*um***gcini-pali**.	**I was** a wicket-keeper.
Nanidlala ntoni ngelaa xesha?	What **were you** (pl.) playing at that time?
Sasidlala umbhoxo.	**We were** playing rugby.
Waye*zi***gcina e**philile ngokuhamba.	**He used to** keep himself fit by walking.
Babe*zi***gcina be**philile ngokubaleka.	**They used to** keep themselves fit by running.
Wawunjani umdlalo wombhoxo ngelaa xesha?	What **was** the game of rugby like at that time?
Yayino*m***dla** imidlalo.	**They were** interesting games.
Lalidlala njani iqela lakho?	How **did** your team **play**?
Ayelung*ile* amaqela ngelaa xesha.	The teams **were** good at that time.
Kwakumnandi ngoko.	It **was** (very) nice then.

As you can see from these examples, '-**be**' or '-**ye**' is omitted except for Classes 1/1a, 4, 6 and 9.

Note: As is the case with the **participial** and the **continuous recent past tense**, '-*si*-' / '-*s*-' also occur in the **continuous remote past tense** with **verbs** of **one syllable** and **vowel verbs** respectively, while '-**nga**-' is inserted in the negative.

How to apply it

CD 2, tr 3, 05:28

1 Listen to the Xhosalized English words and write down the English equivalents

(a) ____________________
(b) ____________________
(c) ____________________
(d) ____________________
(e) ____________________
(f) ____________________
(g) ____________________
(h) ____________________
(i) ____________________
(j) ____________________

2 Okunokwenziwa ngebhola

Unokuyikhaba.	You can kick it.
Unokuyibamba.	You can catch (hold) it.
Unokuyiphosa.	You can throw it.
Unokuyigqithisela.	You can pass it.
Unokuyibetha.	You can hit it.

Now instruct somebody to:

(a) kick it! ________________________________
(b) catch (hold) it! ___________________________
(c) throw it! ________________________________
(d) pass it! ________________________________
(e) hit it! ________________________________

3 Complete the questions with the appropriate interrogative

(a) Uqala ____ umdlalo weqakamba?
(b) Kudlala ___ amaqela namhlanje?
(c) Ngu____ usompempe?
(d) Ngu____ ophume phambili?
(e) Umdlalo udlalwa _____?
(f) Kuphumelele ________?
(g) Kuphumelele ____ iqela?

4 Complete the statements

(a) Ndi______dlala iqakamba.	I **still** play cricket.
(b) _____dlal____ bhola ikhatywayo.	I **don't** play soccer.
(c) ___ndi____dlal___ ntenetya.	I **don't** play tennis **any longer**.
(d) _____ndikade ____dlala intenetya.	I **used to** play tennis.
(e) _____ ndiwudlal___ umbhoxo.	I **never** played rugby.

5 Sports preferences

You express your preferences for certain sports. Ask somebody why he/she prefers a certain sport:

(a) Andithandi mbhoxo. Ndiyacinga ukuba undlongo-ndlongo (*rough*) ungaba nengozi.
Why do <u>you</u> like rugby? ______________________________
(b) Andithandi kuqubha. Ndiyawoyika amanzi.
Why do <u>you</u> like it? ______________________________
(c) Ndithanda intenetya kakhulu.
Why don't <u>you</u> like it? ______________________________
(d) Ndithanda ukunyuka intaba kakhulu. Indalo (*nature*) intle gqitha!
Why don't <u>you</u> like it? ______________________________

6 Past hobbies

Somebody tells you about past hobbies and you ask questions about them:

(a) Ndandikade ndithunga kakhulu.
What did you used to sew? ______________________________
(b) Ndandikade ndinitha yonke imihla.
What did you used to knit? ______________________________

(c) Ndandikade ndicula.
What did you used to sing? ___________________________

(d) Ndandikade ndidanisa kakhulu.
Which dances? ______________________________________

(e) Ndandikade ndiloba kakhulu.
Where? ____

7 Meeting somebody for the first time

You meet someone for the first time. Ask them these questions:

(a) Do you like sport?
(b) Which team do you support?
(c) Do you watch sport on TV?
(d) Do you have hobbies?
(e) Do you like music?

8 Complete appropriately.

Fill in the correct subject concord to complete the following particulars about past soccer personalities:

(a) UJomo Sono _____mele ibhola yaseMzantsi-Afrika phesheya.
(b) UGeorge Thebe ____yintloko yeSANFA.
(c) UMbanya ____dlalela iMorokaSwallows.
(d) UKaizer Motaung ____ngomnye wabadlali abaphambili beOrlandoPirates.

9 Read the dialogue and answer the questions

USIPHO NOVUYANI BADIBANA BANCOKOLE

USipho	Molo, bhuti. Uzifihle phi? Ubuphi? Khange ndikubone ixesha elide.
UVuyani	Mfondini, bendigula inyanga yonke.
USipho	Awu! Ndilusizi. Ubhetele ngoku?
UVuyani	Ewe, ndiphilile kwakhona kangangokuba ndiqale ukuphangela kwakhona namhlanje. Ukhe wambona uNomsa kutshanje? (*recently*)
USipho	Hayi. Ndiva ukuba usesibhedlele.
UVuyani	Uphethwe yintoni?
USipho	Andiqinisekanga. Ingathi waba kwingozi. (*she was in an accident*)
UVuyani	Awu! Ingozi enjani?
USipho	Uyazi, uNomsa udla ngokubaleka. (*usually runs*)

	Ebe*zi*qeqeshela i*Two Oceans*. Ngoku, kuthiwa wawa. Wophuka umlenze.
UVuyani	Torhwana! Imbaleki enje ukuqaqamba. (*she's an outstanding athlete*) Ukwesiphi isibhedlele?
USipho	Andazi.
UVuyani	Ndiza kufowunela umyeni wakhe ukufumanisa (*find out about*) ngesibhedlele.

(a) USipho udibana nabani?
(b) Kutheni engambonanga uVuyani ixesha elide?
(c) Akasebenzanga ixesha elingakanani uVuyani?
(d) Abahlobo bathetha ngabani?
(e) UNomsa udla ngokwenza ntoni?
(f) Kutheni uNomsa esesibhedlele?
(g) Kutheni uVuyani efuna ukufowunela umyeni kaNomsa?

10 Fill in the appropriate missing elements

(a) UVuyani __funa ukufowunela umyeni __mhlobo ___khe.
(b) UVuyani __funa ukufowunela inkosikazi __mhlobo ___khe.
(c) UVuyani __funa ukufowunela abazali ___mhlobo ___khe.

11 Hobbies and pastimes

Read the following about hobbies and pastimes. Fill in the appropriate words and phrases from the list:

(a) inabo nobuchule bokwenza izinto ngezandla (b) abadlala imidlalo (c) Luphulaphula lubukele (d) ukuphulaphula (e) ubomi bangaphandle (f) abaphila, ngomculo (g) ukuqokelela, (h) nokubukela (i) baqokelela and (j) ukufunda.

Bakho abantu abathanda (1) __________ izinto, umzekelo izitampu. Baneencwadi ekuthiwa zii-album, apho kukho izitampu ezininzi ezikhoyo ehlabathini *(from all over the world).* Abantu abambalwa (2) ___________ izinto zakudala, umzekelo ifanitsha *(furniture)* okanye imizobo *(paintings).*

Baninzi abantu abathanda (3) ___________. Ngempela-veki banyuka iintaba, bayabaleka, bakhwela ibhayisekile, baqubha elwandle okanye emilanjeni okanye bayaloba kuba bathanda ukutya iintlanzi.

Inkoliso *(most)* yabantu (4) ________________________ umzekelo initha iijezi, yaluka imilengalenga yodonga, ithunga iilokhwe, iyachwela, yenza izitya ngodongwe okanye isebenza egadini.

Uninzi *(many)* lwabantu luthanda (5) ________kunomathotholo (6) _________ kumabona-kude imini yonke. (7) ____________ _______ iindaba, umculo, imidlalo eqhutywayo, (*serials, lit. plays which are continued)* iifilim, imidlalo enjengombhoxo, iqakamba, isoka njalo, njalo.

Baninzi abantu (8) ____________, ngakumbi isoka, umbhoxo, neqakamba ezithandwa kakhulu.

Abanye abantu bathanda (9) _______ amaphephandaba neencwadi. Bathenga iincwadi okanye baboleka kwithala leencwadi *(from the library).*

CAPE TOWN CITY LIBRARIES
The holder of this card is responsible for items issued on it. Loss of this card must be reported immediately.

KAAPSE STADSBIBLIOTEKE
Houer van hierdie kaartjie is verantwoordelik vir items hierop uitgeloen. Meld verlies van hierdie kaartjie sonder versuim aan.

ITHALA LEENCWADI LESIXEKO SASEKAPA
Umnikazi weli cwecwe uyakuphendula ngazo zonke izinto eziphume ngalo. Ukuba lithe lalahleka masaziswe kwangoko.

Kukho abantu (10) ____________. Bacula ekwayarini, badlala izikhaliso *(musical instruments)* umzekelo ipiyano okanye bayadanisa.

Test yourself

1 Which English form is the **participial** similar to?
2 What are the **participial** subject concords of Classes 1/1a, 2/2a, and 6?
3 What type of verbs insert '**-si-**'in the **participial**?
4 Which **conjunction** is followed by the **participial**?
5 Which **interrogative** and **auxiliary verbs** (two) are followed by the **participial**?
6 What is the prefix that characterizes the **continuous recent past tense** for the 1st person (s. & pl.), the 2nd person (pl.) and the majority of the classes?
7 What are the prefixes for the 2nd person (s.) and Classes 3, 4, 6 and 9?
8 'I am busy' = 'Ndixakekile'. How would say 'I **was** busy'?

9 You know that verbs of one syllable insert '-**si**-' and vowel verbs insert '-**s**-' in the participial as well as in the **continuous recent past tense**. How would you say:

'What were they saying?' 'What were you doing?'

10 How do you say: 'I **was not** working' and 'I **was not** busy'?

If you have done all exercises and answered the questions above correctly, then you are well prepared to proceed to the next unit.

13 Masiye kulaa restyu intsha!
Let's go to that new restaurant!

In this unit you will learn how to:

- ask for a table for the appropriate number in your party
- ask for a particular table
- ask for a menu
- ask what dishes are recommended
- excuse yourself from the table
- comment on your food
- ask for the bill

Incoko

CD 2, tr 4

After the cricket, Peter and Themba, Jenny and Thandi go to a recently opened restaurant specializing in traditional Xhosa fare.

Umphathi-werestyu	Molweni. Namkelekile kwi*Ziko Lethu*. Siyavuya kakhulu ukunibona! Ninjani?
UThemba	Hayi, siphilile ngaphandle kokulamba! Ingaba unayo itafile yabantu abane?
Umphathi-werestyu	Ngokuqinisekileyo! Ndilandeleni.
UThandi	Ingaba singafumana itafile ngasefestileni?
Umphathi-werestyu	Nantsi. Injani le?
UThandi	Ilungile! Siyabulela.

They sit down.

Umphathi-werestyu	Nalu uluhlu lokutya.
UThemba	Ucebisa sithathe ntoni na? Yintoni isipeshali sanamhlanje?
Umphathi-werestyu	Heke, kwizidlo zokuqala sine***sonka samanzi***.

UJenny	Oo! loo nto indikhumbuza ubuntwana bam efama! Ndiyasithanda kakhulu ***isonka samanzi***!
Umphathi-werestyu	Nyhani, Nkosikazi! Nisuka phi?
UJenny	Ndakhulela efama emaXhoseni.
Umphathi-werestyu	Ndawoni?
UJenny	NgaseKomani.
Umphathi-werestyu	Oo, andiwazi loo mhlaba. Mna ndikhulele phesheya kweNciba. Heke, mandibalule n***omphokoqo***, ***umngqusho***, ***umfino***, ***imutton stew nolusu***.
UPeter	Ndilibele, yintoni ***umphokoqo*** kanye?
Umphathi-werestyu	Ngumgubo wombona ophekiweyo.
UPeter	Oo, ewe, ndiyakhumbula ngoku.
UJenny	Ngowuphi ***umfino*** wakho?
Umphathi-werestyu	Sisipinatshi netswele. Ndinganizisela into yokusela elixa nikhetha into yokutya? Kunjani ng***omqombothi***, ***amarhewu*** okanye ***utywala***.
UThemba	Masingcamleni zonke! Sizisele nebhotile yewayini. Ungayivula?
Umphathi	Ngokuqinisekileyo!

The restaurant owner comes back with the open bottle of wine and asks whether they are ready to order.

Umphathi-werestyu	Nilungele uku-odola? Senikhethile?
UThemba	Hayi, asikakhethi. Sisacinga.
Umphathi-werestyu	Kulungile, ndiza kubuya emva kwexeshana.
UJenny	Kanene, Mnumzana, liphi igumbi lokuhlambela?
Umphathi-wesrestyu	Ndilandele, ndiza kukubonisa.
UJenny	Enkosi. Ndixoleleni kancinci.
Abanye	Kulungile.

When Jenny comes back they order and after a while their meal arrives.

Umphathi-werestyu	Naku ukutya!
UJenny	Mm, kunuka mnandi! Kujongeka mnandi kanjalo!
Umphathi-werestyu	Heke, ndiyathemba ukuba niza konwabela ukutya kwenu!

They finish the meal.

Umphathi-werestyu	Ingaba nitye kamnandi?
Abahlobo	Kakhulu!

UJenny	Ndingathanda ukufumana iresiphi yakho yo***mngqusho*** ukuba asilohlebo?
Umphathi-werestyu	Ndiza kukucelela kumpheki.
UJenny	Ndiyabuyela.
Umphathi-werestyu	Heke, kunjani ngesimuncumuncu?
Abahlobo	Enkosi kakhulu kodwa sonke sanele!
UThemba	Singayifumana i-bill ngoku?
Umphathi-werestyu	*Utsho endodeni*!

QUICK VOCAB

Isigama

iziko	hearth
itafile	table
ngokuqinisekileyo	certainly
-landela	follow someone
uluhlu	menu
-cebisa	advise, recommend
isipeshali	speciality
-suka	come from (lit. to go out from)
phesheya	on the other side of / beyond
kweNciba	the Kei River, i.e. Transkei
-balula	select, pick out
umgubo	flour
umbona	maize
-phekiweyo	cooked
isipinatshi	spinach
itswele	onion
elixa	while
-ngcamla	taste
-odola	order
asikakhethi	we haven't chosen yet
-cinga	think
igumbi lokuhlambela	bathroom
ndixoleleni	would you excuse me?
-onwabela	enjoy something
asilohlebo	it isn't a secret
ihlebo	a secret
isimuncumuncu	dessert (lit. something sweet)
-anele / -onele	enough
Utsho endodeni!	Right away! (lit. You say so to a man!)

IZIKO

ULUHLU LOKUTYA

Izidlo zokuqala	Starters
Inkozo zethanga ezojiwe namandongomane	Roasted pumpkin pips and roasted groundnuts
Isigezenga	Steamed green mealie balls
Isonka samanzi	Soft freshly steamed bread
Umphokoqo	Crumbly mealie meal porridge with sour milk
Isipheko Esikhulu	**Main Course**
Idubhayi	Bean & Mealie Stew
Imithwane	Pumpkin Runner Stew
Umngqusho	Samp & beans
Umfino	Spinach & Onion Stew
Ithanga	Boiled Pumpkin
Imifino	Stewed Greens
Ulusu	Tripe
Umkhupha	Porridge of Maize & Beans with Meat
Isimuncumuncu	**Dessert**
Isaladi yeziqhamo ne-ayisikhrim	Fruit salad & ice cream

Insight

*Ama***si** is a much favoured beverage amongst *ama***Xhosa.** If you have read former President Nelson Mandela's autobiography, ***Long Walk to Freedom****, you might recall this passage:

> 'I am very fond of this sour milk, which is known as ***amasi*** among the Xhosa people and is greatly prized as a healthy and nourishing food.
> It is very simple to make and merely involves letting the milk stand in the open air and curdle. It then becomes thick and sour rather like yog[h]urt.'

The idiom '*Ama***si** abekwe *e***lang***eni*' (lit. The sour milk has been put in the sun), means that an outcome is a foregone conclusion. One could very well say:

'*Ama***si** abekwe *e***lang***eni* ngomhla wama 27 Apreli. 1994' referring to South Africa's first democratic election in 1994.

Nelson Rolihlahla Mandela, *Long walk to Freedom, Little, Brown, UK (Randburg MacDonald Purnell, 1994) p. 266.

Some traditional dishes (Izidlo zakwaNtu)

The most popular dish, in its numerous forms, is porridge: porridge made of sorghum – *ama***zimba** – (indigenous to Africa) and maize / mealie – *u***mbona**- (pl. *imi***mbona**) which was introduced to Southern Africa via Western and Central Africa from South America by Portuguese navigators. The word 'mealie' is derived from the Portuguese word for sorghum, 'milho' (cf. Renata Coetzee, ***Funa***, Heinemann, Johannesburg, p. 66).

*isi***dudu**

thin mealie meal porridge (2.5 parts of water, 1 part of meal)

or

sweet milk porridge (1 part ground green mealies, 6 parts fresh sweet milk)

*um***qa**

thick mealie meal porridge mixed with pumpkin (2 parts meal, 1 part water)

*um***phokoqo**

crumbly mealie meal porridge (4 parts of meal, 1-2 parts of water)

CEREAL AND VEGETABLE MIXES

*um***qa** we**thanga** / *in***gubela**

1 medium pumpkin, 250 ml mealie meal

*um***xhaxha**

5 parts pumpkin, 2 parts green mealies

*um***fino / ***um***qubela / ***isi***gibane**

greens and mealie meal

LEGUME DISHES

*Um***ngqusho**

samp (crushed maize) and beans

Umngqusho

Ingredients

125 g beans, soaked overnight
125 g samp, soaked overnight
500 g brisket, cut into cubes
1 onion, chopped
2 tomatoes, chopped
1 green pepper, chopped
salt, pepper, lemon juice to taste

Method

Cook the beans and samp for approx. 3 hours. Brown meat and onion, add salt, pepper and water to cover and simmer until almost done. Add onion, tomato and green pepper and simmer until the ingredients are cooked. Mix with the *um***ngqusho**, add lemon juice to taste, heat through and serve.

(**Renata Coetzee**, *Funa*)

ooo0ooo

'Ukutya kwethu thina maXhosa ngumbona esithi siwenze umngqusho, isidudu, isonka, amarhewu, utywala ukanti abakwaZulu bathanda irayisi kakhulu. [...] Kwezinye indawo yenziwa ngumgubo wamazimba.'

(**K.S. Bongela**; ***IPhulo***, Maskew Miller Longman, 1977)

ooo0ooo

'This same veld offered grazing for our livestock and yielded ***umfino***, wild spinach, to our mothers, in rich variety [. . .]

I do not remember ever being desperately hungry as a child. No. There was always more than enough to eat. New mealies cooked on the cob, dry mealies cooked with beans, mealies roasted, mealies stamped and broken into bits, mealies crushed and ground to powder; pumpkin as vegetable, pumpkin mixed with mealie-meal, other squash, eggs, fruit, sour milk, milk fresh foamy warm, straight from the udder; garden vegetable, wild vegetable, ***amazimba***, and a host of other delectable eatables. Such variety; such ready availability.'

(**Sindiwe Magona**, ***To My Children's Children***, David Philip Publishers, 1990)

How to ...

Ask for a table for the appropriate number in your party

U**na***yo* *i***tafile** y*aba***ntu** *aba***bini** / *aba***thathu** / *aba***ne** / *aba***hlanu**?
Singa**fumana** *i***tafile** ya*ba***ntu** *aba***ne**?

Ask for a particular table

Singa**fumana** *i***tafile** nga*se***festil***eni*?

Ask for a menu

Singa**fumana** *ulu***hlu** lo*ku***tya** / *i***menyu**?
Singa**fumana** *ulu***hlu** lo*ku***sela**?

Ask what is recommended / special

Ubalula ntoni?
Ucebisa ntoni?
Ucebisa si**khethe** **ntoni** na?
Y*intoni** *isipeshali** sa**namhlanje**?
Une*si***dlo** *esi***sodwa namhlanje**?

Excuse yourself from the table

*Ndi***xolele** kancinci.

Comment on your food

Kujongeka mnandi.
Kunuka mnandi.
Kumnandi.

Ask for the bill

Singa*yi***fumana** *i*-**bill**?

How it works

1 Two nouns in possessive relationship in many words to do with food, having meals, etc.

*in*__yama__ *yen*__komo__	beef (lit. **meat** *of* **cow**)
*in*__yama__ *ye*__gusha__	mutton / lamb (lit. **meat** *of* **sheep**)
*in*__yama__ *yen*__kuku__	chicken (lit. **meat** *of* **chicken**)
*in*__yama__ *ye*__hagu__	pork (lit. **meat** *of* **hog**)
*uku*__tya__ *kwase*__lwandle__	sea food (lit. **food** *of* the **sea**)
*i*__suphu__ *yen*__kuku__	chicken soup
*i*__suphu__ *ye*__tumato__	tomato soup
*is*__onka__ *sama*__si__	cheese (lit. **bread** *of* **sour milk**)
*isi*__dlo__ *sa*__kusasa__	breakfast (lit. **meal** *of* **early morning**)
*isi*__dlo__ *sase*__mini__	lunch (lit. **meal** *of* **midday**)
*isi*__dlo__ *sa*__ngokuhlwa__	dinner, supper (lit. **meal** *of* the **evening**)
*i*__gumbi__ *lo*ku__tyela__ (*in*__dlu__ *yo*ku__tyela__)	dining room (lit. **room** *of* **eating** [**for**])
*i*__tafile__ *yo*ku__tyela__	dinner table
*i*__laphu__ *le*__tafile__	tablecloth
*ulu*__hlu__ *lwezi*__selo__	beverages
*ulu*__hlu__ *lwe*__wayini__	wine list

2 More about verbal extensions

The **causative** '-**za**' instead of '-**isa**' (cf. **Unit 4**) is used in the following verbs ending in '-**la**':

Ndiyakhumbula ngoku.	I **remember** now.
I*ndi*khumbuza ubuntwana bam.	It **reminds** *me* of my childhood. (lit. it **makes me remember**)
Khathalela impilo yakho.	**Care for** your health.
Musa uku*zi*khathaza.	You must not **worry** (*yourself*).
Ndiza kuphumla ixeshana.	I'm going to **rest** for a while.
*Zi*phumze ixeshana.	**Rest** (*yourself*) for a while.

The **stative** or **neuter** '**-eka**' indicates a state or condition without referring to the agent causing that condition, similar to the passive voice. The English equivalent would be '**be** (do) **-able**' or 'can **be**' (**done**):

Iyavul**ek**a le festile?	Is this window open**able**? **Can** this window **be** open**ed**?
Ifuman**ek**a lula inyama?	Is meat readily obtain**able**?

-thanda	love	-tya	eat
-thand**w**a	**be** lov**ed**	-ty**iw**a	**be** eat**en**
-thand**ek**a	**be** lov**able**	-ty**ek**a	**be** ed**ible**
-funda	read	-funa	need / want
-fund**w**a	**be read**	-fun**w**a	**be** want**ed**
-fund**ek**a	**be** leg**ible**	-fun**ek**a	**be** necessary (lit. be desir**able**)

Some verbs suffix -**akala** instead of -**eka**:

-bona	see	-qonda	understand
-bon**akala**	be vis**ible**	-qond**akala**	be understand**able**

There are a number of verbal forms ending in -'**ek***ile*' which correspond to English 'to be' + adjectives (→ cf. **Unit 5**):

Ndiqinis**ek***ile*.	I am **certain**.
Ndixak**ek***ile*.	I am **busy**.
Sikhulul**ek***ile*.	We are **free**.
Kubalul**ek***ile*.	It is **important**.

In some instances, verbs with '**-eka**' or '**-wa**' seem to be interchangeable:

Kushiy**ek**a ukutya okuninzi. Kushiy**w**a ukutya okuninzi.	Much food is **left over**.

'-jong**ek**a' < '-jonga' (< 'look') is literally translated as '**looked at as**':

Kujong**ek**a mnandi.	It looks nice!

3 -'ka'- with verb in the negative = 'not yet'

*Asi***kakhethi***i*.	We **have***n't* **chosen yet**.
*Andi***k**azi.	I **do***n't* **know yet**.
*Asi***tyi** *i***langa** linge**katshoni***i*.	We **do***n't* **eat** before sunset. (lit. before the sun has not **yet** gone down)

*Andi***ka***li***fuman***i* *i***xesha** loku**phumla**.

I have *not* **yet found time** to **rest**.

'Ukuba *aku***ka***y**i* *ema***Mpondomis***eni* *m***fundi**, *aku***ka***wa***bon***i* *ama***Afrikakazi** *ama***hle**.' (**AC Jordan**)

If you **have** *not* **yet** been to the land of the Mpondomise, reader, you have **not yet** seen beautiful African women.

How to apply it

1 Give the negative

(a) Ukutya kumnandi.
(b) Ndinambitha (*enjoy*) ukutya.
(c) Isonka sinencasa.
(d) Ndithanda inyama.

2 Answer the question 'How are you?' in a typical Xhosa way

Remember, this involves saying something along the lines of '*I am well except for ...*'.

(a) Ndiphilile ngaphandle ______________ (being very hungry).
(b) ____________________________________ (being very thirsty).
(c) ____________________________________ (the work).
(d) ____________________________________ (the weather).
(e) ____________________________________ (too much studying).

3 Give the opposite description

(a) Imifuno mitsha kakhulu: ______________________________
(b) Ii-apile zimuncu (sour): ______________________________
(c) Isuphu inetyuwa kakhulu: ______________________________
(d) Ndithanda isonka esimdaka: ______________________________
(e) Ndikhetha ukusela iwayini ebomvu: ______________________________
(f) Iitapile zishushu: ______________________________

4 Ask

(a) Do you have a table for two? ______________________________
(b) Do you have a table for three? ______________________________
(c) Do you have a table for four? ______________________________
(d) Do you have a table for five? ______________________________

5 Ask the waiter

(a) whether you can sit outside ______________________________
(b) to bring the menu ______________________________
(c) whether you can order now ______________________________
(d) whether you can have red wine ______________________________
(e) whether you can have vegetables / fruit ______________________________

6 Ask the waiter for something

(Start the sentence off by saying 'Ndingafumana':)

(a) another slice of bread ______________________________
(b) another beer ______________________________
(c) another fork ______________________________
(d) another knife (imela) ______________________________
(e) another spoon ______________________________
(f) another teaspoon ______________________________
(g) another plate (ipleyiti) ______________________________
(h) another cup of tea ______________________________

7 English equivalents

You know that 'igumbi lokutyela' means 'dining room'. Can you guess the English equivalent of:

(a) igumbi lokulala ______________________________
(b) igumbi lokuhlala ______________________________
(c) igumbi lokufundela ______________________________

8 Match these Xhosalized words with the original Xhosa

1	ibhlakfesi	(a)	isonka samasi
2	ilantshi	(b)	uluhlu lokutya
3	idinala	(c)	indlu yangasese (lit. house of privacy)
4	imenyu	(d)	igumbi lokuhlambela
5	itshizi	(e)	isidlo sakusasa
6	ibhafrum	(f)	isidlo sangokuhlwa
7	ithoyilethi	(g)	isidlo sasemini

9 You are asked what you would like

(a) **for breakfast**. Say that you would like:
porridge; two slices of brown (lit. dark) bread; a soft-boiled (-thambileyo) egg; butter and jam (ijam).

____

____

(b) **for lunch**. Say that you would like:
cold meat , salad (isaladi), a slice of white bread and a slice of cheese.

____

____

(c) **for supper**. Say that you would like:
lamb, potatoes, vegetables, fruit.

____

____

10 List all the vegetables you will need to make the soup

Izithako zokupheka

500g yesuphu yenyama yenkomo
1 itswele elikhulu
3 iikomityi zeminqathe
1 ikomityi yeembotyi ezintsha
1 icephe letyuwa
½ itispuni yepepile
1 ikomityi yee-ertyisi
1 ikomityi yeembotyi zeswekile
1 itoti yesuphu yetumato okanye isuphu yemifuno
½ ikomityi yerhasi
intwana yetyuwa yegaliki
2 iitispuni zepasili
3 iitapile

imifuno	vegetables	iimbotyi ezintsha	green beans	QV
irhasi	barley	iminqathe	carrots	
iiertyisi	peas			

11 Read the dialogue and answer the questions

Umncedisi Molo, ndingakunceda ngantoni?
UThandi Mm, iziqhamo zakho zijongeka zintle.
Umncedisi Zitsha *krebhe*, Nkosikazi, ndiziphuthume ngokwam namhlanje ekuseni. Enye into, zitshiphu *bhe*!
UThandi Ndiza kwenza isaladi yeziqhamo. Ndifuna ama-apile, amapere, ipayina, ii-orenji, iipesika neebhanana. Ezi bhanana ziseluhlaza. Unazo ezivuthiweyo?
Umncedisi Nazi ezivuthiweyo, Nkosikazi.
UThandi Enkosi. Iivatala zijongeka mnandi. Zidla malini?
Umncedisi Zidla R7.00 Zimnandi zinamanzi kakhulu. Kunjani ngokungcamla?

UThandi	Enkosi. Ingantle loo nto. Mm, imnandi kakhulu. Ndiphe enkulu leya.
Umncedisi	Kunjani ngamakhiwane neediliya?
UThandi	Hayi, Mnumzana. Ezi ziqhamo zanele.
Umncedisi	Kulungile.

(a) Kutheni uThandi efuna ukuthenga iziqhamo?
(b) Uthenga eziphi iziqhamo?
(c) Zinjani iibhanana?
(d) Injani ivatala?
(e) Idla malini ivatala?
(f) UThandi akathengi ziphi ziqhamo?

QUICK VOCAB

iziqhamo	fruit	ipere (ama-)	pear
ivatala (ii-)	watermelon	-tsha *krebhe*	*very* fresh
i-apile (ama-)	apple	-ngokwam	myself
idiliya (ii-)	grape	-phuthuma	fetch
ikhiwane (ama-)	fig	-tshiphu *bhe*	*very* cheap
ipayina (ii-)	pineapple	-vuthiweyo	ripe
i-orenji (ii-)	orange	-dla malini?	cost how much?
ipesika (ii-)	peach	-namanzi	juicy

12 A friend is helping you prepare a meal. Tell her/him what to do

(a) Please wash (-hlamba) the potatoes.
(b) Don't take the big potatoes, take the small ones.
(c) Peel (-chuba) two onions and an apple.
(d) Chop (-nqunqa) the onions and the pumpkin.
(e) Grate (-tshweza) the carrots.
(f) Wash the lettuce (iletisi) leaves and the tomatoes.
(g) Bring some dishes (izitya).
(h) They are in the cupboard (ikhabhathi) above the sink (isinki).
(i) Open the tin.
(j) Open this one as well.
(k) Please set (-lungisa) the table.

Insight

To address someone you know well in a letter you could write:

Nomsa *o***thandeka***yo*	**Dear** Nomsa (lit. *who* **is loved**)
Mhlobo wam *o***thandeka***yo*	My **dear** friend
Sisi *endim***thanda***yo*	**Dear** sister (lit. *whom I* **love** [*her*])

Bhota = Greetings, is often used in the letter pages of magazines:

Bhota Jeffrey . . .	
Bhota mfundi . . .	**Dear** reader . . .

To end a letter to a person you know very well:

Ngoluthando/Ngolukhulu *u***thando**	With love / with great love
Umhlobo wakho	Your friend
Umhlobo wakho *oku***thanda***yo*	Your loving friend (lit. who you loves)

More formal endings:

*O***wakho** ngenene . . .	Yours truly . . .
. . . *ozi***thobile***yo*	(lit. humbling myself)

13 Writing an invitation

Try to write the appropriate invitation that would have elicited the following answer:

Nomsa othandekayo,

Ndiyabulela kakhulu ngencwadi yakho nangokundimema. Kuza kuba mnandi ukutya isidlo sangokuhlwa nawe. Ndiyazi ukuba ungumpheki wenene ngakumbi kwizidlo zakwaNtu.

Sobonana ngoMgqibelo ke. Undibulisele kubazali bakho.

Bayeza na nabo ekhayeni lakho ngoMgqibelo?

Ngolukhulu uthando Nomvuyo.

NEW AFRICAN CUISINE. Traditional dishes with a modern twist is what party people get when they hire the catering services of **Ubusuku Be-Afrika!** If you are planning a real African party, they will bring along a praise singer, sangoma, artists and a township band to dinner.

Cape Times, 23/10/98.

Test yourself

1 How would you ask for 'beef, mutton, chicken, pork'?

2 Name three verbs where the **causative extension** is '**-za**' instead of '**-isa**'.

3 How do you ask: 'Is this fruit edible?', 'Can this window be opened?', 'Is my writing legible?'

4 Give the English equivalent of: '**Ndixakekile** ngoku, andinakho ukukunceda namhlanje.'

5 In a positive sentence -**sa**- expresses 'still'. What does '**A**ndi**sa**sebenz**i**' mean?

6 How do you say: 'I have **not yet** decided' and 'I **do not** know **yet**'?

7 You begin a letter: 'Sipho **othandekayo'**…' What is the literal meaning of '**othandekayo**'?

8 How do you end a letter to someone you know well?

9 Using the appropriate ideophone, how do you describe something as '*very* fresh' and '*very* cheap'?

10 '*Ama***futha**' means 'fat, oil' and is only used in the plural form. Can you name two other nouns used only in the plural?

If you have done all exercises and answered the questions above correctly, then you are well prepared to proceed to the next unit.

14 Ukuthenga impahla nezinto yinto zakwaNtu (zesiNtu)

Buying clothes and various African arts and crafts

In this unit you will learn how to:

- marvel at something
- discuss size
- ask about colour preference
- compliment someone on their appearance
- discuss price
- say something fits well
- offer a discount
- ask what payment is acceptable
- make more comparisons

Incoko

CD 2, tr 5

Peter and Jenny want to buy some Xhosa handicrafts and traditional clothes.

UJenny	Tyhini! Khawujonge nje zonke ezi zinto zintle! Iinkukho ezolukiweyo, imilengalenga yodonga, izinto zodongwe, iingobozi nenye impahla. Kuza kuba nzima ukukhetha!
UMncedisi	Molweni, ndinganinceda?
UJenny	Inene, ivenkile yakho intle kakhulu! Ndiyazi, ndiza kuchitha imali eninzi namhlanje!
UMncedisi	Enkosi kakhulu. Ningathanda ukujonga kuqala?
UJenny	Ingantle loo.
UMncedisi	Ndibizeni ukuba nifuna uncedo okanye nifuna ukwazi nto.
UJenny	Kulungile, Nkosikazi. Mna, ndingathanda ukuqala ngokujonga iilokhwe nemibhinqo.
UPeter	Lo ngumlengalenga wodonga phaya koluya donga, mhle, Nkosikazi.

UMncedisi	Owuphi, Mnumzana?
UPeter	Lo ubonisa umfazi otshaya inqawa. Wenziwa phi?
UMncedisi	Wenziwa ngabafazi bale ndawo.
UPeter	Yimalini, nkosikazi?
UMncedisi	Ngelishwa le milengalenga yodonga idla imali eninzi kule mihla kuba kaloku yolukwe ngesandla yaye yeyoboya beseyibhokwe.
UPeter	Ndiyeva.

Jenny emerges from the changing room.

Umncedisi	Mm! Ufanelekile, Nkosikazi! Intle kakhulu loo lokhwe! Iyakufanela kunjalo nje!
UJenny	Ewe, kodwa ngathi inobuncinci. Nceda, Nkosikazi, ndiphathele enye enkulu kunale.
UMncedisi	Kulungile, ndiza kubona. Eyiphi isayizi?
UJenny	U36.
UMsebenzi	Ungathanda owuphi umbala?
UJenny	Yiza nelubhelu okanye ebomvu.

The assistant returns with a bigger size.

UMncedisi	Ngelishwa sinemhlophe nentsundu neluhlaza kuphela kwisayizi yakho, Nkosikazi.
UJenny	Kulungile ke, ndiza kulinganisa le intsundu.
UJenny	Heke, indilingana *twatse*! Ndiza kuyithenga! Idla malini, Nkosikazi?
UMncedisi	Ukuba uthenga ilokhwe nombhinqo ndingalihlisa ixabiso. Ziza kudla R225 zombini.
UJenny	Kulungile. Ndiza kuzithenga zombini kodwa andiqinisekanga ukuba ndinemali eyaneleyo. Uyalamkela ikhadi?
UMncedisi	Sukuxhala, Nkosikazi. Samkela imali, itsheki nekhadi.
UJenny	Kulungile kuba ndisafuna ukuthenga nezinye izinto njengezodongwe neengobozi, ngakumbi namaso.
UMncedisi	Utsho ukuthi izihombiso-mzimba ezenziwe ngeentsimbi. Amaso makhulu kuneentsimbi, Nkosikazi!
UJenny	Kakade! Ndilibele!
UMncedisi	Ufuna ntsimbi zini? Ezomqala okanye ezengalo? Uyazithanda zona ezamaqatha?
UJenny	Yho! Zonke zintle kakhulu! Kwakhona kuza kuba nzima kum ukukhetha! Jonga yonke le mibala ngemibala!
UMncedisi	Kulungile, Nkosikazi, thatha ixesha lakho!

QUICK VOCAB

Isigama

tyhini!	gosh!
iinkukho	mats
-olukiweyo	woven
imilengalenga	hangings
udonga	wall
izinto zodongwe	pottery (lit.things of clay)
iingobozi	baskets
nenye impahla	and other goods
-chitha	spend (also, waste)
uncedo	help
iilokhwe	dresses
imibhinqo	skirts
owuphi?	which one?
umfazi	woman
-tshaya	smoke
inqawa	pipe
yimalini?	how much is it? (lit. it is what money?)
-dla	cost (lit. eat)
uboya	wool
yeyoboya	it is of the wool
beseyibhokhwe	being of goats, i.e. mohair
ibhokhwe	goat

ufanelekile	you look very smart (lit. it becomes you)
iyakufanela	it suits you
inobuncinci	it's small
-phathela	bring (for)
eyiphi isayizi?	which size?
owuphi umbala?	which colour?
-linganisa	try on
-lingana *twatse*	fit *perfectly*
-hlisa / -ehlisa	reduce
ixabiso	price
zombini	both
-amkela	accept
itsheki	cheque
amaso	big beads
utsho ukuthi	you mean
izihombiso-mzimba ezenziwe ngeentsimbi	jewellery made from beads
-khulu ku-	bigger than
iintsimbi	smaller beads
ntsimbi zini?	what kind of beads?
ezomqala (of the neck)	necklace
ezengalo (of the arm)	bracelet
ezamaqatha (of the ankles)	anklets

How to ...

Marvel at something

Tyhini! **Khawujonge** nje zonke *ezi zin***to** *zi***ntle**!
Jonga yonke *le mi***bala** nge*mi***bala**!

Discuss size

*Eyi***phi** *i***sayizi**?
Ngathi ino*bu***ncinci** / ino*bu***khulu**.
*Ndi***phathele** *e***nye** *en***kulu** kuna*le* / *e***nye** *e***ncinci** kuna*le*.

Ask about colour preference

*Owu***phi** *um***bala**?
*Eli***phi** *i***bala**?

Compliment someone on their appearance

U**fanelek***ile*!
*In***tle** kakhulu loo **lokhwe**! Iya*ku***fanela** kunjalo nje!

Say something fits well

Ilingana *twatse* leyo!

Offer a discount

Ndinga*li***hlisa** *i***xabiso**.

Ask what payment is acceptable

Uya*l***amkela** *i***khadi**?

How it works

1 Superlative and comparatives

In **Unit 9** you learned how to express '**the best**':

*o***yena** *m***ntu** ***u*****lungile***yo*	the **best** person
*e***lona xesha** ***li*****lungile***yo*	the **best** time
*e***yona** *n***to** / *n***dawo** ***i*****lungile***yo*	the **best** thing / place, etc.

The **superlative** can also be expressed without the qualificative '**-lungile***yo*':

Elona xesha lokubukela iintyatyambo yaseKapa lisentlakohlaza.	The **best time** (of) to see the flowers of the Cape is in spring
Elona hlebo lokuhambela eKapa lisekwindla.	The **best kept secret** (of) to visit Cape Town is in autumn.
Oyena mntu ulungele lo msebenzi nguSipho.	The **best person** for this job is Sipho.

To express '**the most . . of them all**, '**the nicest of them all**' etc., use '**kuna-**' + emphatic pronoun + **-onke**:

Ukhuthele **kuna**bo *b***onke**.	He / she is the **most diligent of** them **all**.
Intle le lokhwe **kuna**zo *z***onke**.	This is the **nicest** dress **of** them **all**.

To express '**best (above) . . . of all**', use **ngaphezu kwa-** + **-onke**:

Ndithanda le milengalenga yodonga **ngaphezu kwe**nto *y***onke**.	I like these wall hangings **best of all** (things).

To express '**bigger than**'; '**more than**' etc., use '**kuna**-:

Ilokhwe ebomvu *in***kulu** **kune**lokhwe emhlophe.	The red dress is **bigger than** the white one.
Loo lokhwe *in***kulu** **kuna**le.	That dress is **bigger than** this.
Iingxowa yakho *in***kulu** **kune**ngxowa yam.	Your bag is **bigger than** my bag.
Eyakho *in***kulu** **kune**yam.	Yours is **bigger than** mine.
Wena unemali *e***ninzi** **kuna**m.	You have **more** money **than** me (I do).

UJenny unemali *e***ninzi kuno**Peter.	Jenny has **more** money **than** Peter.
Uchitha imali *e***ninzi kuna**ye.	She spends **more** money **than** he does.

To express '**more** ... **than**', use '**ngaphezu kwa**-':

Ilokhwe entsundu *i***dulu ngaphezu kw**elokhwe ebomvu.	The brown dress is **more expensive than** the red one.
UJenny uchithe imali e**ninzi ngaphezu** koPeter.	Jenny spent **more** money **than** Peter.
Sahamba **ngaphezu kwee**veki ezimbini.	We travelled for **more than** two weeks.

To express '**less** ... **than**', use '**ngaphantsi kwa**-':

Ndinexesha *eli***ngaphantsi kwe**yakho!	I have **less** time **than** you!

To express '**better than**', use '-**ngcono kuna**-':

Lo mgaqo u**ngcono kuna**lowo.	This road is **better than** that (road).

To expresss '**as** ... **as**', use '**njenga**-':

Ilokhwe ebomvu *i***dulu njenge**mhlophe.	The red dress is **as expensive as** the white one.
Loo lokhwe *i***dulu njenga**le.	That dress is **as expensive as** this (one).
Ixesha lam linexabiso **njenge**xesha lakho.	My time is **as** precious **as** your time.
Ixesha lam linexabiso **njenge**lakho.	My time is **as** precious **as yours**.
Unemali *e***ninzi njenga**m.	You have **as much** money **as** me (I do).
UJenny unomsebenzi *om***ninzi njengo**Peter.	Jenny has **as much** work **as** Peter.
Usebenza kakhulu **njenga**ye.	She works **as much as** he does.

To express '**in comparison to**', use '**kuna**-':

Ndikhetha iti **kune**kofu.	I prefer tea (**in comparison**) to coffee.

To express '**a few more**', use '**-nye**':

Kufuneka ndithenge *ezi***nye** *izi***pho**.	I need to buy **a few more** gifts.

To express '**as soon as**', use '**-kangangoko**':

Yiza kamsinya **kangangoko** unakho.	Come **as soon as** you can.

2 *Various ways of expressing 'much'*

kakhulu (adverb)	**very / much / very much**
Ndiyayithanda **kakhulu**.	I like it **very much**.
gqitha	**very / too much / so**
Inencasa **gqitha**!	It's **too** delicious!
kangaka / kangako	**so much**
Hayi sukuthetha **kangaka**!	Don't talk **so much**!
kangangoko	**as much as**
Zama ukuphumla **kangangoko** unakho.	Try to rest **as much as** you can.
-**ngakanani na**?	**how much**?
Ufuna imali **engakanani**?	How **much** money do you need?
kangangokuba (conjunction)	**so much so that**
U*si*thetha (*isi***Xhosa**) njengomXhosa isiXhosa **kangangokuba** uya*si*fundisa.	She speaks *it* like a Xhosa **so much so that** she teaches *it*.
-**ninzi** (adjective)	**much**
Ufuna imali e**ninzi**?	Do you need **much** money?

3 *The Xhosa equivalent of English 'both' (of)*

The corresponding forms for the 1st and 2nd person plural are:

so*ba***bini**	**both** of **us**
no*ba***bini**	**both** of **you**
bo*ba***bini**	**both** of **them**

The corresponding forms for the noun classes (obviously only the plural classes) are:

yo*mi*bini i*mi*lengalenga	**both** curtains
o*ma*bini a*ma*cici	**both** earrings
zo*zi*bini i*z*andla	**both** hands
zo*m*bini i*z*into	**both** things

Note: An expression often heard when saying thank you: Ndibamba nga**zo zo*zi*bini**. (lit. I hold with **both** [hands].)

From the last set of examples you will see that these forms consist of class concord + **o** + adjectival concord + numeral stem -**bini**:

s-	**+**	**o-**	**+**	*ba-*	+	**-bini**:	**so*ba*bini**
b-	**+**	**o**	**+**	*ba-*	+	**-bini**:	**bo*ba*bini**

To express, for example, 'the **three of us**, the **four of you**, the **five of them**', etc., **numeral stems 3–6** (adjectives) are used in the same way:

so*ba*thathu	the **three** of **us**	**no*ba*ne**	the **four** of **you**
bo*ba*hlanu	the **five** of **them**	**o*ma*thandathu**	the **six** of **them**
(*aba***ntwana**)		(*ama***doda**)	

4 More possessive adjectives

In **Unit 2**, you learned that the **possessive adjectives** of the **1st** and **2nd persons** (s. & pl.), i.e. '**my**', '**our**', '**your**', **follow the nouns** to which they refer and consist of **two parts** (**possessive concord** representing '*of*' which changes according to the noun possessed) and a **second element** (the **possessive stem**) which does not change.

The table below includes the **possessive adjectives** of the **3rd person** (s. & pl.) '**his**'/'**her**', '**its**'/ '**their**'

	-m	**-ithu***	**-kho**	**-inu***	**-khe**	**-bo**
		our	*your*(s.)	*your*(*pl.*)	*his/her/its*	*their*
*um***ntwana**	*wa***m**	*we***thu**	*wa***kho**	*we***nu**	*wa***khe**	*wa***bo**
*um***sebenzi**	*wa***m**	*we***thu**	*wa***kho**	*we***nu**	*wa***khe**	*wa***bo**
*aba***ntwana**	*ba***m**	*be***thu**	*ba***kho**	*be***nu**	*ba***khe**	*ba***bo**
*imi***sebenzi**	*ya***m**	*ye***thu**	*ya***kho**	*ye***nu**	*ya***khe**	*ya***bo**
*ili***zwe** *i***khaya**	*la***m**	*le***thu**	*la***kho**	*le***nu**	*la***khe**	*la***bo**
*ama***qabane**	*a***m**	*e***thu**	*a***kho**	*e***nu**	*a***khe**	*a***bo**
*isi***tshixo**	*sa***m**	*se***thu**	*sa***kho**	*se***nu**	*sa***khe**	*sa***bo**
*izi***tshixo**	*za***m**	*ze***thu**	*za***kho**	*ze***nu**	*za***khe**	*za***bo**
*i***-adelesi**	*ya***m**	*ye***thu**	*ya***kho**	*ye***nu**	*ya***khe**	*ya***bo**
*iin***dondo**	*za***m**	*ze***thu**	*za***kho**	*ze***nu**	*za***khe**	*za***bo**

*ulu***vo**/*u***sapho**	*lwa***m**	*lwe***thu**	*lwa***kho**	*lwe***nu**	*lwa***khe**	*lwa***bo**
*ubu***ntu**	*ba***m**	*be***thu**	*ba***kho**	*be***nu**	*ba***khe**	*ba***bo**
*uku***hamba**	*kwa***m**	*kwe***thu**	*kwa***kho**	*kwe***nu**	*kwa***khe**	*kwa***bo**

* *wa* + *i***thu** > *we***thu** *wa* + *i***nu** > *we***nu**, etc.

However, when it comes to formulating **possessive adjectives** referring to nouns **other than nouns of classes** 1/1a and 2/2a, it is a little more challenging. This is because of the many possible combinations of **possessive concords** and the stems of the **emphatic pronoun (without '–na'**; → see **Unit 9**).

Do you remember the idiom '*In***dlovu** ayisindwa ng*um***boko** *wa***yo**'. (lit. The **elephant** is not burdened by **its trunk**) i.e. No-one ever finds his natural responsibilites too burdensome?

wa- is the **possessive concord** of '*um***boko**' (Class 3)
-yo < **emphatic pronoun** (without '**-na**') referring to '*in***dlovu**' (Class 9)

Some possible combinations of the **possessive concord** and **stem:**

Ngubani *i***gama** *lom***fundi**?	What is the **name** *of* the **student**?
*I***gama** *la***khe** ngu- . . .	*His / her* **name** is . . .
Ngoobani *ama***gama** *aba***fundi**?	What are the **names** *of* the **students**?
*Ama***gama** *a***bo** ngoo-	*Their* **names** are . . .
Ngubani *i***gama** *lom***thi**?	What is the **name** *of* the **tree**?
*I***gama** *la***wo** ngu-. . .	*Its* **name** is . . .
Ngoobani *ama***gama** *emi***thi**?	What are the **names** *of* the **trees**?
*Ama***gama** *a***yo** ngoo- . ..	*Their* **names** are . . .
Ngubani *i***gama** *le***xhego**?	What is the **name** *of* the **old man**?
*I***gama** *la***lo** ngu-. . .	*His* **name** is . . .
Ngoobani *ama***gama** *ama***xhego**?	What are the **names** *of* the **old men**?
*Ama***gama** *a***wo** ngoo- . ..	*Their* **names** are . . .
Ngubani *i***gama** *lesi***kolo**?	What is the **name** *of* the **school**?
*I***gama** *la***so** ngu-. . .	*Its* **name** is . . .
Ngoobani *ama***gama** *ezi***kolo**?	What are the **names** *of* the **schools**?
*Ama***gama** *a***zo** ngoo- . ..	*Their* **names** are . . .
Ngubani *i***gama** *len***tombi**?	What is the **name** *of* the **girl**?
*I***gama** *la***yo** ngu-. . .	*Her* **name** is . . .

Ngoobani *ama***gama** <u>*een*</u>**tombi**?	What are the **names** *of* the **girls**?
*Ama***gama** *a***zo** ngoo- . ..	*Their* **names** are . . .
*um***sebenzi** *oo***gqirha**	the **doctors' work**
*um***sebenzi** *wa***bo**	*their* **work**
*imi***zi** *yemi***mandla**	**homesteads** of the **regions**
*imi***zi** *ya***yo**	*their* **homesteads**
*ama***nzi** *om***lambo**	the **water** of the **river**
*ama***nzi** *a***wo**	*its* **water**
*isi***kolo** *se***dolopho**	the **town's school**
*isi***kolo** *sa***yo**	*its* **school**
*izi***kolo** *zee***dolopho**	*the* **towns' schools**
*izi***kolo** *za***zo**	*their* **schools**
*ulu***vo** lw*aba***zali**	the **parents' opinion**
*ulu***vo** *lwa***bo**	*their* **opinion**
*ubu***bele** *be***xhego**	the **old man's kindness**
*ubu***bele** *ba***lo**	*his* **kindness**
*ukw***azi** *koo***titshala**	the **knowledge** of the **teachers**
*ukw***azi** *kwa***bo**	*their* **knowledge**

5 *Possessive pronouns 'mine', 'yours', etc.*

The **possessive pronouns** are formed by prefixing *a-*, *e-* or *o-* to the **possessive adjectives** (cf. **Unit 2**):

Mine	**Yours**	**Ours**	**Yours (pl.)**	(**Referring to**)
*o***wam**	*o***wakho**	*o***wethu**	*o***wenu**	(*u***nyana** / *um***bhinqo**)
*a***bam**	*a***bakho**	*a***bethu**	*a***benu**	(*aba***ntwana**)
*e***yam**	*e***yam**	*e***yethu**	*e***yenu**	(*imi***bhinqo**)
*e***lam**	*e***lakho**	*e***lethu**	*e***lenu**	(*i***khadi**)
*a***wam**	*a***wakho**	*a***wethu**	*a***wenu**	(*ama***khadi**)
*e***sam**	*e***sakho**	*e***sethu**	*e***senu**	(*isi***kolo**)
*e***zam**	*e***zakho**	*e***zethu**	*e***zenu**	(*iz***andla**)
*e***yam**	*e***yakho**	*e***yethu**	*e***yenu**	(*i***-adelesi**)
*e***zam**	*e***zakho**	*e***zethu**	*e***zenu**	(*ii***lokhwe**)

In the same way you can form possessive pronouns for the 3rd persons:

*o***wakhe** (*u***nyana = son**)	**his / hers**
*a***bakhe** (*oo***nyana = sons**)	**his / hers**
*e***zakhe** (*izi***tshixo = keys**)	**his / hers**

*o***wabo** (*u***nyana = son)**	**theirs**
*a***babo** (*oo***nyana = sons)**	**theirs**
*e*zabo (*izi***kolo** = schools)	**theirs**

Possessive pronouns with the copulative:

*Ngum***ntwana wam**.	***It is*** *my* child.
*Ngo***wam**.	***It is*** *mine.*
*Ngaba***ntwana bethu**.	***They are*** *our* **children**.
*Nga***bethu**.	***They are*** *ours.*
*Sisi***tshixo sabo**.	**It is** *their* **key**.
S*e***sabo**.	***It is*** *theirs.*
Yi-**adelesi yakhe**.	***It is*** *his / her* **address**.
*Ye***yakhe**.	***It is*** *his / hers.*

For emphasis the possessive pronoun can precede the noun:

*O***wam** *u***nyana** *u*sekhaya.	*My* **son** is at home.

6 More about ideophones (izifanekisozwi)

You were first introduced to this distinctive feature of the Xhosa language in **Unit 5**. **Ideophones** occur not only in the spoken but also in the written language. They can be used to emphasize intensity of colour and are often onomatopoeic to indicate movement, action, state, sound, etc. They are mainly used with the verb 'uku**thi**' which has no meaning of its own but simply marks the mood (i.e. indicative, imperative, subjunctive, participial), tense, person, class, number, positive or negative of the predicate, while the **ideophone** carries the **meaning**:

uku**thi** *tu*	be silent	Yi**thi** *tu*!
uku**thi** *shwaka*	disappear	Ilanga li**the** *shwaka*!
uku**thi** *cwaka*	calm down	Umoya wa**thi** *cwaka*.
uku**thi** *thu*	appear suddenly	Kwa**thi** *thu* amafu.
uku**thi** *hlasi*	grab	Wajika **wamthi** *hlasi*.
uku**thi** *vu*	sit down	Ndixakeke andinaxesha lokuthi *vu*.
uku**thi** *ncwaba*	lie very still	Lala u**thi** *ncwaba*.

Ideophones also occur with other verbs in which case the verb retains its original meaning while the **ideophone** functions as an **adverb**:

-**bheka** *ngqo*	go straight	**Bheka** *ngqo* endleleni.
-**buya** *ngqo*	come straight back	*Aba***buy***anga ngqo*.

-**thetha** *ngqo*	talk straight out	**Theth**ani *ngqo*.
-**ma** *nkqo*	stand up straight	*Yi***ma** *nkqo*!
-**funda** *nkqi*	learn quickly	Abantwana ba**funda** *nkqi.*
-**lala** *yoyi*	fall fast asleep	Wa**lala** *yoyi*.
-**phila** *qete*	completely well	Ndi**phile** *qete* ngoku.

Ideophones also occur with **adjectives and relative adjectives** other than colours:

Iziqhamo zi**tsha** *krebhe*!
Iziqhamo zi**tshiphu** *bhe*!

→ cf. **Unit 13**.

Some **ideophones** function as adverbs:

gqitha	very / too much	*In***tle** *qgitha* le lokhwe!
mpela	at all	*Andi***phil***anga mpela.*
qha	only	Ndifuna ilokhwe e**nye** *qha.*
qho	continually	Imvula i**na** *qho* namhlanje.
tu	at all	*Andi***lal***anga tu* phezolo (last night).
	absolutely	Kuthe *cwaka tu.* (It is *absolutely* silent.)
	completely	I-emele i**zele** ithi *tu* ngamanzi. (The bucket is *completely* full of water.)

Another **ideophone** for expressing 'completely' is '*shici*' used mostly in the sense of 'to forget *completely*':

Ithe *shici* kum.	I had *completely* forgotten.
Enkosi ngoku*ndi***khumbuza** sendi**libele** *shici*.	Thanks for **reminding** *me*, I had *completely* **forgotten**.

Ideophones can be used in many contexts to express:

temperature	
futhu	very warm / excited
Lithi *futhu* kwelanga!	It is very *warm!*
ceke	icy (cold)
La manzi a**banda** *ceke*!	This water is *icy*!
state of mind	
nqa	astonishment
Ndithe *nqa*!	I was *astonished*!

qabu	be relieved
Ndithe *qabu*!	I was very *relieved*!

sudden appearance / disappearance

gqi	sudden appearance
Uthe *gqi*!	He appeared *unexpectedly*!
thu	sudden appearance
Wathi *thu*!	He *suddenly appeared*!
shwaka	sudden disappearance
Ilanga lithe *shwaka.*	The sun *suddenly disappeared.*

positions and directions

zwi	stretched out
Naba *zwi*!	**Lie** *stretched out*!
nkqo	straight up
*Yi***ma** *nkqo*!	**Stand** up *straight*!

The vividness of **ideophones** is well illustrated when you compare the following two sentences. They describe someone running into a house, grabbing a child, running out to a car, getting into it and leaving:

Wabaleka wangena endlwini wathatha umntwana waphuma ebaleka wangena emotweni wahamba.	Wabaleka *dyulukudu* endlwini, *hlasi* umntwana, *gqi* phandle, *ngqe*, *khatha* emotweni, watsala!

Some **ideophones** taken from **Sindiwe Magona's** autobiography *Kubantwana Babantwana Bam* (Cape Town, David Philip, 1995):

'UMhla weNkosi yayingumhla onocoselelo; uthe *tse* yaya ungakhululanga konke. (p.26)	The Day of the Lord was a careful day; *correct* (straight) and thoroughly ill at ease.
Thina babengazange baya *nkqu* kuTsolo.' (p.28)	We had not *even* been to Tsolo.
'Ngomhla weKrisimesi wonk' umntwana wayenxiba impahla yeKrisimesi, intsha *kraca* ...' (p.75)	On Christmas Day every child wore *brand* new 'Christmas clothes'.
'Wandithela *thsuphe* ubawo ngonobangela wengxaki endandikuyo.' (p. 8)	Father began *hinting* at what was at the root of my problem.

'*Hebhu hebhu* uThembeka, kungekudala *phekhethe*. [...] Naba bantwana basekhaya *yoyi, yoyi, yoyi, cum.'* (p. 236)	Thembeka *slowly dozed* off till finally she *was out* like a candle One by one, *off, off, off* they went until they too *were out*.
'Lee *thaa* kum ithamsanqa elikhulu elilelam.' (p. 237)	My exceeding good fortune began to *dawn* on me. (lit. It *became clear* to me the great fortune which was mine.)

Cultural background

Beadwork

Beadwork is an integral part of traditional Nguni dress. Before the introduction of glass beads (probably first obtained from Portuguese explorers and traders) natural material was used (and still is): ostrich egg shells, seeds, horn, etc. Decorating with beads has a purpose far beyond mere ornamentation and 'dressing up'. It is also the outward sign of relationships between people, their status in society, their age group, as well as the ritual status or spiritual power of the wearer. Messages were often transmitted through the use of various colours, colour combinations and motifs (peculiar to different regions), e.g. the small rectangular 'love letters' (*ama***phico**) made by teenage girls to indicate their love for a young man.

Traditionally, young girls and women made beadwork with a particular wearer in mind, but also for themselves and other women. Highly prized items of beadwork were handed down from mother to daughter or were made by mothers for daughters. Apart from necklaces, bracelets and anklets they also made aprons, collars, headbands and belts.

Necklaces with many strings of beads, *izi***danga**, were usually worn by chiefs and senior men on ceremonial occasions. The beaded collar worn by Nelson Mandela in this famous picture and the one worn by former US vice-president Al Gore when he was granted the honorary mayorship of Crossroads, Cape Town in June 1997, are called *ama***thumbu** or *ama***cangqi**.

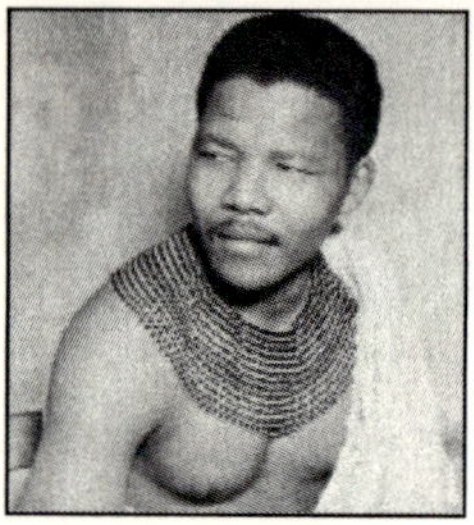

Nelson Mandela
(Courtesy: Mayibuye Centre)

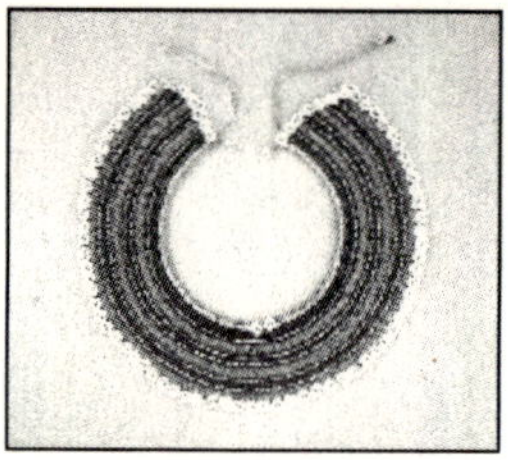

amathumbu
(National Gallery)

Al Gore (*Cape Times* 09/06/98)

Much of the beadwork produced today caters for the tourist trade. This market has led to changes in design, colours and colour combinations. 'The sale of beadwork to strangers has meant that a greater emphasis is placed on its commercial value than on its symbolic meaning.' (*South African National Gallery 10/93*)

Beads are also an integral part of the traditional healer's dress. (*Cape Argus*, 15/01/97)

How to apply it

1 Complete questions appropriately

Complete the following questions which you might ask a shopkeeper by filling in the missing object concords:

(a) Ndinga____fumana phi amacici?
(b) Ndinga____fumana phi iingobozi?
(c) Ndinga____fumana phi imibhinqo?
(d) Uya____thengisa iminqwazi? (*hats*)
(e) Uya____thengisa izinxibo zakwaNtu?

2 A shop assistant needs to know 'which'

(a) Ufuna __________ umbala?
(b) Ufuna __________ isayizi?
(c) Ufuna __________ izihombiso-mzimba?
(d) Ufuna __________ ingobozi?
(e) Ufuna __________ amacici?

3 Read the text and answer the questions

> **EZAKWANTU**
> **Nantoni na eyenziwe ngeentsimbi**
> **Siziincutshe zezakwaNtu**
>
> Sithengisa iimpahla, oonopopi, iinqawa, iingxowa, imilengalenga yodonga, iimagi ezihonjiswe ngeentsimbi, amatsheyini eendondo, iintsimbi zomqala, ezengalo, ezamaqatha njalo, njalo.
>
> Kuphela sifowunele: Siza kukwenzela zonke izinto ngakumbi ezeentsimbi okanye ke ngaphandle kweentsimbi!

(a) What kind of text is it?
(b) What is the active form of '-**ho*nj*iswa**'?
(c) Fill in the correct form of the possessives:
ixabiso ____nopopi; ixabiso ___nqawa (pl.);
ixabiso ____ngxowa
(d) There are two nouns adopted from English. What are they?

4 Read the dialogue and answer the questions

(You might need to consult the Xhosa–English vocabulary.)

A Molo, Nkosikazi. Uthengise izinxibo zakwaNtu na?
B Hayi, ndilusizi, ziphelile. Ndizithengise kakhulu. Zifunwa gqitha kule mihla.
A Uyazi uza kuzifumana nini kwakhona?
B Ngelishwa andazi. Mhlawumbi kule nyanga izayo.
A Andizi kuba kho kule nyanga izayo. Ndiza kubuyela apha kulo nyaka uzayo. Andihlali apha.
B Uvela phi?
A Ndivela eKapa.
B Oo ndiyabona. Mhlawumbi kukho enye into oyinqwenelayo? Sinazo izihombiso-mzimba ezihle zakwaNtu. Sikwanazo neentlobo ngeentlobo zeengobozi ezintle.
A Ndifuna iingobozi, enye enkulu nenye encinci noko.

B Yiza ngapha ukhethe.
A Ndiyasithanda kakhulu isihombo sale, kodwa inzima inkulu gqitha. Andinakuyiphatha.
B Uyithanda njani le?
A Intle. Ikhaphukhaphu. Ndifuna le. Yimalini?
B Yi-R250.00.
A Yhu, idulu kakhulu. Undibiza ixabiso eliqhelekileyo?
B Kakade. Zonke izinto zidulu kule mihla.
A Ungandibonisa le isekoneni. Ndiyayithanda. Ilula kunale. Isihombo sayo sihle kanjalo.
B Le itshiphu kunale inzima.
A Ndiza kuyithenga nale incinane. Ukuba ndithenga ezimbini uza kulihlisa ixabiso kancinci?
B Ewe, Nkosikazi, ndiza kulihlisa nge 10%.
A Ndiyabulela. Athini amaxabiso azo?
B R280.00. Nantoni enye?
A Hayi, kulungile.
B Hamba kakuhle Nkosikazi. Sobonana kulo nyaka uzayo.
A Kulungile.

(a) Uvela phi umthengi?
(b) Kutheni zingekho izinxibo zakwaNtu?
(c) Umthengi uthenga ntoni endaweni yezinxibo?
(d) Umthengisi ulihlisa ixabiso ngepesenti engakanani?
(e) Umthengi ufuna ukubuyela nini evenkileni yezakwaNtu?

5 List the clothes usually worn by men and women

Use the following words: (a) ilokhwe (b) iikawusi (c) ibhatyi (d) ibhatyi yemvula (e) umnqwazi (f) ihempe (g) iqhina (h) izihlangu (i) ibhulukhwe (j) ibhlawuzi (k) isuti (i) iqhiya.

1 Anxiba iimpahla eziphi amadoda?

____

____

____

____

____

____

2 Kunxitywa ntoni ngabafazi?

____

____

____

____

____

____

6 Buying a skirt

Fill in the missing relative concords to describe what kind of skirt you want to buy:

(a) Ndifuna umbhinqo ____namabala _____ninzi.
(b) Ndithanda amabala ____qaqambileyo.
(c) Andithandi mibhinqo ____futshane gqitha.
(d) Zange ndithenge mbhinqo ____dulu gqitha, kodwa andithengi mibhinqa ____tshiphu kanjalo. Ndithanda iimpahla zeempawu ___________ (-hle; of good quality).

7 What goes with what?

Fill in the relative concords:

(a) Ndicinga ukuba iblawuzi ___mhlophe ihamba kakuhle nombhinqo ____mnyama okanye ____luhlaza?
(b) Ucinga ukuba le lokhwe ____bomvu ihamba kakuhle nebhatyi ____ntsundu?
(c) Andicingi ukuba ezi zihlangu ____lubhelu ____kho (your) ziyahamba nebhulukhwe _____pinki!

8 Use the comparative or superlative and say

(a) Ndithanda iintsimbi zomqala nga_____ kwazo __onke izihombiso-mzimba.
(b) Ndicinga ukuba le yeyona ngobozi __lungileyo.
(c) Zihle ezi zihlangu kuna__ __onke.
(d) Le lokhwe __ntle __luhlaza njengengca idulu kuna__ __luhlaza njengesibhakabhaka.

9 Characterize people by comparing them to certain animals

Use this list: ihlosi (leopard), inyosi (bee), ingonyama (lion), indlovu (elephant), undlebende < indlebe = ear + de = long (donkey).

(a) Unamandla kuna- ______________________________

(b) Unamendu kuna- ______________________________

(c) Unenkani kuna- ______________________________

(d) Ukhuthele kuna- ______________________________

(e) Unzima kuna- ______________________________

10 Change the comparisons in Exercise 9 using 'njenga-'

(a) ____

(b) ____

(c) ____

(d) ____

(e) ____

11 Fill in the missing possessives. Keep in mind that 'their' refers to 'abantu':

Kulunge kakhulu ukufunda iilwimi zabanye *aba***ntu** kuba ngaloo ndlela umntu uzuza ulwazi ngemo-ntlalo ______ nezithethe ______ nokuba bangabantu abaluhlobo luni na.

It is very good to learn the languages of other **people** because in that way a person gains knowledge of **their** way of life and **their** customs and what sort of people they are.

12 Fill in the missing possessive pronouns:

(a) *U***nyana** (my) ______ *u*sesikolweni. Uphi (yours) ________? _________ (Mine) *us*ekhaya.

(b) *Um***thi** (my) ______ *u*khula kakuhle. Unjani *u*khula (yours) ________? (Mine) _________ *u*khula kakuhle nawo.

(c) *U***sana** (my) ________ *lu*sekhaya. Luphi (yours) ________? (Mine) _________ *lu*sesibhedlele.

(d) *Uku***tya** (my) _________ *ku*setafileni. Kuphi (yours) _________? (Mine) ___________ *ku*sekhitshini.

13 Answer the questions below:

(a) *Aba***ntwana** *ba***bo** *ba*sesikolweni.
Baphi *a***benu**? ____________(*Ours* are at home.)

(b) *Ame***hlo** *a***m** *a*lungile.
*A***wakho** *a*njani? ____________(*Mine* are good too.)

(c) *Imi***thi** *ya***m** ikhula kakuhle.
*I*njani ikhula *e***yakho**? _________(*Mine* are growing well too.)

(d) Nali *i***khaya** *la***m**.
*Li*phi *e***lakho**? ____________(*Mine* is far away.)

(e) Nasi *isi***kolo** *sa***m**.
*Si*phi *e***sakho**? ____________(*Mine* is far away.)

(f) *In***gxowa** *ya***khe** (intombi) *i*sendlwini.
*I*phi *e***yakho**? _______________(*Mine* is here.)

(g) *Iing***xowa** *za***zo** (iintombi) *zi*sendlwini.
*Zi*phi *e***zenu**? ________________(*Ours* are here.)

14 Read the text and answer the questions

ULindiwe Mabuza ngomnye (a) wamabhinqa anempumelelo (b) ebomini. Ungumyili nomthungi weempahla ophambili. Ungumnini we*Fashion Design Studio*. Igama lakhe laziwa gqitha kwezefashoni kweli (c) naphesheya. Ngo-1995 (d) wamenywa ukuba amele uMzantsi-Afrika Kwi'*Sun Europa Fashion Show*' eParis. Abantu baseFrance bazithanda gqitha iimpahla zakhe. Ungumlawuli nenqununu ye*Lindiwe Academy of Fashion Design*. Ufundisa abathungi abakhasayo (who are still novices Lit. still crawling). ULindiwe uthi (e) uyifumene impumelelo ngenxa yabantwana bakhe ebebesoloko bemkhuthaza. Ukholelwa ukuba 'Xa ufundisa umntwana, ufundisa ilizwe, xa utyebisa ibhinqa, utyebisa ihlabathi.'

(a) What is another word for *i***bhinqa**? You should know its derivation.
(b) ebomini is a **locative**. What is the basic noun?
(c) Which word could you insert here?
(d) What is the **active** of this **passive** form?
(e) What is the **infinitive**?
(f) Find the four **copulative forms** and the three **object concords** in the text.

Test yourself

1 Instead of the superlative '**ngoyena mntu ulungileyo**' in the sentence '**USipho ngoyena mntu ulungileyo**', use '**kunabo bonke**' and '**ngaphezu kwabantu bonke**'.
2 Compare the size of two dresses by saying: 'The red dress is **bigger than** the white dress.'

3 Compare the quality of two dresses by saying: 'This dress is **better than** that (one).'
4 Compare the cost of two dresses by saying: 'The red dress is **as expensive as** the white dress.'
5 In Unit 13 you saw that the adverb '**very**' can be expressed by an ideophone, e.g. *imi***funo** *in***tsha** *krebhe*. Which other two adverbs could you use to express '**very**'?
6 Advise someone: 'Try to drink **as much** water **as** you can.'
7 Inform someone that: 'Both of us will come as soon as we can.'
8 How do you say '**her** name (referring to *in***tombi**), **their** names (referring to *iin***tombi**), **their** dresses (referring to *aba***fazi**)'?
9 Instead of saying 'Y***i*****moto** *ya***m** le', say 'It is mine'; and instead of 'Ng*aba***ntwana** *b***ethu** aba', say 'They are ours'.
10 Ask: 'Can you both come?'

If you have done all exercises and answered the questions above correctly, then you are well prepared to proceed to the next unit.

15 Iinkathazo zohambo
Travel woes

In this unit you will learn how to:

- ask for and give directions
- ask about and describe road conditions
- offer someone a lift
- express irritation at yourself
- express gratitude at someone's fortuitous arrival / presence
- say what is wrong with your car
- make arrangements for car repairs

Incoko

CD 2, tr 6

After making their purchases Jenny and Peter resume their journey but get lost and ask a passerby for directions.

UPeter	Molo tata, kunjani?
Umhambi	Molweni. Hayi, ndisatotoba, mfo wam!
UPeter	Ungasinceda, bawo? Silahlekile. Ingaba le yindlela eya engcwabeni lika**Sandile**?
Umhambi	Hayi, nihamba ngendlela engeyiyo.
UPeter	Siza kuyibamba phi ke ngoku eyiyo?
Umhambi	Buyani umva ngalo mgaqo nize ngawo. Nakufika kwisiphambuka sokuqala, nilandele indlela yasekhohlo. Emva koko, hambani *ngqo.* Emva kwekhilomitha niza kubona isalathiso esithi '***Engcwabeni likaSandile***'.
UPeter	Injani indlela? Yindlela yetha?
Umhambi	Hayi, yindlela yegrabile. Enye into, ilisongololo! Kukho enye indlela apha ngasekunene ekufutshane kunayo. Ngelishwa ayilunganga.

UPeter	Enkosi kakhulu, tata, usincedile. Kanene, uya phi, tata? Ingaba singakukhwelisa?
Umhambi	Hayi enkosi, ndilinde intombi yam apha.

They follow the shorter road and have a puncture!

UPeter	Nx! Ivili ngebe lingagqabhukanga ukuba bendithathe umgaqo wetha!
UJenny	Kusoloko kulula ukuqonda emva kwesithonga!

Luckily a passing motorist stops to give assistance.

Umqhubi	Molweni, yintoni umonakalo? Ndinganinceda?
UPeter	Molo Mnumzana. Ngathi ivili lam ligqabhukile. Ungandiboleka ujack? Ngelishwa owam uthe *shwaka*!
Umqhubi	Hayi, ilishwa! Linda umzuzwana, ndiza kumkhupha ujack ebhuthini. Linomoya ivili lolaleliso?
UPeter	Ngethamsanqa ndilimpompe izolo!

The good Samaritan helps Peter change the tyre.

UJenny	*Kwekhu, tshotsho ufike,* Mnumzana!
UPeter	Inene! Kambe ke, Mnumzana, ingaba ikhona igaraji ekufutshane? Ndiyoyika ngathi siza kuphelelwa yipetroli kamsinyane. Andiyiqondi le nto kuba ndiyizalise izolo itanki!
Umqhubi	Ingaba kukho umngxuma etankini? Uyazi, yenzeka lula loo nto ezindleleni zasemaphandleni! Masikhangele!
UPeter	Oo! ilishwa! Unyanisile! Inene, kukho umngxunyana ongange-ertyisi! Siza kuthini?
Umqhubi	Hayi, mfondini, sukuxhala. Ukuba unayo isepha, ndiza ku*wu*vingca. Emva koko, ungaqhuba uye egaraji.
UPeter	Igaraji ikude kangakanani?
Umqhubi	Ikufuphi, ndilandele.
UPeter	*Nangamso*, Mnumzana. Inene usincedile!

When they reach the garage Peter expresses his gratitude again. They exchange names and addresses before taking leave of each other. Peter then arranges for the petrol tank to be repaired.

Umkhandi	Molo, ndingakunceda ngantoni, Mnumzana?
UPeter	Molo, Mnumzana. Ngelishwa kukho umngxunyana kwitanki yepetroli yam. Ungayilungisa kwangoku?
Umkhandi	Eh, ndinomsebenzi omninzi kodwa ndiza kuzama.
UPeter	Oo ndiyabulela. Kuza kuthatha ixesha elingakanani ukwenza loo nto?

Umkhandi	Mm, mandibone, malunga neeyure ezimbini.
UPeter	Ungandixelela, uza kubiza malini lo msebenzi?
Umkhandi	Kunzima ukutsho kanye, Mnumzana. Malunga neR350
UPeter	Kulungile, Mnumzana. Masiyishiye ke imoto. Sobonana va!

Isigama

-totoba	totter along	-boleka	borrow / also lend
-lahleka	be lost	ujack	jack
ingcwaba	grave	umzuzwana	moment
indlela engeyiyo	the wrong road (lit. the road which is not)	-khupha	take out
		ibhuthi	boot
-buya umva	turn back	ivili lolaleliso	spare wheel
umgaqo	road	*kwekhu, tshotsho ufike!*	*thank goodness you arrived!*
nakufika	when you arrive at		
isiphambuka	intersection	-phelelwa	used up completely
isalathiso	sign	umngxu<u>**m**</u>a	hole
itha	tar	umngxu***ny***ana	small hole
igrabile	gravel	amaphandle	countryside, rural areas
ilisongololo	it's winding like a millipede	siza kuthini?	what are we going to do?
-khwelisa	give a lift	-ngange-ertyisi	like a pea
nx!	damn!	isepha	soap
-gqabhuka	burst	-vingca	close up
ukuqonda	to be wise	kangakanani?	how far?
emva kwesithonga	after an event	-lungisa	repair
isithonga	loud bang / report	-ngakanani?	how long?
umonakalo	trouble / damage	mva	later

How to ...

Ask for and give directions

Ingaba le ***yin*dlela *e*ya** *e*____________________?
Siza ku*yi***bamba phi** ke *in***dlela** *e***ya** *e*_________?
*U***xolo** nginga**fikelela njani** *e*________________?

Hamba*ni* *ngqo*.
Nihamb<u>e</u> kw*isi***phambuka** so*ku***qala**, ni**landel**<u>e</u> *in***dlela** yase**kunene**.
Buya*ni* umva **nga***lo* *m***gaqo.**
U**phantse ufik**<u>e</u>! (You're nearly there!)

Ask about and describe road conditions

Injani *in***dlela**?

Ilung*ile.*
Im**bi**.
*Ayi***lung***anga.*
*Yin***dlela** **yetha**.
*Yin***dlela** **yegrabile**.
*In***dlela** i*li***songololo**.
*Yin***dlela** *e***kufutshane**.
*Yin***dlela** *e***kude** kakhulu.

Offer someone a lift

Singa*ku***khwelisa**?

Express irritation at oneself

Nx! Nxa!

Express gratitude at someone's fortuitous arrival / presence

Kwekhu, tshotsho ufike!
Kwekhu, tshotsho ube kho!

Say what is wrong with your car

Ingathi kukho *um***ngxuma** *e***tanki** ye**petroli**.
*I***moto** yam **yaphuk***ile.*
*I***moto** yam **ixing***ile* (stuck).
*I***moto** yam *ayi***qhwithi** *i* (won't start).
*I***moto** yam **ifuna** *ama***nzi**.
*I***moto** yam **iphelel<u>w</u>e** *yi***petroli**.
*Izi***bane** *azi***sebenz***i.*
*I***bhetri** ye**moto** yam **iflethi**.

Make arrangements about car repairs

Unga*yi***lungisa** kwangoku?
Kuza ku**thatha** *i***xesha** *eli***ngakanani** uku*yi***lungisa**?
Unga*yi***tsala** *i***moto** yam? (tow)
Uza ku**dla** **malini** lo *m***sebenzi**?
Uza ku**xabisa** **malini** lo *m***sebenzi**?

How it works

1 How to express: 'I am not', 'you are not', 'we are not', 'he / she is not', 'they are not' + noun (copulative)

The **negative** of the **copulative construction** is formed from the **negative SC** + copulative '*-ng-*' + **o** + **prefix** of the noun **minus initial vowel**:

*Andingom***qhubi** unamava.	**I am not** an experienced **driver**.
*Asingoba***qhubi** banamava.	**We are not** experienced **drivers**.
*Akungom***qhubi** mbi.	**You are not** a bad **driver**.
*Aningoba***qhubi** banamava.	**You are not** experienced **drivers**.
*Akangom***qhubi** ulungileyo.	**He /she is not** a good **driver**.
*Abangoba***qhubi** balungileyo.	**They are not** good **drivers**.

With nouns belonging to Classes 3–15, the non-concording '*asi-*' replaces the negative subject concord:

*Asingom***gaqo ulungile***yo*.	**It** *is not* a good road.
*Asiyomi***gaqo ilungile***yo* .	**They** *are not* good roads.
*Asilo***cebo** lihle elo.	**It** *is not* a good idea.
*Asisosi***bhedlele** sikhulu.	**It** *is not* a big hospital.
*Asiyon***dlela ilungile***yo*.	**It** *is not* a good road.

2 How to express 'it is not me' / 'you' / 'us', etc.

'**Asi**'- is also prefixed to the copulative of **emphatic pronouns** to form the negative (cf. **Unit 11**). Compare these positives and negatives:

*Ndi***m**.	It is **me**.
***Asindi*m**.	It ***is not*** **me**.
*Si***thi.**	It *is* **us**.
***Asisi*thi**.	It ***is not*** **us**.
*Ngu***we**.	It *is* **you** (s.).
***Asingu*we**.	It ***is not*** **you** (s.).
*Ni***ni**.	It *is* **you**. (pl.)
***Asini*ni**.	It ***is not*** **you**. (pl.)
*Ngu***ye**. (*um***qhubi**)	It *is* **him / her**.
***Asingu*ye**.	It ***is not*** **him / her**.

*Nga***bo**. (*aba***qhubi**)	It *is* **them**.
Asinga**bo**.	It ***is not*** **them**.
*Nga***wo**. (*um***gaqo**)	It *is* **it**.
Asinga**wo**.	It ***is not*** **it**, etc.
*Yi***yo**. (*in***dlela**)	It *is* **it**, etc.
Asiyi**yo**.	It ***is not*** **it**, etc.

Negative copulatives with possessive pronouns:

Asing*o*wam.	It is **not** *mine*. (the child)
Asing*o*bethu.	They are **not** *ours*. (the children)
Asis*o*sabo.	It is **not** *theirs*. (the key)
Asiy*o*yakhe.	It is **not** *his / hers*. (the address)

3 Negative forms of relative adjectives and adjectives

In **Unit 8** you saw that simply prefixing the subject concord to the relative stem forms the predicate:

Ndilusizi, *i*moto yam **i**mdaka.	I **am** sorry, my car **is** dirty.

To form the negative, simply prefix the **negative subject concord**:

*Um***gaqo** *awu***banzi**.	The road *is not* **wide**.
*Imi***gaqo** *ayi***banzi**.	The roads *are not* **wide**.
*In***dlela** *ayi***banzi**.	The road *is not* **wide**.
*Iin***dlela** *azi***banzi**.	The roads *are not* **wide**.

Negative forms of **adjectival stems** (cf. **Unit 8**), however, insert the **adjectival concord** between the **negative subject concord** and the **adjectival stem**:

*Um***gaqo** *m***hle**.	The road *is* **good**.
*Um***gaqo** *awum***hle**.	The road *is not* **good**.
*Imi***gaqo** *mi***tsha**.	The roads *are* **new**.
*Imi***gaqo** *ayimi***tsha**.	The roads *are not* **new**.
*In***dlela** *im***bi**.	The road *is* **bad**.
*In***dlela** *ayim***bi**.	The road *is not* **bad**.
*Iin***dlela** *zim***bi**.	The roads *are* **bad**.
*Iin***dlela** *azim***bi**.	The roads *are not* **bad**.
*Is***alathiso** *si***ncinci**.	The sign *is* **small.**
*Is***alathiso** *asisi***ncinci**.	The sign *is not* **small**.

Note: In colloquial speech the **negative** form of adjectives and relative adjectives will often be heard ending in '**-anga**':

*Um***gaqo** *awum***hlanga**.	The road *is not* **good**.
*Imi***gaqo** *ayimi***tshanga**.	The roads *are not* **new**.
*In***dlela** *ayim***banga**.	The road *is not* **bad**.
*Iin***dlela** *azim***banga**.	The roads *are not* **bad**.
*Aku***shushwanga** namhlanje.	It *is not* **hot** today.

4 *Interrogative adjective '-ni?' = 'of what sort / kind?'*

This construction may be used with reference to new-born babies and animals to find out whether they are male or female:

Ufuna **m***ntwana* *m***ni**? Inkwenkwe okanye intombazana?

Uthanda	*m***ntu**	*m***ni**?	Uthanda	*ba***ntu**	*ba***ni**?
Ukhetha	*m***sebenzi**	*m***ni**?	Ukhetha	*mi***funo**	*mi***ni**?
Ufuna	**phepha**	*li***ni**?	Ufuna	*ma***so**	*ma***ni**?
Ukhetha	*si***qhamo**	*si***ni**?	Ufuna	*zi***qhamo**	*zi***ni**?
Ukhetha	*n***ja**	**ni**?	Uthanda	*zin***gobozi***	*zi***ni**?

Wenza *lu***thambo*** (exercise) *lu***ni**?
Ukhetha *bu***tywala*** (alcohol) *bu***ni**?
Ukhetha *ku***tya** *ku***ni**?

As you can see the **initial vowel** of the **prefix** of the noun has been omitted and its corresponding adjectival concord is prefixed to '**-ni**'.

***Note**: the reappearance of the consonant associated with nouns of **Class 10** (*z*), **Class 11** (*l*) and **Class 14** (*b*).

Note also: This occurs in the **locative** in **Classes 10** and **11**:

*iin***taba**	> *ezin***tab***eni*	*on / at* the **mountains**
*iin***dlela**	> *ezin***dlel***eni*	*on* the **roads**
*iin***dawo**	> *ezin***daw***eni*	*at* **places**
*iin***xweme**	> *ezin***xwem***eni*	*at* the **coasts**
*iin***donga**	> *ezin***dong***eni*	*at / on* the **walls**
*u***nxweme**	> *elu***nxwem***eni*	*at / on* the **coast**
*u***donga**	> *elu***dong***eni*	*at / on* the **wall**

5 *Exclamations*

There are a number of frequently used exclamations in Xhosa which add 'spice' to the language. Here are some examples:

Annoyance

I-i...! / ish!	Go away! You tire me out!
Nxa! Nx!	Damn!

Assertion

Nako ke!	There you are!

Comfort

Ngxesiii!	Let me kiss it better! (to a child)

Compassion

Mawo-o-o!	I'm sorry!
Yeha!	Oh dear!
Torho! / Torhwana	Shame! (cf. Afrikaans 'tog')

Congratulations

Halala! Huntshu!	Hurrah!

Emphatic affirmation

E-e!	Yes!
Hayi ke!	Sure!
Heke!	Well then!
Ngxatsho ke!	Excellent! / To the point!

Emphatic negation

Hayi bo!	No way!
Hayi khona!	Absolutely not!

Pain

Shu!	Ouch!

Regret

Owu!	Alas!
Ngxe!	Sorry!
Hayi ilishwa!	Oh dear!

Relief

Qabu!	What a relief!
Kwekhu, tshotsho ufike!	Thank goodness you arrived!

Surprise, astonishment

(Oo / Awu) Nkosi yam!	Dear Lord!
Yho! / Yhu!	Gee whizz!
Tyhini!	Gosh!
Tyho! Tyhu!	Good heavens!

Kwowu!	Oh!
Mawo!	My! / Wonderful!
Nyhani!	Really!
Kazi!	I wonder!

Warning

Heyi ... heyi ... heyi (andifuni loo nto)	(accompanying gesture of shaking one's finger at a person)

How to apply it

1 Match the road signs with the English equivalent

The equivalents are: (a) Dangerous curve (b) Dead end (c) Caution (d) Road closed (e) No overtaking (f) Do not enter (g) Roadworks ahead (h) Road flooded (i) Emergency exit (j) Drive carefully.

1 Indlela iyaphela
2 Indlela ivaliwe
3 Indlela iyalungiswa phambili
4 Igophe eliyingozi
5 Qhuba kakuhle
6 Eyakuphuma ngesiquphe
7 Lumka
8 Ungangeni
9 Indlela igqunywe ngamanzi
10 Ungayigqithi enye imoto

2 Ask about the condition of the road

(a) Is the road good? Ingaba ____________________________
(b) Is the road safe? ____________________________________
(c) Is it a tar road? _____________________________________
(d) Is it a gravel road? __________________________________
(e) Is the road still under construction?_____________________
(f) Is the road already open to traffic? Ingaba ______________
_____________________kwizithuthu?

3 You are lost in a town and ask a passerby for directions

(a) *Excuse me sir. Could you help me? I am lost.*
Ufuna ukuya phi?

(b) *I want to go to a shop called Kwantu Crafts. Do you know it*?
Ewe, ndiyayazi. Ikufutshane kakhulu xa ulapha. Ndiza kukucacisela indlela. Hamba *ngqo*. Ekoneni yokuqala ujike ngasekunene. Uza kudlula ezinye iivenkile. Ekoneni elandelayo ecaleni lasekhohlo uza kubona ivenkile yezaKwantu. Ungathanda ukuba ndikukhaphe?

(c) *No, thank you, I understand where to find the shop. It seems very near indeed. First I go straight, then right and then I must turn left*.
Kulungile. Hamba kakuhle.

(d) *Thank you very much, sir. Goodbye*.

4 Complete the questions

(a) ___ma phi iiteksi?
(b) ___khona iibhasi ___ya eRhini?
(c) Kukho ibhasi __ya eRhini namhlanje?
(d) ___phi isikhululo ____bhasi?
(e) __ma phi ibhasi ___ya esitishini?
(f) Iiteksi ___nqabile na ku___ ndawo?

5 Ask

(a) ___khona ____________ (a garage) endleleni?
(b) ________ ____________ (a shop) endleleni?
(c) ________ isikhululo samapolisa endleleni?

6 Ask for the nearest

(a)	shop	Indawoni ______________	_kufutshane?
(b)	hospital	Sindawoni ______________	_kufutshane?
(c)	police station	Sindawoni ______________	_kufutshane?
(d)	phone	Indawoni ______________	_kufutshane?
(e)	doctor	Undawoni ______________	_kufutshane?
(f)	petrol station	Indawoni ______________	_kufutshane?
(g)	place ('dorp')	Indawoni ______________	_kufutshane?

7 Ask somebody

(a)	to give you a lift	Unga______________________?
(b)	to help you	Unga______________________?
(c)	to lend you a jack	Unga______________________?
(d)	to show you the way to Grahamstown	Unga______________________?

8 Tell the mechanic what's wrong with your car

(a)	The lights are not working.	Izibane ____sebenzi.
(b)	The hooter is not working.	Uphondo ____sebenzi.
(c)	The handbrake is not working.	Ibhreki ___sandla ____sebenzi.
(d)	The fan belt is broken.	Ifenibelti ____sebenzi.
(e)	The windscreen wiper is not working.	Isihlambi ___festile ____ngaphambili ____sebenzi.
(f)	My left rear light is not working.	Isibane sam ___ngasemva __sekhohlo ___sebenzi.

9 What can be wrong with your car?

(a)	I have a flat tyre.	Ndin__vili ____ngen__moya.
(b)	My right front tyre is flat.	__vili ___m ___ngaphambili __sekunene __flethi.
(c)	My car has broken down.	Imoto __m __aphukile.
(d)	My car is stuck.	Imoto __m __xingile.
(e)	My car won't start.	Imoto __m ___qhwithi.
(f)	It needs water.	__funa amanzi.
(g)	It has run out of petrol.	__phelelwe ___petroli.
(h)	My car battery is flat.	Ibhetri __moto __m __file.
(i)	My car must be towed.	Kufuneka imoto __m _tsalwe.

10 What has been stolen?

(a) Imoto yam ___biwe.
(b) Ujack __m ___biwe.
(c) Ivili __m lolaleliso __biwe.
(d) Isipaji (wallet) __m __biwe.
(e) Ingxowa ___nkosikazi __m __biwe.

11 Read the dialogue and answer the questions

A Uxolo, Mnumzana, ungandixelela ukuba kukude kangakanani ukusuka apha ukuya eCala? Kukude kakhulu?
B Hayi, akukude. Kukufuphi.
A Ziikhilometha ezingaphi?
B Ndicinga ukuba malunga neekhilometha ezilishumi.
A Ingaba indlela intle?
B Ayimbi gqitha, kodwa ayintle kanjalo.
A Asiyondlela yetha?
B Hayi, asingomgaqo wetha, ngumgaqo wegrabile kodwa ngethamsanqa awumxinwa, ubanzi noko.

A Kulungile. Phambi kokuya eCala singathanda ukubuka idolophu yakho kancinci. Unokusixelela apho kukho indawo ekhuselekile yokumisa imoto?

B Ewe ikhona. Hamba *ngqo*, kwisiphambuka esilandelayo ujike ngasekhohlo uza kubona ibala lokupaka elikhulu elikhuselekileyo ecaleni lasekunene.

A Enkosi kakhulu, Mnumzana.

B Ndlela ntle.

(a) Umqhubi ufuna ukuya phi?
(b) Ziikhilomitha ezingaphi ukuya apho?
(c) Injani indlela?
(d) Yindlela ni?
(e) Kutheni umqhubi efuna indawo yokumisa imoto yakhe?
(f) Ufuna ukupaka imoto yakhe ndawoni?

Test yourself

1 Give the literal translation and explain the formation of '**Indlela engeyiyo**.' = 'The wrong road.'

2 What do you say when expressing gratitude/relief at someone's presence?

3 Describe the following road conditions:

(a) It's a gravel road. (b) It's a good road.
(c) It's a narrow road, not wide. (d) It's a tarred road.
(e) It's the wrong road. (f) It's the right (i.e. appropriate) road.

4 Negate the following: 'Zama ukuwuthatha umgaqo wegrabile. ' 'Bendinemoto kunyaka ophelileyo.'

5 What does 'Úng*um*q**hubi** on*ama***va**' mean and what is the negative form?

6 What is the negative of: 'Licebo elihle elo.'?

7 What are the **negative forms** of the copulatives of the following **emphatic pronouns?**

Ndim Sithi Nguye (umqhubi) Yiyo (imoto)

8 What must you remember when using the locative form of nouns prefixing '*iin-*'(Class 10), e.g. '*iin***taba**' = mountains and '*u-*' (Class 11), e.g. '*u***nxweme**' = the coast, when saying: 'We like to walk **in the mountains**.' 'We also like to walk **along** the **coast**.'

9 Give the positive ('Yes, it is.') as well as negative answer ('No, it is not.') to the following question: Ingaba yeyona ndlela imfutshane eya edolophini? (Is this perhaps the shortest way to town?)

10 What is the difference between '**-ni**' in 'Ufuna**ni**'? and '**-ni**' in 'Ufuna ziqhamo zi**ni**'?

If you have done all exercises and answered the questions above correctly, then you are well prepared to proceed to the next unit.

16 Umzila welifa likaXhosa
Xhosa heritage trail

In this unit you will learn how to:

- ask about someone's holiday
- ask where someone went
- describe travel routes
- express delight

Incoko

CD 2, tr 7

The Murrays discuss their recent trip with the Thamsanqas.

UThemba	Belinjani ikhefu lenu emaXhoseni? Nibe nohambo olumyoli?
UPeter	Belungummangaliso nangona besineenkathazo zemoto ezimbalwa kodwa ngethamsanqa sancedwa ngabantu abanobubele gqitha!
UThandi	Heke, ngesiqhelo kunjalo ke emaphandleni. Kanene, beniye phi kanye?
UJenny	Siluqale ukhenketho lwethu e**Peddie**. Ukususela kwiintsuku zam zokufunda isiXhosa eyunivesithi, soloko ndafuna ukutyelela iindawo zembali yamaXhosa eMpuma-Koloni. Kanene, yintoni 'iPeddie' ngesiXhosa? Ndilibele.
UThandi	Yi**Ngqushwa**, wethu!
UJenny	Oo, ewe, kanene. Heke, siye e**Ngqushwa** kuba besifuna ukubuka laa mthi wodumo – umthi wo*mqwashu.* Emva koko, sasinga e**Qonce** kwimyuziyam yeKaffrarian apho kukho khona inkitha yezinto zakwaNtu ezidala umdla kakhulu. Emva kwemini saya kwikhaya lika**Steve Biko**. Sabona kwanendawo apho wafihlwa kuyo.
UPeter	Ngemini elandelayo, yekoko ukusinga ku**Belekazana**; sihambe ngokugwegweleza sadlula ku**Qoboqobo** saya kutsho kummandla w**Amalinde**.

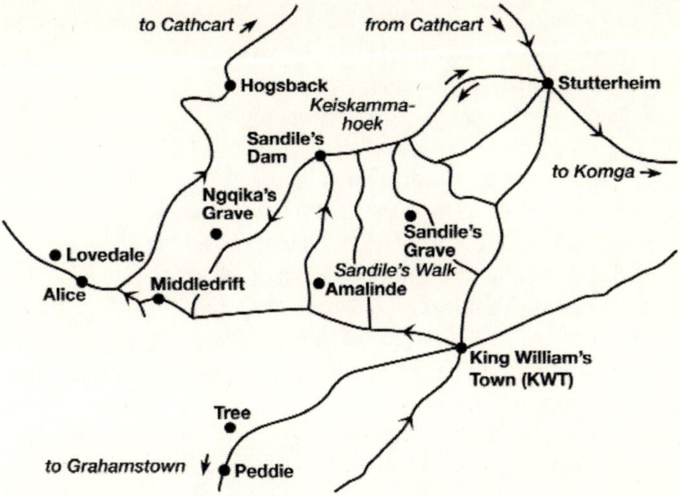

UThemba	Oo **Amalinde**! Niyazi, kulapho kwaliwa khona elinye lamadabi amabi kwimbali yamaXhosa.*
UJenny	Kakade! Lidabi elo elixelwa kumbongo kaJolobe '***UThuthula***', *omnye wemibongo yethu eyunivesithi.
UThemba	Wonke ummandla lowa ngasezintabeni z**Amathole** uzele ziindawo zembali yamaXhosa. Kukho iindawo ezininzi ezithiywe ngamakhosi ama**Rharhabe**.
UPeter	Unyanisile. Sidlule idama lika**Sandile** kwaye sibone nengcwaba lika**Ngqika** endleleni eya *e***Dikeni**.
UPeter	E**Dikeni** sibe nomdla kakhulu ukutyelela i**Lovedale College** ne**Yunivesithi yaseFort Hare** apho uNelson Mandela wayengumfundi khona kunye nezinye iinkokeli zanamhlanje.
UJenny	Mna, ndisand' ukufunda incwadi *The Ochre People* ebhalwe ngu**Noni Jabavu**. Ngoko ke bendifuna kakhulu ukufumana umzi kayise, u**Profesa Jabavu,** owayehlala e**Xesi** xa wayenguprofesa weelwimi zakwaNtu e**Fort Hare**. Ingaba nina nakhe na*yi*funda le ncwadi?
UThandi	Ewe. U**Noni Jabavu** ubhala kakuhle kakhulu, atsho ububone ubuhle balo mmandla. Enye into uzoba umfanekiso omhle

*See later in this unit for historical context.

ngemo-ntlalo nezithethe zamaXhosa ngaloo maxesha. Niyifundile kanjalo enye incwadi yakhe u*Drawn in Colour*?

UJenny Ewe, andithi kanene waqala ngayo?

UThemba Nawufumana ke umzi ka**Jabavu**?

UJenny Hayi, ngelishwa asibanga nampumelelo!

UThandi Nasinga phi emva koko?

UPeter Sahlala ku**Belekazana** iintsuku ezimbalwa. Yho! Ubuhle baloo mmandla buqaqambile. Uxolo olulapho! Nokuzola! Amahlathi elo zwe neengxangxasi *ezixhomis' amehlo*, neentaka ezintlobo-ntlobo nentsholo yazo zizinto ezingummangaliso ukuzibona!

UThemba *Bekuxhelw' eXhukwane* kuwe, Peter, wena mntu wendalo!

UPeter Yitsho uphinde! Yiyo loo nto sigqibe sihlala phaya zonke ezo ntsuku.

UJenny Indawo elandelayo esityelela kuyo ibiyi**Cumakala**. Besifuna ukubona ingcwaba lika**Sandile** kodwa salahleka sancama. Sathi masilande kumkhondo wakhe kodwa saphelelwa lixesha.

UPeter Ngemini elandelayo, sasinga e**Mtata**. Endleleni, sicande amadlelo amahle, iinkomo neegusha zithe *gqa gqa gqa* emathambekeni ukudlula kooma**Qumrha**, nooma**Gcuwa**, nooma**Dytuwa**. Sinjani ukunqwenela ukutyelela i**Qunu** apho wazalelwa khona u**Nelson Mandela**. Ngelishwa, ikhaya elo lakhe lobuntwana alisekho kodwa sisekho sona isikolo sakhe.

UThemba Nibe nalo ixesha lokuya elunxwemeni?

UPeter Kakade! Sihlale e**Mzimvubu** iintsuku zantathu. Indalo apho! Iinduli ezihla ukuya elunxwemeni, amanqugwala namasimi ombona! Inene *ilizwe liyintombazana* kwelo!

Wild Coast, Eastern Cape (Courtesy T.V. Bulpin)

UThemba Hayi, mfowethu, utsho ndanekhwele!

UJenny Endleleni eya e**Mzimvubu** sidlule ivenkile yangaphandle yakudala e**Libode**. Yandikhumbuza isincoko sika**Jolobe** '*Ivenkile Yangaphandle*'. Kodwa eyona ndawo ebesifuna ukuya kuyo kuse**Cala**.

UThandi Nibizwa yintoni *e***Cala**?

UJenny Besimenywe ngabahlobo bethu.

UThandi Nenza ntoni ke apho?

UJenny Sithabathe inxaxheba ebomini bemihla ngemihla. Yaye, ububele esibufumene kubantu balapho buyamangalisa. Ngorhatya singqonge umlilo siphulaphule iintsomi njengemihla yakudala!

Isigama

uhambo	trip	eXesi	at Middledrift
nangona	although	atsho ububone	so that you see
ummangaliso	a delight	imo-ntlalo	way of life
ububele	kindness	isithethe	custom
ukhenketho	trip	andithi kanene?	aren't I right
ukususela kwa-	since		in saying?
imbali	history	-qaqambile	stunning
udumo	fame	ukuzola	tranquillity
umthi womqwashu	milkwood tree	amahlathi elo zwe	indigenous forests
-singa e- / ku-	head for	ingxangxasi	waterfall
eQonce	to KWT	ezixhomis' amehlo	sight for sore eyes
imyuziyam	museum	izintlobo-ntlobo	different kinds
-fihlwa	be hidden,	intsholo	singing
	i.e. buried	-xhelw' eXhukwane*	be delighted
apha wafihlwa	where he	umntu wendalo	nature lover
	was buried	yitsho uphinde!	say that again!
kuyo	at it	eCumakala	at Stutterheim
yekoko ukusinga	and off we went	salahleka	we got lost
kuBelekazana	to Hogsback	sancama	we gave up
-gwegweleza	make a detour	sathi	we wanted
-dlula	pass	masilande	to follow
ummandla	region	umkhondo	track
idabi	battle	-canda	cut through
umbongo	poem	amadlelo	pastures
-zele + cop.	filled with	iinkomo	cattle
-thiywa	be named	iigusha	sheep
idama	dam	-thi gqa gqa gqa	dotted
eDikeni	to Alice	amathambeka	slopes
inkokeli	leader	iGcuwa	Butterworth
ndisand' ukufunda	I've just read	unxweme	coast
umzi kayise	her father's home		

*lit. An animal has been slaughtered at **Xhukwane**.

Xhukwane in the **Middledrift** district was known as a residential area where the people lived in dire poverty and where meat was a rarity. When, therefore, anyone slaughtered a beast it was cause for rejoicing for all the inhabitants. This saying was coined by **AC Jordan** in *Ingqumbo Yeminyanya (The Wrath of the Ancestors)*: 'Kwaku**xhelwe eXhukwane** kuDingindawo asakubona ngathi zimbi ngakuZwelinzima.' (Dingindawo was **delighted** to see that the tables were turning on Zwelinzima.)

eMzumvubu	at Port St John	isincoko	essay
induli	hill	-menywa (<mema)	be invited
inqugwala	round hut	-ngqonga	sit around
amasimi	fields	umlilo	fire
ilizwe liyintombazana	*the country is beautiful* (lit. the country is a young girl)	intsomi	folktale
		njengemihla yakudala	like days of old
ndanekhwele	you've made me quite jealous!		
ivenkile yangaphandle	country store		

How to ...

Ask about someone's holiday

Belinjani *i***khefu** lakho / lenu?
Ibinjani *i***holide** yakho / yenu?
Benibe no**hambo** *olu***myoli**?

Ask where someone went

Ubuye phi kanye?
Beniye phi kanye?
Nibe **na***lo* *i***xesha** lo*ku***ya** *elu***nxwem***eni*?
Nenz*e* **ntoni** ke apho?

Say how and where you went

Si*lu***qal***e* *u***khenketho** lwethu *-e-... / ku-...*
Besifuna uku**bukela** ...
Emva koko sa**singa** *e-... / ku-...*
Nge**mini** *e***landela***yo*, yekoko uku**singa** *e-... / ku-...*
Nge**mini** *e***landela***yo* sa**singa** *e-... / ku-...*
Si**hamb***e* ngoku**gwegweleza** sa**dlula** *e-... / ku-...*
Sa**hlala** *e-... / ku-... iin***tsuku** *ezi***mbalwa**.
*In***dawo** *e***landela***yo* *e*si**tyelele** **ku***yo* **ibi***yi*...
*En***dlel***eni* si**cand***e* *ama***dlelo** *ama***hle**.

Express delight

Belu*ngum***mangaliso**!
*Ubu***hle** baloo *m***mandla** bu**qaqamb***ile*!
*In***dalo** apho!
Bekuxhelw' eXhukwana kum!
Ilizwe yintombazana!
*Ama***hlathi** elo **zwe** nee**ngxangxasi** *ezixhomis' amehlo*!
*Iin***taka** *ezin***tlobo-***n***tlobo** ne*n***tsholo** yazo **zi***zin***to** *ezingum***mangaliso** ukuz*i***bona**!
*Ubu***bele** *esibu***fumane** ku*ba***ntu** balapho buya**mangalisa**.

How it works

1 Place names

Many Xhosa place names derive from geographical features such as rivers, ponds, cliffs, mountains, plants and even animals found in a particular area. **Lusikisiki** takes its pleasant name from the sound of the reeds rustling in a nearby marsh, **Gonubie** (< *i***Qunube)** from the wild bramble berries which grow along the banks of the river. **Keiskamma**, shining water, **Tsitsikamma** clear water, are derived from the Khoi languages as are many other place names recognizable by their clicks. A number of Xhosa place names, especially the cities, have been adopted from English and Afrikaans:

■ **Major cities**	**Izixeko ezikhulu**	**Known derivations**
Cape Town	*i***Kapa** (*e***Kapa**)	< Xhosalized '**Cape**'
East London	*i***Monti** (*e***Monti**)	< Afrikaans '**mond**' i.e. the mouth of the Buffalo River
Durban	*i*Theku (*e*Thek*wini*)	< Xhosa '**itheku**' = 'bay'
Johannesburg	*i***Goli** (*e***Goli**)	< English '**gold**'
	*i***Rhawuti** (*e***Rhawut***ini*)	< Afrikaans '**goud**'
Port Elizabeth	*i***Bhayi** (*e***Bhayi**)	< Xhosalized '**bay**'
Pietermaritzburg	*um*Gungundlovu (*e***M**gungundlovu)	= place of the elephant
Pietersburg	*i*Polokwane	
Pretoria	*i***Pitoli** (*e***Pitoli**)	< Xhosalized 'Pretoria'

Some Towns in the Eastern Cape	Ezinye Iidolophu zaseMpuma-Koloni	
Alice	*i***Dike** (*e***Dik***eni*)	< Xhosa '*i***dike**' = pool
Butterworth	*i***Gcuwa** (*e***Gcuwa**)	
Fort Beaufort	*i***Bhofolo** (*e***Bhofolo**)	(< English Beaufort)
Grahamstown	*i***Rhini** (*e***Rhini**)	
Healdtown	*i***Nxukhwebe** (*e***Nxukhwebe**)	
Keiskammahoek	*u***Qoboqobo** (*ku***Qoboqobo**)	
King Williams Town	*i***Qonce** (*e***Qonce**)	
Lady Frere	*i***Cacadu** (*e***Cacadu**)	
Middledrift	*i***Xesi** (*e***Xesi**)	
Peddie	iNgqushwa (*e***Ngqushwa**)	
Port St. Johns	*u***Mzimvubu** (*e***Mzimvubu**)	(at the home of the hippos)
Queenstown	*u***Komani** (*ku***Komani**)	
Somerset East	*u***Nojoli** (*kwa***Nojoli**)	(< *i***joni** = English soldier)
Stutterheim	*i***Cumakala** (*e***Cumakala**)	
Uitenhage	*i***Tinarha** (*e***Tinarha**)	

Terminology related to administrative divisions

location, settlement, village	*i***lali** (< Afrikaans 'laager')
village	*i***dolophana**
town	*i***dolophu** (< Afrikaans 'dorp')
city	*isi***xeko**
capital	*i***komkhulu**
district	*isi***thili**
area, constituency	*in***gingqi**
region	*um***mandla**
province	*i***phondo**

Insight

You know that many Xhosa words are adopted from English and/or Afrikaans, e.g:

*i***kofu** (coffee) *i***ti** (tea) *i***rediyo** (radio) *i***tikiti** (ticket)

→See **Unit 5** and Xhosa–English Vocabulary for more examples.

This 'cross-pollination' also works the other way around. For example, one often refers to someone who is an expert in a particular field or who is particularly bright as being a '**fundi**' < *um***fundi** = a student, i.e. someone who studies/who is learned.

English speakers often describe a notable event as being 'quite an *in***daba**' < *iin***daba** = news.
The Xhosa word for a 'wall' is *u***donga**. It has been adopted by English speakers with the meaning of 'a huge hole in the ground'.

Many Xhosa words have acquired a second meaning from their original meaning. In this way, Xhosa has manifested itself as a dynamic, vibrant, virile language adaptable to, and developing in harmony with, the changing environment in that it sprouts new words and expressions to accommodate new concepts and cultural items and, to an even greater extent, absorbs and Xhosaizes foreign words and terms.'(Pahl, H.W. ed., *The Greater Dictionary of Xhosa*, Vol 3, p.xxxii)

Below are a number of examples of this aspect of the Xhosa language, some of which you have already come across in this book.

2 *Word adaptations*

- **confer degrees**, **cap** = uku**thwesa** *isi***danga** – original meaning of 'uku**thwesa**' = to **crown**, put something on the head; original meaning of '*isi***danga**' = necklace of many strings of beads

  'Waye**thweswa** *isi***danga** sembeko sobugqirha boncwadi (iD Litt) yiyunivesithi yaseFort Hare ngowe-1974 yokumbulela ngokubhala kwakhe isiXhosa.'

- **capital** i.e. money = *in***kunzi** – original meaning of '*in***kunzi**' = 'a bull'. Cattle (*iin***komo**) have always been the centre and pride of Xhosa life, representing wealth and respect. Apart from supplying milk, meat and leather for clothing, they play a very important part in ancestral sacrifice and in bridal payment (*i***lobolo**). In urban life money, '**capital**', has largely replaced cattle as a symbol of wealth.

- **way**, **road** = *um***gaqo** –
  original meaning: **animal track**
  rules, **regulations** = *imi***gaqo**
  grammar = *imi***gaqo**-*n***tetho**
  constitution = *imi***gaqo**-*si***seko**

■ **headquarters, depot**	=	*i***ziko** – original meaning: **hearth** in centre of **hut**
polling **booth**	=	*i***ziko** lo**voto**
civic **centre**	=	*i***ziko** lo**luntu**
■ **electricity**	=	*um***bane** – original meaning: **lightning**
■ **telephone**	=	*um***nxeba** – original meaning: **rope**
■ **library**	=	*i***thala** le**ncwadi** – original meaning: **shelf in a hut**
■ **book**, **letter**	=	*in***cwadi** – original meaning: thin transparent **coat of the poisonous bulb** *buphane disticha*': '*in***cwadi**'
■ **page**	=	*i***khasi** – original meaning: **ensheathing leaf of mealie cob**
■ **source**, **channel**	=	*i***jelo** – original meaning: **tube**, **reed** to spurt water through when smoking
news **channels**	=	*ama***jelo** een**daba**
reliable **sources**	=	*ama***jelo** *a***thembekile***yo*
■ weather **forecaster**	=	*is***anuse** semo**zulu** – original meaning: '*is***anuse**' = diviner (< -**nuka** = to smell).

How to apply it

In this unit, instead of the usual variety of exercises, you will find a number of Xhosa texts where you can exercise your **reading skill**. Some English texts are also included and these, together with the ones in Xhosa, should whet your appetite to learn more about Xhosa literature, history, culture and traditions.

UJAMES JAMES RANISI JOLOBE (1902–1976)

Ulibone ilanga ngowa-25 Julayi ngonyaka we-1902 e**Ndwe** ngase**Cala** apho uyise wayengumfundisi khona. Wafumana imfundo yokuqala *e***Ndwe** nase**Matatiele**. Ngo1916 wathunyelwa e**Mthwaku**. Ukususela ngo-1919 ufundise kwizikolo ngezikolo.

Ngelo xesha wayehlala ngase**Mt.Frere** apho kuthethwa isiBhaca, isiHlubi nesiSuthu khona. Ngoko ke isiXhosa sakhe sasibuthathaka. Incwadi yakhe yokuqala *UZagula* yalungiswa kunene ngu**S.E.K. Mqhayi**, Imbongi yeSizwe. Phofu, xa wayengutitshala e**Bhobhotyane** nase**Mankazana**, wafunda isiXhosa esithethwa ngamaNgqika omgquba. (→ See next page) Ngo-1926 uye e**Fort Hare** e**Dikeni**. Apho waqeqeshwa kwimfundo yobufundisi waza waphumelela neB.A. Ukususela ngelo xesha upapashe iincwadi ezininzi – umzekelo *Umyezo, Amavo, Elundini loThukela* nezinye. *UThuthula* yimbalasane kwizibongo zikaJolobe ngakumbi ezothando. Ngumbongo-mbaliso osikhumbuza ngoHelen of Troy.

Wahlela iincwadi ezininzi. Kananjalo ukwaguqulele ezinye esiXhoseni. Ngo-1952 wathiwa *jize* ngeMbasa kaVilakazi* yiYunivesithi yaseWitwatersrand. Wayethweswa isidanga sembeko sobugqirha boncwadi (iD.Litt.) yiyunivesithi yase**Fort Hare** ngowe-1974 yokumbulela ngokubhala kwakhe isiXhosa.

UGqirha Jolobe usweleke ngomhla we-16 Meyi ngo-1976.

UJolobe akasayi kulityalwa kwimbali yolwimi lwamaXhosa kuba ulutyebisile watyebisa *nkqu* isithethe sawo.

wathunyelwa	was sent	umbongo-mbaliso	narrative poem
izikolo ngezikolo	different schools	wahlela	he edited
iindawo ngeendawo	different places	wathiwa *jize*	he was awarded
sasibuthathaka	was weak	iMbasa kaVilakazi*	the Vilakazi Medal
yalungiswa kunene	was extensively corrected	yokumbulela	in acknowledgement
		usweleke	he died
Imbongi yeSizwe	Poet Laureate	akasayi	he will never
upapashe	he published	kulityalwa	be forgotten
yimbalasane	is the outstanding	ulutyebisile watyebisa *nkqu* isithethe sawo	he has enriched it (the language) and even Xhosa culture
kwizibongo	among the poems		
ezothando	lit. of things of love		

*Prof. BW Vilakazi was the first black lecturer to be appointed at the University of Witwatersrand. This award, in his name, is given to scholars who have made significant contributions to African languages.

HISTORICAL CONTEXT OF THE BATTLE OF AMALINDE

At the beginning of the 18th century there was a great deal of fighting between **Ngqika** (1778–1829), and his uncle **Ndlambe**, son of **Rharhabe** and brother of **Mlawu (Ngqika's** father), who died, together with his father **Rharhabe**, in a battle against **abaThembu** in 1782. **Ngqika** was only four years old when his father died. **Ndlambe**, therefore, ruled as regent for **Ngqika**. He handed over power before **Ngqika** reached his 20th birthday but continued to try to exercise power which angered **Ngqika** whose ambition it was to rule all ama**Xhosa**. With the help of alliances with other Xhosa chiefs and with the Boers and the British of the Cape Colony, **Ngqika** and **Ndlambe** were engaged in bitter battles. One of the reasons for such bitterness and hostility was **Ngqika**'s abduction of the beautiful **Thuthula**, one of **Ndlambe**'s wives. This action resulted in widespread rebellion. Eventually peace was restored through an agreement whereby **Ndlambe** recognized **Ngqika** as his senior. However, in the great battle of **Amalinde**, fought in 1818, **Ngqika** was defeated by **Ndlambe** but soon after that he secured a victory over his uncle with the help of the British troops. (c.f. Peires)

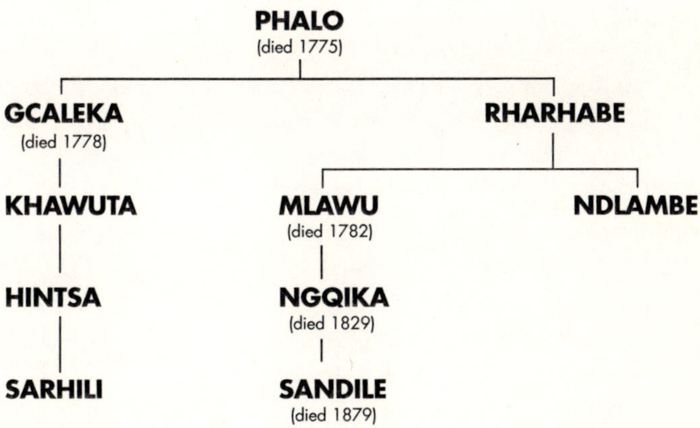

UNontando – Noni Jabavu was born on 20 August, 1919 at Middledrift in the Eastern Cape Province. At the age of 14 she was sent to England in the care of English friends and went to school in York. Her studies at the Royal Academy of Music were interrupted by the Second World War when she joined the first group of women trained as semi-skilled workers and became an oxy-acetylene welder in the aircraft industry. She met her husband Michael Cadbury Crosfield, a film director, while still at school. Their families had first became associated when her grandfather, **John Tengo Jabavu**, politician and journalist who founded and was the first editor of *Imvo Zabantsundu*, led a deputation to the Houses of Parliament to protest against the policies to be implemented in South Africa. It was during this time that he met George Cadbury of the chocolate firm and Joseph Crosfield, Noni's husband's grandfathers. Her father, Davidson Don Tengo Jabavu (1885-1959), was the first Xhosa professor of African languages and Latin at the University of Fort Hare in the Eastern Cape.

Scenes from a South African life

'The hum of conversation was deafening. Every buyer was helped to make his or her choice by the others standing about and who all spoke in the usual terrific tones as if addressing people far off up mountains. From time to time, someone would turn aside, remove his or her pipe that was as long as your arm from the mouth and indulge in a splendid hard jet-like spit on to the floor boards. You had to keep a sharp look-out and leap out of the way.

The Europeans spoke Xhosa, and seemed relaxed, unhurried, like their customers. I pushed my way through and stood at the counter next to a woman in the act of announcing that she had at last reached 'the moment of being about to buy'. She shouted, 'Come, European, I am ready for you.'

Her shoulders were bare, for she had wound her shawl under her armpits and over the married woman's modesty bib in order to free her hands. She now lifted them to her huge turban. The brass bangles from wrist to forearm gleamed. She felt in the folds of the turban, patting the folds back into place – all the while keeping up a powerful running commentary on the reasons why she had decided on the goods she had picked in preference to other specimens of the same, interrupting it to repeat, 'Come, European.'

Then she began to untie the knotted rag. She took out of it some pound and ten-shilling notes. They were grubby, and wrapped around coins: half-crowns, florins, shillings, sixpences, even 'tickeys' – the tiny silver threepenny bits.

'Come, man! What is the matter with this European – is he pretending not to want money?' Her every move was watched, men and women sucking their long pipes, eyes glued on her fingers as she fumbled. One man called out after the last tickey had been unwrapped, 'Where are the pennies and halfpennies?'

'Oh, I keep those in my purse', she said. That in turn was inside a twill bag decorated with black piping and suspended from her waist. She counted out the money. One of the Europeans now sauntered up and joined in the watching. She counted the money a second time, and a third time through, then paused. She raised her face to the ceiling and burst out in loud lament, 'Oh God, these Europeans are killing me! Why do you kill me, European, taking all my money?'

I leapt back a step for she 'threw' her voice like an actress, within inches of my ear. You could have heard her from the back row of a theatre, yet the shopkeeper was only across the counter. He was not disturbed but replied quietly, blandly, in Xhosa, his brown eyes scanning the money spread out in front of him, 'Have you not come of your own volition then, to be killed?'

(Noni Jabavu, *The Ochre People*, pages 64-5, John Murray, London, 1963)

Abantu (Photo: Jean Morris)

Cape Times, 18/3/98

IVENKILE YANGAPHANDLE

Courtesy: T.V. Bulpin

Nokuba ungumhambi akunzima ezilalini zethu ukwazi ukuba ivenkile yiyiphi na kuba iba nguwona mzi uzindlu zibalulekileyo umzi kananjalo ojikelezwe yimithi. (p.69) Abantu abaNtsundu abaninzi bayoyiswa kukubiza amagama abantu abaMhlophe kwaye nangaphandle koko bathanda ukumnika igama lentetho yabo umntu oMhlophe osebenza phakathi kwabo – igama elidla ngokulandela izimbo zomninilo lowo. Ngenxa yezi ndawo wofumana ukuba abeLungu beevenkile bonke ezilalini phaya banamagama esiNtu. Okuya bezingekandi kakhulu iintsimbi zamehlo phakathi kwabaNtsundu ubesakuthi Mhlophe ofike enxiba zona kwa-oko kube sekuthiwa nguMehlomane ukubizwa kwakhe. Umfo osisiqololwane enengxeba isiqingqi sendodana ebenganyali ukuzizuzela igama lokuba nguMafutha. Umfo oyindlezane ububele ubesele eya kubizwa ngokuba nguThandabantu. (p.70–71) Mhlawumbi wena uba kule venkile kuthengwa ngemali ngabo bonke abantu ukanti akunjalo. Le venkile ifana nendawo yentengiso ngezinye iindawo. Abanye ukuze bathenge kufuneka bona ngokwabo bathengise kwakumnini-venkile. Omnye uza namaqanda kwakunye nodaba olubangela ukuba ananise ngawo. (p.71) Lo mzi uyivenkile akwanele ukuba kuthengwe kuthengiswe kuwo kuphela, neposi yesithili esi iphuma kwakuwo apha. Yinto leyo oya kufika iincwadi ziyimfumba kwityeyana ebethelelwe eludongeni phaya. (p.72) Ngaphandle kwezi ndawo sezikhankanyiwe, ivenkile yangaphandle, ivala nelinye ikroba entlalweni yabantu bengingqi leyo ikuyo. Ifana nendawo yembutho, indawo yokubonana kwabantu neyokuthululwa kwemiyalezo eya kumacala abengenakufikelela kuwo lula umntu. Evenkileni uyazi ukuba uya kumbona nokuba mnye umntu oya ngakwelo cala. Andithethi ngolutsha lona kuba luse lusazi ukuba apho lungabonana khona kusevenkileni. (p.72–73)

(J.J.R. Jolobe, *Amavo*, Witwatersrand University Press, Johannesburg, 1973)

(Translation in key at the end of the book.)

SAMUEL EDWARD KRUNE MQHAYI (1875–1945)

Courtesy: Imvo

IKHULU LEMINYAKA

KWILITYE lengcwaba likaSamuel Edward Krune Mqhayi kubhalwe kwathiwa "Apha kulele imbongi yesizwe nombhali wencwadi, iphakathi lesizwe sakwaXhosa siphela, inkokheli ekwangumKrestu wenene, makaphumle ngoxolo, umoya wakhe mawuhlale usikhokela isizwe".

'In my final year at Healdtown, an event occurred that for me was like a comet streaking across the night sky. Towards the end of the year, we were informed that the great Xhosa poet, **Krune Mqhayi**, was going to visit the school.'

*(See pages 38–40 in **Long Walk to Freedom**, McDonald Purnell, 1994, for the full account of this momentous occasion in the life of the young Nelson Mandela.)*

This editorial in **Imvo** was written on the occasion of the centenary of the birth of '**Imbongi** ye**Sizwe Jikelele**' – **The Poet of the Nation**, **Samuel Edward Krune Mqhayi**. **Mqhayi** , playwright, poet and praise singer extraordinaire, was born at Tyhume near Alice. His formative years were spent at the Great Place of his uncle Chief Nzanzana where he remained for six years absorbing the traditional atmosphere and studying the customs and traditions of the Xhosa. He listened attentively to the discussions on customary law grasping the intricacies of legal procedure which he would later use as the basis for his chef d'oeuvre *Ityala Lamawele*. He received his education at Lovedale and became a teacher and wrote *Ityala Lamawele* in 1914 while teaching at Macleantown. He was a prolific writer producing many books including poetry, plays and biographies.

After teaching for a year in East London he became assistant editor of *Izwe Labantu* and edited *Imvo Zabantsundu* from 1920–1921, during the last months of Jabavu's life.

In 1927 he wrote seven additional stanzas of *Nkosi Sikelel' iAfrika* and in 1939 he published his autobiography. Among his well-known publications are *Don Jadu, Imihobe nemibongo* and *Inzuzo.*

The editor of *Abantu Batho,* the official organ of the African National Congress named him *iMbongi yeSizwe Jikelele* – the Poet of the Nation. On his retirement he went to Ntab' oZuko near Berlin, where he died in 1945.

The Telling of Folktales (Ukwenziwa Kweentsomi)

It was, and is still to some extent, a Xhosa custom for grandmothers to tell their grandchildren **iintsomi** – folktales. Their purpose was to enforce and support some point of family discipline or custom. They upheld conduct that was for the good of society or the welfare of the community.

Folktales always start with: *Kwathi ke kaloku ngantsomi* (Once upon a time) while the grandchildren usually respond by saying *Chosi!* (Hush!).

> 'Always, however, there was at least one adult, usually grandmama, sitting with us around the fire. To keep us children awake, she would tell *iintsom*i, the fairytale of amaXhosa.
>
> There were tales about ogres and giants, about animals of the forests, great beasts, and about little hopping creatures of the veld. There were tales about animals of the river, huge scale-covered reptiles that could swallow people and animals whole, crushing them to death as they did so. And later on, when hungry, bring them up and chew them as cud.

There were happy tales also: princes and princesses, kings and queens, and chiefs and chieftainesses: stories that we listened to and believed. Stories that were told with such vivid detail and in such modulation of voice that we children saw them in our minds and lived them in our feelings; crying when a little orphaned girl, on her way to her uncle or her grandparents who would look after her (this would-be guardian angel always lived far, far away) fell into the hands of an ogre disguised as a kindly little old lady, with designs to have her for his dinner. We roared with laughter – the kind of laughter that leaves you feeling weak in your belly, tears streaming down your face; honest no-nonsense and no-decorum laughter – whenever cruel giants and cannibals came to grief, usually by inadvertently falling prey to the very traps intended for their victims.

Oh, no doubt, we were blood-thirsty little people ourselves, but we felt self-righteous about it as long as it was the bad, terrible, cruel, ugly ogre, or some such, who thus met his demise.

Some of these stories told us of the origin of man, others were about natural phenomena, and others still were designed to teach us, the unwary audience, some aspect of morality. Looking back now, I see clearly how *iintsomi* are an essential and integral part of the socialization of the child among amaXhosa.'

Sindiwe Magona, *To My Children's Children*, David Philip Publishers (Pty) Ltd, Cape Town 1990

Imbangi yokuba imbila iswele umsila

CD 2, tr 7, 09:00

Kwathi ke kaloku ngantsomi ebutsheni belizwe zonke izilwanyana zazingenamsila. Zonke zazonwabile ngaphandle kokumkani wezilo, ***iNgonyama***.

Ithe ke ngenye imini yagqiba ukuba zonke zamkele izipho ukuze zijongeke zintle kakhulu. Yazimema zonke ukuba zize enkundleni. Izilo zaphambana luvuyo ngaphandle kwee***mbila***.

Endaweni yokuya enkundleni zona zakhetha ukuhlala zigcakamele ilanga. Zazisonqena kakhulu kodwa zazizifuna zona izipho. Ngoko ke, zacela ***iinkawu*** ukuba zize zizamkele izipho ezo. ***Iinkawu*** zavuma zaya enkundleni apho zonke izilo zazihlangene khona. ***INgonyama*** yazibulisa yazamkelisa izipho zonke. Ngasinye samkela umsila! Noko ke ukumkani lo wayesel' emdala kakhulu namehlo emadala waza ke ngoko wenza iimpazamo ezininzi. Umzekelo, wanika ***indlovu***, isilo esikhulu kakhulu umsilana omncinane kodwa ***unomatse***, emncinci enjalo, wamnika umsila omkhulukazi. ***Iinkawu*** ke zanikwa imisila yazo zanikwa neyee***mbila*** imisila. Zahamba zonwabile. Zadlula ekhayeni leembila ezo. Zabuza ***iimbila*** ngetheko. ***Iinkawu*** zahleka zaveza imisila yazo emitsha ngokuzidla okukhulu zatsho zisithi: 'Zizipho zokumkani ezi.' Zabongoza zathi ***iimbila***: 'Sinikeni imisila yethu! Ncedani nisinike imisila yethu!' Kodwa ***iinkawu*** zahleka zagigitheka zalatha isihlomelo ngaphantsi koboya emsileni zathi: 'Khangelani. Nantsi imisila yenu. Anizikhathazanga ngokuya kuyamkela, saza ke thina sayihlomela kweyethu.' Zatsho zathi *shwaka* ***iinkawu***. Zaqumba kakhulu ***iimbila*** kodwa azaba nakwenza nto. Zisayiswele imisila ***iimbila*** kude kube nanamhla oko. Kodwa ke, azonqeni njengoko zazinjalo ebutsheni belizwe.

Phela phela ngantsomi!

(**Note**: The proverb closely related to this intsomi is '***Imbila yaswela umsila ngokuyalezela***'.)

Why the rock rabbit has no tail

Once upon a time when the world was young (lit. at the newness of the land) all animals did not have tails. All were happy except for the king of the beasts, the ***Lion***.

So one day he decided that all the animals should receive presents so that they should look beautiful. He invited all to come to his court. The animals were overjoyed (lit. mad with joy) except for the ***rock rabbits***.

Instead of going to the court they preferred to bask in the sun. They were very lazy but they still wanted to receive their presents. Therefore they asked the ***monkeys*** to go and get their presents. The ***monkeys*** agreed and went to the court where all the animals were gathered. The ***Lion*** greeted them and gave out their presents. Each one received a tail. It happened that this king was already very old and his eyes, too, were old with the result that he made many mistakes. For example, he gave the ***elephant***, a very big animal, a very small tail but to the ***squirrel*** which is very small, he gave a huge tail. The ***monkeys*** were then given their tails and were also given those of the ***rock rabbits***. They left happy. They passed by the home of those ***rock rabbits***. The ***rock rabbits*** asked them about the party. The ***monkeys*** laughed and proudly showed off their tails and said: 'These are the gifts from the King.' The ***rock rabbits*** pleaded saying: 'Give us our tails. Please give us our tails'. But the ***monkeys*** laughed and giggled and pointed to a joint under the fur on the tail: 'Look, here are your tails. You couldn't be bothered to go and get them yourselves, so we joined them onto ours!' Having said so the ***monkeys*** disappeared. The ***rock rabbits*** were very angry but they could not do anything. So they are tailless till this day, but they are not nearly as lazy as they were when the world was young!

That is the end of the story!

(lit. The dassie [rock rabbit] has no tail because he sent someone on his behalf, i.e. don't rely on others to do your bidding!)

Test yourself

1 From which language do the place names Gonubie, Keiskamma and Tsitsikamma originate? What is their meaning?

2 What are the two names for Johannesburg and from which languages are they borrowed?

3 What would you **suffix** to '*i***dolophu'** (< Afrikaans 'dorp') meaning **town** to change the meaning to 'village'?

4 The original meaning of '*in***kunzi**' = 'a bull' and of '*um***bane**' = 'lightning'. What is their other meaning?

5 What are the two meanings of '*um***gaqo**'? Name two compound nouns which incorporate the plural '*imi***gaqo**'.

6 The **Battle of Amalinde** was the subject of the poem '**Thuthula**'. Who wrote it?

7 Which prominent Eastern Cape family could boast of having in their midst the editor of the first Xhosa newspaper, Imvo Zabantsundu, a professor of languages and a well-known author?

8 Who wrote the first verse of '**Nkosi Sikelel' iAfrika**? Who wrote the seven additional stanzas? (He was named '*Im***bongi** ye*Si***zwe Jikelele**'– The Poet of the Nation.)

9 What is the introductory and the final sentence when relating a folktale?

10 Give the literal translation of the proverb '*Imbila yaswela umsila ngokuyalezela.*'

Congratulations!

You have finished all the Test yourself questions!

Selected summaries

1 *Summary of the ways of expressing 'and'*

- with **nouns**: **na**- (with vowel coalescence taking place, cf. **Unit 2.8**):

ubisi n**a** + **a**manzi	> ubisi **na**manzi	milk **and** water
ikofu n**a** + **i**ti	> ikofu n**e**ti	coffee **and** tea
amanzi na + ubisi	> amanzi **no**bisi	water **and** milk

- with **locatives** -**s**- is inserted after **na**-:

emilanjeni **nas**elwandle	in rivers **and** in the sea

- with **verbs**:
  second verb ends in **-e** (subjunctive) (cf. **Unit 8.2**).

intlungu zifika zimk**e**?	Does the pain come **and** go?

- connecting **clauses**: **yaye** or **kwaye**:

Kungenwa simahla **yaye** kuhanjwa simahla.	Free entrance **and** free transport (lit. It is freely entered **and** freely gone.)
Uphilile **kwaye** unamandla.	He / she is well **and** is strong.

2 Summary of use of negative 'nga-'- and 'nge-'

- **-nga-** with **verbal predicates**

infinitive	Ndikhetha uku**nga**qhubi ebusuku.	I prefer **not to drive** at night.
imperative (instruction)	U**nga**hambi! (or musa ukuhamba)	Do**n't** go!
subjunctive	Kufuneka a**nga***wu*thathi *um*gaqo wegrabile.	He should **not** take the gravel road.
participial	Ndikhule *e***nga**thethi siXhosa.	I grew up **not** speaking Xhosa.
relative	Nceda ulungise *izi***bane** *ezi***nga**sebenzi*yo*.	Please repair the lights that are **not** working.
continuous recent past tense:	Bendi**nga**sebenzi	I was **not** working.
continuous remote past tense:	Ndandi**nga**sebenzi	I did**n't** used to work.

- '**-nge-**' with **non-verbal predicates**

continuous recent past tense:	Bendi**nge**namoto	I did **not** have a car.
	Bendingekho ekhaya izolo.	I was **not** at home yesterday.
relative clauses:	Imoto yam ine**vili** *eli***nge**namoya.	My car has a **flat** tyre. (lit. wheel *that* has **no** pressure)
	*Yin***dlela** *e***nge**yiyo.	It's the **wrong** road. (lit. the road *that* is **not**)
with '**-ka-**' = **not yet**:	Asityi ilanga li**ngeka**tshoni.	We do**n't** eat before sunset. (lit. before the sun **not yet** gone down)

3 Summary of formatives

- **-ya- / -y-** inserted between the **subject concord** and the **verb stem** in **the long form** of the **present tense indicative:**

Ndiy**a**funda. / Ndiyazi.	I am learning. / I know.

and between the **subject concord** and the **object concord** in **the long form** of the **present tense indicative:**

Ndi**yasi**funda isiXhosa.	I (it) am learning Xhosa.

- **-sa- / = still-** inserted between the **subject concord** and the **verb stem**:

Ndi**sa**funda. / Ndisoyika.	I am **still** learning. / I am **still** afraid.
Bendi**sa**funda.	I was **still** learning.

- **-sa- /-s-** in a **negative** sentence = **any longer** inserted between the negative **subject concord** and the **verb stem**:

Andisafundi. / **Andis**oyiki.	I am **no longer** studying. / I am **no longer** afraid.

- -se- = **still** with non-verbal predicates:

Usemtsha.	He / she is **still** young.

- **locative -s-** and **-l-**:

Usekhaya?	**Are** you at home?
Ulapha?	**Are** you here?

- **-si / -s-** inserted between the **subject concord** and a **monosyllabic verb stem** in the **participial mood**:

Ndiqhwalela ndisiye.	I am limping **going** along.
Ndilungisela ukutya ndisoya inyama.	I am preparing the food while roasting the meat.

4 Summary of the use of the emphatic pronoun

		As for *me*	copula + Abs. pr. *It is me*	na- + Abs. pr. and/with *me*	nga- + Abs. pr. about *me*	ku- + Abs. pr. to *me*, etc.
1st		*m*na	*ndim*	na*m*	nga*m*	ku*m*
		*thi*na	*sithi*	na*thi*	nga*thi*	ku*thi*
2nd		*we*na	*nguwe*	na*we*	nga*we*	ku*we*
		*ni*na	*nini*	na*ni*	nga*ni*	ku*ni*
Noun classes						
3rd	1/a	*ye*na	*nguye*	na*ye*	nga*ye*	ku*ye*
	2/2a	*bo*na	*ngabo*	na*bo*	nga*bo*	ku*bo*
P	3	*wo*na	*nguwo*	na*wo*	nga*wo*	ku*wo*
	4	*yo*na	*yiyo*	na*yo*	nga*yo*	ku*yo*
e	5	*lo*na	*lilo*	na*lo*	nga*lo*	ku*lo*
	6	*wo*na	*ngawo*	na*wo*	nga*wo*	ku*wo*
r	7	*so*na	*siso*	na*so*	nga*so*	ku*so*
	8	*zo*na	*zizo*	na*zo*	nga*zo*	ku*zo*
s	9	*yo*na	*yiyo*	na*yo*	nga*yo*	ku*yo*
	10	*zo*na	*zizo*	na*zo*	nga*zo*	ku*zo*
o	11	*lo*na	*lulo*	na*lo*	nga*lo*	ku*lo*
	10	*zo*na	*zizo*	na*zo*	nga*zo*	ku*zo*
n	14	*bo*na	*bubo*	na*bo*	nga*bo*	ku*bo*
	15	*ko*na	*kuko*	na*ko*	nga*ko*	ku*ko*

5 Summary of sound changes

Vowel sound changes

In Xhosa words two dissimilar **vowels** are never juxtaposed. Throughout this book you have come across the various ways this is avoided which results in various **sound changes.** These **sound changes** facilitate **pronunciation**:

1 Vowel elision – the falling away of the first vowel

the '**a-**' of y**a**- falls away:

ndiy**a** + **a**zi	> Ndiy**a**zi	I know
ndiy**a** + **o**nwaba	> Ndiy**o**nwaba	I become happy

the '**a-**'of b**a**- falls away:

b**a**- + **a**kha ngoku	> B**a**kha ngoku	They are building now
b**a**- + **e**nza ntoni?	> B**e**nza ntoni?	What are they doing?

the '**a-**' of ak**a**- falls away:

ak**a**- + **e**nzi nto	> Ak**e**nzi nto	He / she does not do anything
ak**a**- + **o**nwabi	> Ak**o**nwabi	He / she is not happy

the '**i**-' of 'nd**i**-'/'s**i**-' falls away:

and**i**- +-**a**zi	> And**a**zi	I don't know
mas**i** + -**o**nwab<u>e</u>	**>** Mas**o**nwab<u>e</u>	Let us be happy

the '**i**-' of 'is**i**-' falls away:

is**i**- + -**o**nka	> is**o**nka	bread

the '**u**' of uk**u-** falls away:

uk**u**- + -**o**ja	> uk**o**ja	to roast

Note: After **No**- (the prefix for girls' names) the initial vowel of the prefix of the noun falls away:

No + *i***khaya**	> **No**khaya	home
No + *ubu***ntu**	> **No**buntu	humanity

2 Consonantalization – the change of 'u-'- and 'i- to 'w-' and 'y-' respectively

uk**u**- + -**a**zi	> ukwazi	to know
ul**u**- + -**a**zi	> ulwazi	knowledge
ù- + -**e**nza	> **W**enza ntoni?	What are you doing?
k**u**- + **i**kliniki	> **kwi**kliniki	in / at / from the clinic
i + -**a**kha	> **Y**akha indlu.	He / she is building a house.
i + enza	> **Y**enza iti	He / she is making tea.
i + -**o**ja	> **Y**oja inyama	He / she is roasting meat.

3 Vowel coalescence – the merging of two dissimilar vowels to form one vowel

When nouns follow '**na-**' = and, with, also:

a + **a** > **a:**

U**na** + **a**bantwana	> U**na**bantwana?	= Do you **have** (lit. you with) children?

a + **i** > **e:**

Ewe, unyana na- + **i**ntombi	> unyana **ne**ntombi	= a son **and** a daughter

a + **u** > **o**:

Ewe, intomb**i** + **u**nyana	> intombi **no**nyana	= a daughter **and** a son

When nouns follow **nga-** = about, in, **by**, **by means of**, **with**:

a + **a** > **a:**

pheka nga + amafutha	> Pheka **nga**mafutha.	= Cook **with** oil.

a + **i** > **e:**

sihamba nga- + imoto	> Sihamba **nge**moto.	= We are going **by** car.

a + **u** > **o**:

sihamba nga + **u**loliwe	> Sihamba **ngo**loliwe.	= We are going **by** train.

In nominal possessives:

a + **i** > **e:**

ikomityi ya- + ikofu	> ikomityi yekofu	= a cup **of** coffee

a + i > ee:

abasebenzi ba- + iinkampani > abasebenzi beenkampani = staff **of** companies

a + u > o:

isicelo sa- + umsebenzi > isicelo somsebenzi = application **of** a job

kw**a- + u > ko:**

ukwenziwa + kwa- + ubusi > ukwenziwa kobusi* = the making **of** honey

*'**w**' is omitted before '**o**' for ease of pronunciation.

With a few frequently used **one-syllable verbs** containing a so-called latent '**i**':

a + i > e: siya + (i)**za** > Siy**eza**. = We are coming.

siya + (i)**ma** > Siy**ema**. = We are stopping.

aka- + **(i)va**> Ak**eva**. = He / she does not hear.

aba-+ (i)**va** > Ab**eva**. = They do not hear.

4 Separation of two vowels by a consonant

- In the present tense negative of the 2nd person (s.) and Classes 1, 3, 4, 6 & 9:

a- + ùphungi	> **Aku**phungi.	= **You don't** drink.
a- + ùthethi	> **Aka**thethi.	= **He / she does not** speak.
a- + u**khuli**	> Awukhuli.	= **It** (tree) **does not** grow.
a- + i**khuli**	> Ayikhuli.	= They (trees) **do not** grow.
a- + a**band**i	> Akabandi.	= It (water) **is not** cold.
a- + **ithethi**	> Ayithethi.	= He (the man) **does not speak**.

- in the **object concord** of the **2nd** person (s.):

ndiya + uthanda > Ndiya**ku**thanda. = I love **you**.

- in the **remote past tense:**

ú + akhulela > **W**akhulela efama. = **He / she** grew up on a farm.

- after **ma**- = let in Classes 1 & 6

ma + **a**zole > Makazole. = **Let** them (the men) be calm.

Consonant sound changes

Palatalization: When '-**w**'- is brought into proximity with the consonants **b** and **m** and with the consonant combination **mb** (known as bilabial consonants as they are formed by the lips), the following **sound changes** occur: (cf. **Unit 10.1**)

b > ty

-gqib- + wa	>-gqitywa	= **be finished**

bh > j

-bhubhel- + wa	>-bhujelwa	= **be bereaved** (lit. **be died** for)

m > ny

-fuman- + wa	>-funyanwa	= **be found**

mb> nj

-hamb- + wa >	>-hanjwa	= **be gone**
-khumbul + wa	>-khunjulwa	= **be remembered**

ph > tsh

-khuph- + wa	>-khutshwa	= **be taken out**

Palatalization also occurs in:

- the **locative**:
  ihlobo = summer *e*hloty*eni* = *in* summer
- the **diminutive:**
  umlomo > umlony*ana* = *little* mouth
  umsebenzi > umsetyenz*ana* wokuzonwabisa = a hobby
  (lit. *little* work of making oneself happy)

Nasalization: When '**n**' is brought into proximity with certain consonants, the following sound changes occur:

- when '**n**' precedes '**b**', '**f**', '**p**' & '**v**':

n + b > mb:	zin + bini	> Zimbini.	= They are two.
n + f > mf:	in + fundo	> imfundo	= education
n +p > mp:	in + pilo	> impilo	= health
n + v >mv:	in + vume	> imvume	= agreement

- when '**n**' and '**m**' precede aspirated consonants **kh** , **ph** and **th**:

n +kh > nk:	in + khululek-	> inkululeko	= freedom
n + th > nt:	zin + thathu	> Zintathu.	= They are three.
m + ph > mp:	im + phumelel-	> impumelelo	= success

- when '**n**' precedes '**s**' / '**sh**':
  n + **s** > **nts**: i**n** + -**s**ikelel- > i**nts**ikelelo = blessing
  n +**sh** > **ntsh**: i**n** + **sh**ukum- > i**ntsh**ukumo = movement
- when '**n**' precedes '**hl**':
  n + **hl** > **ntl**: zi**n** + **hl**e > Zi**ntl**e = They are beautiful.
- when '**n**' precedes '**ty**:
  n+ **ty** > **ndy**: i**n** + -**t**yeb- > i**ndy**ebo = wealth
- when two '**n**'s are juxtaposed:
  n + **n** > **n**:e**n** + **n**ye > e**n**ye = one, another

Translations of dialogues

It goes without saying that word-for-word translations from one language to another are virtually impossible. For literal translations consult the vocabulary boxes in each unit.

Unit 1 Getting acquainted on an aeroplane

Stewardess	Good day, ladies and gentlemen. Welcome to flight 301 going to Cape Town.
Thandi	Hello, how are you today?
Jenny	I am well.
Thandi	Oh! You speak Xhosa well! I am Thandi Thamsanqa.
Jenny	I am Jenny Murray. I am glad to meet you. How are you?
Thandi	(No), I am well, thanks. I'm also glad to meet you.
Jenny	Do you live in Cape Town, Thandi?
Thandi	Yes, we live in Pinelands.
Jenny	Oh! I also live in Pinelands.
Thandi	Where exactly?
Jenny	Near Forest Drive. Where do you live exactly?
Thandi	Near Pinelands High School.
Stewardess	Excuse me, ladies and gentlemen. Fasten your seat belts. We'll shortly be arriving in Cape Town. Thank you for choosing Rainbow Airlines. I hope we'll see each other again soon! Welcome to Cape Town! Goodbye.
Jenny	Goodbye, Thandi. It was nice to speak to you.
Thandi	We'll see each other again!

Unit 2 Meeting again at the Murrays' house

Jenny	Hello, come in!
Thandi	How are you?
Jenny	We are well. It's nice to see you again.
Thandi	This is my husband, Themba.
Jenny	Hello, Themba. I'm very glad to meet you. This is my husband Peter.
Themba	I'm glad to meet you.
Peter	We are also glad to meet you. Welcome to our home. This is our son.
Thandi	Hello, my child. What's your name?
David	I am David.
Themba	Do you go to school, David?
David	Yes, I go to Grove.
Thandi	Where are you learning to speak Xhosa?
David	I'm learning it at school (*Nkosikazi*).
Peter	Do you have children?
Themba	Yes, we have a son and a daughter.
Peter	Do they go to school?
Themba	Yes, they do. They go to Westerford.
Jenny	What about something to drink? Would you prefer tea or coffee or something cold?
Thamsanqas	Whatever. Yes, whatever.
Peter	Would you like to sit inside or outside?
Thandi	Let's sit outside. It's beautiful. May I help you Jenny?
Jenny	Thank you Peter and Themba. You can chat (in the meantime).
Peter	Okay!

Unit 3 Knowing how to speak Xhosa

Themba	Peter, you speak Xhosa well. Tell me, where did you learn to speak it so well?
Peter	I grew up on a farm near Grahamstown. Then I continued to learn it at school. Unfortunately, I've forgotten a lot. Also, I know that I make a lot of mistakes, but I'm trying (my best).
Themba	That doesn't matter, making mistakes. What is important is that you try to speak it every day.
Peter	You're right. You must tell me though when I make mistakes.

Themba Fine, but you do follow (understand) well.
Peter Yes, if one speaks slowly.
Themba Well then, I'll also try to speak slowly.
Peter Thanks, because I don't speak as well as Jenny. She also grew up on a farm in the Eastern Cape. She learned it at school and university. She speaks as well as a Xhosa-speaking person – so much so that she teaches it now.
Themba That's lovely! You know, the Dutch saying: *'So veel tale as jij kan, so veel male is jij man.'*
Peter That's so true!

Unit 4 Speaking about work

Peter Tell me, Themba, what's your line of work?
Themba I work for an airline as a personnel manager.
Peter Oh, (that's) personnel manager in English?
Themba You're spot on!
Peter You obviously communicate and work well with people.
Themba Yes, I like to work with people very much. You know the Xhosa idiom: *A person is a person through other persons.*
Peter You are so right!
Themba What's your work, Peter?
Peter I am a horticulturist at Kirstenbosch.
Themba Mm, that's interesting!
Peter Yes, it's interesting work. It is such a beautiful place to work at. Does Thandi also work?
Themba Yes, she also likes to work with people. She is a doctor. She works at the Red Cross Children's Hospital. She goes there in the mornings only. In the afternoon she works at a Primary Health Care clinic.
Peter She also works very hard then.
Themba At which school does Jenny teach?
Peter She doesn't teach at a school. She teaches adults who want to learn to speak Xhosa. You know, there are many people who want to learn to speak Xhosa now, especially business people and staff of companies, housewives, doctors and nurses, etc., etc.
Themba Well, as they say in English: '*Better late than never*!'
Peter How do you say that in Xhosa?
Themba I don't know. Language is like that. It is not always easy to translate, especially when it comes to idioms.

Unit 5 How do you like your coffee?

Peter	At last! Let's quench (our) thirst!
Jenny	Sorry for letting you wait (such) a long time. We were chatting! I'm sure that you must be thirsty.
Peter	Yes, we are very thirsty. We are also hungry.
Themba	No, that's okay, we were also chatting.
Jenny	Thandi, how do you like your coffee? Do you want milk and sugar?
Thandi	Milk only, thanks.
Jenny	And you, Themba, do you want coffee with milk?
Themba	Yes, thanks, and two teaspoons of sugar.
Jenny	Here is the sugar. Help yourself.
Peter	How about some cake and sandwiches, Thandi?
Thandi	Thanks, Peter. May I have a small slice of cake? It looks lovely!
Peter	Indeed, it is delicious. Here's a slice!
Thandi	Thanks. Mm! This cake is delicious, Jenny, may I have the recipe?
Jenny	Sure! Just remind me. Themba, can I also give you a slice of cake?
Themba	Thanks Jenny. I love sweet things very much!
Jenny	Peter, please pass Themba the cake (while) I pour your coffee.
Peter	Okay. Thandi, what about another cup of coffee?
Thandi	No, thanks. One cup of coffee is enough for me.
Peter	Gosh, the sun has disappeared. It's getting cool now. Shouldn't we go inside?
Jenny	Yes, it's suddenly got cold. I am cold. Aren't you cold too?
Thandi	A little.
Jenny	Well, let's go inside then! Peter, please close the door.

oooOooo

Thandi	Jenny, don't forget to give me the recipe for the cake.
Jenny	I haven't forgotten. Here it is. If you prefer chocolate icing you can dissolve a spoon of cocoa powder in a spoon of boiling water and beat well into the icing.

Unit 6 Are you warm enough?

Peter	Are you warm enough or should I switch on the heater?
Themba	No thanks, we don't need a heater. It's not that cold.

Jenny	The Cape weather is like that. One minute the sun is shining, the next (minute) it is raining.
Thandi	No man, don't exaggerate. And don't complain about the Cape weather! The rain is better than drought. We need rain in South Africa. It's scarce.
Peter	Jenny, you sound like the Gautengers! They don't like our weather; they complain about the rain in winter and about the wind in summer!
Themba	But let's be honest, the weather is beautiful in Gauteng in winter. It's dry, it doesn't rain.
Thandi	But the thunderstorms and lightning there in summer!
Jenny	No, let's admit it, every place has its advantages and disadvantages.
Thandi	You're right. For instance, in Durban, the winter is pleasant, but the humidity there in summer is intolerable.
Jenny	Yes, it's exactly like that.
Peter	I hope that the weather will be fine this coming weekend because there is a big cricket match at Newlands. Do you like cricket, Themba?
Themba	Very much! Like Makhaya Ntini says on TV: '*I don't like cricket, I love it!*'
Peter	Well, I'm going on Saturday with David. Would you and your son like to come with us?
Themba	Yes, I would like that very much.
Peter	Okay, I'll phone you on Friday so that we can arrange where and when to meet.

Unit 7 Jenny at work – 'Let's speak Xhosa'

Jenny	Hello, students! Today **you** are going to speak Xhosa, and **I** am going to listen! Who wants to start?
Mark and Paul	We'll start, Jenny.
Mark	I'll be the petrol attendant, Paul will be the motorist.
Jenny	All right, students, talk!

At the garage

Attendant	Good day, sir. How are you, today? How can I help you?
Motorist	Good day, *Mnumzana*. How are you?
Attendant	No, nothing wrong. I'm okay despite the problems. And you?

Motorist	I'm also fine, thanks.
Attendant	Should I fill the tank today?
Motorist	No, give me only 50 rands' worth today.
Attendant	All right sir. How are the tyres?
Motorist	It seems the left front tyre needs a little air. Please check all round.
Attendant	All right, sir. How much air?
Motorist	Pump them to 210 all round. Please don't forget to check the water and oil.
Attendant	No sooner said than done, sir!
After a few moments	
	Well, everything is okay in front. Should I also wipe the windows?
Motorist	That would be helpful!
Attendant	Well, I've finished, sir.
Motorist	I am grateful. Thank you. Here's the money for the petrol. Here's also something for tobacco (tip).
Attendant	Thank you. Goodbye, sir.
Motorist	Goodbye, *Mnumzana*. We'll see each other again.
Jenny	Mark and Paul, you've done well. Congratulations! Well, Val and Sally, let's hear your conversation!
Val and Sally	All right.
At the supermarket	
Val	Sorry, *Nkosikazi*! Did I hurt you?
Lady	No, it's nothing. Oh! You speak Xhosa?
Val	I'm trying.
Lady	No, you're not just trying, you speak it! Where do you know Xhosa from?
Val	Sorry, I didn't understand. Please say that again.
Lady	I said, where did you learn it?
Val	Oh now I understand! I attend Xhosa classes.
Lady	Who is teaching you? (By whom are you being taught?)
Val	A Mrs Murray. She grew up with Xhosa-speaking people, *emaXhoseni*.
Lady	I too am from *emaXhoseni*.
Val	Where is your home?
Lady	In Cacadu.

Val Oh, isn't that Lady Frere in English?
Lady Gosh! You're right. Indeed, you do know Xhosa!
Val Where do you live, *Nkosikazi*?
Lady In Claremont. Where do you live?
Val In Kenilworth, but I work here in Claremont.
Lady I also work here in Claremont. I have a restaurant in Fir Avenue called *'Ningene'* (*Come in*).
Val Really! Perhaps I'll visit you there. Gosh, I nearly forgot, my name is Val Todd.
Lady I'm pleased to meet you, Val. I am Xoliswa Silinga.
Val I'm also glad to meet you, Xoliswa. It was very nice to talk to you. I hope we'll see each other again. I'm going to tell my teacher and the class about your restaurant. Perhaps we'll all visit you there soon.
Xoliswa That would be nice. Goodbye.
Val Goodbye Xoliswa. I'm sure we'll see each other again at the restaurant!
Jenny You also did very well, Val and Sally. I'm happy. I'm very happy with your progress! Congratulations! Now let me wish you all a pleasant holiday.

Unit 8 Thandi at work – 'I am Dr Thamsanqa'

Thandi Good morning, *Nkosikazi*. Hello, my child. Please come in. I am Dr Thamsanqa.
Sit down. Here's a chair. What's your name, *Nkosikazi*?
Mother I am Nonceba Majola.
Thandi And you, my child, what's your name?
Child Lindiwe.
Thandi No, don't cry my child. Don't worry. I won't hurt you. Here's a doll. Do you want to hold it? Well then, *Nkosikazi*, tell me, why have you come to see us here at the hospital?
Mother It's this little one, doctor.
Thandi What is the matter (with her)?
Mother She's complaining of a bad headache, doctor. Another thing, she is coughing. She is coughing a lot.
Thandi How old is she?
Mother Five, doctor.
Thandi Did you bring her *Road to Health* Card?

Mother	Yes, here it is.
Thandi	That's fine. Well then, my child, show me, where exactly is your head sore? Can you point to where your head is sore?
ULindiwe	It's sore here.
UThandi	Is your throat sore?
ULindiwe	No.
UThandi	Are your ears sore?
ULindiwe	Yes.
UThandi	Is there any discharge from her ears, *Nkosikazi*?
UMama	Yes. there is.
Thandi	How long has your child been ill, Mrs Majola?
Mother	This is the third day.
Thandi	Tell me, have you given her something to alleviate the pain?
Mother	Yes, I gave her Panado, but it didn't help at all.
Thandi	Has she (this child) ever had a headache before?
Mother	No, doctor.
Thandi	Has she ever been sick before?
Mother	No, doctor.
Thandi	Has she (this child) any other problems?
Mother	Yes, doctor, she is not eating well.
Thandi	All right, Mrs Majola. I would like to examine her now. Please undress her and lie her down here on the bed.

Unit 9 Peter at work at Kirstenbosch

Peter	Good morning, pupils. Welcome to Kirstenbosch! My name is Peter Murray. This is my colleague Mrs Phumla Bongela. We are both horticulturists here at Kirstenbosch. Mrs Bongela will tell you about the waterwise gardens and the Outreach Gardening Project. This project was started to help schools to establish gardens suitable to your area. But first, I'm going to tell you a little about Kirstenbosch (itself). This garden, famous all over the world for its beauty, was founded in 1913. It is much acclaimed for its collection of South African plants. Look at these pictures taken at the Chelsea Flower Show in London where year after year Kirstenbosch has won many medals.
	oooOooo
Phumla	Well then, pupils, I'm going to visit you at your school so

	that we can start a waterwise garden. I'll bring plants and garden tools, but I also want you to participate in this exercise by trying to prepare the soil at the school.
Pupils	How can we do that, *Nkosikazi*?
Phumla	The best way to start is to make compost. You can start by collecting kitchen waste. For instance, vegetable peelings, egg shells, leaves, bones, grass cuttings, dead flowers, feathers and ash. But don't put in tins, plastic or paper. I'll visit your school next week. We'll choose a suitable spot to make a compost heap. Until then, you can put everything you have collected into these bags. Well then, pupils, I am grateful to you for listening so attentively. Have a nice picnic now but I ask you please to keep the garden clean. Don't forget to pick up all your wrappers before you leave and put them into the rubbish bins. Goodbye. We'll see each other next week.

Unit 10 Themba at work – an interview

Themba	Good morning, Miss Green. Please sit down. I'm glad to see you. How are you?
Miss Green	Good morning, Mr Thamsanqa. Thank you. I'm fine except for feeling a little nervous.
Themba	No, Miss Green, don't be anxious. Relax! It seems that you speak Xhosa well. Tell me, where do you know it from?
Miss Green	I started to speak it when I was still small because my parents worked at a hospital near Keiskammahoek.
Themba	Oh, then you know the pure Xhosa! Can you also write it?
Miss Green	Yes, Mr Thamsanqa, I learned Xhosa at school and also at university.
Themba	Do you know any other languages as well?
Miss Green	Yes, I speak Afrikaans and a little French but the latter less.
Themba	Well then, Miss Green, please tell me a little about yourself.
Miss Green	I was born in 1969 in Cape Town. My parents moved to Keiskammahoek when I was still small, therefore I did the lower standards from Sub A to Std 5 at Keiskammahoek.
Themba	Where did you do your higher standards?
Miss Green	At boarding school in Port Elizabeth. I passed Matric in 1986. After that I studied for a BA degree at Rhodes University in Grahamstown.

Themba	What were your majors?
Miss Green	English and Xhosa.
Themba	Who taught you Xhosa?
Miss Green	Professor Majola. Do you perhaps know him?
Themba	Oh, very well! We studied together. He is a very bright man.
Miss Green	What a teacher! He helped me a lot. Well, I graduated in 1989. I started to work as a teacher. In 1994 I was promoted and became vice-principal.
Themba	Please tell me, why do you want to change jobs now?
Miss Green	I'm afraid many teachers are going to be retrenched. Besides, I am a 'people person'. I would very much like to work with different people. And I think I can make a contribution to your company.
Themba	Well then, Miss Green, do **you** have any questions?
Miss Green	Yes, Mr Thamsanqa. Do you think that I have a chance of being appointed?
Themba	Yes, I think that you have a very good chance!
Miss Green	When can I expect to hear whether I have been successful?
Themba	We'll let you know at the end of next week.
Miss Green	Thank you very much, Mr Thamsanqa.
Themba	All right, Miss Green. It was nice to meet you. Goodbye.
Miss Green	Goodbye, Mr Thamsanqa.

Unit 11 May I speak to Mr Thamsanqa?

Peter	Hello, may I speak to Mr Thamsanqa? Is he perhaps there?
Secretary	May I ask who would like to speak to him?
Peter	Yes, this is Peter Murray speaking.
Secretary	Please hold on, Mr Murray. I'll just look and see whether he is in his office.
Peter	Okay.
Secretary	Mr Murray, I'm sorry, Mr Thamsanqa is not here at the moment. He went out.
Peter	Do you know when he'll be back?
Secretary	I'm sorry, he didn't say. Would you like to leave a message?
Peter	Yes, please tell him that I wanted to get in touch with him about the cricket tomorrow. Perhaps he can phone me at home this evening.

Secretary	All right Mr Murray. I'll tell him. What's your telephone number?
Peter	It's 531-3767.
Secretary	All right, Mr Murray.
Peter	Thank you. Goodbye.
Secretary	Goodbye, Mr Murray.

David	David Murray speaking.
Themba	Hello, David. How are you, my boy?
David	Oh, hello, Mr Thamsanqa. I'm fine thanks. And you?
Themba	No, I'm fine. Is your father perhaps there, David?
David	Yes. Wait a moment. I'll call him.

Themba	Hello, Peter. It's Themba here. Thanks for phoning. Unfortunately I was at a meeting the whole day. I got your message when it was already late (evening).
Peter	It doesn't matter. I know you are busy.
Themba	What time shall we meet tomorrow?
Peter	What about 9.30?
Themba	That's fine. Where?
Peter	In front of the main gate.
Themba	Okay, we'll be there at 9.30. We'll see each other then.
Peter	We'll see each other.

Jenny	Hello!
Thandi	Hello, may I speak to Mrs Murray?
Jenny	Hello, Thandi, it's me!
Thandi	Oh, sorry, my dear, I didn't recognize your voice. What's wrong?
Jenny	Oh, I've just got a little cold.
Thandi	Oh, I'm sorry. I'm phoning you because Themba and I are going to that new Xhosa restaurant on Saturday evening. We would like to invite you and Peter to join us. Can you come? Do you think you will be better by then?
Jenny	Oh, that would be lovely. I read about that restaurant in the paper last weekend. My mouth was watering. The (description of the) food brought back childhood memories. We used to eat all those traditional dishes on the farm!

Thandi	Well then, let me fetch you so that we can meet Peter and Themba after the cricket game.
Jenny	Thank you, my dear. We'll see each other.

Unit 12 At the cricket

Themba	It's lovely to see so much interest in cricket these days. Look at all these budding Makhaya Ntinis playing cricket.
Peter	Indeed. Wherever you look these days there are boys playing cricket. Did you play cricket when you were at school, Themba?
Themba	Yes, I liked playing cricket very much. I was a wicket-keeper–batsman. In fact, I opened the innings!
Peter	Really!
Themba	And you, mate, which sports did you play?
Peter	Well, I played tennis and rugby at school. Unfortunately, I broke my arm when I was still playing under 15s. After that I never played rugby again.
Themba	What position did you play?
Peter	I was a scrumhalf. Though I didn't play cricket I like to watch it very much, especially when we play overseas teams. Did you play rugby or soccer?
Themba	I played rugby.
Peter	What position?
Themba	I was eighth man.
Peter	What about soccer? Did you play it?
Themba	Yes, I played, it but I preferred rugby.
Peter	It is very interesting how sport has the power to unite a nation.
Themba	You're right. Remember the support the whole country gave *AmaBhokobhoko* at the world cup final! Who can forget how everyone sang, *Tshotsholoza*, as if in one voice.
Peter	Indeed, I'm sure that the way the crowd sang gave *AmaBhokobhoko* the impetus they needed to win the world cup!
Themba	Wow! Who could forget the pride on President Mandela's face when he wore the No.6 jersey and held the trophy aloft together with François Pienaar.

Peter — *Bafana Bafana* also got support like that when they won the African Cup of Nations. By the way, what do you do these days to keep yourself fit?

Themba — E-e, I try to run three times a week, and I play squash regularly. And you?

Peter — I cycle, and I try to walk up the mountain on Sundays. But sometimes it's difficult to find the time because my hobby is woodwork.

Themba — Mine is photography. But the problem is just to find the time!

Peter — Look, the players have come back. Lunch is finished. The game is going to start now. Let's go back to our seats.

Unit 13 Let's go to that new restaurant!

Restaurateur — Good evening. Welcome to *iZiko Lethu*. We are very glad to see you. How are you?

Themba — No, we are fine except that we are hungry! Do you perhaps have a table for four?

Restaurateur — Of course! Follow me.

Thandi — Can we perhaps have a table near the window?

Restaurateur — Here it is. How is this?

Thandi — It's fine! Thank you.

Restaurateur — Here is the menu.

Themba — What do you recommend? What are the specials today?

Restaurateur — Well, to start with we have *isonka samanzi*.

Jenny — Oh! That reminds me of my childhood on the farm. I really loved *isonka samanzi*.

Restaurateur — Is that so, *Nkosikazi*! Where do you come from?

Jenny — I grew up on a farm *emaXhoseni*.

Restaurateur — Where exactly?

Jenny — Near Queenstown.

Restaurateur — Oh, I don't know that region. I grew up in Transkei. Well, let me also recommend *umphokoqo*, *umngqusho*, *umfino*, mutton stew and tripe.

Peter — I have forgotten, what exactly is *umphokoqo*?

Restaurateur — It's cooked mealie meal.

Peter — Oh yes, I remember now.

Jenny — How is your *umfino* (made)?

Restaurateur — It's made with spinach and onion. May I bring you

	something to drink while you are deciding? How about *umqombothi, amarhewu* or beer?
Themba	Let's taste them all! We have brought a bottle of wine. Can you open it?
Restaurateur	Of course!

Restaurateur	Are you ready to order?
Themba	No, we haven't chosen yet.
Restaurateur	Fine, I'll come back in a little while.
Jenny	By the way, *Mnumzana*, where is the cloakroom?
Restaurateur	Follow me, I'll show you.
Jenny	Thank you. Excuse me for a little while.
The others	That's fine.

Restaurateur	Here's the meal!
Jenny	Mm, it smells delicious! It also looks delicious!
Restaurateur	Well then, I hope that you'll enjoy your meal!

Restaurateur	Have you eaten well?
The friends	Very much so!
Jenny	I would like to get your recipe of *umngqusho* if it is not a secret?
Restaurateur	I'll ask the cook for it.
Jenny	I would be grateful.
Restaurateur	What about (some) dessert?
The friends	Thanks very much but we've all had enough (to eat).
Themba	May we have the bill now?
Restaurateur	No sooner said than done!

Unit 14 Buying clothes and various African arts and crafts

Jenny	Gosh! Please just look at all these beautiful things! Woven mats, wall hangings, pottery, baskets and clothing. It's going to be difficult to choose!
Assistant	Good day, may I help you?
Jenny	Your shop is really very beautiful! I know I'm going to spend a lot of money today!
Assistant	Thanks very much. Would you like to look around first?

Jenny	That would be nice.
Assistant	Call me if you need help or you want to know anything.
Jenny	Okay, *Nkosikazi*. I would like to start looking at dresses and skirts.
Peter	That wall hanging on that wall over there is beautiful, *Nkosikazi.*
Assistant	Which one, sir?
Peter	That one with the woman smoking a pipe. Where was it made?
Assistant	It was made by the local women.
Peter	How much does it cost, *Nkosikazi*?
Assistant	Unfortunately these wall hangings cost a lot of money nowadays because they are made by hand and are of mohair.
Peter	I understand.

Assistant	Oo! You look very smart, *Nkosikazi*! That dress is very beautiful! It really suits you!
Jenny	Yes, but it's a bit small. Have you got it in a bigger size?
Assistant	I'll look for a bigger size. What size?
Jenny	36.
Assistant	What colour would you like?
Jenny	Yellow or red.
Assistant	Unfortunately we only have white, brown and green in your size.
Jenny	That's fine, I'll try on the brown one.

Jenny	It fits me perfectly. I'll take it! How much is it?
Assistant	If you buy the dress and the skirt I can reduce the price. They'll cost R225 together.
Jenny	Fine. I'll buy both but I don't have enough money. Do you accept credit cards?
Assistant	Don't worry, *Nkosikazi*. We accept cash, cheques and credit cards.
Jenny	That's good, because I still want to buy other things like pottery, basketware, and especially (jewellery) beads. (*amaso*)
Assistant	You mean '*iintsimbi*'. '*Amaso*' are bigger than *iintsimbi*.
Jenny	Of course! Now I remember!
Assistant	What sort of beads do you want? Necklaces, bracelets? Do you like these anklets?

Jenny	Gosh! Everything is very beautiful. Again it's going to be very difficult for me to choose! Look at all the colours!
Assistant	That's okay, *Nkosikazi*, take your time!

Unit 15 Travel woes

Peter	Good day, *tata*, how are you?
Passerby	Good day. No, I am still tottering along, my chap.
Peter	Can you help us, *bawo*? We are lost. Is this perhaps the road leading to *Sandile*'s grave?
Passerby	No, you are on the wrong road.
Peter	Where do we get (on) the right road then?
Passerby	Turn back on the road you are on now. When you come to the first intersection follow the road to the left. After that, go straight. After one kilometre you'll see the sign '*To Sandile's Grave*'.
Peter	What is the road like? Is it a tarred road?
Passerby	No, it's a gravel road. It is also rather winding like a millipede! There is another road to the right which is shorter. Unfortunately it is not good.
Peter	Thank you very much, *tata*. By the way, where are you going? Can we give you a lift?
Passerby	No, thank you, I'm waiting here for my daughter.
oooOooo	
Peter	Damn! The tyre wouldn't have burst if we had taken the tarred road!
Jenny	One is always wise after the event!
Motorist	Hello, What's the trouble? Can I help you?
Peter	Hello, *Mnumzana*. My tyre seems to have burst. Can you lend me your jack? Unfortunately mine has disappeared.
Motorist	What a shame! Wait a minute, I'll get the jack out of my boot. Has your spare got air?
Peter	Fortunately I pumped it up yesterday.
Jenny	Thank goodness, you arrived, *Mnumzana*!
Peter	Indeed! By the way, is there a garage nearby? I'm afraid we are soon going to run out of petrol. I can't understand it because I filled the tank yesterday!

Motorist Perhaps there is a hole in the tank? You know, that happens quite easily on country roads. Let's have a look!

Peter Oh, heavens! You are right. Indeed, there is a little hole the size of a pea. What are we going to do now?

Motorist No, don't worry. If you have some soap I'll close it up. After that you will be able to drive to the garage.

Peter How far is the garage?

Motorist It's nearby, follow me.

Peter Thank you, *Mnumzana*. You've really helped us.

Mechanic Good day, can I help you, sir?

Peter Good day, *Mnumzana*. Unfortunately, there is a little hole in my petrol tank. Can you repair it immediately?

Mechanic Eh, I have a lot of work but I'll try.

Peter Oh I thank you. How long will it take?

Mechanic Mm, let me see, perhaps two hours.

Peter Can you tell me how much it will cost?

Mechanic It's difficult to tell exactly. About R350.

Peter Fine, *Mnumzana*. Let's leave the car. We'll see each other later.

Unit 16 Xhosa heritage trail

Themba How was your holiday *emaXhoseni*? Did you have a pleasant trip?

Peter It was wonderful, though we had some problems with the car but luckily we were helped by some very kind people.

Thandi Well, it's usually like that in the rural areas. But where exactly did you go?

Jenny We started our trip in **Peddie**. Since my university days when I was studying Xhosa, I've always wanted to visit the historical places of the Eastern Cape. By the way, what is **Peddie** in Xhosa? I've forgotten.

Thandi It's *Ngqushwa*.

Jenny Oh, yes, of course. Well, we went to **Peddie** because we wanted to see that famous tree, the white milkwood tree. After that we headed for **King William's Town** to visit the **Kaffrarian Museum** where there is a very interesting collection of traditional artifacts. In the afternoon we went to **Steve Biko**'s house. We also visited his grave.

Peter	The following day, we went off to **Hogsback** making a detour and passing through **Keiskammahoek** into the *Amalinde* region.
Themba	Oh *Amalinde*! You know, it was in that region that one of the bloodiest battles in Xhosa history was fought.
Jenny	Of course! That's the battle that is described in the poem *UThuthula* by **Jolobe**, which was one of our (prescribed) poems at university.
Themba	The whole region near the *Amathole* Mountains is full of Xhosa history. There are many places which are named after *Rharhabe* chiefs.
Peter	Yes, we passed *Sandile*'s Dam and also saw *Ngqika's* grave on the way to **Alice**. In **Alice** we were very interested to visit Lovedale College and **Fort Hare University** where **Nelson Mandela** was a student together with many other present-day leaders.
Jenny	I had just finished reading *The Ochre People* written by **Noni Jabavu**. I therefore very much wanted to find the house in **Middledrift** where her father, Professor Jabavu, lived when he was professor of African languages at **Fort Hare**. Have you ever read this book?
Thandi	Yes, **Noni Jabavu** writes very well so much so that one can actually see the beauty of this region. She describes so beautifully the way of life and customs of the Xhosa people of that time. Have you also read her other book *Drawn in Colour*?
Jenny	Yes, am I not right in saying that that was her first book?
Themba	Did you find **Jabavu**'s house after all?
Jenny	No, unfortunately we didn't.
Thandi	Where did you head for after that?
Peter	We stayed at **Hogsback** for a few days. Gosh! The beauty of that region is breathtaking. The peace! And the tranquillity! The indigenous forests and the waterfalls are quite stunning, and the many species of birds and their singing are just too wonderful to experience.
Themba	You must have been in your element, Peter, person of nature that you are!
Peter	You can say that again! Therefore we decided to stay there several days.

Jenny	The next place we visited was **Stutterheim**. We wanted to see *Sandile's* grave but we got lost and gave up. We wanted to follow *Sandile's* walk but we had no time.
Peter	The following day we headed for **Umtata**. On the way, we cut through beautiful pastures, with cattle and sheep dotting the slopes, passing through **Komga**, **Butterworth** and **Idyutywa**. We wanted to visit **Qunu** where **Nelson Mandela** was born. Unfortunately, his childhood home is not there any more but his school is still there.
Themba	Did you have time to go to the coast?
Peter	Of course! We stayed at **Port St Johns** for three days. The nature there! The hills descending to the coast, the round huts and the maize fields! Indeed, the country is still so unspoilt (it is like a young maiden!).
Themba	No, you've made me quite jealous!
Jenny	On the way to **Umtata**, at **Libode**, we passed by an old country store. It reminded me of **Jolobe**'s essay *Ivenkile Yangaphandle*. We actually wanted to go to **Cala**.
Thandi	What attracted you to **Cala**?
Jenny	We were invited there by friends.
Thandi	What did you do there?
Jenny	We took part in the daily activities. And the kindness we found there was so heartwarming. In the evenings, we even sat around the fire and listened to folktales like in days of old!

Key to exercises and Test yourself questions

Unit 1

1 (a) Molo Thandi. (b) Molo mama. (c) Molo tata. (d) Molo sisi. (e) Molo bhuti. (f) Molo nkosikazi. (g) Molo mnumzana/ mhlekazi. (h) Molo nkosazana. (i) Molo mntwan'am. (j) Molweni manene namanenekazi. (k) Ndingu... (l) Ndiyavuya ukukwazi. **2** (a) Unjani (namhlanje)? (b) Uhlala eKapa? (c) Ndawoni kanye? **3** (a) Namkelekile eKapa, manene namanenekazi. (b) Ndiyaphila, enkosi. (c) Ndiyavuya ukukwazi. (d) Ndihlala eKapa. (e) Bekumnandi ukuthetha nawe. (f) Bekumnandi ukudibana nawe. (g) Sobonana kwakhona kamsinya. (h) Sala kakuhle. (i) Salani kakuhle. (j) Hamba kakuhle. (k) Hambani kakuhle. **4** (a) Uphila njani? / Unjani namhlanje? (b) Uhlala phi? (c) Ndawoni kanye? **5** Nam ndiyavuya ukukwazi Jenny. **6** knowledgeable person; news/affair; danger; opportunity/chance; try, strive. **7** (a) ibhafrum – bathroom (b) ibhedi – bed (c) ikhabhathi – cupboard (d) idrowa – drawer (e) iwodrophu – wardrobe (f) ishelefu – shelf (g) ibhokisi – box (h) itipoti – teapot (i) ifolokhwe – fork (j) iwotshi – watch (k) ipensile – pencil (l) irediyo – radio (m) iheji – hedge (n) igaraji – garage (o) ibhayisikile – bicycle (p) imoto – motor(car) (q) ilori – lorry (r) iteksi – taxi (s) ifomu – form (t) imali – money.

Test yourself

1. Molo sisi! **2**. Wamkelekile! Namkelekile! **3**. Ndingu… is prefixed to the name, *e.g.* NdinguJohn or NdinguJenny. **4**. Subject concords. They never stand alone but are prefixed to the verb or an interrogative, e.g. Uphila njani? Unjani? **5**. Yes, because it shows an interest in the well-being of the whole family. **6**. Ndiphilile/Ndikhona. or: Siphilile/Sikhona. **7**. Uhlala phi? The interrogative comes after the verb, unlike English. **8**. By intonation or by adding '**na**'. **9**. '**Hamba** kakuhle' is said to a person **leaving,** '**Sala** kakuhle' is said to a person **staying**. **10**. **Salani** kakuhle!

Unit 2

1 (a) Ngubani igama lakho? / Ùngubani? (b) Ùnjani namhlanje? (c) Uyafunda? (d) Ufunda phi ukusithetha isiXhosa? **2** wakho; wam; wakho; wam. **3** (a) Ngena. (b) Kumnandi kakhulu ukudibana nawe. (c) Hlala phantsi. (d) Kunjani ngokuphunga okanye ngokusela? (e) Hamba kakuhle. **4** (a) Ùfuna (ukuphunga) ikofu? (b) Ùfuna (ukuphunga) iti? (c) Ùfuna ukudibana noPeter? (d) Ùfuna ukuthetha noThemba? (e) Ufuna ukuthetha isiXhosa? (f) Ufuna ukuhlala ngaphandle? (g) Ufuna ukuhlala ngaphakathi? (h) Ufuna ukuhamba ngoku? **5** (a) Nifuna (ukuphunga) ikofu? (b) Nifuna (ukuphunga) iti? (c) Nifuna ukudibana noPeter? (d) Nifuna ukuthetha noThemba? (e) Nifuna ukuthetha isiXhosa? (f) Nifuna ukuhlala ngaphandle? (g) Nifuna ukuhlala ngaphakathi? (h) Nifuna ukuhamba ngoku? **6** (a) Ukhetha iti okanye ikofu? (b) Ukhetha ukuhlala ngaphakathi okanye ngaphandle? (c) Ukhetha ukuthetha isiXhosa okanye isiNgesi? **7** (a) Masingene! (b) Masihlale phantsi! (c) Masithethe isiXhosa! (d) Masiphunge ikofu! (e) Masiphunge iti! (f) Masisele into ebandayo! (g) Masihlale ngaphandle! (h) Masincokole! (i) Masisale! (j) Masiye / Masihambe. **8** (a) Bahlala; eKapa / ePinelands. (b) Ùfunda; esikolweni. (c) Úfunda; esikolweni. (d) Bahlala; ePinelands. **9** (a) Ngubani igama lakho? (b) Ùhlala phi? (c) Ùphila njani namhlanje? Possible answers: (a) NdinguJohn Smith. (b) Ndihlala eKapa. (c) Ndiphila kakuhle. **10** UJenny: Molo Thandi, wamkelekile. UThandi: Molo, sisi. UJenny: Ngena. Kunjani namhlanje? UThandi: Ndisaphila. Unjani wena? UJenny: Ndikhona, sisi. Ufuna into yokusela? UThandi: Hayi, Jenny, ndikhetha ikofu. UJenny: Kulungile. Masiphunge. Ufuna ukuhlala ngaphakathi? UThandi: Hayi, sisi. Masihlale ngaphandle. Lihle namhlanje. Ndingakuncedisa? UJenny: Ewe, ungandincedisa.

Test yourself

1. Ngubani igama **lakho**? (lit. It is who name of your?) Ngubani ifani **yakho**? (lit. It is who surname of your?) (Note that the possessive adjective **follows the noun in Xhosa**.) **2**. There is a distinction in tone. The 2nd person has a low tone and the 3rd person a high tone. To avoid misunderstanding one could add '**wena**' = '**as for you**': **Wena**, uphila njani? **3**. No, **Ú**thetha isiXhosa can translate '**He**' or '**she**' speaks Xhosa depending on whether the person referred to is male or female. **4**. No, there are two words: *uku***phunga** = *to* **drink** hot liquid and *uku***sela** = *to*

drink cold liquid: Ndithanda *uku***phunga** *i***ti.** *Um***ntwana** wam ukhetha *uku***sela** *in***to** *e***banda***yo*. **5**. There are two forms of the present tense: the long form: Ndi**ya**funda. The short form: Ndifunda isiXhosa. The verb ends in **-a** for all persons. **6**. I am **still** learning. **May** I go? **7**. Uya*ndi*fundisa. Uya*si*fundisa. **8**. Masihlale phantsi! **9**. '**and**' / '**with**' / '**also**' but when used between a subject concord and a noun it means '**have**' / '**has**', e.g.: Ndi**na**bantwana. (There is no verb for 'to have'.) **10**. A **clan name** = *isi***duko**.

Unit 3

1 (a) Ndifuna ukuthetha isiXhosa. (b) Ndingathetha isiNgesi? (c) Ndithanda ukuthetha isiXhosa. (d) Ndizama ukuthetha isiXhosa. (e) Ndithetha isiXhosa kancinci nje. (f) Ndisafunda. (g) Ndisaphazama kakhulu xa ndithetha isiXhosa. (h) Nceda ndilungise. **2** (a) Andiqondi. (b) Nceda uphinde kwakhona. (c) Andilandeli. (d) Uxolo, ùthini? **3** (a) Hayi, andikwazi. (b) Hayi, andisithethi kakuhle. (c) Hayi, andiqondi. (d) Hayi, andiphilanga. (e) Hayi, andikhumbuli. (f) Hayi, andifuni (kuphunga) kofu. (g) Hayi, andifuni manzi. (water) **4** (a) Nceda uthethe isiXhosa / Ndicela uthethe isiXhosa. (b) Nceda uzekelele / Ndicela uzekelele. (c) Nceda uphinde kwakhona / Ndicela uphinde kwakhona. (d) Nceda uzame kwakhona / Ndicela uzame kwakhona. (e) Nceda undixelele / Ndicela undixelele. **5** (a) When was President Nelson Mandela born? (b) He was born on July 18, 1918. (a) Where did he grow up? (b) He grew up in Qunu in the Eastern Cape Province. (a) Where did he go to school? (b) He went to a Weslyan school. After that he went to the University of Fort Hare. (a) What did he do after that? (b) He worked as a policeman on the mines but he carried on with his law studies. **6** (a) Kuthethwa isiNgesi, isiBhulu nesiXhosa. (b) Kuthethwa isiXhosa, isiNgesi nesiBhulu. (c) Kuthethwa isiTswana nesiBhulu. (d) Kuthethwa isiSuthu nesiBhulu. (e) Zonke iilwimi zithethwa eGauteng. (f) Kuthethwa isiSwati, isiTsonga, isiZulu, isiNdebele nesiBhulu. (g) Kuthethwa isiZulu nesiNgesi. (h) Kuthethwa isiTswana, nesiBhulu. (i) Kuthethwa isiVenda, isiPedi nesiBhulu. (j) Kuthethwa isiXhosa eMpuma-Koloni naseNtshona-Koloni. (k) Kuthethwa isiZulu kwaZulu-Natal eMpumalanga naseGoli. (l) Kuthethwa isiTswana eMntla-Ntshona naseMntla-Koloni. (m) Kuthethwa isiSuthu eFreyistata. **7** (a) UmZulu uthetha isiZulu. AmaZulu athetha isiZulu. (b) UmSwati uthetha isiSwati. AmaSwati athetha isiSwati. (c) UmNdebele uthetha isiNdebele. AmaNdebele athetha isiNdebele. (d) IBhulu lithetha isiBhulu. AmaBhulu athetha isiBhulu. (e) UmVenda uthetha isiVenda. AmaVenda athetha isiVenda. (f) INgesi lithetha isiNgesi. AmaNgesi athetha isiNgesi. (g) UmTswana uthetha isiTswana. AbeTswana bathetha isiTswana. (h) UmSuthu uthetha isiSuthu. AbeSuthu bathetha isiSuthu.

Test yourself

1. No. Classes 14 (*ubu-*) and 15 (*uku-*) have no plural. **2.** *ama***nzi** = water. **3**. They have a short and a long prefix depending on the length of the noun stem: Nouns of Class 5 prefix *i-* with stems of more than one syllable, e.g. *i***gama** = *name* but prefix *ili-* with stems of one syllable: e.g. *ili***zwe** = *country.* (The subject concord in both cases is **li**-.) Nouns of Class 11 prefix *u-* with stems of more than one syllable, e.g. *u***lwimi** = *tongue/language* but prefix *ulu-* with stems of one syllable: e.g. *ulu***ntu**= *community.* (The subject concord in both cases is **lu**-.) **4**. *um***Xhosa** – *ama***Xhosa**; *um***Zulu** – *ama***Zulu**; *um***Swati** – *ama***Swati** **5**. *Abe***Suthu**; *i***Ngesi**; *i***Bhulu** **6**. Because '**n**' is never followed by an aspirated consonant, in this case 'kh'. **7.** No. It denotes emphasis and contrast only, so it is used **as well as** the subject concord, e.g. **Mna**, **ndi**yahamba ngoku. (As for me) **I** am going now. **Wena**, **ù**phila njani? (As for you) How are **you**? **8**. *Umntu ngumtu ngabantu. = A person is a person through other people.* **9**. The subject concord incorporates a long '**â**' (falling tone): Nd**a**khulela efama = I grew up on a farm. **10**. By using the verb -**cela** or -**nceda**: Ndi**cela** uhlale phantsi. **Nceda** uhlale phantsi.

Unit 4

1 (a) ootitshala (b) balungile (c) ntoni? (d) Ungumfundi (e) ntoni? (f) abazali bakho? (g) Uyingcaphephe yezityalo (h) ungutitshalakazi (i) ntoni? (j) isiXhosa (k) nesiNgesi (l) abazali (m) ungumphathi (n) ungugqirha. **2** umakhi, umbhali, umcoci, umculi, umfoti, umguquli, umlawuli, umlimi, umphathi, umqeqeshi, umsasazi, umthengisi, umthwali (*porter), umzobi. **3** (a) UThemba ungumphathi. (b) USipho ungumakhi. (c) ULinda ungumcoci. (d) UNozipho ungumsasazi. (e) USindi ungumbhali. (f) ULumkile ungumlimi. (g) UThandeka ungumculi. (h) UXoliswa ungumguquli. (i) UYizani ungumthengisi.

(j) UThandi ungugqirha. **4** Ngabantwana; ngabazukulwana; yintombi: ngutata; ngumama; ngutat'omkhulu; ngumakhulu. **5** (a) Lo ngunyana wam. (b) Ngabazali bam. (c) Yintombi yam. (d) Lo ngutat'omkhulu wam. (e) Lo ngumama wam. (f) Yinkosikazi yam. (g) Ngabantwana bam. (h) Lo ngumyeni wam. **6** (a) Uvela efama ngaseRhini. (b) Uhlala eKapa ngoku. (c) Uya eKirstenbosch yonke imihla. (d) Uvela eMpuma-Koloni. (e) Ufundisa abantu abafuna ukufunda ukuthetha isiXhosa, oosomashishini, abasebenzi beenkampani njalo, njalo. (f) Usebenza kwisibhedlele sabantwana iRed Cross. (g) Uya kwikliniki yePrimary Health Care. (h) Usebenzela inkampani yeenqwelo-moya. **7** (a) Ndivela e__; (b) Ndihlala e___ ngoku; (c) Nding___ / Ndil____; Ndiy____; (d) Ndisebenza e___ / Ndisebenzela ___ **8** (a) ndisebenzela (b) iphekela (c) uyandifundisa (d) ufundela (e) bayathandana. **9** (a) Masifundisane! (b) Masidibane! (c) Masincedisane! (d) Masakhane! **10** (a) ndihambe ngoku (b) ndiye emsebenzini (c) ndisebenze ngoku (d) ndiye esibhedlele (e) ndigoduke (f) ndithethe isiXhosa yonke imihla (g) ndihlawule ngekhadi. **11** (a) ngebhasi; nge-eropleni (b) nge-eropleni; ngemoto (c) ngokomsebenzi; ndingumphathi (d) kwishishini; e-ofisini (e) nangokuhlwa; ngamanye (f) ngento. **12** Bangumthi; Bayinyoka; Uyinyoka; Ungumkhombe; Uyindlovu. **13** UJenny: Thandi, usebenza kwesiphi isibhedlele? UThandi: Ndisebenza kwisibhedlele sabantwana iRed Cross. UJenny: Oo, wenza umsebenzi omkhulu. Usebenza khona imini yonke? UThandi: Hayi, ndisebenza esibhedlele kusasa kuphela. Emva kwemini ndisebenza kwikliniki yePrimary Health Care. UJenny: Ngumsebenzi onzima kanjalo.UThandi: Nawe usebenza kakhulu, Jenny. UJenny: Masiye ngaphandle ngoku. Nantsi ikofu nekeyiki. Ndigqibile ekhitshini. (a) Jenny and Thandi (b) about their work (c) in the kitchen.

Test yourself

1. To Classes 2, 2a (*aba*-, *oo*-) **ng***aba*fundi/**ng***oo*titshala and Class 6 (*ama*-) **ng***ama*Xhosa **2**. Class 5: **-l-**: Class 7:**-s-**: Class 8: **z-**: Ndiligqwetha. = I **am** a lawyer. Umzantsi-Afrika **l**ilizwe.= South Africa **is** a country. Usisithethi sepalamente. = She **is** the speaker of parliament. Bazizithethi zepalamente. = They **are** speakers of parliament. **3**. It is a **feminine** suffix: *In***kosi**kazi = *chief's wife, lady;* an **augmentative** suffix indicating greatness of size or importance: *ili***zwe**kazi = *continent*. (lit. large country); a suffix indicating some relationships: *u***bawo**kazi = paternal uncle. **4**. It is omitted: e.g. Molo Sipho! Molo tata! **5**. It means 'to teach' (lit. to cause to learn). **6**. *uku***fundis**ana = *to* **teach** each other **7**. **for** (What are you studying **for**?) **8**. Ndihlala **ngase**yunivesithi. Uhamba **nge**moto? Ewe, kodwa **nga**manye amaxesha ndihamba **nge**bhasi. **9**. **-e**: *Ndi***incede**! **10**. *Uchan'ucwethe! = You're spot on!*

Unit 5

1 (a) Iphi iswekile? (b) Luphi ubisi? (c) Iphi ikeyiki? (d) Liphi icephe? (e) Iphi ikofu? (f) Iphi iti? (g) Iphi itispuni? **2** (a) Nantsi iswekile. (b) Nalu ubisi. (c) Nantsi ikeyiki. (d) Nali icephe. (e) Nantsi ikofu. (f) Nantsi iti. (g) Nantsi itispuni. **3** (a) Ndiya*yi*thanda. (b) Ndiya*wa*thanda. (c) Ndiya*zi*thanda. (d) Ndiya*zi*thanda. (e) Ndiya*yi*thanda. **4** (a) Yizalise. (b) Wabilise. (c) Luzise. (d) Yigqithise. (e) Zincede. **5** (a) Unjani namhlanje? (b) Banjani abantwana? (c) Unjani umyeni wakho? (d) Injani inkosikazi yakho? (e) Banjani abazali bakho? (f) Unjani umsebenzi? (g) Linjani izulu? (h) Injani ikeyeki? (i) Zinjani iisengwitshi? **6** (a) (Ionti) yenze shushu; (*u*bisi) unga*lu*bilisi; (umxube) *wu*zamisele (b)$1\frac{1}{4}$ iikomityi zecastor sugar; 2 iikomityi zeflawa; ikomity yobisi; 90gm yemajarini; $1\frac{1}{2}$ iitispuni zevanilla essence; indlela yokwenza; umxube wobisi; iitin zekeyiki; ipakethe ye-icing sugar; 250 gm yemajarini; icephe lecocoa powder; icephe lamanzi.
7 Amaqanda; iflawa; ibhotholo; iswekile; ubisi; imajarini; i-icing sugar. **8** ikofu; amanzi; ikofu; ubisi; ubisi; ubisi; ubisi; ubisi. **9** 1(c) 2(d) 3(g) 4(a) 5(e) 6(h) 7(b) 8(f).

Test yourself

1. *yourself*:'*Zi***ncede**' = **help** (the equivalent of the English reflexive pronoun); '*-zi-*' in 'Ndiya**zi**thanda *izin***to** *ezi***mnandi** = I **like** *them* sweet things: is an object concord referring to *izin***to**. **2**. *i***kofu** < coffee; *i***swekile** < Afrikaans suiker (sugar); *i***tispuni** < teaspoon; *isi***layi** < slice; *i***keyiki** < cake; *i***sengwitshi** < sandwich; *i***resiphi** < recipe; *i***komityi** < Afrikaans koppie (cup); *isi***layi** belongs to Class 7. **3**. *i***khitshi** = kitchen, *i***polisa** = policeman, *i***vili** = wheel belong to Class 5, therefore their plural is: *ama***khitshi,** *ama***polisa,** *ama***vili**. **4**. The 2nd person (s) SC = u, OC = *-ku-*. Class 1/1a: SC = ú-, OC = *-m*; Class 3: SC = u-, OC = -*wu-*; Classes 4 and 9: SC = i, OC = *-yi-* ; Class 6: SC = a-, OC = *-wa-* **5**. *Aba***sebenzi** **bee**nkampani. **6**. '*to* **remind**' (lit. cause to remember) **7**. Ndilapha; Ndisesikolweni **8.** *uku***hamba** means '*to* **go**, walk, **travel**' (or as noun '**travel/traveling**'), *uku***ya** means '*to* **go to**' followed by a locative: Ndiya eKapa. **9**. No, 'are' is understood: U**phi**? (lit. you where?) **10**. Yes: -**njani**?: U**njani**? = **How** (are) you?

Unit 6

1 1(b) 2(d) 3(a) 4(e) 5(c) 6(f). **2** (a) Ndiyagodola; kuyabanda (b) Ndifudumele; kufudumele (c) Kuyaphola; kupholile (d) Kuza kuna ngomso; akuzi kuna namhlanje. **3** (a) Yimini entle (b) embi (c) epholileyo (d) eshushu (e) Bubusuku obupholileyo. **4** (a) Siza (b) ningathanda (c) Sinamanye (d) ndingathanda (e) kuxhomekeke (f) uvuthuza (g) luza kulwa (h) Ndiyoyika (i) asizi kuya (j) kuvuthuza gqitha (k) Niza kuya (l) kuyanetha? (m) andoyiki (n) Niza kuya (o) kushushu (p) andikhathazeki / asikhathazeki. **5 Weather forecast**: (a) winter (b) summer

Makhe sikhangele ukuba imozulu yangomso iza kuba njani na. Liza kusibekela libanda linentshizane **eNtshona-Koloni** kodwa liqhaqhazelise amazinyo embindini emva kwemini kude kuwe nekhephu kwimimandla ephakamileyo nasezintabeni. Siya phaya **eMpuma-Koloni**. Gqaba amafu lipholile linemvulana. Iimvula ziza kunwenwela ngasempuma ngomso. Ziya kuphela emva kwemini. (*Let's just have a look at what the weather will be like tomorrow. It will be overcast and cold with drizzle in the* ***Western Cape*** *but in the interior it will be so cold as to make your teeth chatter and there will even be snow falling in the high regions and on the mountains. We go over to the* ***Eastern Cape****. Scattered clouds, cool with light rain. The rain will spread towards the east tomorrow in the afternoon.*) Izanuse zemo-zulu zilumkise ukuba liza kuzola de ilanga *ligqatse ubhobhoyi* eNtshona-Koloni ngomso. Kanti kuza kubhudla umoya ongephi kodwa uza kutsho ngamandla kufutshane nonxweme ngokuhlwa. EMpuma-Koloni liya kuzola lithe gqaba amafu, kanti kungakho neendudumo mva. (*The weather forecasters warn that it will be fine becoming so hot that the sun will scorch even the African hoopoe bird in the* ***Western Cape*** *tomorrow. There will be a slight wind but it will be stronger near the coast towards evening. In the* ***Eastern Cape*** *it will be fine with a few scattered clouds and there could even be thunder later.*)

6 (a) Uyakwazi ukuthetha isiXhosa? Hayi, ndikwazi ukuthetha isiZulu kancinci kuphela / qha. (b) Uyakwazi ukuthetha isiNgesi? Ewe, ndisifunda esikolweni. (c) Ungandinceda? Kakade, ndiza kukunceda.

Ndilusizi, andinakho ukukunceda / andinakukunceda. (d) Unokuza ngoLwesihlanu? Ndilusizi, andinakuza. Ndixakekile gqitha. (e) Ndingakufowunela ngomso? Kulungile. (f) Ndingakugalelela enye ikomityi yekofu? Hayi, enkosi. Ikomityi enye yanelekum. (g) Ndingangena? Ewe, ndicela ungene. **7** (a) Ndikhetha izinto ezimnandi. (b) Ndikhetha ikofu enobisi neswekile. (c) Ndikhetha iisengwitshi. (d) Ndikhetha imajarini (e) Ndikhetha iwayini emhlophe. **8** (1) imnyama (2) ilubhelu (3) iluhlaza (4) imhlophe (5) ibomvu (6) iblawu / iluhlaza. **9** 'Now we (have) hope for peace, Now we (have) hope for happiness / Through the coming of the summer rains / Because summer has now come.' From a summer rain region, i.e. Eastern Cape.

Test yourself

1. *uku***godola** refers to people: Uya**godola** (na)? = 'Are you cold?'; *uku***banda** refers to something inanimate: Kuya**banda** (namhlanje) = 'It is cold (today)'. **2**. Kuya**phola** = 'It is **getting cool**' describes the process; ku**pholile = it** is **cool** describes the state (stative verb). **3**. *in***tlakohlaza** = 'spring' belongs to Class 9; *i***hlobo** = 'summer' Class 5; *ukw***indla** = 'autumn' (lit. season of eating the first ripe grain) Class 15 (*uku-*); *ubu***sika** = 'winter' (lit. season of cutting < *uku***sika** = *to* **cut**) belongs to Class 14. **4**. **u**- (SC of *um***ntu**) + onke > **w**onke; **i**- (SC of *imi***hla**) + -onke > **y**onke **5**. An adjective is placed **after a noun**: *Aba***ntu** *aba***ninzi** bafunda *isi*Xhosa. **6**. The concords i.e. Classes 1/1a/3: **om**hle (AC) Class 4: **emi**hle (AC) Class 6: **ama**hle (AC) Class 9: **en**tle(AC) Class 10: **ezin**tle (AC) **o**lula (RC) **e**lula (RC) **a**lula (RC**e**lula (RC) **ezi**lula (RC) **7**. Ng*um***sebenzi** *o***nomdla.** Ng*ama***doda** *a***namandla.**
8. **Andi**thandi **ku**pheka. **9**. **Musa** *uku***libala** = **Don't** forget! (s.) **Musa***ni* *uku***libala!** (pl.) (**Musa + infinitive** (s.): **Musa***ni* **+ infinitive** (pl.) **10**. Ndi**nga**ngena? Uyakw**azi** ukuthetha isiXhosa? U**nakho** ukuza? (often shortened to **Unokuza**?)

Unit 7

1 (a) Uxolo, ndikwenzakalisile? (b) Uxolo ngokukuphazamisa. (c) Ndilusizi, ndileyithi. (d) Uxolo, ndilibele. (e) Uxolo ngokukulindisa. (f) Uxolo, andisithethi kakuhle isiXhosa. **2** 1(c) 2(a) 3(e) 4(b) 5(d).

3 (a) Yiza apha. Kulungile, ndiyeza. (b) Yima! Kulungile, ndiyema. (c) Yenza iti ngoku. Kulungile, ndiza kuyenza ngoku.
4 Ewe, ndifuna ipetroli. / (u-97) Ndifuna u-97/ Nceda ugalele u-97. / Hayi, ndiphe nge-50 rand qha namhlanje. / Nazi. / Hayi, kodwa unokukhangela amavili. / Faka 210. / Ewe. Musa ukulibala ukukhangela amanzi. / Enkosi. Nali icuba. **5** (a) Wazalelwa (b) ndazalelwa (c) bafudukela (d) Ndakhulela (e) wazalelwa (f) ndazalelwa (g) ndahlala (h) Utshatile? (i) sisebenza (j) Utshatile wena? (k) ndineentombi (l) unabantwana? (m) sinabantwana / ndinabantwana (n) isencinci (o) Kufuneka (p) Ndileyithi / Kuleyelithi (q) Bekumnandi.
6 (a) Ube nempela veki emnandi eRhini. (b) Ube neholide emnandi. (c) Ndikunqwenela impumelelo emsebenzini wakho. (d) Ubhale kakuhle. (e) Ube neKresmesi emyoli nonyak' omtsha omnandi. (f) On birthdays. At weddings. (On the occasion of President Mandela's marriage to Graca Machel, family members sang this song which is traditionally only sung at weddings.) **7** 1(i) 2(j) 3(b) 4(h) 5(g) 6(d) 7(c) 8(e) 9(f) 10(a). **8** Title.

Test yourself

1. Because '*ukuza*' belongs to a group of one-syllable verbs whose stems contain a **latent i**. Therefore ndiya- + -(i)**za** > ndiy**e**za. **2**. **Enkosi** (kakhulu); **undincedile**; **ndiyabulela**. **3**.(a) You have helped me. (b) You have helped us. (c) We have helped you (s.). (d) We have helped you (pl.) (e) You (pl.) have helped me. (f) You (pl.) have helped us.
4. -**a**zisa = introduced -**e**nza = make, do; -**o**nwaba = become happy.
5. The subject concord '**ù**-' before a vowel verb > **w**: **ù** + -enza > **w**enza; the vowel of the subject concord is dropped: **ni**- + -**a**mkelekile > **n**amkelekile the 'i' of the subject concord being dropped. **6**. Vowel verbs prefix '**Y**- ' **Y**enza/ **Y**enzani! Latent (i) and monosyllabic verbs prefix '**Yi**'-: **Yi**ma/**Yi**mani!/**Yi**tsho/**Yi**tshoni! **7**. The **remote past tense,** characterized by a **long â** (falling tone) in the subject concord: **Wa**gqiba; **wa**hamba; **wa**yifumana; **wa**yibopha; **wa**yithatha; **wa**yigoduka. **8**. By prefixing **khawu**-, e.g. **khawu**linde! **9**. **Ùgqibile**? **Ùgqibe** nini? **10**. -lib**ala** > -lib**ele**; -l**ala** > -l**ele**; -fum**ana** > -fum**ene;** -ph**atha** > -ph**ethe; -dibana** na- **> -dibene** na-.

Unit 8

1 amehlo; iindlebe; iingalo, izandla; iminwe; imilenze; iinyawo; iinzwane; amazinyo; amadolo. **2** (a) Unjani umntwana wakho? Usesesibhedlele? (b) Ndilusizi ukuba ubhetele kancinci kuphela/qha kodwa ndonwabile ukuba usekhaya kwakhona. (c) Utheni ugqirha? (d) Masithembe ukuba uza kuphila kamsinyane kwakhona. **3** (a) iflu (b) ifiva (c) ibhedi (d) usisi. **4** (a) Molo mama. (b) Unjani namhlanje? (c) Ndilusizi ukuba usesibhedlele ugula. (d) Ndingakunceda ngantoni? (e) Uneentlungu? (f) Ndithemba / ndinqwenela ukuba uya kuchacha ngokukhawuleza. (g) Sala kakuhle, mama. **5** 1(f) 2(d) 3(b) 4(c) 5(a) 6(e). **6** (c) (a) (d) (f) (b) (e). **7** (a) Unesibindi. (b) Unentliziyo kakhulu. (c) Banomqolo kakhulu. (d) Unomlomo. (e) Unesandla. **8** He/she has a cold hand. (b) He/she has a hot hand. (c) He/she gives with a beautiful heart. (d) He/she has a white heart. (e) Do you have heavy knees? **9** (a) My heart is sore. (b) He/she has a dark/black heart. (c) He/she has a pure heart. **10** (a) oluphi ulwimi (b) eziphi iilwimi (c) nezinye iilwimi ... kwelinye ilizwe? (d) oluphi ulwimi? (e) ngowuphi unyaka? (f) ngeyiphi inyanga? (g) Ngeyiphi imini? (h) kweliphi ilizwe? (i) Kweyiphi idolophu? (j) kwesiphi isikolo? (k) kweliphi ibanga? (l) kweyiphi iyunivesithi?

Test yourself

1. The subject concord, e.g: ndi**lusizi**. **2**. Izulu lihle namhlanje. Lizulu elihle namhlanje. **3**. Class 9: *en-* > *in-*, e.g. *i***fama** *in***kulu** **4**. By using **-se-**, e.g.: U**se**mncinci (*um***ntwana**) = He/she (the child) is **still** small. **5**. The second verb ends in **-e**: Iintlungu zifika zimk**e**? **6**. **Wakhe wa**gula ngaphambili? Hayi andi**zange nda**gula ngaphambili. **7**. **Kutheni**: **Kutheni** ùfunda isiXhosa?; **-elani**: **Ùfundelani** isiXhosa? (present tense); **-eleni**: **Ùfundeleni** isiXhosa? (past tense); **ngoba**: Ùfunda isiXhosa **ngoba**? **8**. They are distinguished **by tone only** in the **strong classes** (i.e. where the subject concord begins with a consonant): **Baphi** abantwana = **Where** (are) the children? **high tone**; **Baphi** abantwana = **Which** children? **low tone, and** by **tone and a different concord** in the weak classes (i.e. where the subject concord is a vowel only: *I***phi** *in***cwadi** = *Where* (is) the **book**?; *Yi***phi** *in***cwadi** = *Which* **book**? **9**. **-kazi**: *i***xhegokazi**. **10**. Une*mi***nyaka** *emi*ngaphi *um***ntwana** *wa***kho**? or Mingaphi *imi***nyaka** *yom***ntwana** *wa***kho**? or **Wazalwa** nini *um***ntwana** *wa***kho**?

Unit 9

1 (a) kaNkosikazi Bongela (b) likaRycroft (c) bakaPeter (d) kaPeter (e) kaPhumla. **2** It is the coming of Nxele. **3** Umgquba, imbewu, imithi, izixhobo. **4** (a) Uphi – Unaye? nangu. (b) Ziphi – Unazo? nanzi. (c) Iphi – Unayo? Nantsi. (d) Liphi – Unalo? Nali. (e) Siphi – Unaso? Nasi. (f) Iphi – Unayo? Nantsi. (g) Liphi – Unalo? Nali. (h) Iphi – Unayo? Nantsi. (i) Iphi – Unayo? Nantsi. (j) Uphi – Unawo? Nanku. **5** 1(f) 2(g) 3(d) 4(c) 5(h) 6(a) 7(b) 8(e). **6** (a) ezi zinto (b) loo kiriva (c) le mithi (d) loo mithi (e) ezaa zithole (f) laa heji. **7** (a) le (b) lo (c) lo (d) le (e) esi (f) lo (g) le (h) le. **8** (a) Eyona (b) Eyona; (c) eyona (d) eyona (e) lelona (f) eyona. **9** (a) -qokelela (b) yahlukanisani (c) Fakani (d) -bole (e) -gcine (f) -thatha (g) -nkcenkceshele (h) -tyaleni (i) -zaliseni (j) -tyaleni (k) -gcineni (l) -fe (m) Khumbulani (n) nqabe (o) -zama (p) -londoloza (q) nkcenkceshelani (r) -nkcenkceshela (s) nkcenkceshelani (t) Lumkani (u) -moshi (v) Jikelezani (w) -gcine.

Test yourself

1. (a) **each** pupil / student (b) the garden is renowned **for** (its) **beauty** (c) year **after** year. **2**. **ka**-: Umsebenzi **ka**Peter, *ubu***chule** *bu***ka**Peter. **3**. Prefix the consonant associated with the noun in the 'strong' classes to **-ona**: *aba***fundi** *b***ona** etc; in the 'weak' classes prefix '**w**' or '**y**' to **-ona**: *um***sebenzi** *w***ona**, *i***gadi** *y***ona** etc. Exception: Class 1 and 1a: *um***fundi** *ye***na**, *u***Peter** *ye***na** **4**. U**nawo** *ama***nzi**? Ewe, ndi**nawo**. **5**. Kulungile **ku***m*. Ndixelele **nga***we*. **6**. Ubuza *o***wona** *m***buzo** **u**nzima. **7**. Lo mthi. Loo mthi. Laa mthi. **8**. Yes, for emphasis in which case the noun retains its prefix, e.g. *I***dumile** *i***gadi** *le*. **9.** Class 11, the plural is *iin***tlobo** (Class 10) with the sound change *iin*- + **-hlobo** > *iin***tlobo**. **10**. **kuba** = because; **ukuba** = that / if; **kodwa** = but; **xa** = when.

Unit 10

1 1(c) 2(b) 3(d) 4(a). **2** (a) The dough is eaten by the dog. (b) The soil is beaten by the sun. (c) The children were entered by a bird. (d) It was gone by the custom. (e) This thing is deprived of time. (f) The depth of a pool is felt by a stick. **3** Horoscope; obituary. **4** (a) Bancokola e-ofisini / emsebenzini. (b) Kakuhle. (c) Baya ekhefi baphunge. (d) Ngoba/Kuba uMary unyuselwe emsebenzini. (e) Entlanganisweni. **5** 1 (c)

Ndiyireceptionist; 2 (a) Ndingumpheki; 3 (b) Ndiyintatheli. **6** (a) **Social worker** (wanted). *Our company is looking for the service of an energetic hard-working person (who can work hard) in child protection. A driver's licence and knowledge of Xhosa are essential. Experience in childcare and speaking English and Afrikaans well is an advantage. Salary is negotiable according to work experience. Send your CV and the names of three referees who can be contacted and the job application to _____. Closing date is ____.* (b) **Receptionist / secretary** (wanted). *A well-known garage (place that repairs and sells cars) is looking for a receptionist / secretary. The applicant must have the following skills: be computer literate; able to write and send accounts; write and answer all letters; communicate with people; speak Xhosa, English and Afrikaans well. Experience in secretarial work is also required. This includes: answering calls and enquiries; dealing with visitors; writing letters and posting outgoing mail; looking after all stationery; preparing meetings. Fax CV and three contactable references to __.* **7** (a) good (b) bad (c) interesting (d) brave (e) popular (beloved) (f) energetic (g) knowledgeable (h) kind (i) lonely (j) experienced (k) calm (l) diligent (m) famous (n) busy.

Test yourself

1. Si**funa** umpheki. Umpheki uya**funwa**. **2**. **Palatalization** (see selected summary **5**). **3**. –ty**iwa**; -enz**iwa**. **4.** *uku***phuma** **5**. Abafundi babuze *imi***buzo** *emi***ninzi**. *Imi***buzo** *emi***ninzi** i**buzwe** ngabafundi.
6. Ndi**phelelwe** ngumsebenzi. **7**. No entry. No smoking. No parking. No swimming. **8.** Ndikhetha ukuhamba **ndedwa**. Ndi**ndedwa** ekhaya.
9. Ndi**ne**thamsanqa. Bendi**ne**thamsanqa. **10**. Ndinqwenela ukuba u**be** **ne**thamsanqa.

Unit 11

1 (a) akakho (b) akazi kuba kho (na) (c) akazi kubuya (d) akakho, usekhaya. (e) awukho (f) ayikho. **2** (a) ndingathetha (b) Ndilusizi (c) usaxakekile (d) ukushiya umyalezo (e) Mxelele ukuba ndiza kuzama ukumfowunela kwakhona emva kwemini. **3** For example, Wrong number. (Inombolo ewrongo) **4** (a) Ufuna ukuthetha noNksk. Bizo. (b) Hayi, akakho. (c) Uvile ukuba uNksk. Bizo ufuna umntu oza kumncedisa kwishishini lakhe. Ufuna ukwenza isicelo. (d) Uza kuzama ukufowuna ngentsimbi yesithandathu. **5** (a) Ndithethe noVal namhlanje. (b) Siza kuya kubukela ifilim ngeCawa. (c) Ungahamba nathi? (d) UVal uza kundiphuthuma ngentsimbi yesihlanu. **6** (a) Ndinabantwana abathathu, iintombi ezimbini nonyana omnye. (b) imiyalezo emine (c) iinombolo zefowuni ezimbini (d) amatikiti amahlanu (e) iincwadi ezintandathu. **7** UThandi: Molo sisi. UNomsa: Ewe ke, sisi. Kunjani? UThandi: Ndikhona, sisi, ngaphandle nje komsebenzi. Unjani wena? UNomsa: Ndiphilile, enkosi. Uxakekile? UThandi: Ewe, kufuneka ndiye evenkileni. Sifuna ukulungiselela itheko ngoMgqibelo. Ukuba lihle singenza ibrayi ngokuhlwa. Singathanda ukuba nize wena noSipho? Siza kumema nabanye abahlobo. UNomsa: Enkosi ngokusimema. Ndingathanda ukuza kodwa ndiza kuthetha noSipho kuqala. Ndiza kukufowunela ngokuhlwa okanye ngomso. UThandi: Ndiyathemba ukuba uSipho unokuza. UNomsa: Nam ndiyathemba. UThandi: Awu, nkosi yam, seyi-5 o'clock. Kufuneka ndikhawuleze ndiye evenkileni. Sobonana ngoMgqibelo mhlawumbi. UNomsa: Kamnandi. (a) yes (b) yes (c) no (d) no (e) yes. **8** 1(e) 2(b) 3(g) 4(c) 5(f) 6(a) 7(h) 8(d). **9** (a) nabani? (b) Ngubani (c) bani? (d) eyiphi (e) Ngubani (f) Ithini (h) Ithini (i) Ithini (j) ntoni? (k) ngantoni? (l) Yintoni (m) ntoni? **10** 1(d) 2(b) 3(e) 4(a) 5(c).

Test yourself

1. 'It is who, who is speaking'? A **relative clause**. **2. Ngubani ixesha**?/**Lithini ixesha**? **3**. **Ngubani** ixesha' = **What is** the time? and **Ngabani** ixesha' = **At what** time? **4**. UThemba usebenza **apha.** UThemba u**khona**? **5**. Hayi, **akakho**. **6**. *om***nye** *um***ntwana** = *another* **child**; *um***ntwana** *om***nye** = *one* **child**. 7. No, **1–6** are **adjectives** and prefix the **adjectival concord** of the preceding noun, **7–10** are **nouns** consisting of a **prefix** and **stem. 8.** Hlala **phantsi**! Ndifumene isitshixo **phantsi kwe**tafile. **9**. *izi***nto 10**. **Ùfunani**?

Unit 12

1 (a) isenta – centre (b) iflenki – flank (c) iflyhafu – flyhalf (d) ihoka – hooker (e) ilokhu – lock (f) isikramhafu – scrumhalf (g) irenka / front rank (h) isikoro – score (i) isoka – soccer (j) amatikiti – tickets.
2 (a) Yikhabe! (b) Yibambe! (c) Yiphose! (d) Yigqithise! (e) Yibethe!

3 (a) nini (b) awaphi (c) ngubani (d) ngubani (e) njani / ngubani (f) bani (g) eliphi. **4** (a) Ndisadlala (b) Andidlali (c) Andisadlali (d) Ndandikade ndidlala (e) (Andi)zange ndiwudlale. **5** (a) Kutheni wena uwuthanda umbhoxo? (b) Kutheni wena ukuthanda? (c) Kutheni wena ungayithandi? (d) Kutheni wena ungakuthandi? **6** (a) Wawukade uthunga / Wawuthunga ntoni? (b) Wawukade unitha / Wawunitha ntoni? (c) Wawukade ucula / Wawucula / ntoni? (d) Wawukade udanisa yeyiphi imidaniso? (e) Wawukade uloba phi? **7** (a) Uyayithanda imidlalo? (b) Uxhasa eliphi iqela? (c) Uyayibukela imidlalo kumabona-kude? (d) Unemisetyenzana yokuzonwabisa? (e) Uyawuthanda umculo? **8** (a) wayemele (b) wayeyintloko (c) wayedlalela (d) wayengomnye. **9** (a) USipho udibana noVuyani. (b) Ebegula. (c) Ebegula inyanga yonke. (d) Bathetha ngoNomsa. (e) Udla ngokubaleka. (f) Wawa, wophuka umlenze. (g) Ufuna ukufowunela umyeni wakhe kuba ufuna ukufumana isibhedlele. **10** (a) UVuyani ufuna ukufowunela umyeni womhlobo wakhe. (b) UVuyani ufuna ukufowunela inkosikazi yomhlobo wakhe. (c) UVuyani ufuna ukufowunela abazali bomhlobo wakhe. **11** 1(g) 2(i) 3(e) 4(a) 5(d) 6(h) 7(c) 8(b) 9(j) 10(f).

Test yourself

1. The English -ing form. **2**. **e-** **be-** **e-** **3. Monosyllabic verb**, e.g: Ndiqhwalela ndi**si**ya = I'm limping going along! (Possible answer to the question 'Ùnjani?') **4**. **xa** = 'when'
5. interrogative **kutheni** = 'why?'; auxiliary verbs **sel**(e) = 'already' and **soloko** = 'always'. **6**. **be-**, e.g. **Be**ndisebenza. **7**. 2nd person (s) and Class 3: **ubu-**; Class 1/1a: **ebe-** or **ube-** cl 2a: **bebe-**; Class 4 & Class 9: **ibi-**; Class 6: **ebe-** (so-called weak classes) **8**. By prefixing **be-**: **Be**ndixakekile. **9**. Bebe**si**thini; Ubu**s**enza ntoni? **10**. **Be**ndi**nga**sebenz**i**. Bendi**nga**xakekek**anga.**

Unit 13

1 (a) Ukutya akumnandi. (b) Andinambithi kutya. (c) Isonka asinancasa. (d) Andithandi nyama. **2** (a) kokulamba (b) kokunxanwa (c) komsebenzi (d) kwezulu (e) kokufunda gqitha. **3** (a) Imifuno midala kakhulu. (b) Ama-apile amnandi. (c) Isuphu ayinatyuwa (konke). (d) Ndithanda isonka esimhlophe. (e) iwayini ebomvu. (f) Iitapile azishushu / ziyabanda. **4** (a) Unayo itafile yabantu ababini (b) abathathu (c) abane

(d) abahlanu? **5** (a) Ndingahlala ngaphandle? (b) Nceda / Ndicela uzise uluhlu lokutya / imenyu. (c) Ndingaodola ngoku? (d) Ndingafumana iwayini ebomvu? (e) Ndingafumana imifuno / iziqhamo?
6 Ndingafumana (a) esinye isilayi sesonka (b) obunye utywala (c) enye ifolokhwe (d) enye imela (e) elinye icephe (f) enye itispuni (g) enye ipleyiti (h) enye ikomityi yeti. **7** (a) bedroom (b) sitting room / lounge (c) study. **8** 1(e) 2(g) 3(f) 4(b) 5(a) 6(d) 7(c). **9** (a) Ndingathanda isidudu, izilayi ezibini zesonka esimdaka, iqanda elithambileyo, ibhotolo nejam. (b) Ndingathanda inyama ebandayo, isaladi, isilayi esinye sesonka esimhlophe nesilayi esinye sesonka samasi (setshizi). (c) Ndingathanda inyama yegusha, iitapile, imifuno neziqhamo.
10 itswele elikhulu, iminqathe, iimbotyi ezintsha, iiphizi, iimbotyi zeswekile, igaliki, ipasili, iitapile. **11** (a) (Kuba) ufuna ukwenza isaladi yeziqhamo. (b) Ama-apile, amapere, ipayina, ii-orenji, iipesika, iibhanana nevatala. (c) Ezinye ziluhlaza, ezinye zivuthiwe. (d) Ivatala imnandi inamanzi kakhulu. (e) Idla R7. (f) Akathengi makhiwane neediliya. **12** (a) Nceda uhlambe iitapile. (b) Musa ukuthatha iitapile ezinkulu, thatha ezi ezincinci. (c) Chuba amatswele amabini ne-apile (elinye). (d) Nqunqa amatswele (kunye) nethanga. (e) Tshweza iminqathe. (f) Hlamba amagqabi eletisi neetumato. (g) Zisa ezinye izitya. (h) Zisekhabhathini phezu kwesinki. (i) Vula itoti. (j) Vula nale. (k) Khawulungise itafile. **13** Nomvuyo othandekayo, Ndingathanda ukukumema kwisidlo sangokuhlwa ngoMgqibelo. Asibonananga ixesha elide ngoko ke kungamnandi ukuncokola kwakhona. Ndithemba ukuba uMgqibelo ngokuhlwa ulungile kuwe. Ngothando Nomsa.

Test yourself

1. Ndifuna *in***yama** ye*n***komo** (lit. meat of a cow); *in***yama** ye**gusha** (lit. meat of a sheep); *in***yama** ye*n***kuku** (lit meat of a chicken); *in***yama** ye**hagu** (lit meat of a pig). **2** *uku***khumbuza** = '*to* **remind**' (lit. cause to remember); *uku***phumza** = *to* make someone **rest**; *ukuzi***khathaza** = *to* **worry** oneself. **3**. Ezi ziqhamo zi**tyeka** na? Iya**vuleka** le festile? Ukubhala kwam kuya**fundeka** na? **4.** 'I'm busy now, I can't help you'. **5**. I am **no longer** working. **6.** Andi**ka**gqibi. Andi**ka**zi. **7.** 'who is lovable'. **8**. Ngolukhulu uthando. **9**. **-tsha** *krebhe*; **-tshiphu** *bhe*. **10**. *ama***nzi** = 'water', *ama***si** = 'sour milk'.

Unit 14

1 (a) Ndingawafumana (b) Ndingazifumana (c) Ndingayifumana (d) Uyayithengisa (e) Uyazithengisa. **2** (a) owuphi (b) eyiphi (c) eziphi (d) eyiphi (e) awaphi. **3** (a) advertisement (b) ukuhombisa (c) likanopopi; leenqawa; lengxowa (d) iimagi < mug(s); iitsheyini < chain(s). **4** (a) Uvela eKapa (b) Ziphelile (c) Uthenga iingobozi ezimbini (d) Ulihlisa nge-10% (e) Kulo nyaka uzayo. **5** 1 (b) (c) (d) (e) (f) (g) (h) (i) (k); 2 (a) (b) (c) (d) (e) (h) (i) (j) (l). **6** (a) onamabala amaninzi (b) aqaqambileyo (c) mifutshane (d) udulu; itshipu; ezintle. **7** (a) emhlophe; omnyama; oluhlaza (b) ibomvu; entsundu (c) zilubhelu zakho; epinki. **8** (a) ngaphezu; zonke (b) ilungileyo (c) kunazo zonke (d) intle iluhlaza; kunayo iluhlaza. **9** (a) kunengonyama (b) kunehlosi (c) kunondlebende (d) kunenyosi (e) kunendlovu. **10** (a) njengonyama (b) njengehlosi (c) njengondlebende (d) njengenyosi (e) njengendlovu. **11** *ya*__bo; *za*__bo **12** (a) *wa*__m__; *o*__wakho__; *o*__wam__ (b) *wa*__m__; *o*__wakho;__ *o*__wam__ (c) *lwa*__m;__ *o*__lwakho;__ *o*__lwam__ (d) *kwa*__m;__ *o*__kwakho;__ *o*__kwam 13__ (a) *A*__bethu__ basekhaya (b) *A*__wam__ *a*lungile __na__*wo*. (c) *E*__yam__ *i*khula kakuhle __na__*yo*. (d) *E*__lam__ *li*kude. (e) *E*__sam__ *si*kude. (f) *E*__yam__ *i*khona. (g) *E*__zethu__ *zi*khona. **14** (a) inkosikazi / umfazi; from umbhinqo 'skirt' (b) ubomi (c) lizwe (d) wamema (e) ukufumana (f) ngomnye; ungumyili; ungumnini; ungumlawuli; bazithanda; uyifumene bemkhuthaza.

Test yourself

1. USipho ulungile kunabo bonke. USipho ulungile ngaphezu kwabantu bonke. **2.** Ilokhwe ebomvu inkulu kunelokhwe emhlophe. **3.** Le lokhwe ingcono kunaloo. **4.** Ilokhwe ebomvu idulu njengelokhwe emhlophe. **5.** Imifuno emitsha **kakhulu/gqitha**. **6.** Zama ukusela amanzi **kangangoko** unakho. **7.** **Sobabini** siza kuza kangangoku sinakho. **8.** igama layo, amagama azo, iilokhwe zabo. **9.** *Y*eyam; *N*gabethu. **10.** Ninakho ukuza nobabini.

Unit 15

1 1(b) 2(d) 3(g) 4(a) 5(j) 6(i) 7(c) 8(f) 9(h) 10(e). **2** (a) indlela ilungile? (b) ayinangozi? (c) yindlela yetha? (d) yindlela yegrabile? (e) indlela isakhiwa (f) indlela sel' ivuliwe na. **3** (a) Uxolo Mnumzana. Ungandinceda na? Ndilahlekile. (b) Ndifuna ukuya kwivenkile

ingu*Kwantu Crafts*/ evenkileni egama lingu*Kwantu Crafts*. Uyayazi? (c) Hayi enkosi. Ndiyaqonda apho ndiyifumana khona ivenkile. Ngathi ikufutshane nam. Kuqala ndiza kuhamba ngqo, emva koko ndijike ngasekunene, emva koko kufuneka ndijike ngasekhohlo. (d) Enkosi kakhulu, Mnumzana. Kamnandi / Hamba kakuhle. **4** (a) Zima (b) Zikhona iibhasi eziya (c) eya (d) Siphi isikhululo seebhasi (e) Ima phi ibhasi eya (f) zinqabile kule. **5** (a) Ikhona igaraji (b) Ikhona ivenkile (c) Sikhona. **6** (a) ivenkile e- (b) isibhedlele esi- (c) isikhululo samapolisa esi- (d) ifowuni e- (e) ugqirha o- (f) igaraji e- (g) idolophu e-. **7** (a) Ungandikhwelisa na? (b) Ungandinceda na? (c) Ungandiboleka ujack? (d) Ungandibonisa indlela eya eRhini? **8** (a) azisebenzi (b) alusebenzi (c) Ibhreki yesandla ayisebenzi (d) ayisebenzi (e) Isihlambi sefestile yangaphambili asisebenzi (f) Isibane sangasemva sasekhohlo asisebenzi. **9** (a) Ndinevili elingenamoya. (b) Ivili lam langaphambili lasekunene lifleti. (c) Imoto yam yaphukile. (d) Imoto yam ixingile. (e) Imoto yam ayiqhwithi. (f) Ifuna amanzi. (g) Iphelelwe yipretoli. (h) Ibhetri yemoto yam ifile. (i) imoto yam itsalwe.
10 (a) Imoto yam ibiwe (b) Ujack wam ubiwe (c) Ivili lam lolaleliso libiwe (d) Isipaji sam sibiwe (e) Ingxowa yenkosikazi yam ibiwe.
11 (a) eCala. (b) Malunga neekhilometha ezilishumi. (c) Ayintle kangako. (d) Ngumgaqo wegrabile. (e) Ungathanda ukubuka idolophu. (f) Apho kukho indawo ekhuselekileyo khona.

Test yourself

1. The road which (it) is not: **e-** = relative concord referring to *in***dlela** + negative '–**nge**–'-' **yi**'- = it is (copulative) + '**-yo**' = it (emphatic pronoun referring to *in***dlela**). **2.** Kwekhu, tshotsho ube kho!
3. (a) Ngumgaqo wegrabile. (b) Ngumgaqo omhle/olungile (c) Ngumgaqo omxinwa, awubanzi. (d) Ngumgaqo wetha. (e) Ngumgaqo ongeyiyo. (f) Ngumgaqo ofanekileyo. **4**. Zama uku**nga***wu*thathi *um***gaqo** we**grabile**. Bendi**nge**namoto kunyaka ophelileyo. **5**. 'He / she is an experienced driver**. Akango***m***qhubi** *u***n***ama***va**. **6. Asilocebo** *li***hle** *elo*. **7**. **Asi**ndim; **Asi**sithi; **Asi**nguye; **Asi**yiyo. **8**. The consonant associated with these classes reappears, i.e. '**z**' in the case of *iin***taba** and '**l**' in the case of *u***nxweme**: Sithanda ukuhamba e**z**intabeni. Sithanda ukuhamba e**l**unxemeni kanjalo. **9**. Ewe, yiyo. Hayi, asiyiyo. **10**. **-ni** is an **interrogative** in'Ufuna**ni**'? and **-ni** is an **interrogative adjective** in:'Ufuna *zi***qhamo** *zi***ni**'? = 'of what sort'?

The initial vowel of the prefix of the noun is omitted and the corresponding adjectival concord is prefixed to **-ni**.

Unit 16

JJR Jolobe was born on 25 July 1902 at Indwe near Cala where his father was a minister. He first went to schools at Indwe and Matatiele. In 1916 he was sent to St Matthews. From 1916 onwards he taught at different schools. At that time he lived near Mt Frere where the Xhosa dialects 'isiBhaca' and 'isiHlubi' and Sotho are spoken. Therefore, his Xhosa was weak. His first book, *UZagula*, was extensively corrected by SEK **Mqhayi**, Poet Laureate. However, when he was a teacher in Bhobhotyane and Mankazane he learned pure Xhosa (lit. which is spoken by the amaNgqika). In 1926 he went to Fort Hare in Alice. There he trained as a minister and received a BA degree. From that time onwards he published many books: *Umyezo* ('Orchard'), *Amavo* ('Stories'), *Elundini lo Thukela* ('On the banks of the Thukela') and others. *UThuthula* is the most outstanding among **Jolobe**'s poems, especially his love poems. It is a narrative poem which reminds us of Helen of Troy. He edited many books. He also translated others into Xhosa. In 1952 he was awarded the **Vilakazi** medal by the University of the Witwatersrand. In 1973 he received a DLitt in acknowledgement of his Xhosa writing from the University of Fort Hare. **Dr Jolobe** died on 16 May 1976. He will never be forgotten in the history of the Xhosa language because he enriched it and its culture.

The Country Store

Even if you are a stranger it is not difficult to recognize a country store in our villages because it is the homestead with the most prominent buildings and which is also surrounded by trees. [...] Many black people are uneasy about calling white people by their names, and moreover, they like to give the white person who works among them a name in their language – a name that usually refers to the pecularities of its owner. Therefore, you will find that all the white shopkeepers in the villages have Xhosa names. As spectacles were not very common among blacks, a white who arrived wearing them was immediately called '*Four Eyes*'. A short, chubby person would earn himself the name of '*Fatty*'. A chap oozing human kindness would be called '*Lover of the People*'. [...] Perhaps you may assume that at that store trade was conducted with money only, but this is not so. This store resembles a market place in other respects. For some to buy goods it is necessary that they themselves sell goods to the shopkeeper. One brings eggs together with the sad news behind what necessitates their sale. [...] At this store it is not enough that only buying and selling takes place, it is also where the mail of the area comes. Thus you will find a pile of letters in the little chest nailed to the wall over there. [...] Apart from the points already mentioned, the country store fills another gap in the lives of the people of the area. It is also a gathering place where people meet one another and where messages going to areas not easily accessible are disseminated. At the store, you know that you'll meet at least one person who is going that way. To say nothing of the youth because the young people already enjoy the certainty of knowing that the store is the place to meet. [...]

Test yourself

1. Khoisan: Gonubie = wild bramble berries growing along the banks of a river; Keiskamma = shining water; Tsitsikamma = clear water. **2**. iGoli < English 'gold'; iRhawutini < Afrikaans 'goud'. **3**. diminutive suffix –**ana**: idoloph**ana**. **4**. *in***kunzi** = capital; *um***bane** = electricity. **5**. road and track; *imi***gaqo-***n***tetho** = grammar, *imi***gaqo-***si***seko** = constitution **6.** James James Ranisi Jolobe. **7**. The Jabavu family. **8.** Enoch Sontonga, Samuel E. Mqhayi. **9**.'**Kwathi ke kaloku ngantsomi** …' the equivalent of '**Once upon a time** … ; Phela, phela ngantsomi! **10**. The rock rabbit (dassie) lacks a tail by giving an order (for). Don't rely on others to do your bidding.

Xhosa–English vocabulary

Nouns and verbs are listed in alphabetical order according to the **first letter of** the **stem**, e.g. *u***hambo**, *uku***hamba**, *ukw***azi**, *ub***omi**, *is***onka**.

However, the question of where the division between prefix and stem in many **Class 9 and 10 nouns** 'presents an insoluble problem' (Pahl, H.W. [ed.] p. xxxv), e.g.:

ingozi:	*in***gozi**	or	*i***ngozi**
incwadi:	*in***cwadi**	or	*i***ncwadi**

To avoid possible confusion between these nouns and those that belong to **Class 5**, which also prefix 'i-' (but '*ama-*' in the plural), the **Class 9** prefix throughout this book is '*in-*' e.g. *in***gozi**, *in***cwadi**.

Nouns where '*g*' or 'k' is inserted for reasons of pronunciation, e.g.:

*ing***qokelela** (< *uku***qokelela**)
*ink***xaso** (< *uku***xhasa**)

are listed according to the **stem of the verb** from which they are derived. The **bold numbers** indicate the unit in which the word first appears or is explained.

Note In cases where one noun is combined with another by menas of a possessive concord, e.g. *i***sanuse** s**emozulu** *weather forecaster* the plural form *iz***anuse** z**emozulu** is not given. This also applies for the English–Xhosa vocabulary. Refer to Unit 5.2 should you want to learn the plural of the nouns.

A

*is***aci** (*iz-*) *saying, idiom* **4**
*ukw***ahlula** *to separate* **9**
-ahlukene *be divorced* **7**
*ukw***akha** *to build* **4**
*um***akhi** (*ab-*) *builder* **4**
*is***akhiwo** (*iz-*) *building* **16**
*is***alathiso** (*iz-*) *sign* **15**
*ukw***aluka** *to weave* **12**
*ukw***amkela** *to welcome* **1**; *accept* **14**
*am***andla** *strength, power* **12**
*um***andlalo** (*im-*) *mat, bed* **8**
*is***andla** (*iz-*) *hand* **8**

-anele *be enough* **5**
*is***anuse** (*iz-*) *diviner* **16**
*is***anuse** semo**zulu** *weather forecaster* **16**
apha *here* **6**
apho *there* **6**
apho … khona *where ...* **8**
*ukw***aphuka** *to break* **8**
*i-***apile** (*ama-*) *apple* **13**
-asekhohlo *left* **15**
-asekunene *right* **15**
*ukw***azana** *to get acquainted* **1**
*ukw***azela** *to know from* **7**
*ukw***azi** *to know* **1**; *knowledge* **3**
*ukw***azisa** *to introduce* **2**
*is***aziso** *advertisement* **10**

B

*uku***ba** *to be, become* **10**
*uku***ba** *to steal* **15**
*uku***balisa** to *relate* **4**
*um***bala** (*imi-*) *colour* **5 /** *i***bala** (*ama-*) **14**
*i***bala** *open space* **15**
*im***balela** *drought* **6**
-balele *to be intensely hot* **6**
*uku***baleka** *to run* **12**
*im***baleki** *(iim-) athlete, runner* **12**
*im***balisi** (*iim-*) *historian* **4**
*im***bali** *history* **16**
*uku***balula** *to recommend* **13**
-balulek*ile to be important* **3**
*uku***bamba** *to hold on* **11**; *catch* **15**
*uku***banda** *to be cold* **5**
*i***banga** (*ama-*) *standard* (at school) **8**
*um***bane** (*imi-*) *lightning* **6**; *electricity* **16**
*isi***bane** (*izi-*) *light* **15**
-bani? *who?* **2**
-banzi *wide* **8**
*u***bawo** (*oo-*) *(my) father* **1**
*u***bawokazi** (*oo-*) *(my) paternal uncle* **2**
*uku***baxa** *to exaggerate* **6**
*uku***beka** *to put, place, lay* **9**
*ubu***bele** *kindness* **10**
*im***bewu** (*iim-*) *seed* **9**
*i***bhafrum** (*ii-*) *bathroom* **1**
*uku***bhaka** *to bake* **5**
*isi***bhakabhaka** *sky* **6**
*uku***bhala** *to write* **4**
*um***bhali** (*aba-*) *writer* **4**
*i***bhanti** (*ama-*)*(seat) belt* **1**
*i***bhasi** (*ii-*) *bus* **4**
*i***bhatyi** (*ii-*) *jacket, coat* **11**
*i***bhayisekile /** *i***bhayisikile** (*ii-*) *bicycle* **1**
*i***bhedi** (*ii-*) *bed* **1**
*isi***bhedlele** (*izi-*) *hospital* **4**
-bhethele *better* **5**
*i***bhetri** (*ii-*) *battery* **7**
*um***bhinqo** (*imi-*) *skirt* **14**
*i***bhinqa** (*ama-*) *woman* **14**
*uku***bhitya** *to lose weight* **8**
-bhity*ile thin* **5**
*i***bhlawuzi** (*ii-*) *blouse* **14**
*i***bhokisi** (*ii-*) *box* **1**
*i***bhokhwe** (*ii-*) *goat* **16**
*i***bhola** *e***kha***tywa***yo** *football, soccer* **12**
*i***bhola** yom**nyazi** *netball* **12**
*i***bhotolo** *butter* **5**
*um***bhoxo** *rugby* **12**
*i***bhreki** (*ii-*) *brake* **15**
*uku***bhubha** *to die* **10**
*uku***bhudla** *to blow* (wind) **6**
*i***Bhulu** (*ama-*) *Afrikaner* **3**

*isi***chotho** *hail* **6**
*uku***cothoza** *to go slowly* **7**
*i***cuba** *tobacco* **7**
*uku***cula** *to sing* **4**
*um***culi** (*aba-*) *singer* **4**
*um***culo** *music* **12**
*in***cutshe** (*iin-*) *specialist* **14**
*in***cwadi** (*iin-*) *book, letter* **8**
*u***cwethe** (*oo-*) *shrew* **4**

D

*i***dabi** (*ama-*) *battle* **16**
*uku***dada** *to swim* **10**
*u***dadewabo** *his / her / their sister* **2**
*u***dadewethu** *my sister* **2**
*u***dadewenu** *your sister* **2**
*u***dad'***o***bawo** (*oo-*) *paternal aunt* **2**
-dala *old, stale* **6**
*uku***dala** *to create* **16**
*in***dalo** *nature* **12**
*i***dama** (*ama-*) *dam* **16**
*uku***dambisa** *to alleviate* **8**
*isi***danga** (*izi-*) *degree, necklace* **10**
*uku***danisa** *to dance* **12**
*um***daniso** (*imi-*) *dance* **12**
*in***dawo** (*iin-*) *place* **4**
*n***dawo***ni*? *whereabouts?* **1**
-de *long* **5**; *tall*
*in***debe** (*iin-*) *trophy* **12**
*uku***dibana na-** *to meet (with)* **1**
*u***didi** *quality* **14**
-dikidiki *lukewarm* **8**
*i***dilesi** (*ii-*) *address* **7**
*ii***diliya** *grapes* **13**
*i***dinala** *dinner* **13**
*um***dla** *interest* **4**
*uku***dla** *to eat* **10**; *to cost* **14**
-dla ngoku- *usually* **8**
*uku***dlala** *to play* **12**
*uku***dlala** *ama***nqindi** *to box* **12**
*um***dlalo** (*imi-*) *game* **6**; *play* **12**
*um***dlali** (*aba-*) *player* **12**
*um***dlalo** *o***qhu***ty***wa***yo* *serial* **12**
*um***dlalo** w*ama***nqindi** *boxing* **12**
*in***dlebe** (*iin-*) *ear* **8**
*in***dleko** (*iin-*) *expense* **10**
*i***dlelo** (*ama-*) *pasture* **16**
*in***dlela** (*iin-*) *way, road* **14**
*u***dliwano-***n***dlebe** (*iin-*) *interview* **10**
*isi***dlo** (*izi-*) *meal* **10**
*isi***dlo** sak**usasa** *breakfast* **13**
*isi***dlo** sa**ngokuhlwa** *supper* **13**
*isi***dlo** sase**mini** *lunch* **12**
*izi***dlo** zakwa**Ntu** *traditional fare* **13**
*uku***dlokova** *to roll (ship)* **6**
*in***dlovu** (*iin-*) *elephant* **4**
*in***dlu** (*izin-*) *house* **13**
*in***dlu** ya**ngasese** *toilet* **13**
*uku***dlula** *to pass by* **15**
*in***doda** (*ama-*) *man* **3**
*in***dodakazi** (*ama-*) *sister-in-law* **4**
*i***dolo** (*ama-*) *knee* **8**
*i***dolophu** (*ii-*) *town* **15**
*iin***dondo** *spectacles / glasses* **14**
*u***donga** (*iin-*) *wall* **7**
*u***dongwe** *clay* **14**
*i***drowa** (*ii-*) *drawer* **1**
*isi***dudu** *porridge* **5**
*iin***dudumo** *thunder* **6**
*in***duli** (*iin-*) *hill* **16**
-dulu *expensive* **8**
*uku***duma** *to become famous* **9**
-dum*ile* *be famous* **7**
*u***dumo** *fame* **16**

*ulu***dwe** (*izin-*) *list* **9**
*ulu***dwe** *lokutya* *menu* **13**

E

ecaleni kwa- *next to* **11**
ekugqibeleni *at last* **5**
ekupheleni kwa- *at the end of* **10**
*i-***emele** (*ii-*) *bucket* **9**
emva *behind* **11**
emva kwa- *after / behind* **4**
emva kwemini *in the afternoon* **4**
*am***endu** *speed* **14**
enkosi *thank you* **1**
*ukw***enza** *to do, make* **4**
*ukw***enzakala** *to injure, hurt* **8**
*ukw***enzakalisa** *to cause to hurt* **8**
*ukw***enzeka** *to happen* **5**
*i-***eropleni** (*ii-*) *aeroplane* **1**
*i-***ertyisi** (*ii-*) *pea* **13**
ewe *yes* **1**
ezantsi *below, downstairs* **11**

F

*uku***fa** *to die* **9**
*uku***faka** *to put in* **9**
*i***fama** (*ii-*) *farm* **3**
*um***fana** (*aba-*) *young man* **1**
*uku***fana na-** *to be like* **6**
*uku***fanela** *to suit* **14**
-**fanele** *ought* **5**
-**fanelekile***yo appropriate* **9**
*i***fani** (*ii-*) *surname* **2**
*i***fanitsha** (*ii-*) *furniture* **12**
*um***fazi** (*aba-*) *woman* **8**
*im***fazwe** (*ii-*) *war* **7**
*i***fenibelti** (*ii-*) *fanbelt* **15**
*i***festile** (*ii-*) *window* **7**
*uku(zi)***fihla** *to hide (oneself)* **10**
*uku***fihlwa** *to be buried* **16**
*uku***fika** *to arrive* **1**
*i***filimu** (*ii-*) *film* **11**
*um***fino** *wild spinach* **13**
*i***flawa** *flour* **5**
*um***fo** (*aba-*) *fellow* **1**
*i***folokhwe** (*ii-*) *fork* **1**
*i***fomu** (*ii-*) *form* **1**
*m***fondini**! *(my) fellow*!
*uku***fota** *to take photographs* **4**
*um***foti** (*aba-*) *photographer* **4**
*uku***fowun(el)a** *to phone (for)* **6**
*i***fowuni** / *i***foni** *telephone* **5**
*isi***Frentshi** *French* (language*)* **3**
*i***friji** (*ii-*) *fridge* **5**
*isi***fuba** (*izi-*) *chest* **8**
*uku***fudukela** *to move to* **7**
uku**fudumala** *to become warm* **6**
-**fudumele** *be warm* **6**
*isi***fudumezi** (*izi-*) *heater* **6**
*um***fula** (*imi-*) *stream* **9**
*uku***fuma** *humidity* **6**
*uku***fumana** (-**fumene**) *to get, find* **5**
*uku***fumaneka** *to be obtainable* **13**
*uku***fumanisa** nga- *to find out about* **12**
*uku***funa** *to want* **2**
*uku***funda** *to learn* **2**
*uku***fundela** *to study (for)* **3**
*um***fundi** (*aba-*) *student, pupil, learner* **4**
*uku***fundisa** *to teach* **3**
*uku***fundisisa** *to read carefully* **4**
*isi***fundo** *lesson / unit* **10**
*isi***fundo** *esiyin***tloko** *major subject* **10**
*ku***funeka** *it is necessary, must* **3**
-**funeka***yo necessary* **5**
*im***funeko** *necessity* **9**
*imi***funo** *vegetables* **9**

-**fuphi** *near* **6**
*ama***futha** *fat* **13**
futhi *often* **6**
-**futshane** *short* **6**

G

*i***gaba** (*ama-*) *hoe* **9**
*i***gadi** (*ii-*) *garden* **9**
*uku***galela** *to pour* **5**
*i***galelo** (*ama-*) *contribution* **10**
*in***galo** (*iin-*) *arm* **8**
*isi***gama** *vocabulary* **1**
*i***gama** (*ama-*) *name* **2**; *word*
*um***gaqo** (*imi-*) *road, animal track* **15**
*imi***gaqo** *n***tetho** *grammar* **16**
*imi***gaqo** si**seko** *constitution* **16**
*i***garaji** (*ii-*) *garage* **1**
*in***gca** *grass* **6**
-thi ***gca gca gca*** *dotted* **16**
*in***gcaphephe** yez*i***tyalo** *horticulturist* **4**
*uku***gcina** *to look after* **8**; *keep* **9**
uku<u>*z*</u>*i***gcina** -**phil***ile to keep* <u>*oneself*</u> *fit* **12**
*in***gobozi** (*iin-*) *basket* **9**
*uku***godola** *to be cold (humans)* **5**
*uku***goduka** *to go home* **4**
*i***gophe** (*ama-*) *curve / bend* **15**
*in***gozi** *danger, accident* **12**
*i***gqabi** (*ama-*) *leaf* **9**
*uku***gqabhuka** *to burst (of a tyre)* **15**
*uku***gqiba** *to decide* **13**
-**gqib***ile to have finished something* **4**
*in***gqiniba** (*iin-*) *elbow* **8**
*u***gqirha** (*oo-*) *doctor, western practitioner* **4**
*i***gqirha** (*ama-*) *traditional practitioner* **4**
gqitha *very, too much* **5**
*uku***gqithis(el)a** *to pass (for)* **5**
*um***gqomo** (*imi-*) *bin* **9**
*um***gquba** *compost* **9**
*uku***gquma** *to cover* **9**
*i***gqwetha** (*ama-*) *lawyer* **4**
*ubu***gqwetha** *legal profession* **3**
*i***grabile** *gravel* **15**
*um***gubo** *flour* **5**
*in***gubo** (*iin-*) *blanket* **6**
-**gugi***le* *be worn out* **5**
*i***gugu** *pride* **12**
*uku***gula** *to be ill* **6**
*i***gumbi** (*ama-*) *room* **5**
*i***gumbi** *loku***fundela** *study* **13**
*i***gumbi** *loku***hlala** *lounge* **13**
*i***gumbi** *loku***hlambela** *bathroom***13**
*i***gumbi** *loku***lala** *bedroom* **13**
*i***gumbi** *loku***phekela** *kitchen* **5**
*i***gumbi** *loku***tyela** *dining room* **13**
*uku***guqula** *to translate* **4**
*um***guquli** (*aba-*) *translator* **4**
*i***gusha** (*ii-*) *sheep* **13**
*uku***gwegweleza** *to make a detour* **16**
*in***gxangxasi** (*iin-*) *waterfall* **16**
*i***gxalaba** (*ama-*) *shoulder* **8**
*i***gxobha** *marsh* **9**
*in***gxowa** (*iin-*) *bag* **7**

H

*i***hagu** (*ii-*) *pig, hog* **13**
halala! *hurray*! **7**
*uku***hamba** *to go, walk* **1**
*uku***hamba na**- *to go with* **14**
*uku***hamba** ***ngqo*** *to walk straight along* **5**

*uku***hambisa** *to continue* **4**
*u***hambo** *trip* **16**
*i***harika** (*ii-*) *rake* **9**
*i***hashe** (*ama-*) *horse* **12**
hayi *no* **1**
*i***heji** (*ii-*) *hedge* **1**
heke *well then* **3**
*i***hempe** (*ii-*) *shirt* **14**
*um***hla** (*imi-*) *day* **3**; *date* **10**
*um***hla** *woku***zalwa** *birthday* **7**
yonke *imi***hla** *every day* **3**
*uku***hla** *to come down* **7**
*um***hlaba** *soil* **9**
*uku***hlaba** *to stab* **8**
*i***hlabathi** *world* **9**
*um***hlakulo (imi-**) *spade* **9**
*uku***hlala** *to stay, live, sit* **1**
-hleli *be seated* **7**
*uku***hlamba** *to wash* **8**
*isi***hlambi** se**festile** *windscreen wiper* **15**
*um***hlangala** (*imi-*) *mongoose* **9**
*isi***hlangu** (*izi-*) *shoe* **14**
*i***hlathi** lelo **zwe** (*ama-*) *indigenous forest* **16**
*uku***hlawula** *to pay* **4**
-hle (**-ntle**) *beautiful* **2**
*ubu***hle** *beauty* **9**
*i***hlebo** (*ama-*) *secret* **13**
*um***hlekazi** (*aba-*) *sir* **1**; *(your) Excellency* **4**
*uku***hlisa** *to reduce, bring down* **14**
*um***hlobo** (*aba-*) *friend* **1**
*i***hlobo** *summer* **6**
*u***hlobo** (*iin***tlobo)** *kind / sort / way* **10**
*ubu***hlobo** *friendship* **12**
*i***hlosi** (*ama-*) *leopard* **14**
*ulu***hlu** *list* **5**
*ulu***hlu** lo*ku***tya** *menu* **13**
*ulu***hlu** lwe*zi***selo** *beverage / menu* **13**
*isi***hlwele** (*izi-*) *crowd* **12**
*i***hoki** *hockey* **12**
*i***holide** *holiday* **7**
*uku***hombisa** *to adorn, decorate* **14**
*izi***hombiso-***m*zimba *jewellery* **14**
*isi***hombo** (*izi-*) *pattern* **14**
*i***hotele** (*ii-*) *hotel* **10**
huntshu! *hurray*! **5**
*ukw***indla** *autumn* **6**

J

*in***ja** (*izin-*) *dog* **10**
*isi***Jamani** *German* (language) **3**
*isi***Japani** *Japanese* (language) **3**
*i***jelo** (*ama-*) *channel, tube, reed* **16**
*i***jezi** (*ii-*) *jersey* **12**
jikelele *(all) round* **7**
*uku***jikeleza** *to surround* **9**
*in***jineli** (*iin-*) *engineer* **4**
*in***jingalwazi** (*iin-*) *professor* **4**
*uku***jonga** *to look at* **6**
*uku***jongeka** *to look as if* **5**
*in***jongo** (*iin-*) *aim* **9**
*i***joni** (*ama-*) *soldier* **4**

K

kabini *twice* **6**
kahle! *hold on*! (exclamation) **6**
kakubi *badly* **6**
kakhulu *very* **1**
kakuhle *well* **1**
kamnandi *nicely/goodbye* **6**
*in***kampani** *(iin-) company* **4**
kamsinya(ne) *soon, shortly* **1**
kananjalo *also* **4**
kancinci *a little* **3**
kanene *indeed* **4**

*in***kani** *obstinacy* **14**
kanjalo *also, as well* **3**
kanjalo *like this* **6**
kangaka *so (much)* **3**
kangako *so* **6**
kangangokuba *so much so* **3**
*u***kanina** (*oo-*) *cousin (mothers are sisters)* **2**
kaninzi *often* **6**
kanye *once, exactly* **4**
*i***kawusi** (*ii-*) *sock* **14**
*u***kayise** (*oo-*) *cousin (fathers are brothers)* **2**
ke *then* **3**
*isi***kere** *soku***thena** *pruning shears* **9**
*i***ketile** (*ii-*) *kettle* **5**
*i***keyiki** (*ii-*) *cake* **5**
*i***khabathi** (*ii-*) *cupboard* **1**
*i***khadi** (*ama-*) *card* **4**
*uku***khala** *to cry, complain* **8**
*uku***khalaza** (nga-) *to complain* (about) **6**
*isi***khaliso** (*izi-*) *musical instrument* **12**
*uku***khanda** *to repair (car)* **10**
*uku***khangela** *to look, check* **7**
*uku***khapha** *to accompany* **6**
*uku***khanya** *to shine* **6**
-khaphukhaphu *light and fluffy* **5**
*um***khasa***yo* (*aba-*) *novice* **14**
*i***khasi** (*ama-*) *page* **16**
*uku***khathazeka** *to mind, worry* **6**
*ukuzi***khathaza** *to worry (oneself)* **8**
*i***khaya** (*ama-*) *home* **2**
*uku***khawuleza** *to hurry* **10**
*i***khefi** *café* **10**
*i***khefu** *holiday* **10**
*um***khenkethi** (*aba-*) *tourist* **10**
*u***khenketho** *trip* **16**
*uku***khetha** *to choose* **1**; *prefer* **2**
*i***khitshi** (*ama-*) *kitchen* **5**
*i***khiwane** (*ama-*) *fig* **13**
*uku***khohlela** *to cough* **7**
*uku***kholwa** *to believe* **10**
*um***khombe** (*imi-*) *rhino* **4**
*uku***khombisa** *to point* **8**
khona *there* **4**
-khona *here, present* **1**
*um***khondo** (*imi-*) *track* **16**
*i***khonsethi** (*ii-*) *concert* **6**
*um***khuhlane** *cold, flu* **8**
*uku***khula** *to grow* **12**
*uku***khulela** *to grow up at* **3**
-khulu *big* **6**
*uku***khulula** *to undress* **8**
*uku***khululeka** *to free, be comfortable* **7**; *relax* **10**
*isi***khululo** (*izi-*) sama**polisa** *police station* **15**
*isi***khululo** se**bhasi** *bus stop* **15**
*um***khuluwa** (*aba-*) *elder brother* **2**
*uku***khumbula** *to remember* **7**
*uku***khumbuza** *to remind* **5**
*uku***khupha** *to take out* (also *vomit*) **15**
*u***khuphiswano** (*iin***kuphiswano**) *match, competition* **6**
*uku***khusela** *to protect* **10**
-khuselek*ile* *to be safe* **15**
*uku***khuthaza** *to encourage* **14**
-khuthele *be diligent* **10**
*uku***khwela** *i***bhayisekile** *to ride a bike* **12**
*uku***khwela** *i***hashe** *to ride a horse* **12**
*uku***khwelisa** *to give a lift to* **15**
*i***kiriva** (*ii-*) *wheelbarrow* **9**

L

-**leyithi** *late* **7**

*uku***libala** (-**libele**) *to forget* **3**

*uku***lila** *to weep / cry* **8**

*uku***lima** *to farm, cultivate* **4**

*um***limi** (*aba-*) *farmer* **4**

*uku***lindela** *to wait for* **11**

*uku***lindisa** *to keep someone waiting* **5**

*uku***lingana** *to try on* **14**

*uku***loba** *to fish* **11**

*u***loliwe** (*oo-*) *train* **3**

*i***lokhwe** (*ii-*) *dress* **14**

*um***lomo** (*imi-*) *mouth* **8**

*uku***londoloza** *to save* **9**

*i***lori**, also *i***loli** (*ii-*) *lorry* **1**

-**lubhelu** *yellow* **5**

-**luhlaza** *green, blue* **5**

-**lula** *easy* **4**; *light* **6**

*uku***luma** *to bite* **8**

*uku***lumka** *to be careful* **9**

-**lungile***yo* *good* **6**

*uku***lungisa** *to prepare* **9**; *set the table* **13**; *repair* **15**

-**lusizi** *sorry, sad* **6**

*uku***lwa** *to fight* **6**

*u***lwandle** (*ii-*) *sea* **6**

*u***lwimi** (*ii-*) *tongue, language* **3**

M

*uku***ma** *to stop, stand* **7**

*u***mabona-kude** (*oo-*) *TV* **12**

*u***mafungwashe** *eldest sister* **2**

*i***magi** (*ii-*) *mug* **14**

*u***makazi** (*oo-*) *(my) maternal aunt* **4**

*u***makhulu** (*oo-*) *grandmother* **1**

*u***maleko** (*oo-*) *layer* **5**

*i***mali** *money* **1**

*u***malume** (*oo-*) *maternal uncle* **2**

*u***mama** (*oo-*) *mother* **1**

*uku***mamela** *to listen* **9**

malunga na- *concerning* **9**

*um***mandla** (*imi-*) *region* **16**

*um***mangaliso** (*imi-*) *delight, wonder* **16**

*u***mantyi** (*oo-*) *magistrate* **4**

-**manzi** *wet* **6**

*i***maphu** (*ii-*) *map* **9**

*u***matshini** *woku***cheba** *i***ngca** *lawn mower* **9**

*oo***mawokhulu** *grandparents* **2**

*uku***mba** *to dig* **7**

*u***mbona** (*imi-*) *maize* **13**

-**mdaka** *dirty* **8**

*i***meko** (*ii-*) *situation* **10**

*i***mela** (*ii-*) *knife* **13**

*uku***mela** *to represent* **12**

*uku***mema** *to invite* (passive - **menya***)* **11**

*i***menyu** (*ii-*) *menu* **13**

mhlawumbi *perhaps* **7**

-**mhlophe** *white* **5**

*i***mini** *day* **4**

emva kwe**mini** *in the afternoon* **4**

*uku***mka** *to go away* **6**

mna *as for me* **4**

-**mnandi** *nice, pleasant* **1**; *sweet, delicious* **5**

-**mnyama** *black* **5**

*i***mo-ntlalo** *way of life* **16**

molo / molweni *hello* **1**

*uku***mosha** *to damage* **9**

*i***moto** (*ii-*) *(motor)car* **1**

*u***moya** (*imi-*) *wind* **6**; *air* **7**

*uku***mpompa** *to pump* **7**

-**msulwa** *pure, innocent* **8**

-**muncu** *sour* **6**

*isi***muncumuncu** *dessert* **13**

-mxinwa *narrow* **8**
-myoli *lovely* **16**

N

*uku***na** *to rain* **6**
na- *and / with*; *(to) have* **2**
... **na**? *to denote a question* **1**
*uku***naba** *to stretch* **14**
nabani *anybody* **16**
-nakho/-nako *can* **6**
*um***nakwabo** *his/her/their brother* **2**
*um***nakwethu** *my/our brother* **2**
*um***nakwenu** *your brother* **2**
nam *me too / and / with me* **1**
-namandla *strong* **6**
-namanzi *juicy* **13**
-namava *experienced* **10**
*uku***nambitha** *to enjoy, relish* **13**
-namendu *speedy* **8**
namhlanje *today* **1**
nangona *although* **16**
*i***nani** (*ii-*) *number* **10**
nanini na *any time* **16**
nantsi (*i***kofu**) *here it is* **4**
naphina *everywhere* **16**
na*se*- *and in* **3**
nawe *with you / and you* **1**
*uku***nceda** *to help someone* **5**
*ukuzi***nceda** *to help oneself* **5**
*uku***ncedisa** *to help someone with something* **2**
*um***ncedisi** (*aba-*) *assistant* **9**
*u***ncedo** *help* **14**
-ncinane *small, little* **6**
-ncinci *small, little* **5**
*uku***nci***ph***isa** *reduce* (passive **-nci***tshi***iswa**) *reduced* **10**
*uku***ncokola** *to chat* **2**
*isi***ncoko** (*izi-*) *essay* **16**
ndawonye *together* **5**
*isi***Ndebele** *Ndebele* (language) **3**
-ndlongo-ndlongo *rough* **12**
*u***ndwendwe** (*iin-*) *guest, visitor* **9**
-nencasa *delicious* **5**
*i***nene** *truth* **5**; *indeed* **5**
*i***nene** (*ama-*) *gentleman* **1**
*i***nenekazi** (*ama-*) *lady* **1**
-nenkani *stubborn* **14**
*uku***netha** *to rain* **6**
-nga- *may, can* **2**
(i)**ngaba** *perhaps* **11**
ngabani ixesha? *at what time?* **11**
-ngakanani? *how much?* **7**
ngakumbi *especially* **3**
nga*ma***nye** *ama***xesha** *sometimes* **4**
ngaphakathi *inside* **2**
ngaphambili *in front* **7**; *before* **8**
ngaphandle *outside* **2**
ngaphandle kwa- *outside of / besides* **11**
ngaphantsi *underneath* **11**
ngaphantsi kwa- *less than* **14**
ngaphezu kwa- *more than* **14**
-ngaphi? *how many*? **6**
ngase- *in the vicinity of* **1**
(i)**ngathi** *(it) seems* **5**
*uku***ngcamla** *to taste* **13**
-ngcono (kuna-) *better (than)* **8**
*i***ngcwaba** (*ama-*) *grave* **15**
ngelishwa *unfortunately* **3**
*uku***ngena** *to come in* **2**
ngenene *indeed* **5**
ngenxa *ya- because of* **6**
ngesaquphe *suddenly* **5**
*i***Ngesi** (*ama-*) *English person* **3**
*isi***Ngesi** *English* (language) **2**
ngethamsanqa *luckily* **4**

ngoku *now* **2**
ngokufanelekile*yo properly* **9**
ngokuhlwa *in the evening* **4**
ngokukhawuleza *quickly* **6**
ngokuqinisekile*yo certainly* **5**
ngokwanele*yo enough, sufficiently* **6**
ngomso *tomorrow* **6**
ngononophelo *carefully* **9**
*uku***ngqonga** *to sit around something* **16**
-**ngqukuva** *round* **5**; *blunt* **8**
ngubani? / **ngoobani**? *who is / are*? **2**
-**ngxam***ile be in a hurry* **5**
*um***ngxuma** (*imi-*) *hole* **15**
*um***ngxu***nya***ana** *little hole* **15**
*uku***nika** *to give* **5**
*uku***nika** *u***moya** *to give spirit, i.e. support* **12**
*um***nikazi-khaya** (*aba-*) *housewife* **4**
nina *as for you* (pl.) **2**
*um***ninawa** (*aba-*) *younger brother* **2**
nini? *when?* **3**
*um***nini(kazi)** (*aba-*) *owner* **4**
-**ninzi** *many* **4**
*u***ninzi** *majority, many* **12**
*uku***nitha** *to knit* **12**
njalo *like that* **6**
njalo njalo *and so on, etc.* **4**
njani? *how*? **1**
nje *just* **3**
njenga- *like, as* **3**
*u***njingalwazi** (*oo-*) *professor + name* **4**
*uku***nkcenkceshela** *to water* **9**
*u***nobhala** (*oo-*) *secretary* **4**
*u***nogadi** (*oo-*) *guard* **4**
noko *in a small way* **3**; *though* **14**
nokuba yin**toni** *whatever* **2**
-**nolwazi** *knowledgeable* **9**
*u***nomathotholo** (*oo-*) *radio* **12**
*i***nombolo** ye**foni** *telephone number* **7**
-**nomdla** *interesting* **4**
*u***noncwadi** (*oo-*) *librarian* **4**
*u***nondyebo** (*oo-*) *treasurer* **4**
*u***nongendi** (*oo-*) *nun* **4**
nonke *you all* **1**
*u***nontlalo-ntle** (*oo-*) *social worker* **4**
*u***nopopi** (*oo-*) *doll* **8**
*u***noposi** (*oo-*) *postman* **4**
*u***nosilarha** (*oo-*) *butcher* **4**
*u***novenkile** (*oo-*) *shopkeeper* **4**
-the ***nqa*** *be surprised* **5**
-**nqab***ile be scarce* **6**
*i***nqaku** (*ama-*) *written article* **10**
*um***nqathe** (*imi-*) *carrot* **13**
*i***nqindi** (*ama-*) *fist* **12**
*uku***nqunqa** *to chop* **13**
*i***nqugwala** (*ama-*) *round hut* **16**
*um***nqwazi** (*imi-*) *hat* **14**
*uku***nqwenela** *to wish, want* **7**
*aba***ntakwethu** *my / our siblings* **2**
*aba***ntakwenu** *your siblings* **2**
*aba***ntakwabo** *his / her siblings* **2**
umntla *north* **3**
entla *in the north* **3**
ntoni? *what?* **4**
-**ntsundu** *brown* **6**
*um***ntu** (*aba-*) *person* **3**
*aba***ntu** *aba***dala** *adults* **4**
*ubu***ntu** *human decency* **3**
*um***ntwana** (*aba-*) *child* **1**
*ubu***ntwana** *childhood* **11**

O

P

phakathi kwa- *between* **5**; *among; inside* **11**
-**phambili** *forward, in front* **11**; *outstanding* **12**
*isi***phambuka** (*izi-*) *intersection* **15**
phandle *outside* **11**
*uku***phangela** *to work* **4**
phantse *nearly* **15**
phantsi *down* **1**
phantsi kwa- *under* **11**
*uku***phatha** *to manage, rule* **4**; *to hold / bring* **7**
*uku***phathela** *to bring for* **14**
*um***phathi** (*aba-*) *manager* **4**
*um***phathi**-*ba***sebenzi** *personnel manager* **4**
*um***phathiswa** (*aba-*) *cabinet minister* **10**
phaya *over there* **6**
*uku***phazama** *to make mistakes* **3**
*uku***phazamisa** *to interrupt* **4**
*uku***pheka** *to cook* **4**
*um***pheki** (*aba-*) *cook* **4**, *chef* **10**
*uku***phela** *to come to an end* **6**
*uku***phelelwa** *to be used up completely* **15**
-**phelile***yo past, last* **6**
*uku***phendula** *to answer* **6**
*i***phepha** (*ama-*) *paper* **5**
*i***phepha**-*n***daba** (*ama-*) *newspaper* **7**
*i***phepha** lo*ku***qhuba** *driver's licence* **10**
-**phesheya** *overseas* **12**
phesheya *kwa- on the other side of* **13**
phezulu *up, upstairs* **11**
phezu kwa- *on top of, above* **5**
phi? *where?* **1**
*uku***phila** *to be well, be alive* **1**
*uku***phila** ***qete*** *to be completely well* **5**
*uku***phinda** *repeat* **3**
*isi***pho** (*izi-*) *gift* **14**
phofu *then* **12**
*um***phokoqo** *maize meal porridge* **13**
*uku***phola** *to become cool* **5**
-**phol***ile to be cool* **5**
*u***phondo** (*iim***pondo**) *horn, hooter* **15**
*uku***phosa** *to miss* **10**
*uku***phulaphula** *to listen* **7**
*uku***phuma** *to go out* **7**
*uku***phumelela** *to manage, succeed* **4**
*uku***phumla** *to rest, relax* **5**
*ukuzi***phumza** *to rest oneself* **13**
*uku***phunga** *to drink (hot liquid)* **2**
*isi***Phutukezi** *Portuguese* (language) **3**
*uku***phuthuma** *to fetch* **11**
*isi***pili** (*izi-*) *mirror* **3**
*i***pilisi** (*ii-*) *pill* **8**
*isi***pinatshi** *spinach* **13**
*i***pleyiti** (*ii-*) *plate* **13**
*i***polisa** (*ama-*) *policeman* **4**
*u***profesa** (*oo-*) *professor* **4**
*im***pumalanga** *east* **3**
*im***pumelelo** *success* **7**

Q

qabu! *relief!* **5**
*um***qa** *thick maize porridge* **13**
*uku***qabula** *to quench (thirst)* **5**
*um***qala** (*imi-*) *throat* **8**
*uku***qala** *to begin* **8**
*i***qakamba** *cricket* **6**

*um***qamelo** (*imi-*) *pillow* **5**
*in***qanawa** (*iin-*) *ship* **6**
*i***qanda** (*ama-*) *egg* **5**
*uku***qaqamba** *to shine* **6**; *to throb* **8**
-qaqamb*ile be bright* **14**; *stunning* **16**
*in***qawa** (*iin-*) *pipe* **14**
*i***qela** (*ama-*) *team* **12**
*uku***qeqesha** *to train* **4**
*um***qeqeshi** (*aba-*) *trainer* **4**
*um***qeshwa** (*aba-*) *employee* **10**
qha *only* **5**
*uku***qhagamshelana na-** *to contact* **10**; also **-qhakamshelana** *na-*
*i***qhalo** (*ama-*) *proverb* **10**
*isi***qhamo** (*izi-*) *fruit* **13**
-qhelek*ile be normal, usual* **14**
*i***qhina** (*ama-*) *tie* **14**
qhiwu (*uku***thi**) *hold up* **12**
*i***qhiya** (*ii-*) *head covering* **14**
qho *always* **6**
*uku***qhobosha** *to fasten* **1**
*uku***qhuba** *to continue* **3**; *to drive* **4**
*uku***qhubela phambili** *to progress* **7**
*um***qhubi** (*aba-*) *driver* **4**
*uku***qhuqha** *to beat together* (*ingredients*) **5**
*uku***qhuqhisisa** *to beat very well* **4**
*uku***qhwalela** *to limp* **7**
*uku***qhwitha** *to start (a car)* **15**
*uku***qina** *to become stiff* **5**
-qinisek*ile to be sure* **5**
*i***qobokazana** (*ama-*) *girls, young ladies* **7**
*uku***qokelela** *to collect* **9**
*ing***qokelela** *(iin-) collection* **7**
*i***qokobhe** (*ama-*) *shell* **9**
*um***qolo** (*imi-*) *spine, backbone* **8**
*um***qombothi** *kind of beer* **5**
*uku***qonda** *to understand* **3**
*uku***qondakala** *to be understandable* **13**
*i***qondo** (*ama-*) *degree* **10**
*i***qondo** lo*bu***shushu** *temperature* **6**
*uku***qubha** *to swim* **10**
*i***qunube** (*ama-*) *berry* **7**
*in***qununu** (*iin-*) *principal* **10**
*um***ququzelelikazi** (*aba-*) *stewardess* **1**
*in***qwelo-moya** (*iin-*) *aeroplane* **1**

R

*i***rediyo** (*ii-*) *radio* **1**
*i***resiphi** (*ii-*) *recipe* **5**
*i***restyu** (*ii-*) *restaurant* **7**
*i***rhasi** *barley* **13**
*u***rhatya** *dusk* **16**
*ama***rhewu** *non-alcoholic beer* **5**
rhoqo *regularly* **9**

S

-sa- *still* **2**
*um***sakwethu** *my / our sister* **2**
*uku***sala** *to stay, remain* **1**
*i***saladi** (*ii-*) *salad* **13**
*u***sana** (*iint-*) *baby* **8**
*i***sengwitshi** (*ii-*) *sandwich* **5**
*i***sango** (*ama-*) *entrance, gate* **9**
*u***sapho** (*iint-*) *family* **4**
*i***sarha** (*ii-*) *saw* **9**
*uku***sasaza** *to broadcast* **4**
*um***sasazi** (*aba-*) *broadcaster* **4**
*uku***sebenza** *to work* **4**
*uku***sebenzela** *to work for* **4**
*um***sebenzi** (*aba-*) *employee* **4**

*um***sebenzi-gadi** (*aba-*) *gardener* **9**
*aba***sebenzi** *staff* **4**
*um***sebenzi** (*imi-*) *work* **4**
*uku***sebenzisa** *to use* **5**
*uku***seka** *to establish, found* **9**
*i***sekela**-*in***qununu** (*ama-*) *vice-principal* **10**
*uku***sela** *to drink (cold liquid)* **2**
*i***sele** (*ama-*) *frog* **4**
*i***senta** *ye***gadi** (*izi-*) *garden centre* **9**
*i***sepha** *soap* **15**
*um***se***ty***enzana** (*imi-*) wo*kuz***onwabisa** *hobby* **10**
*i***shelefu** (*ii-*) *shelf* **1**
*i***shishini** (*ama-*) *factory* **4**
*i***shishini** lee*n***cwadi** *publishing house* **4**
*i***shishini** lem**pahla** *clothing factory* **4**
*uku***shiya** *to leave* **11**
*uku***shiyeka** *to be left over* **13**
-shushu *hot* **3**
*ubu***shushu** *heat* **6**; *fever* **8**
shwaka (*uku***thi**) *disappear* **5**
*ama***si** *sour milk* **13**
*ubu***si** *honey* **5**
*u***siba** (*iint-*) *feather, pen* **8**
-sibekele *to be overcast* **6**
*uku***sika** *to cut* **9**
*ubu***sika** *winter* **3**
*i***siko** (*ama-*) *custom* **10**
simahla *free, gratis* **16**
*i***sinala** (*ii-*) *boarding school* **10**
*uku***singa** *to head for* **16**
*i***sinki** *sink* **13**
*u***sisi** (*oo-*) *sister* **1**
*ili***so** *eye*; *ame***hlo** *eyes* **8**
*ama***so** *big beads* **14**
-soloko *always* **4**
*u***Somandla** *the Almighty* **4**
*u***somashishini** (*oo-*) *businessman* **4**
*uku***sombulula** *to solve* **10**
*u***sompempe** (*oo-*) *referee* **4**
*i***songololo** (*ama-*) *millipede* **15**
soze *never will* **8**
*u***sozigidi** (*oo-*) *millionaire* **11**
*isi***su** (*izi-*) *stomach, abdomen* **8**
*uku***suka** *to come from* **13**
*u***suku** (*iint-*) *24-hour day* **6**
*uku***sula** *to wipe* **7**
*i***suphu** (*ii-*) *soup*
*uku***susela nga-** … *uku***ya nga-** … *from … till …* **11**
*i***suti** (*ii-*) *suit* **14**
*isi***Suthu** *Sotho* (language) **3**
*isi***Swati** *Swati* (language) **3**
*i***swekile** *sugar* **5**

T

*in***taba** (*iin-*) *mountain* **4**
*in***tabakazi** *high mountain* **4**
*i***tafile** (*ii-*) *table* **13**
*in***taka** (*iin-*) *bird* **6**
*in***tamo** (*iin-*) *neck* **8**
*isi***tampu** (*izi-*) *stamp* **12**
*i***tanki** *tank* **7**
*i***tapile** (*ii-*) *potato* **13**
*u***tata** (*oo-*) *father* **1**
*in***tatheli** (*iin-*) *journalist* **9**
*u***tatomkhulu** (*oo-*) *grandfather* **1**
*i***teksi** (*ii-*) *taxi* **1**
*in***tenetya** *tennis* **12**
*isi***tephu** (*izi-*) *step izi***teps** *steps* **8**
*in***tetho** (*iin-*) *saying* **4**
*i***tha** *tar* **15**

*uku***thabatha** *in***xaxheba** *to take part* **9**
-**thabathek***ile to be impressed* **7**
*izi***thako** *ingredients* 5
*i***thala** (*ama-*) lee*n***cwadi** *library* **12**
*i***thambeko** (*ama-*) *slope* **16**
-**thambile***yo soft* **5**
*i***thambo** (*ama-*) *bone* **9**
*u***thambo** (*ii***ntambo**) *(physical) exercise* **12**
*um***thana** (*imi-*) *shrub (small tree)* **9**
*uku***thanda** *to love, like* **4**
-**thandeka***yo beloved* **6**; *dear* **13**
*u***thando** *love* **13**
*isi***thandwa** *beloved* **6**, *darling* **11**
*i***thanga** (*ama-*) *pumpkin* **13**
*uku***thatha** *to take* **5**
*uku***thathela** *to take for* **4**
*i***themba** (*ama-*) *hope* **10**
*uku***themba** *to hope* **1**
*uku***thenga** *to buy* **4**
*uku***thengisa** *to sell* **4**
*um***thengisi** (*aba-*) *shop assistant* **4**
*uku***thetha** *to speak* **1**
*isi***thethe** (*izi-*) *custom* **14**
*isi***thethi** (*izi-*) *speaker* **4**
*um***thetho** (*imi-*) *law* **3**
*i***theyiphu** (*ii-*) *tape* **12**
*um***thi** (*imi-*) *tree* **4**
*ulu***thi** (*izin***ti**) *stick* **3**
*uku***thi** *to say* **2**
-**thile** *certain* **8**
*uku***thiywa** *to be named* **16**
*ukuzi***thoba** *to humble oneself* **13**
*izi***thole** *seedlings* **9**
*i***thoyilethi** *toilet* **13**
*i***thuba** (*ama-*) *chance* **10**
*i***thumbu** *lama***nzi** *hose* **9**
*i***thumbu** *beaded collared necklace* **14**
*uku***thumela** *to send to* **8**
*uku***thunga** *to sew* **4**
*um***thungi** (*aba-*) *tailor*
*um***thungikazi** (*aba-*) *seamstress* **4**
*um***thunzi** (*imi-*) *shade* **9**
*izi***thuthu** *traffic* **15**
*u***thuthu** *lween***kuni** *ash* **9**
*uku***thwala** *to carry* **4**
*um***thwali** (*aba-*) *porter* **4**
*i***ti** *tea* **2**
*i***tikiti** (*ama-*) *ticket* **5**
*in***tini** *Cape otter* **9**
*i***tipoti** (*ii-*) *teapot* **1**
*i***tispuni** (*ii-*) *teaspoon* **5**
*in***tlakohlaza** *spring* **6**
*u***titshala**(**kazi**) (*oo-*) *teacher* **4**
*i***titshala**(**kazi**) (*ii-*) *teacher* **4**
*in***tlalo** *manner of life* **14**
*in***tlama** (*iin-*) *batter, dough* **5**
*in***tlanganiso** (*iin-*) *meeting* **10**
*in***tlanzi** (*iin-*) *fish* **6**
*in***tliziyo** *heart* **8**
*in***tloko** *head* **8**
*iin***tlungu** (pl.) *pain* **8**
*in***to** (*izin***to**) *thing* **3**
*in***to eninzi** *a lot* **3**
enye *in***to** *another thing* **3**
*in***to** yo*ku***sela** *something cold to drink* **2**
*uku***tolika** *to translate* **4**
*i***toliki** (*ii-*) *translator / interpreter* **4**
*in***tombi** (*iin-*) *girl, daughter* **1**
*in***tombazana** *little girl* **1**
amantombazana **tombazana** *little girls* **1**

torho! *shame!* **7**
torhwana! *shame!* **12**
*i***toti** (*ii-*) *tin* **9**
*uku***totoba** *to totter along* **7**
*isi***tovu** (*izi-*) *stove* **3**
*uku***tsala** *to tow* **15**
*uku***tsalela** *to phone someone* **11**
-tsha *young, fresh* **6**
-tsha ***krebhe*** *very fresh* **13**
*um***tshana** (*aba-*) *niece / nephew* **2**
*uku***tshata** *to marry* **5**
-tshat*ile to be married* **5**
*in***tshatsheli** (*iin-*) *champion* **12**
*uku***tshaya** *to smoke* **7**
*i***tsheki** (*ii-*) *cheque* **14**
*i***tsheyini** (*ii-*) *chain* **14**
-tshiphu *cheap* **8**
-tshiphu *to be very cheap* **13**
*uku***tshintsha** *to change* **10**
*uku***tshisa** *to burn something* **6**
*isi***tshixo** (*izi-*) *key* **7**
*i***tshizi** *cheese* **13**
*uku***tsho** *to say so* **2**
*uku***tshona** *to go down (sun)* **5**
*in***tshonalanga** west **3**
*uku***tshweza** *to grate* **13**
*in***tsimbi** (*iin-*) *bell, small bead* **14**
*in***tsimbi** y*ama***qatha** *anklet* **14**
*in***tsimbi** ye*n***galo** *bracelet* **14**
*in***tsimbi** yo*m***qala** *necklace* **14**
*in***tsimbi** *clock* **11**; also *bell, iron*
nge*n***tsimbi** *ya- at ... o'clock* **11**
-tsolo *pointed* **8**
*in***tsomi** (*iin-*) *folktale* **16**
*isi***Tsonga** *Tsonga language* **3**
*isi***Tswana** *Tswana language* **3**
*i***tswele** (*ama-*) *onion* **13**
*isi***tulo** (*izi-*) *chair* **8**
*in***twasahlobo** *early summer* **6**
twatse (*uku***thi**) *to fit perfectly* **14**
*um***tya** (*imi-*) *string* **9**
*ili***tya** (*ama-*) *stone* **9**
*isi***tya** (*izi-*) *dish* **12**
*uku***tya** *to eat, food* **5**
*i***tyala** (*ama-*) *debt* **10**
*uku***tyala** *to plant* **7**
*isi***tyalo** (*izi-*) *plant* **9**
*in***tyatyambo** (*iin-*) *flower* **5**
*uku***tyebisa** *to enrich* **14**
*ubu***tyebi** *resource* **9**
*uku***tyelela** *to visit* **7**
tyhini*! gosh!* **14**
*i***tyuwa** *salt* **13**
*u***tywala** (Class 14) *beer, alcohol* **5**

U

ukuba *that; if* **3**
ukususela *kwa- since* **16**
ukususela *ku-* **... ukuya** *ku- from ... until / to* **11**
ukuze *(so) that + subjunctive* **6**

V

*ama***va** *experience* **10**
*um***va** / *m***va** *back* **15**
*uku***va** *to hear, understand* **3**
*uku***vala** *to close* **5**
*i***vatala** (*ii-*) *watermelon* **13**
*uku***vela** *to come from* **4**
*um***veleli** (*aba-*) *visitor* **10**
*isi***Venda** *Venda* language **3**
*i***venkile** (*ii-*) *shop, store* **16**
*i***venkile yangaphandle** *country store* **16**
*i***vili** (*ama-*) *wheel, tyre* **5**
*i***vili** l**olaleliso** *spare wheel* **15**
*uku***vingca** *to close up* **15**
*uku***vuka** *to wake up* **7**
*im***vula** (*imi-*) *rain* **6**

ukuvula *to open* **12**
ukuvuma *to agree, admit* **6**
ivumba (*ama-*) *fragrance* **9**
ukuvumela *to allow (for)* **10**
-vunyelwa *allowed* **10**
ukuvumelana *to be in harmony* **7**
isivundiso *fertilizer* **9**
-vuthiweyo *ripe* **13**
ukuvuthuza (*ko***moya**) *to blow* **6**
ukuvuya *to be glad* **1**
ukuvuyisana na- *to rejoice with* **7**
ukuvuza *to leak, discharge* **8**
umvuzo (*imi-*) *salary* **10**

W

ukuwa *to fall* **8**
iwayini *wine* **5**
wena *as for you* **1**
iwodrophu (*ii-*) *wardrobe* **1**
-wonke-wonke *public* **11**
iwotshi (*ii-*) *watch* **1**

X

xa *when(ever)* **3**
elixa (< **ixesha**) *while* **13**
ixabiso *price* **9**
ixabiso eliphantsi *low price* **9**
-xakekile *to be busy* **5**
ingxaki (*iin-*) *problem* **8**
inxalenye *rest* **12**
inkxaso (*iin-*) *support* **12**
ukuxela *to tell* **4**
ukuxelela *to tell to* **3**
ixesha (*ama-*) *time* **5**
ixesha lo**bandlululo** *apartheid* **7**
ixeshana *a little while* **13**
ukuxhala *to be anxious* **10**
ukuxhapha *to lap up* **11**
ukuxhasa *to support* **12**
umxhasi (*aba-*) *supporter* **12**
ixhego (*ama-*) *old man* *7*
ixhegokazi (*ama-*) *old woman* **8**
ukuxhentsa *to dance (traditional)* **12**
umxhentso (*imi-*) *traditional dance* **12**
izixhobo *tools* **9**
ukuxhoma *to hang* **11**
-xhomekeke ku- *depending on* **6**
isiXhosa *Xhosa* (language) **1**
ixhwele (*ama-*) *herbalist* **4**
ukuxilonga *to examine* (medically) **8**
-xingile *to be stuck* **15**
ukuxolela *to forgive* **13**
ixolo (*ama-*) *peel* **9**
uxolo *peace; pardon / excuse me* **1**
ukuxuba *to mix* **5**
umxube (*imi-*) *mixture* **5**
ukuxubisisa *to mix very well* **4**

Y

ukuya *to go to* **1**
umyalezo (*imi-*) *message* **11**
inyama *meat* **13**
inyameko *attention* **9**
inyanga (*ii-*) *month, moon* **8**
inyani *truth* **6**
inyaniso *truth* **3**
yaye *and* **6**
ukuyeka *to stop* **6**
umyeni (*aba-*) *husband* **2**
iyeza (*ama-*) *medicine* **8**
umyili (*aba-*) *designer* **14**
uyise (*oo-*) *her / his father* **16**
inyoka (*iin-*) *snake* **4**
iyunivesithi (*ii-*) *university* **2**
iyure (*ii-*) *hour* **10**

Z

*uku***za** *to come*

-**za***yo coming, next* **6**

*um***zali** (*aba-*) *parent* **2**

*um***za** (*aba-*) *cousin (parents brother and sister)* **2**

*uku***zalisa** *to fill* **5**

*uku***zalelwa** *to be born in / at* **3**

*uku***zalwa** *to be born* **3**

*uku***zama** *to try* **3**

*uku***zamisela** *to stir* **5**

*um***zantsi** *south* **3**

*isi***zathu** (*izi-*) *reason* **10**

*uku***zekelela** *to speak slowly* **3**

*um***zekelo** (*imi-*) *example* **6**

-**zele** + copulative *full of* **16**

-zi- myself, yourself, etc. **5**

*um***zi** (*imi-*) *homestead* **16**

*isi***ziba** (*izi-*) *deep pool in a river* **10**

*i***ziko** (*ama-*) *hearth* **13**

*i***ziko** *lolu***ntu** *civic centre* **16**

*um***zimba** (*imi-*) *body* **8**

*i***zinyo** (*ama-*) *tooth* **8**

*uku***zisa** *to fetch, bring* **5**

*uku***zoba** *to paint, draw* **4**

*um***zobi** (*aba-*) *artist* **4**

*um***zobo** (*imi-*) *illustration* **5**; *painting* **12**

*uku***zola** *tranquillity* **16**

-**zol***ile to be calm* **6**

*i***zolo** *yesterday* **6**

-**zondelela***yo energetic* **10**

*um***zukulwana** (*aba-*) *grandchild* **2**

*i***zulu** / *imo***zulu** *weather* **5**

*isi***Zulu** *Zulu* (language) **3**

*uku***zuza** *to win* **9**; *obtain* **10**

*um***zuzu** (*imi-*) *minute* **6**

*um***zuzwana** (*imi-*) *moment* **5**

*u***zwane** (*iin-*) *toe* **8**

*ili***zwe** (*ama-*) *country* **3**

*ili***zwekazi** (*ama-*) *continent* **4**

*isi***zwe** *nation* **12**

*ili***zwi** (*ama-*) *voice* **11** (also *spoken word)*

English–Xhosa vocabulary

above **phezulu**
accept, to *ukw***amkela**
accident *in***gozi** (*iin-*)
accompany, to *uku***khapha**
acquainted, to get *ukw***azana**
address *i-***adelesi** (*ii-*), *i***dilesi** (*ii-*)
adult *um***ntu** *om***dala,** adults *aba***ntu** *aba***dala**
advertize, to *ukw***azisa**; *uku***bhengeza**
advertisement *is***aziso** (*iz-*); *isi***bhengezo** (*izi-*)
advice *i***cebiso** (*ama-*), *ing***cebiso** (*iin-*)
advise, to *uku***cebisa**
aeroplane *in***qwelo-moya** (*iin-*); *i-***eropleni** (*ii-*)
afraid, to be *uk***oyika**
Afrikaans *isi***Bhulu**
Afrikaner *i***Bhulu** (*ama-*)
after **emva kwa-**
after that **emva koko**
afternoon **emva kwemini**
again **kwakhona**
age *ubu***dala**
agree, to *uku***vuma**
aim *in***jongo** (*iin-*)
aim, to *uku***chana**
air *u***moya**
all **-onke**
alleviate, to *uku***dambisa**
allow, to *uku***vumela**
Almighty *u***Somandla**
alone **-odwa**
also **kanjalo**, **kananjalo**
although **nangona**
always **qho**, *l***onke** *i***xesha**, **rhoqo, -soloko**
and **na-**, **kwaye, yaye**
and so on **njalo njalo**
animal *isi***lo**; *isi***lwanyana** (domestic) (*izi-*)
ankle *i***qatha** (*ama-*)
anklet *in***tsimbi** y*ama***qatha**
answer, an *im***pendulo** (*iim-*)
answer, to *uku***phendula**
anxious, to be *uku***xhala**
any time **nanini na**
anybody **nabani**
anywhere **naphina**
apartheid *i***xesha** lo**bandlululo**
apple *i-***apile** (*ama-*)
applicant *um***celi-msebenzi** (*aba-*)
application *isi***celo** (*izi-*)
appropriate -**fanelekile***yo*
arm *in***galo** (*iin-*)
arrive, to *uku***fika**
article (written) *i***nqaku** (*ama-*)
artist *um***zobi** (*aba-*)

ash *u***thuthu** lwee*n***kuni**
ask, to *uku***buza**
ask for, to *uku***cela**
assist, to *uku***ncedisa**
assistant *um***necedisi** (*aba-*)
at last **ekugqibeleni**
athlete *im***baleki** (*iim-*)
attention *in***yameko**
autumn *ukw***indla**

baby *u***sana** (*iint̲-*)
back **umva, mva**
bad -**bi**
badly **kakubi**
bag *in***gxowa** (*iin-*)
bake, to *uku***bhaka**
barley *i***rhasi**
basket *in***gobozi** (*iin-*)
bathroom *i***gumbi** lo*ku***hlambela**, *i***bhafrum**
battery *i***bhetri** (*ii-*)
battle *i***dabi** (*ama-*)
be, to *uku***ba**
be like, to *uku***fana na-**
beach *u***nxweme** (*ii-*)
bead, big *ili***so** (*ama-*), small *in***tsimbi** (*iin-*)
beans (green) *iim***botyi**
beat together (ingredients), to *uku***qhuqha**
beautiful -**hle**; beauty *ubu***hle**
because **kuba**
because of **ngenxa ya-**
become, to *uku***ba** + copulative
bed *um***andlalo** (*im-*); *i***bhedi** (*ii-*)
bedroom *i***gumbi** loku**lala**
beer *u***tywala**
before **phambi kwa-**
begin, to *uku***qala**
behind **emva** (adv.) **emva kwa-** (prep.)
believe, to *uku***kholwa**
below **ezantsi**
bell *in***tsimbi** (*iin-*)
belt (seat-) i**bhanti** (*ama-*)
bend *i***gophe** (*ama-*)
berry *i***qunube** (*ama-*)
besides **ngaphandle kwa-**
better -**bhetele**
better than **ngcono kuna-**
between **phakathi kwa-**
beverage (menu) *ulu***hlu** lwe*zi***selo**
bicycle *i***bhayisikile** (*ii-*)
big -**khulu**
bin *um***gqoma** (*imi-*)
bird *in***taka** (*iin-*)
birthday *um***hla** woku**zalwa**
bite, to *uku***luma**
bitter -**krakra**
black -**mnyama**
blanket *in***gubo** (*iin-*)
blouse *i***blawuzi** (*ii-*)
blow (wind), to *uku***vuthuza**, *uku***bhudla**
blue -**luhlaza okwesibhakabhaka**; -**blowu**
boarding school *i***sinalo** (*ii-*) (< seminary)
boat *i***phenyane** (*ama-*); *in***qanawa** (*iin-*)
body *um***zimba** (*imi-*)
boil something, to *uku***bilisa**
boiled -**bila***yo*
bone *i***thambo** (*ama-*)
book *in***cwadi** (*iin-*)
born, to be (at) *uku***zal**(el)**wa**
borrow, to *uku***boleka**

box *i***bhokisi** (*ii-*)
box, to *uku***dlala** *ama***nqindi**
boxing *um***dlalo** w*ama***nqindi**
boy *in***kwenkwe** (*ama***k<u>h</u>wenkwe**),
little boy *in***kwenkwana**
bracelet *in***tsimbi** yen**galo**
brake *i***bhreki** (*ii-*)
bread *is***onka**
break, to *ukw***aphuka**
breakfast *isi***dlo** *sa***kusasa**;
*i***blakfesi**
bright -**qaqambile**
bring, to *uku***zisa**, *uku***phatha**
bring for *uku***phathela**
broadcast *uku***sasaza**
broadcaster *um***sasazi** (*aba-*)
brother *u***bhuthi** (*oo-*), elder
brother *um***khuluwa** younger
brother *um***ninawa**
brown -**ntsundu**
bucket *i-***emele** (*ii-*)
build, to *ukw***akha**
builder *um***akhi** (*ab-*)
building *is***akhiwo** (*iz-*)
bull *in***kunzi** (*iin-*)
burn something, to *uku***tshisa**
burst, to (tyre) *uku***gqabhuka**
bus *i***bhasi** (*ii-*)
bus stop *isi***tishi** *se***bhasi** (*izi-*)
businessman *u***somashishini** (*oo-*)
busy, be -**xakek***ile*
but **kodwa**
butcher *u***nosilarha** (*oo-*)
butter *i***bhotolo**
buy, to *uku***thenga**

cabinet minister *um***phathiswa**
(*aba-*)
cake *i***keyiki** (*ii-*)
call, to *uku***biza**
calm, be -**zol***ile*
can -**nakho** *uku-*
capital *in***kunzi** (*iin-*)
car *i***moto** (*ii-*)
card *i***khadi** (*ama-*)
careful, to be *uku***lumka**
carefully **ngononophelo**
carrot *um***nqathe** (*imi-*)
carry, to *uku***phatha,** *uku***thwala**
catch, to *uku***bamba**
cattle *iin***komo**
celebrate, to *uku***bhiyoza**
certain -**thile**
certainly **ngokuqinisekileyo**
chain *i***tsheyini** (*ii-*)
chair *isi***tulo** (*izi-*)
champion *in***tshatshali** (*iin-*)
chance *i***thuba** (*ama-*)
change, to *uku***tshintsha**
channel *i***jelo** (*ama-*)
chat, to *uku***ncokola**
cheap -**tshiphu**
check *i***tsheki** (*ii-*)
check, look at, to *uku***khangela**
cheese *i***tshizi**
chest *isi***fuba** (*izi-*)
chicken *in***kuku** (*iin-*)
chief *in***kosi** (*ama***k<u>h</u>osi**)
child *um***ntwana** (*aba-*)
childhood *ubu***ntwana**
choose, to *uku***khetha**
chop, to *uku***nqunqa**
Christmas *i***Kresmesi**
church *i***cawa** (*ii-*)
city *isi***xeko** (*izi-*)
civic centre *i***ziko** lo*lu***ntu**
clean, to -*uku***coca**
clean, be -**cocek***ile*

cleaner *um***coci** (*aba-*)
climb, to *uku***nyuka**
close, to *uku***vala**
close up, to *uku***vingca**
cloth *i***laphu** (*ii-*)
clothes (also goods, luggage) *iim***pahla**
clothing factory *i***shishini** le*m***pahla** (*ama-*)
coast *u***nxweme** (*ii-*)
coat *i***bhatyi** (*ii-*)
coffee *i***kofu**
cold, to be *uku***banda**
cold, to feel *uku***godola**
collect, to *uku***qokekela**
collection *in***gqokekela** (*iin-*)
colour *um***bala** (*imi-*); *i***bala** (*ama-*)
come, to *uku***za**
come down, to *uku***hla**
come from, to *uku***vela**
come in, to *uku***ngena**
come to an end, to *uku***phela**
comfortable, to be -**khululek***ile*
coming -**za***yo*
company *in***kampani** (*iin-*)
competition *u***khuphiswano**
complain (about), to *uku***khala**(**za**)
compost *um***gquba**
concerning **malunga na-**
concert *i***khonsethi** (*ii-*)
congratulate, to *uku***vuyisana na-**
conserve, to *uku***londoloza**
contact to, *uku***qhagamshelana na-**
continent *ili***zwekazi** (*ama-*)
continue, to *uku***hambisa**, *uku***qhuba**
contribution *i***galelo** (*ama-*)
conversation *in***coko** (*iin-*)
cook, to *uku***pheka**
cool, to become *uku***phola**
cool, to be -**phol***ile*
cost, to *uku***dla**
cough, to *uku***khohlela**
count, to *uku***bala**
country *ili***zwe** (*ama-*)
cousin *u***kanina** (*oo-*), *u***kayise** (*oo-*), *um***za** (*aba-*)
cousins *aba***zala**
cover, to *uku***gquma**
cow *in***komo** (*iin-*)
create, to *uku***dala**
cricket *u***qakamba**
crowd *isi***hlwele** (*izi-*)
cry, to *uku***lila**
cultivate, to *uku***lima**
cup *i***komityi** (*ii-*)
cupboard *i***khabathi** (*ii-*)
curtain *um***lengalenga** (*imi-*)
curve *i***gophe** (*ama-*)
custom *i***siko** (*ama-*); *isi***thethe** (*izi-*)
customer *um***thengi** (*aba-*)
cut, to *uku***sika**

damage *um***onakalo** (*imi*)
dance *um***daniso** (*imi-*), (traditional) *um***xhentso** (*imi-*)
dance, to *uku***danisa**, (traditional) *uku***xhentsa**
danger *in***gozi**
darling, beloved *isi***thandwa** (*izi-*)
date *um***hla** (*imi-*)
daughter *in***tombi** (*iin-*)
day *i***mini** (*ii-*), *um***hla** (*imi-*), 24-hour day *u***suku** (*iint***suku**)
dear (beloved) -**thandeka***yo*

debt *i***tyala** (*ama-*)
decency (human) *ubu***ntu**
decide, to *uku***gqiba**
decorate, to *uku***hombisa**
decrease, to *uku***hlisa**
deep -**nzulu**; depth *ubu***nzulu**
degree *i***qondo** (*ama-*)
delicious -**mnandi** / -**nencasa**
depending on -**xhomekeke** ku-
depth *ubu***nzulu**
designer *um***yili** (*aba-*)
dessert *isi***muncumuncu**
detour, to make a *uku***gwegweleza**
die, to *uku***bhubha** (humans)
*uku***fa** (animals)
difficult -**nzima**; difficulty
*ubu***nzima**
dig, to *uku***mba**
diligent -**khuthele**
dining room *i***gumbi lo***ku***tyela**
dinner *isi***dlo** sango**kuhlwa**,
*i***dinala**
direct, to *uku***lawula**
director *um***lawuli** (*aba-*)
discuss, to *uku***bonisana**; *uku***xoxa**
dish *isi***tya** (*izi-*)
dissolve, to *uku***nyibilikisa**
diviner *is***anuse** (*iz-*)
divorced, to be -**ahlukene**
do, to *ukw***enza**
doctor *u***gqirha** (*oo-*), *i***gqirha**
(*ama-*) traditional healer
dog *in***ja** (*izin-*)
doll *u***nopopi** (*oo-*)
door *u***cango** (*iing-*)
doorway *um***nyango** (*imi-*)
dough *in***tlama** (*iin-*)
down **phantsi**
draw, to *uku***zoba**
dress *i***lokhwe** (*ii-*)
dress, to (also wear) *uku***nxiba**
drink, to *uku***sela** (cold)
*uku***phunga** (hot)
drink (cold) *in***to** yo*ku***sela** (*izin***to**
zo*ku***sela**)
drive, to *uku***qhuba**
driver *um***qhubi** (*aba-*)
driver's licence *i***phepha**(-**mvume**)
lo*ku***qhuba**
drought *im***balela**
dry, be -**om***ile*
dusk *u***rhatya**

ear *in***dlebe** (*iin-*)
early **kusasa**
earring *i***cici** (*ama-*)
Easter *i***Pasika**
easy -**lula**
eat, to *uku***tya,** *uku***dla**
egg *i***qanda** (*ama-*)
elbow *in***gqiniba** (*iin-*)
electricity *um***bane**
elephant *in***dlovu** (*iin-*)
employee *um***qeshwa** (*aba-*),
*um***sebenzi** (*aba-*)
encourage, to *uku***khuthyaza**
energetic -**zondelela***yo*
engineer *in***janeli** (*iin-*)
English (language) *isi***Ngesi**
English person *i***Ngesi** (*ama-*)
enjoy, to (something)
*uku***nambitha** (*uk***onwabela**)
enjoy oneself, to *ukuz***onwabisa**
enough, to be -**anele,**
ngokwanele*yo*
enrich, to *uku***tyebisa**
enter, to *uku***ngena**
entrance *i***sango** (*ama-*)

especially **ngakumbi**
essay *isi***ncoko** (*izi-*)
evening, in the **ngokuhlwa**
every -**onke**; everyday **yonke** *imi***hla**
exactly **kanye**
exaggerate, to *uku***baxa**
examine (medically) *uku***xilonga**
example *um***zekelo** (*imi-*)
excuse (me)! *u***xolo**! (lit. peace)
exercise (physical) *u***thambo** (*iin***tambo**)
exhibition *um***boniso** (*imi-*)
expense *in***dleko** (*iin-*)
expensive -**dulu**
experience *ama***va**
experienced -*nama***va**
expert *in***cutshe** (*iin-*)
explain, to *uku***chaza**
eye *ili***so** (eyes *ame***hlo**)

factory *i***shishini** (*ama-*)
fall, to *uku***wa**
fame *u***dumo**
family *u***sapho** (*iint-*)
famous, to become *uku***duma**, to be -**dum***ile*
far **kude**
farm *i***fama** (*ii-*)
farmer *um***limi** (*aba-*)
fast **ngokukhawuleza**
fasten, to *uku***qhobosha**
fat *ama***futha**
fat, to be -**tyeb***ile*
father *u***tata** (*oo-*); my father *u***bawo** (*oo-*)
fear *u***loyika**
fellow *um***fo** (*aba-*), my fellow *m***fondini**

fertilizer *isi***vundiso**
fetch, to *uku***landa,** *uku***phuthuma,** *uku***zisa**
few -**mbalwa**
fig *i***khiwane** (*ama-*)
fight, to *uku***lwa**
fill, to *uku***zalisa**
find, to *uku***fumana**
fine -**hle**
finger *um***nwe** (*imi-*)
finish, to *uku***gqiba**; finished -**gqib***ile*
fire *um***lilo** (*imi-*)
first -*oku***qala**; firstly *ku***qala**
fish *in***tlanzi** (*iin-*)
fish, to *uku***loba**
fist *i***nqindi** (*ama-*)
flag *in***dwe** (*izin-*); *i***flegi** (*ii-*)
flour *in***gubo,** *i***flawa**
flower *in***tyatyambo** (*iin-*)
flu *um***khuhlane**
folktale *in***tsomi** (*iin-*)
follow, to *uku***landela**
food *uku***tya**
foot *u***nyawo** (*ii-*)
forest (indigenous) *i***hlathi** (**lelo zwe**) (*ama-*)
forget, to *uku***libala**
forgive, to *uku***xolela**
fork *i***folokhwe** (*ii-*)
forward **phambili**
fragrance *i***vumba** (*ama-*)
free, to *uku***khululeka**
free (gratis) **simahla**
fresh -**tsha**
friend *um***hlobo** (*aba-*)
friendship *ubu***hlobo**
frog *i***sele** (*ama-*)

from ... until **ukususela kwa-** ... **ukuya ku** ...
fruit *izi***qhamo**
full -**zele**

garbage *in***kunkuma**
garden *i***gadi** (*ii-*)
gardener *um***sebenzi-gadi**
gate *i***sango** (*ama-*)
gentleman *i***nene** (*ama-*)
German *i***Jamani** (*ama-*)
German (language) *isi***Jamani**
get, to *uku***fumana**
get acquainted, to *ukw***azana**
gift *isi***pho** (*izi-*)
girl *in***tombi** (*iin-*)
give, to *uku***nika**; *uku***pha**
give a lift, to *uku***khwelisa**
glad, to be *uku***vuya**
glasses (spectacles) *iin***dondo**
go, to (with) *uku***hamba (na-**)
go down, to (sun) *uku***tshona**
go home, to *uku***goduka**
go out, to *uku***phuma**
go slowly, to *uku***cothoza**
go to, to *uku***ya**
goat *i***bhokwe** (*ii-*)
good -**lungi**le*yo*
goods *im***pahla**
goodbye **hamba**(ni) / **sala**(ni) **kakuhle**
grandchild *um***zukulwana** (*aba-*)
grandfather *u***tat'omkhulu** (*oo-*)
grandmother *u***makhulu** (*oo-*)
grandparents *oo***mawokhulu**
grapes *ii***diliya**
grass *in***gca**
grate, to *uku***tshweza**
grateful, to be *uku***bulela**
gratis **simahla**
grave *i***ngcwaba** (*ama-*)
great -**khulu**
green -**luhlaza okwengca**
greet, to (for) *uku***bulis(el)a**
grow, to *uku***khula**
grow up at, **ukukhulela**
guard *u***nogadi** (*oo-*)
guest *u***ndwendwe** (*ii-*)

hail *isi***chotho**
hair *u***nwele** (*ii***nwele**)
hand *i***sandla** (*iz-*)
hang *uku***xhoma**
happen, to *ukw***enzeka**
happy, to become, happiness *uk***onwaba**
happy, to be -**onwab***ile*
hat *um***nqwazi** (*imi-*)
head *in***tloko** (*iin-*); headache -**nentloko**
head for, to *uku***singa**
hear, to *uku***va**
heart *in***tliziyo** (*iin-*)
hearth *i***ziko** (*ama-*)
heat *ubu***shushu**
heater *isi***fudumezi** (*izi-*)
heaviness *ubu***nzima**
heavy -**nzima**
help, to *uku***nceda**; help *u***ncedo**
help oneself, to *ukuzi***nceda**
help someone with something, to *uku***ncedisa**
herbalist *i***xhwele** (*ama-*)
here **apha**
hide (oneself), to *uku*(zi)**fihla**
high -**phakamile***yo*
hill *in***duli** (*iin-*)
historian *im***balisi** (*iim-*)

history *im***bali**
hobby *um***setyenzana**
wo*kuz***onwabisa**
hoe *i***gaba** (*ama-*)
hold, to *uku***phatha**
hold on, to *uku***bamba**
hole *um***ngxuma** (*imi-*)
holiday *i***holide**; *i***khefu** (a breather, lit. a gap)
home *i***khaya**; at home *e***khaya**
homestead *um***zi** (*imi-*)
honey *ubu***si**
hooter, horn *u***phondo** (*iim***pondo**)
hope *i***themba** (*ama-*)
hope, to *uku***themba**
horse *i***hashe** (*ama-*)
horticulturalist *in***gcaphephe**
ye*zi***tyalo**
hose *i***thumbu** l*ama***nzi**
hospital *isi***bhedlele** (*izi-*)
hot -**shushu**, (intensely) -**balele**
hour *i***yure** (*ii-*)
house *in***dlu** (*izin-*)
housewife *um***nikazi-khaya** (*aba-*)
how? **njani**?
how big, much? -**ngakanani**?
how many? -**ngaphi**?
humble oneself, to *ukuz*i**thoba**
humidity *uku***fuma**
hungry, be -**lamb***ile*
hurt, be -**enzakalis***ile*
hurry, to *uku***khawuleza**
hurry, be in a -**ngxam***ile*
husband *um***yeni** (*aba-*)
hut (round) *i***nqugwala** (*ama-*)

idea *i***cebo** (*ama-*)
idiom *is***aci** (*iz-*)
if **ukuba**
ill, to be *uku***gula**
illustration *um***zobo** (*imi-*)
immediately **kwangoko**
important -**balulekile***yo*
impressed -**thabathekile***yo*
in front of **phambi kwa-**
indeed **inene**
information *ukw***azisa**
ingredients *izi***thako**
injured, to be -**enzakalis***ile*
innocent -**msulwa**
inside **ngaphakathi** (adv)
phakathi kwa- (prep)
instead of **endaweni ya-**
interpreter *i***toliki** (*ii-*)
interest *um***dla**; interesting
-nom**dla**
interrupt, to *uku***phazamisa**
intersection *isi***phambuka** (*izi-*)
interview *u***dliwano-ndlebe** (*iin-*)
introduce, to *ukw***azisa**
invite, to *uku***mema**

jacket *i***bhatyi** (*ii-*)
jersey *i***jezi** (*ii-*)
jewellery *izi***hombiso-***m***zimba**
job applicant *um***celi-***m***sebenzi**
(*aba-*)
journalist *in***tatheli** (*iin-*)
juicy -**namanzi**
just **nje**

keep, to *uku***gcina**
keep someone waiting, to
*uku***lindisa**
kettle *i***ketile** (*ii-*)
key *isi***tshixo** (*izi-*)
kindness *ubu***bele**
kitchen *i***khitshi** (*ama-*); *i***gumbi**

*loku***phekela**
knee *i***dolo** (*ama-*)
knife *i***mela** (*ii-*)
knit, to *uku***nitha**
know, to *ukw***azi**
know from, to *ukw***azela**
knowledge *ulw***azi**
knowledgeable **-nolwazi**

lady, madam *in***kosikazi** (*ama***khosikazi**), *i***nenekazi** (*ama-*)
language *u***lwimi** (*ii-*)
large -**khulu**
last -**okugqibela, -phelile***yo*
late -**leyithi, emva kwexesha**
law *um***thetho** (*imi-*)
lawyer *i***gqwetha** (*ama-*)
layer *u***maleko** (*im-*)
leader *in***kokeli** (*iin-*)
leaf *i***gqabi** (*ama-*)
leak, to *uku***vuza**
learn, to *uku***funda**, learner *um***fundi** (*aba-*)
leave, to *uku***hamba**, *uku***mka**, *uku***shiya**
left -**asekhohlo**
left over, to be *uku***shiyeka**
leg *um***lenze** (*imi-*)
lend, to *uku***boleka**
leopard *i***hlosi** (*ama-*)
lesson *isi***fundo** (*izi-*)
letter *in***cwadi** (*iin-*); *i***leta** (*ii-*)
lettuce *i***letisi** (*ii-*)
librarian *u***noncwadi** (*oo-*)
library *i***thala** (*ama-*) lee*n***cwadi**, *i***layibhri** (*ii-*)
lie down, to *uku***lala phantsi**
light *isi***bane** (*izi-*)
lightning *um***bane**
life *ub***omi**
like, to *uku***thanda**
like **njenga-**
limp, to *uku***qhwalela**
list *ulu***dwe** (*izin-*), *ulu***hlu** (*izin***tlu**)
listen, to *uku***mamela**; *uku***phulaphula**
little -**ncinci**; -**ncinane;** a little **kancinci**
live, to (i.e. reside) *uku***hlala**
liver *isi***bindi** (*izi-*)
long -**de**
long ago **kudala**
look, to *uku***jonga**, *uku***khangela** (to check)
look after, to *uku***gcina**
look as if, to *uku***jongeka**
look for, to *uku***funa**
lorry *i***lori**, *i***loli** (*ii-*)
lose weight *uku***bhitya**
lost, be -**lahlek***ile*
lounge *i***gumbi** lo*ku***hlala**
love *u***thando**
love, to *uku***thanda**
lovely -**myoli**
low -**phantsi**
luck *i***thamsanqa**; luckily nge**thamsanqa**
lukewarm -**dikidiki**
lunch *isi***dlo** sas*e***mini**, *i***lantshi**

magistrate *u***mantyi** (*oo-*)
maize *u***mbona** (*imi-*)
majority *in***koliso,** *u***ninzi**
make, to *ukw***enza**
make mistakes, to *uku***phazama**
man *in***doda** (*ama-*), old man *i***xhego** (*ama-*)

manage, to *uku***phatha**
manager *um***phathi** (*aba-*)
many -**ninzi**
map *i***maphu** (*ii-*)
marry, to *uku***tshata**, married, be -**tshat***ile*
mat *in***kukho** (*iin-*), *um***andlalo** (*im-*)
match (in sport) *u***khuphiswano** (*iin***k̲uphiswano**)
meal *isi***dlo** (*izi-*)
meat *in***yama**
medicine *i***yeza** (*ama-*)
meet with, to *uku***dibana na-**
meeting *in***tlanganiso** (*iin-*)
menu *i***menyu**; *ulu***hlu** *loku***tya**
message *um***yalezo** (*imi-*)
milk *u***bisi**, sour milk *ama***si**
millionaire *u***sozigidi** (*oo-*)
millipede *i***songololo** (*ama-*)
minute *um***zuzu** (*imi-*)
mirror *isi***pili** (*izi-*)
miss, to *uku***phosa**
miss *in***kosazana** (*ama***kh̲osazana**)
mist *in***kungu**
mistake, to make a *uku***phazama**
mix *uku***xuba**
mixture *um***xube** (*imi-*)
moment *um***zuzwana** (*imi-*)
money *i***mali**
mongoose *um***hlangana** (*imi-*)
month; moon *in***yanga** (*iin-*)
morning, in the **kusasa**
mother *u***mama** (*oo-*)
motorcycle *isi***thuthuthu** (*izi-*)
mountain *in***taba** (*iin-*)
mouth *um***lomo** (*imi-*)
move to, to *uku***fudukela**
mug *i***magi** (*ii-*)
music *um***culo**

name *i***gama** (*ama-*)
named, to be *uku***thiywa**
narrow -**mxinwa**
nation *isi***zwe** (*izi-*)
nature *in***dalo**
near **kufutshane**
near (to) **kufuphi na-**
nearly **phantse**
necessary, it is **kufuneka** …
necessity *im***funeko** (*iim-*)
neck *in***tamo** (*iin-*)
necklace *isi***danga** (*izi-*), *in***tsimbi** yo*m***qala**
need, to *uku***funa**
nephew *um***tshana** (*aba-*)
netball *i***bhola** yo*m***nyazi**
new -**tsha**
news *iin***daba**
newspaper *i***phepha**-*n***daba** (*ama-*)
next (coming) -**landela***yo* (-**za***yo*)
next to **ecaleni kwa-**
nice -**mnandi**, nicely **kamnandi**
niece *um***tshana** (*aba-*)
night *ubu***suku**; *at* **night** *e***busuku**
no **hayi**
normal -**qhelekile***yo*
north *um***ntla**, in the north e**ntla**
nose *im***pumlo** (*iim-*)
novice *um***khasayo** (*aba-*)
now **ngoku**
number *i***nani** (*ama-*) (telephone) *i***nombolo** ye**foni**
nun *u***nongendi** (*oo-*)
nurse *um***ongi**(**kazi**) (*ab-*)

obstinacy *in***kani**
obtain, to *uku***fumana,** *uku***zuza**

obtainable, to be *uku***fumaneka**
office *i-***ofisi** (*ii-*)
often **futhi**, *ama***xesha** *ama***ninzi**, **kaninzi**
oil *i-***oyile**; *ama***futha**
old -**dala**
once **kanye**
onion *i***tswele** (*ama-*)
only **kuphela**, **qha**
open, to *uku***vula**, be open -**vul***ile*
opportunity *i***thuba** (*ama-*)
or **okanye**
order, to *uku-***odola**
organization *um***butho** (*imi-*)
others *aba***nye**
outside (**nga**) **phandle**
oven *i-***onti** (*ii-*)
over there **phaya**
overcast -**sibekele**
overseas -**phesheya**
owner *um***nini**(**kazi**) (*aba-*)

packet *i***pakethe** (*ii-*)
page *i***khasi** (*ama-*)
pain *iin***tlungu**; painful -**buhlungu**
paint, to *uku***zoba**
paper *i***phepha** (*ama-*)
pardon! *u***xolo**! (lit. peace)
parent(s) *um***zali** (*aba-*)
park, to *uku***paka**
parliament *i***palamente** (*ii-*)
pass by, to *uku***dlula**
passenger *um***hambi** (*aba-*)
patient *um***guli** (*aba-*)
pattern *isi***hombo** (*izi-*)
pay, to *uku***hlawula**
pea *i-***ertyisi** (*ii-*)
peace *u***xolo**
pear *i***pere** (*ama-*)
peel *i***xolo** (*ama-*)
peel, to *uku***chuba**
pen *u***siba** (*iintsiba*)
pencil *i***pensile** (*ii-*)
people *aba***ntu**
perch, to *uku***chopha**
perhaps **mhlawumbi**; (i)**ngaba**
person (people) *um***ntu** (*aba-*)
petrol *i***petroli**
photographer *um***foti** (*aba-*)
pick up, to *uku***chola**
pig *i***hagu** (*ii-*)
pill *i***pilisi** (*ii-*)
pillow *um***qamelo** (*imi-*)
pineapple *i***payina** (*ii-*)
pipe *in***qawa** (*iin-*)
place *in***dawo** (*iin-*)
place, to *uku***beka**
plan *i***cebo** (*ama-*)
plant *isi***tyalo** (*izi-*)
plant, to *uku***tyala**
plate *i***pleyiti** (*ii-*)
play, to *uku***dlala**, a / the play *um***dlalo** (*imi-*)
player *um***dlali** (*aba-*)
pleasant -**mnandi**
please! **nceda**!
poem *um***bongo** (*imi-*)
poet *im***bongi** (*iim-*)
point, to *uku***khombisa**
pointed -**tsolo**
policeman *i***polisa** (*ama-*)
police station *isi***khululo** *sama***polisa**
pond *i***chiba** (*ama*)
porridge *isi***dudu**, maize meal porridge *um***phokoqo**, *um***qa**
porter *um***thwali** (*aba-*)
postman *u***noposi** (*oo-*)

pot *im***biza** (*iim-*)
potato *i***tapile** (*ii-*)
pour, to *uku***galela**
power *ama***ndla**
precise -**chanekile***yo*
prefer, to *uku***khetha**
prepare, to *uku***lungisa**
present, at **okwangoku**
president *um***ongameli** (*ab-*)
price *i***xabiso** (*ama-*) (low *eli***phantsi**)
pride *i***gugu**
principal *in***qununu** (*iin-*)
problem *ing***xaki** (*iin-*)
professor *u***njingalwazi** (*oo-*), *u***profesa** (*oo-*)
progress, to *uku***qhubela phambili**
promoted, to be *uku***nyuselwa**
properly **ngokufanelekileyo**
protect, to *uku***khusela**
proverb *i***qhalo** (*ama-*)
pruning shears *isi***kere** so*ku***thena**
public phone *i***fowuni** ka**wonke-wonke**
publish, to *uku***papasha**
publishing house *i***shishini** lee*n***cwadi**
pumpkin *i***thàngà** (*ama-*)
pure -**msulwa**
put (on), to *uku***beka**
put into, to *uku***faka**

quench (thirst), to *uku***qabula**
question *um***buzo** (*imi-*)
quickly **ngokukhawuleza**
quiet, to be *uku***thula**

radio *u***nomathotholo** (*oo-*) **rediyo** (*ii-*)
rain *im***vula** (*iim-*)
rain, to *uku***na**; *uku***netha**
rake *i***harika** (*ii-*)
read, to *uku***funda**
ready, to be (finished) -**gqib***ile*
reason *isi***zathu** (*izi-*)
receive, to *uku***fumana**
recently **kutshanje**
recipe *i***resiphi** (*ii-*)
recommend, to *uku***cebisa**, *uku***balula**
recover, to *uku***chacha**
red -**bomvu**
reduce, to *uku***hlisa**, *uku***nciphisa**
referee *u***sopempe** (*oo-*)
region *um***mandla** (*imi-*)
regularly **rhoqo**
rejoice with, to *uku***vuyisana na-**
relate, to *uku***balisa**
relax, to *uku***khululeka**
remember, to *uku***khumbula**
remind, to *uku***khumbuza**
repair, to *uku***lungisa**; *uku***khanda** (car)
repeat, to *uku***phinda**
reply, to *uku***phendula**
represent, to *uku***mela**
request, to *uku***cela**
request *isi***celo** (*izi-*)
resemble, to *uku***fana na-**
resource *ubu***tyebi**
rest, to *uku***phumla**
restaurant *i***restyu** (*ii-*)
return from *uku***buya**
return to *uku***buyela**
rhino *um***khombe** (*imi-*)
ride, to ukukh**hwela** (in a car, on a horse)
right -**asekunene**

right, be -**nyanis***ile*
ripe -**vuthiwe***yo*
river *um***lambo** (*imi-*)
road *in***dlela** (*iin-*); *um***gaqo** (*imi-*)
room *i***gumbi** (*ama-*)
rope *um***nxeba** (*imi-*)
rot, to *uku***bola**
rough -**ndlongo-ndlongo**
round -**ngqukuva**
rubbish *in***kunkuma**
rugby *um***bhoxo**
rule over, to *uk***ongamela**
run, to *uku***baleka**
runner *im***baleki** (*iim-*)

sad -**lusizi**
safe -**khuselekile***yo*
salary *um***vuzo** (*imi-*)
salt *i***tyuwa**
sandwich *i***sengwitshi** (*ii-*)
save, to *uku***londoloza**
saying *in***tetho** (*iin-*)
saw *i***sarha** (*ii-*)
say so *uku***tsho**
say, to *uku***thi**
scarce, be -**nqabile**
school *isi***kolo** (*izi-*)
sea *u***lwandle**
seamstress *um***thungikazi** (*aba-*)
secret *i***hlebo** (*ama-*)
secretary *u***nobhala** (*oo-*)
see, to *uku***bona**
seed *im***bewu** (*ii-*) cf. *uku***mba** = *to* dig
seedling *izi***thole** (*izi-*)
sell, to *uku***thengisa**
send to *uku***thumela**
separate, to *ukw***ahlula**
service (religious) *in***konzo** (*iin-*)
settlement *i***lali** (*ii-*)
sew, to *uku***thunga**
shade *um***thunzi** (*imi-*)
shame! **torho**! **torhwana**!
sharp -**bhukali**, -**krelekrele** (bright)
sheep *i***gusha** (*ii-*)
shelf *i***shelefu** (*ii-*)
shell *i***qokobhe** (*ama-*)
shine, to *uku***khanya**, *uku***qaqamba**
ship *in***qanawa** (*iin-*)
shirt *i***hempe** (*ii-*)
shoe *isi***hlangu** (*izi-*)
shop *i***venkile** (*ii-*)
shop assistant *um***thengisi** (*aba-*)
shopkeeper *u***novenkile** (*oo-*)
short -**futshane**
shoulder *i***gxalaba** (*ama-*)
show, to *uku***bonisa**
shrub *um***thana** (*imi-*)
siblings (my) *aba***ntwakwethu**, (your) *aba***ntwakenu**
side *i***cala** (*ama-*)
sign *i***salathiso** (*iz-*)
since **ukususela kwa-**
sing, to *uku***cula**
singer *um***culi** (*aba-*)
sister *u***sisi** (*oo-*), eldest sister *u***mafungwashe**
sit (down), to *uku***hlala** (**phantsi**)
sit around, to *uku***ngqonga**
situation *i***meko** (*ii-*)
skill *ubu***chule**
skirt *um***bhinqo** (*imi-*)
sky *isi***bhakabhaka**
sleep (well), to *uku***lala** (**kakuhle**)
slice *isi***layi** (*izi-*)
slope *i***thambeko** (*ama-*)

slowly **kade**; **ngokucothayo**
small -**ncinci**, -**ncinane**
smell, to *uku***nuka**
smoke, to *uku***tshaya**
snake *in***yoka** (*iin-*)
so (much) **kangako (kangaka)**
soccer *i***bhola** *e***khatywa***yo*
social worker *u***nontlalo-ntle** (*oo-*)
sock *i***kawusi** (*ii-*)
soft -**thambile***yo*
soil *um***hlaba**
soldier *i***joni** (*ama-*)
solve, to *uku***sombulula**
sometimes *ama***nye** *ama***xesha**
son *u***nyana** (*oo-*)
soon **kamsinya(ne)**
sore -**buhlungu**
sorry, to be -**lusizi**, sorry! **uxolo**!
sort (type) *u***hlobo** *(iint-)*
soap *i***sepha**
sour -**muncu**
spade *um***hlakulo** (*imi-*)
speak, to *uku***thetha**
speak slowly, to *uku***cothisisa**; *uku***zekelela**
speaker *isi***thethi** (*izi-*)
special -**odwa**
special (offer) *isi***peshali**
specialist *in***cutshe** (*iin-*)
spectacles *iin***dondo**
speed *am***endu**
speedy -**namendu**
spend, to *uku***chitha**
spinach *isi***pinatshi**
spine *um***qolo** (*imi-*)
spoon *i***cephe** (*ama-*)
sport *um***dlalo** (*imi-*)
spring *in***tlakohlaza** (*iin-*)
stab, to *uku***hlaba**

staff *aba***sebenzi**
stamp *isi***tampu** (*izi-*)
stand, to *uku***ma**
standard (at school) *i***banga** (*ama-*)
star *in***kwenkwezi** (*iin-*)
start, to *uku***qala**
start (car) *uku***qhwitha**
station *isi***tishi** (*izi-*)
stay, to (i.e. reside) *uku***hlala**
stay, to (i.e. remain) *uku***sala**
steal, to *uku***ba**
step *isi***tephu** (*izi-*) (cf. *izi***teps**)
stewardess *um***ququzelelikazi** (*aba-*)
stick *ulu***thi** (*izin***ti**)
stiff, to become *uku***qina**
still -**sa**- (ndi**sa**funda); -**se**- (u**se**mtsha)
stir, to *uku***zamisela**
stone *ili***tya** (*ama-*)
stop, to *uku***ma**; *uku***misa**; *uku***yeka**
story *i***bali** (*ama-*); *in***tsomi** (*iin-*)
stove *isi***tovu** (*izi-*)
stream *um***fula** (*imi-*)
street *isi***talato** (*izi-*)
strength *ama***ndla**
stretch, to *uku***naba**
string *um***tya** (*imi-*)
strong -**namandla, -omelele***yo*
stubborn -**nenkani**
stuck -**xingile**
student *um***fundi** (*aba-*)
study (for), to *uku***fund(el)a**
study *i***gumbi** lo*ku***fundela**
succeed, to *uku***phumelela**
success *im***pumelelo**
suddenly **ngesaquphe**
sufficiently **ngokwaneleyo**

suit, to *uku***fanela**
summer *i***hlobo**, early
summer*in***twasahlobo**
sun *i***langa**
supper *isi***dlo** sa**ngokuhlwa**;
*i***dinala**
support *in***kxaso** (*iin-*)
support, to *uku***xhasa**
sure, to be -**qinisek***ile*
surname *i***fani** (*ii-*)
surround, to *uku***jikeleza**
sweet -**mnandi**
sweet *i***lekese** (*ii-*)
swim, to *uku***qubha,** *uku***dada**
switch on, to *uku***layita**

table *i***tafile** (*ii-*)
tailor *um***thungi** (*aba-*)
take, to *uku***thatha**; *uku***thabatha**
take out, to *uku***khupha**
take part in, to *uku***thabatha**
*in***xaxheba**
talented -**nesiphiwo**
talk, to *uku***thetha**
tall -**de**
tape *i***theyiphu** (*ii-*)
tar **itha**
taste, to *uku***ngcamla**
taxi *i***teksi** (*ii-*); by taxi **ngeteksi**
tea *i***ti**
teapot *i***tipoti** (*ii-*)
teaspoon *i***tispuni** (*ii-*)
teach, to *uku***fundisa**
teacher *u***titshala**(**kazi**) (*oo-*),
*i***titshala**(**kazi**) (*ii-*)
team *i***qela** (*ama-*)
telephone, to *uku***fowun(el)a**,
*uku***tsalela**
telephone *i***fowuni** / *i***foni** (*ii-*);
*um***nxeba** (*imi-*)
television *u***mabona-kude**
tell (to), to -**xel(el)a**
temperature *i***qondo** lo*bu***shushu**
tennis *in***tenetya**
thank, to *uku***bulela**; thanks **enkosi**
that (conj) **ukuba**, **ukuze**
+ subjunctive
then **ke**, **phofu**
there **apho**, **khona**
thin -**bhityile**
thing *in***to** (*izin-*)
think, to *uku***cinga**
thirsty -**nxaniwe**; thirst *u***nxano**
throat *um***qala** (*imi-*)
throb, to *uku***qaqamba**
thunder *iin***dudumo**
ticket *i***tikiti** (*ama-*)
tie *i***qhina** (*ama-*)
time *i***xesha** (*ama-*); on time
ngexesha
tin *i***toti** (*ii-*)
tired, to be -**diniwe**
tired, to become *uku***dinwa**
tobacco *i***cuba**
today **namhlanje**
toe *u***zwane** (*iin-*)
together (with) **kunye na**-,
ndawonye
toilet *in***dlu** ya**ngasese**; *i***thoyilethi**
tomorrow **ngomso**
too (much) **gqitha**
tools *izi***xhobo**
tooth *i***zinyo** (*ama-*)
totter along, to *uku***totoba**
tourist *um***khenkethi** (*aba-*)
tow, to *uku***tsala**
town *i***dolophu** (*ii-*)
track *um***khondo** (*imi-*)

traditional fare *izi***dlo** zakwa**Ntu**
traditional healer *i***gqirha** (*ama-*)
train *u***loliwe** (*oo-*); *i***treyini** (*ii-*)
trainer *um***qeqeshi** (*aba-*)
train, to *uku***qeqesha**
traffic *izi***thuthu**
tranquillity *uku***zola**
translate, to *uku***guqula**; *uku***tolika**
translator *um***guquli** (*aba-*)
travel, to *uku***hamba**
traverse, to *uku***canda**
treasurer *u***nondyebo** (*oo-*)
tree *um***thi** (*imi-*)
trim, to *uku***cheba**
trip *u***hambo**; *u***khenketho**
trophy *in***debe** (*iin-*)
trouble *um***onakala** (*im-*)
trousers *i***bhulukhwe** (*ii-*)
truth *in***yaniso**, *i***nene**
try, to *uku***zama**
try on, to *uku***lingana**
turn towards, to *uku***jika nga-**
twice **kabini**
tyre *i***vili** (*ama)*, spare wheel *i***vili** *lo***laleliso**

ugly -**bi**
under **phantsi kwa-**
underneath **ngaphantsi**
understand, to *uku***qonda**; *uku***va**
understandable, to be *uku***qondakala**
undress, to *uku***khulula**
unfortunately **ngelishwa**
up **phezulu**
use, to *uku***sebenzisa**
usually **ngesiqhelo, -dla noku-**

vegetables *imi***funo**
very **kakhulu**
vice-principal *i***sekela**-*in***qununu** (*ama-*)
vicinity, in the **ngase-**
village *i***lali**; *i***dolophana** (*ii-*)
visible, to be *uku***bonakala**
visit, to *uku***tyelela**; *uku***hambela**
visitor *u***ndwendwe** (*ii-*), *um***veleli** (*aba-*)
vocabulary *isi***gama** (*izi-*)
voice *ili***zwi** (*ama-*)

wait (for), to *uku***lind**(**el**)**a**
wake up, to *uku***vuka**
walk, to (straight) *uku***hamba** (**ngqo**)
wall *u***donga** (*iin-*)
wallet *isi***paji** (*izi-*)
want, to *uku***funa**
war *im***fazwe** (*iim-*)
wardrobe *i***wodrophu** (*ii-*)
warm, to become *uku***fudumala**
warm, to be -**fudumele**
wash, to *uku***hlamba**
waste, to *uku***chitha**
watch *i***wotshi** (*ii-*)
watch, to (i.e. TV) *uku***bukela**
water *ama***nzi**
water, to *uku***nkcenkceshela**
waterfall *in***gxangxasi** (*iin-*)
watermelon *i***vatala** (*ii-*)
way *in***dlela** (*iin-*)
way of life *i***mo-ntlalo**
weak -**buthathaka**
wear, to *uku***nxiba**
weather *i***zulu**; *im***ozulu**
weather forecast *u***qikelelo lwemozulu**
weather forecaster *is***anuse**

semozulu
weave, to *ukw***aluka**
week *i***veki** (*ii-*)
weekend *im***pela-veki** (*iim-*)
weight *ubu***nzima**
welcome!
wamkelek*ile*/**namkelek***ile*!
welcome, to *ukw***amkela**
well **kakuhle**
well, to be *uku***phila**
well then **heke**
west *in***tshonalanga**
wet -**manzi**
what? **ntoni**? / -**ni**?
whatever **nokuba yintoni**
wheel *i***vili** (*ama-*)
wheelbarrow *i***kiriwa** (*ii-*)
when **xa**, when? **nini**?
where? **phi**? whereabouts?
ndawoni?
where **apho** … **khona**
while eli**xa**
while, a little *i***xeshana**
white -**mhlophe**
who? -**bani**?
why? **kutheni**?
wide -**banzi**
wife *in***kosikazi** (*ama***k<u>h</u>osikazi**)
wind *u***moya** (*imi-*)

window *i***festile** (*ii-*)
windscreen wiper *isi***hlambi**
se**festile**
wine *i***wayini** (*ii-*)
wipe, to *uku***sula**
wish, to *uku***nqwenela**
woman *um***fazi** (*aba-*); *i***bhinqa**
(*ama-*), old woman *i***xhegokazi**
wonder *um***mangaliso** (*imi-*)
woodwork, to do *uku***chwela**
wool *ub***oya**
word *i***gama** (*ama-*)
work *um***sebenzi** (*imi-*)
work, to *uku***sebenza**;
*uku***phangela**
world *i***hlabathi**
worry, to *uku***khathazeka**
worry oneself, to *uku<u>zi</u>***khathaza**
woven -**olukiwe***yo*
write, to *uku***bhala**
writer *um***bhali** (*aba-*)

year *u***nyaka** (*imi-*), new year
*unyaka om***tsha**
yellow -**lubhelu**
yes **ewe**
yesterday **izolo**
young -**tsha**
young man *um***fana** (*aba-*)

Bibliography

Xhosa language

Dowling, T. (ed.), *Speak Xhosa with Us,* Cape Town, African Voices 2006.

Kirsch, B. and **Skorge**, S., *Masithethe isiXhosa*, Cape Town, Juta & Co. 1995.

Kirsch, B. and **Skorge**, S., *Clicking with Xhosa*, Cape Town, David Philip 2001.

Lanham, L.W., **Riordan**, J., **Mathiso**, M., **Davey**, A.S., **Bentele**, S.V. and **Mahlasela**, B. *Lumko Self-instruction Course in Xhosa*, Grahamstown, Institute of Social and Economical Research, Rhodes University, 1969.

McLaren, J., *A Xhosa Grammar* 4th edn., Cape Town, Longman, 1955.

Pahl, H.W., *IsiXhosa* 3rd edn., Johannesburg, Educum, 1985.

Satyo, S.C., *Igrama Noncwadi LwesiXhosa Ibanga 10*, Via Afrika, 1992.

Schonstein Pinnock, P, *Xhosa, a Cultural Grammar for Beginners,* Cape Town, African Sun Press, 1994.

Zotwana, Z. S., *Xhosa in Context – from Novice to Intermediate*, Cape Town, Perskor, 1991.

Dictionaries

Fischer, A., **Weiss**, E., **Mdala**, E. and **Tshabe**, S., *English–Xhosa Dictionary*, Cape Town, Oxford University Press, 1985.

Godfrey, R., *A Xhosa–English Dictionary* 2nd edn., Lovedale Mission Press, 1918.

McLaren, J., *A New Concise Xhosa–English Dictionary* 2nd edn., Cape Town, Longmans, 1963.

Pahl, H.W. et al. (eds.) *The Greater Dictionary of Xhosa* vols. 1–3. Alice, University of Fort Hare, 1989–2006.

South African *Multi-Language Dictionary and Phrase Book*, The Reader's Digest Association, Cape Town, 1991.

Literature and further reading

Bongela, K.S., *IPhulo*, Cape Town, Maskew Miller Longman, 1977.

Jabavu, N., *The Ochre People*, London, John Murray, 1963.

Jolobe, J.J.R., *Amavo*, Johannesburg, Witwatersrand UP, 1973.

Jolobe, J.J.R. (ed), *Indyebo Yesihobe*, Johannesburg, Educum, 1970.

Jordan, A.C., *Towards an African Literature – The Emergence of Literary Form in Xhosa*, Berkeley and Los Angeles, University of California Press, 1973.

Louw, J.A., 'The Development of Xhosa and Zulu as Languages' in *Language Reform. History and Future*. Fodor, I and Hagège G. (eds), vol.2, pp. 371–92, Hamburg, 1983.

Magona, S., *To My Children's Children*, Cape Town, David Philip, 1990.

Magona, S., *Kubantwana Babantwana Bam*, Cape Town, David Philip, 1995.

Mandela, N.R., *Long Walk to Freedom*, Randburg, Purnell, 1994.

Mesatywa, E.W.M., *Izaci namaQhalo EsiXhosa*, Cape Town, Longman Southern Africa (Pty) Ltd, 1954.

Peires, J.B., *The House of Phalo*, Johannesburg, Ravan Press, 1981.

Index